VIEW OF THE FALLS AND VICINITY IN 1872.

FOR HISTORY OF SEYMOUR.

HISTORY of SEYMOUR CONNECTICUT

—*with*—

Biographies and Genealogies

W. C. Sharpe

HERITAGE BOOKS
2010

HERITAGE BOOKS
AN IMPRINT OF HERITAGE BOOKS, INC.

Books, CDs, and more—Worldwide

For our listing of thousands of titles see our website
at
www.HeritageBooks.com

A Facsimile Reprint
Published 2010 by
HERITAGE BOOKS, INC.
Publishing Division
100 Railroad Ave. #104
Westminster, Maryland 21157

Originally published
Record Print
Seymour, Conn.
1879

— Publisher's Notice —
In reprints such as this, it is often not possible to remove blemishes from the original. We feel the contents of this book warrant its reissue despite these blemishes and hope you will agree and read it with pleasure.

International Standard Book Numbers
Paperbound: 978-0-7884-1389-6
Clothbound: 978-0-7884-8571-8

PREFACE.

In the summer of 1876 several historical sketches were published in the SEYMOUR RECORD, and the same type was made up in book form like pages 9 to 20, with the intention of making only a small pamphlet. From that beginning the following work has grown, and in consequence the arrangement is different from what it would otherwise have been. This is compensated for in some degree by a very complete index.

Beside the articles on the Congregational and Episcopal churches by Rev. S. C. Leonard and B. W. Smith, the author acknowledges the receipt of much valuable information from C. C. Baldwin of Cleveland, Ohio, and Rev. Sylvester Smith. The following works have been used for reference or quotation: Savage's Dictionary of the Early Settlers, Dwight's Travels, Lambert's History of New Haven Colony, Trumbull's History of Connecticut, Barber's Connecticut Historical Collections, Colonial Records of Connecticut, Peters' History of Connecticut, Cothren's History of Woodbury, and Orcutt's History of Wolcott. The major part of the work has however been compiled from the records of the towns of Derby and Seymour, school district and society records, old manuscripts, family records and the recollections of elderly people who have long resided here and have been familiar with the occurrences of which they speak.

Hoping not only that the perusal of the work may be a source of pleasure to all its readers, and that our elderly friends who have been familiar with many of the occurrences described may be gratified with the memories of "Auld Lang Syne," but that it may be found valuable for future reference, the volume is respectfully submitted by   THE AUTHOR.

Earliest Mention.

THE early settlers were too much occupied in the arduous labors required in establishing homes in the wilderness to pay any unnecessary attention to the recording of their transactions, and the merest mention here and there, with occasional documents which have been handed down, afford but scant material for a narration of their lives, labors and liberties. This portion of the valley of the Nangatuck was first distinguished by the Falls, as the most remarkable feature of the kind in the length of the river. The long ridge of rock, through an opening of which the water rushed, foaming and tossing, into the depths below, were well known to the whites, as well as the red men, at a very early date. The especially fine fishing below the rocks, and the abundant game on the forest-clothed hills and in the natural meadows of the vales, were grand attractions to the hunter, trapper and fisherman, whether of aboriginal or Anglo-Saxon blood. Dr. Trumbull, is his history of Connecticut, says that as early as 1633 there was a tribe of Pequot Indians at the "Falls of the Naugatuc."

It appears from the early colonial records that the lands were generally purchased of the Indians by the early settlers at a fair valuation; indeed, Dr. Trumbull, (p. 174-5) says that "many of the adventurers expended more in making settlements than all the lands and buildings were worth after all the improvements they had made upon them." In the account of the settlement of the controversy between Connecticut and Massachusetts in regard to the boundary line, the 107,973 acres awarded to Connecticut were "sold in sixteen shares, in 1716, for * * * a little more than a farthing an acre, and shows of what small value land was esteemed at that day. It affords also a striking demonstration, that, considering the expense of purchasing them of the natives, and of defending, they cost our ancestors five, if not ten, times their value."

In 1664, Okenance or Akenanco was sachem of "Pagassett,"[*] and Ansantwan (sometimes written Ansantawae,) were chiefs, as appears in a deed given by them to Lieut. Thomas Wheeler, April 4th, 1664. Towtaemoe was then a sachem of another portion of the valley, according to a deed given Jan. 6th, 1664, by Lieut. Thomas Wheeler of Pagassett to Alexander Bryan of Milford. The land conveyed was "bounded with Potatuck river southwest, Naugatuck river northeast, & bounded on the northwest with trees marked by Towtaemoe, sachem, containing forty acres, more or less."

---
[*] This name is spelled in various ways, as Paugassett, Paguasuck, &c. Also the Naugatuck varies in orthography from Nau-ko-tunk to Naguatock. In copying old manuscript records the original spelling of the names is followed, although there are sometimes different spellings in the same document.

Of the grants to settlers by the proprietors, in lawful meeting, the following from the Derby records is a specimen.

"The inhabitants of Paugassett met together on April the 5th, 1671, and have granted to Ebenezer Johnson a tract of land bounded on the north side with the common land, and on the west side with the great river, and on the south side with the Devil's Jump, so called, and on the east with the common land, and the said Ebenezer Johnson is engaged to build and fence and inhabit on this land within the space of time of two years after the date hereof: and if the said Ebenezer fulfill not the terms hereof the land is to return to the inhabitants again: and the said Ebenezer is to make a sufficient highway between his fence and the hill, and so maintain it."

On the first of April, 1692, "Huntawah and Conchupatany, Indians of Paguasuck," sold to David Wooster "a certain parcell of land on the northwest side of Naguatuck river, in the road that goeth to Rimmon, the long plain soe called in the bounds of Derby, be it bounded with Nagatuck river south and east, and north and west with the great rocks."

'Conquepotana and Ahuntaway, chieftains at Paugusset, on the 17th of June, 1685, in behalf of themselves and other Indians, sold to Robert Treat, Esq., Samuel Eells, Benjamin Fenn, Thomas Clark, and Sylvanus Baldwin, agents of Milford, a tract of land "lying above the path which goeth from New Haven to Derby, and bounded with said path south, and a brook called Bladen's brook, (on the south side of Scucurra,* or Snake Hill,) north, with the line that is the bounds between New Haven and Milford, east, and the line that is the bounds between Derby and Milford, west, which said land was a mile and six score rods in breadth throughout the length of it." The Indians "reserved the liberty of hunting on this ground."'

'A purchase was made on the 29th of February, 1700, by Robert Treat, Esq., Mr. Thomas Clark, Sen., Samuel Buckingham, Sen., Lieut. Sylvanus Baldwin, and Ensign George Clark, agents for Milford, of a tract of land "lying northward of Bladen's brook, unto a brook called Lebanon brook, bounded north by said Lebanon brook, east by New Haven land, south by Bladen's brook, and west by the line between Derby and Milford; said land being a mile and six score rods in breadth." The consideration given for this land was £15 in pay,† and 15s. in silver. The deed was signed by nine Indians, viz: Conquepotana, Ahantaway, Rasquenoot, Waurarrunton, Wonountacun, Pequit, Suckatash, Durquin, and Windham. This tract of land was divided and laid out, in 1759, into one hundred and ninety-five shares or rights and is commonly called the "two bit purchase," from the circumstance of each buyer of a right paying for the same two Spanish bits, of eight twelve and a half cent pieces. This purchase now forms the northwest part of Woodbridge.' (Milford Record, Vol. 11.)

'Another and the last purchase of land within the old patent bounds of Milford, was made by the same committee, on the 23d of February, 1702, of the same Indians, for £5 in money, or otherwise, £7 10s. in pay,† bound south by Lebanon brook, east by Milford and New Haven line, north by Beacon Hill river or Waterbury line, and west by the line between Derby and Milford; being a mile and six score rods in width. This was called the "one bit purchase," and was laid out in 1769, into one hundred and eighty-seven whole share rights. This land is now the western part of Bethany. (Milford Record, Vol. 15, page 281.) Thus it appears that Milford once extended twenty miles north to Waterbury line, but its territory has been ceeded to

* Now called Skokorat.   † See explanation of currency terms on page 8.

help form other towns, till it is now contracted into a little triangle, of about six miles in length on each side.'—*Lambert's History of the Colony of New Haven.*

On the 15th of Aug., 1693, a tract of land "known by ye name of Acesquantook and Rockhousehill, bounded south with ye Four Mile Brook, north with ye Five Mile Brook, east with Woodbury road as it now is, and west with ye Great River," was sold to "Wm. Tomlinson, Senior and Junior, and widow Hannah Tomlinson, James Hard, Johnathan Lum and Timothy Wooster," for twenty pounds, by Mawquash, Cheshconeeg, Neighbor Rutt, Cockapatouch, Nonnawauk, Wouson, Keuxon, Raretoon, Tarchun, Rashkannoot, Chomasfeet, proprietors of Weeseantook, with the consent of their sagamores. The acknowledgement was made before Justice Ebenezer Johnson. Four Mile Brook is the stream flowing into the Housatonic at Squantuck, and Five Mile Brook is the first considerable stream above.

On the 16th of April, 1700, Cockupatain, sachem, and Runsaway, gentleman Indians of Derby, for four pounds ten shillings, sold to Capt. Ebenezer Johnson and Ensign Samuel Riggs a piece of land "bounded southward with ye littel river, eastward & northward with David Wooster his land & ye above sd Captain's & Ensign's land & nugatuick river, westward & north with * * * indian purchase." The same day "Cockupatain and Huntaway, Indians of Derby," sold to Capt. Ebenezer Johnson & Ensign Samuel Riggs "a certain parcel of meadow and upland lying at ye upward of Chestnut Tree Hill, containing twenty acres, more or less."

Derby, including what is now Seymour, was taken from Milford, one of the six towns of the New Haven colony. It was incorporated by the authority of New Haven in 1675, when there were in it only twelve families. The bounds between Derby and Milford were not laid out till 1680.

The following list contains the names of all settlers of the town who had taken the freeman's oath down to 1708.

Maj. Ebenezer Johnson,
Ens. Samuel Riggs,
Lieut. Thomas Wooster,
William Nashbon,
John Johnson,
Ebenezer Harger,
John Durand,
Samuel Conors,
Josiah Colding,
Deacon Isaac Nichols,
John Davis,
Stephen Pierson,
Joseph Hawkins,
Timothy Wooster,
Samuel Brinsmaid,
Edward Riggs,
Joseph Moss,
William Tomlinson,
Ens. Joseph Hulls,
David Wooster,
Henry Wooster,
Ephraim Smith,
John Riggs,
Francis French,
Dea. Abel Holbrook,
John Thoobals,
John Chatfield,
Jeremiah Johnson,
John Pringle,
Samuel Nichols,
Johnathan Lum,
James Hard.

That wolves and panthers were still common is evident by the passage of an act by the General Assembly in October, 1713, offering a bounty of forty shillings to any person who should kill a wolf, catamount or panther, "and half as much for every wolves' whelp."

In 1720, "it being moved by the proprietors of, and within the town of Derby, that a deed of release and quit-claim of and in the lands of said town," the Assembly granted that such deed be executed.

Among the military appointments by the General Assembly were those of Joseph Hulls as ensign of the local "trainband" in May, 1707, lieutenant in 1809, and captain in 1716. Serj^t Thomas Wooster was by the General Assembly appointed Lieutenant in October, 1706, and commissioned accordingly.

Samuel Nichols was appointed ensign in 1709. In 1716 John Riggs was appointed lieutenant, and in 1722 was made captain. He was one of the deputies to the General Assembly in 1717, and again in 1722. Ebenezer Johnson was a lieutenant colonel in the expedition to Port Royal, (N. S.), in August, 1710, and soon after was promoted colonel. Ebenezer Johnson, Jr., was appointed ensign in 1816, and lieutenant in 1722. Samuel Bassett was appointed ensign in 1822.

The duties of the train-band were often difficult and dangerous. The Indians were numerous, and the history of the colony in those early days shows but too well that constant vigilance was a condition of safety.

The tract of land just over the Oxford line and west of Little River, consisting of about one hundred acres, and known as the Park, was enclosed about the middle of the last century by a Mr. Wooster for the purpose of keeping deer. On one side of the inclosure there was an overhanging rock from which the hunted deer would sometimes leap into the inclosure, much to the discomfiture of the disappointed huntsmen. This was one of the parks referred to by Peters in his history of Connecticut published in 1781.

In the olden time they were particular to give every man his title: magistrates and ministers were called Mr., church members were called brethren and sisters, and those who were not in church fellowship were simply goodman and goodwife. As there were frequent demands upon the military, they were held in high respect and all military titles were scrupulously observed. The early records abound with the titles—ensign, sergeant, lieutenant, captain and colonel. In christening infants scriptural names and religious terms were most common, as for example, Content, Charity, Deliverance, Desire, Experience, Faith, Grace, Hope, Justice, Love, Mercy, Makepeace, Patience, Pity Praisegod, Prudence, Rejoice, Sillence, Thankful, &c.

On account of the lack of money payments were often made in produce of various kinds. The following extract from the "Travels of Madam Knight," who made a journey from Boston to New York about 1695, gives a good representation of the currency of the time.

"They give the title of merchant to every trader who rate their goods according to the time and specie they pay in, viz., pay, money, pay as money, and trusting. Pay is grain, pork, and beef, &c., at the prices set by the general court that year; money is pieces of 8, ryals, or Boston or Bay shillings, (as they call them,) or good hard money, as sometimes silver coin is called by them; also wampum, viz., Indian beads, wch. serves for change. Pay as money, is provisions as aforesaid, one third cheaper than as the Assembly or generall court sets it, and trust as they and the merchant agree for time. Now when the buyer comes to ask for a commodity, sometimes before the merchant answers that he has it, he sais, is your pay *ready?* Perhaps the chap replies, yes. What do you pay in? sais the merchant. The buyer having answered, then the price is set; as suppose he wants a 6d. knife, in pay it is 12d., in pay as money, 8d., and hard money, its own value, 6d. It seems a very intricate way of trade, and what 'Lex Mercatoria' had not thought of."

The Congregational Church.

A sermon delivered in the Congregational Church by Rev. S. C. Leonard, July 9, 1876.

He that goeth and weepeth,
Bearing precious seed,
Shall doubtless come again with rejoicing,
Bringing his sheaves with him.—Psa. 126: 6.

On the 12th day of March, 1817, (a little less than 59¼ years ago), five men had a meeting at our village—the influences of which are around us to-day. There was a house of worship—old and uncomfortable, but a house within which God had been honored, and where He had recorded His name—standing on the hill on the other side of the river, and it is not unlikely that the meeting was held within it.

The five men who had come together from different points for this council were well able to consider a matter. They composed, indeed, a more remarkable company than they could then have known themselves to be.

One was the Rev. Nathaniel W. Taylor, known, at that point of time, as the young and promising pastor of the Center Church in New Haven, 31 years of age, ordained to the work he was then performing—with his whole heart in it—five years, lacking a month, before. The theological department of Yale College, in which he was to grow to the stature of a giant, and do a work, and wield an influence which will never die, had not then been opened for instruction. It was opened in 1822.

Another of the men was the Rev. Samuel Merwin, pastor of the North Church and Society in New Haven. He was a somewhat older man, and had been in the position which he was then faithfully and successfully occupying for twelve years. It is of special personal interest to me that his coming here was the very year after he had received to membership in his church four sisters, tenderly attached to each other, one of whom was my own dear mother—the four, by this act, joining another of their number who had united with the same church previously; the names of each of the sisters awaking memories of a happy childhood in my mind. They are all up higher now. It was before I was born that they, together with 13 others (one of whom was my father), united at the early spring communion season with Mr. Merwin's church, and you will not wonder that the figures which stand for that year have interest for me. Mr. Merwin was the pastor whom I loved, and from whom I received religious instruction in my childhood. The first Sunday school I ever attended was under his pastorate. The affectionate pressure of his hand, one day when I was a child, as he met me at the close of a service, in a season of religious interest, I have never lost the feeling of—through the 45 years between—to this day. He had been told that I was desiring to become a follower of Christ, and as he took my hand in his, it seemed to me, that without speaking a word, he condensed into the loving pressure of his hand a soul full of interest in my welfare. I never see his name without feeling a thrill of joy.

Another of the five men who came together for the meeting at our village was the Rev. Bennett Tyler, then of South Britain, pastor of the Congregational church there, and at this time 34 years of age. The Theological Seminary at East Windsor, with which his now distinguished name is associated in our thoughts, was 17 years in the future, when the South Britain pastor came to the meeting at Humphreysville, as our village was called then. Nobody could have conjectured, at that time, that the names of Taylor and Tyler, so peaceably associated at this meeting would ever come to have such relation to each other, as they did in after years.

Another of the five men was the Rev. Bela Kellogg. Seventeen years before (class of 1800) he had been graduated at Williams College and had afterwards studied theology with the vigorous and famous, and astute pastor of the church in Franklin, Mass., the man who took a seventy years course of hard study and never got tired of it—enjoyed it all the way through;—who never shunned a subject because it was difficult, and never hesitated over any results to which his logic brought him.

The remaining member of the party was the Rev. Zephaniah Swift, who had then been for four years pastor of the ancient church in Derby, a church 136 years old, when he was called to it, and when he answered the call by beginning a genuine life work with and for it—commencing a pastorate which was to prove to be of more than a third of a century (35 years) in length.

The object of this meeting of these men at our village was to organize a church of Christ here, if it should seem to be best.

They prepared themselves for the work which they had been called to perform by appointing the Rev. Zephaniah Swift moderator, and Nathaniel W. Taylor scribe. When they were ready, nine persons presented themselves before them, producing letters of good standing in other Churches of Christ, and asking to be organized into a church. The nine persons were: Joel Beebe and wife, Bradford Steele and wife, Ira Smith and wife, Louis Holbrook, Hannah P. Johnson and Sally Wheeler.

The question was considered by the council, the church was organized, and the name by which it was called was

THE VILLAGE CHURCH.

The vote which the council left on record of the result which they reached on that day is very brief, but as distinct as it is brief. These are the words of it: "Voted, The above named persons be and are hereby organized into a church in this village.

This is not, however, the earliest church constituted here. Twenty-eight years before this, on the 3d day of November, 1789, twenty-six persons signed a certificate setting forth that they had joined the Congregational society (evidently formed then) in this part of the town and withdrew from the Congregational church in Derby, then 112 years old, to form a society in this portion of the town. I have in my hand the document which lies at the basis of the first Church of Christ ever formed in what is now our village. [The document is published at the close of this article.]

A vigorous entering upon their new work this earlier christian company seem to have had the will and found the way to make.

Few in number though they were, they resolutely procured a pastor and built a house of worship.

The house of worship which was put up at this time is of interest to us as *the first house of worship ever erected in our village.* It was placed on land which had been owned by Mr. Isaac Johnson, and where the M. E. Church now stands. It was built at a sacrifice; it was built as those who erected it could build it, with the means which they could command. There was faith and prayer mingled with the work, as it went forward, I have no question. One who often worshipped within it (Mrs. Sarah Jones, afterwards of Erie, Pa., daughter of Bradford Steele) wrote concerning it 20 years ago, to her sister:

"I feel a peculiar interest in that church, well knowing its history from the first. This is not its first struggle. I well remember, when but a mere child, of seeing the anguish of my mother's heart for its depression. * * * The building was where the Methodist church now stands. I well remember when it was done off (what doing off there was). It was divided off into pews. It was neither lathed or plastered, and but poorly clapboarded. Many times have I brushed the snow off the seats before sitting down. Its exterior resembled a barn more than a church. Still it was beloved, and probably had as true worshippers in it as those of modern style. * * * You, my dear sister, know, as yet, but very little of the struggles of our ancestors to perpetuate the blessings we have enjoyed."

The man who was called by this early church to minister to it the gospel of the grace of God, was the Rev. Benjamin Beach, grandfather of one of our respected citizens, Sharon Y. Beach. The Rev. Benjamin Beach preached the gospel to these earnest christian people for about fifteen years. The house, which was built either for or by him, for a parsonage, is standing now, and is the second dwelling east of the present house of worship of the M. E. Church— next the new and tasteful parsonage which has been built within the year past by the Methodist society. The building which was to be the first pastor's home was ready

SEYMOUR AND VICINITY.

for its occupants very promptly—within a few months after the organization of the little church (things seem to have been done with a will then)—and Mr. Beach moved into it in March, 1790, having waited for a time for an opportunity to bring his household goods from North Haven on snow, which did not, however, fall that winter, so as to render it possible for him to do so.

Two outlines of sermons preached by the Rev. Benj. Beach are before me. Time, you see, has left traces of its passage on the old manuscripts. One of them was preached in the year 1798, from Luke, 9: 42. The other is a fast day sermon, preached from II Kings, 19: 14—20, on the 25th of April, 1799, at the point of time when difficulties with France were assuming a threatening, and even warlike, aspect; difficulties which were, to the joy of all, adjusted, after a single, or rather a double naval engagement, in which the French frigate Insurgente, and the American frigate Constellation were prominent. The sermon was preached a year and five months before the treaty, by which peace was restored, was concluded, and nine months before the death of Washington. Of the genuine patriotism of the writer, it leaves no room for question. It has the true ring of the words which were spoken abundantly from our loyal Connecticut pulpits, in the latter part of the last century. There is vigor of thought indicated by these old time-worn manuscripts; there was a live man behind them once. They indicate, I judge, the possession, by this first pastor of our village, of a good deal of the power of putting things in a telling way. They were, evidently, well adjusted to the time to which they belonged, as every sermon ought to be. One of them was preached several times, and as the marks on the margin of it show, once at Waterbury. The remains of this first pastor of our first church lie in Milton, a parish of the famous town of Litchfield; famous not so much for its rocks and its pure air, as for its MEN.

How large the church became within these fifteen years of the faithful ministrations of its first pastor, I have not been able to ascertain. I fear there are no records of it in existence. The Rev. Mr. Beach completed his work here, and removed to Milton, in 1805.

Then the church was for a time scattered. But its members had the heart to worship God and they went, some to Oxford, some to Great Hill, some to Bethany, as they most conveniently could. After a time the Rev. Zephaniah Swift became pastor of the church in Derby, and, with a genuine interest in the welfare of the church, preached for it occasionally.

But a new element had, in the meantime, been introduced into our village. It had taken a new name, and was the scene of a new and busy life. One could not have told, at that point of time, into *what* prominence it might rise. That man of eminence, regarded as an ornament to the period in which he lived, scholar, historian, poet and patriot, GEN. DAVID HUMPHREYS, had fixed upon this spot in our valley to work out a noble idea which had taken possession of his mind. He had gained his honors before he established his interests here. His experience of life had been very varied. He had seen the world in different phases of it; had seen it, and had helped to mould it. He had been a successful military man. He had been a personal friend and associate of the great Washington. He had been intimately connected with the brave and unfortunate Kosciusko. He had been ambassador to two important foreign courts, from which he returned, bringing back to his native land—and to this, his native town—the *"true golden fleece,"* as the phrase is in the inscription on the shaft of granite which marks the resting place of his remains, in the old cemetery in New Haven. He died Feb. 21, 1818. He entered Yale college when he was 15 years old, only, and was graduated when he was 19;—(class of 1771). He commenced his enterprise here—returning to his native valley from his residence abroad —when he was 52, enriched by all his experience, using his wealth freely, gathering into his plans all his broad resources, and employing them without stint or narrowness. He laid the foundation of his work, on the bank of our beautiful river—and at one of the most beautiful points upon it—in the year 1804; and in 1810, when the new manufacturing company was incorporated, the village was wearing his name.

The enterprise which Gen. Humphreys established here was, for its time, one to be looked at by the whole region, and it carried the name of our village (HUMHREYSVILLE) to different and distant points; made it familiar at our nation's capitol, and honored by the presidents of our republic. Dr. Dwight, the able president of Yale College, who was personally, (and I think intimately) acquainted with Gen. Humphreys, says of it:

"In Europe great complaints have been made of manufacturing establishments as having been, very commonly, seats of vice and disease. Gen. Humphreys began this with a determination either to prevent these evils, or if this could not be done, to give up the design. With regard to the health of the people it is sufficient to observe, that from the year 1804 to the year 1810, not an individual belonging to the institution died, and it is believed that among no other equal number of persons there has been less disease. (Dwight's Travels, vol. III, p. 393.)

A journey, of which a very graphic record has come down to us, was made by Pres. Dwight across our valley in the interval marked by the establishment of this manufacturing institution—in the autumn of 1811. He speaks of it with enthusiasm. He had an eye for natural beauty, and he found it here. His words are fairly aglow as he writes about the spot which lies a few rods north of the place on which this house stands. He says:

"The scenery at this spot is delightfully romantic. The fall is a fine object. The river, the buildings belonging to the institution, the valley, the bordering hills, farms and houses, groves and forests united, form a landscape in a high degree interesting." (Travels, vol. III, p. 394.)

Pres. Dwight seems to have been especially interested in the moral aspects of the manufacturing enterprise of which he gives a detailed and very valuable account, established here by Gen. Humphreys.

When Dr. Dwight wrote the account of this journey he was near the end of his life. He died a year and a month earlier than Gen. Humphreys, and two months before this church was reorganized.

Of course, in the year 1817, when the council of which Dr. Taylor was scribe assembled here, our village was much larger than when the earlier church was organized. With the infusion of new life which it had received, it had gained a new outlook. It had passed through vicissitudes. The war of 1812 had affected the manufacturing industries of the place very greatly, at first prosperously and then adversely. But the new Church of the Living God which was planted on that March day of 1817, had opportunity broad enough of bearing fruit for the Master, on our hillsides and in our valley; and it seems to have desired to improve it. The facts are these: The church was constituted on the 12th of March. Eighteen days later, on the 30th of March, the Rev. Zephaniah Swift, of Derby, was present at one of its meetings, and received 18 others into membership. One of the 18 who united with the new church, on that day, is living now, a respected—and the oldest—member of our church, and is spending on this Sabbath, her 86th birthday, Mrs. Daniel White.

Two months after the church was organized, the Rev. Bela Kellogg received other members. In the following September, six months after its organization, others still presented themselves to unite with it, so that when the church entered upon the second year of its new existence, it had within it—their names enrolled on its records—between thirty and forty men and women, who had chosen to stand up to declare themselves for Christ, and their readiness to do work for him. Thirty-four men and women in vital earnest, can do a great deal. The christian age was introduced with a company which could have been counted more easily than this.

These 34 disciples of Christ, thus formed into a new church, so beginning anew in the christian work, wanted to dedicate to the Master a new house of worship. So they prayed to God, and talked the matter over with each other. The result was that, to the M. E. society, which had been previously formed, the old building, endeared to many hearts, was sold, Sept. 22, 1818, and the vigorous Church of the New Beginning, in due time, as it could, built for itself a new house, on the spot overlooking the river, on the eastern side of it, where the old Congregational burying ground is now. The church began at once, in 1818, to prepare for the work of building, meeting for a time in the Bell school-house. The steeple was added to complete the edifice in 1829.

Of those who ministered the gospel to the church in the house of worship overlooking the river, some are remembered very distinctly by individuals here to-day. One of the earliest and most constant friends of the church seems to have been the Rev. Zephaniah Swift, of Derby. He gave it counsel; he gave it time; he gave it work. At one period of its early history he was placed at liberty, by vote of his own church, to preach for it a fourth of the time, receiving from it a fourth of his salary. This church owes much under God to that man, of stately dignity of bearing, but with a warm heart beating within him, good, and true, and faithful; the man who made so powerful an impression on at least one who came under his influence, as to lead him with extravagance of expression to say, that it would be joy enough for him, if he could ever get to heaven, to meet Zephaniah Swift there.

The Rev. Bela Kellogg was never pastor of the church, but ministered to it for a time, not far from its beginning.

The Rev. Ephraim G. Swift was pastor of the church from 1825 to 1827. He died in August, 1858.

On the 11th day of May, 1828, the Rev. Amos Pettingil received to membership of the church several individuals, among whom were Isaac Sperry and wife, Albert Carrington, Adaline and Emeline Sperry, and Olive Merriam. Of those who united with the church while the Rev. Ephraim G. Swift was pastor, one only is a member now, Mrs. Henry P. Davis.

The name of the Rev. Charles Thomson first appears under date of July 20, 1828. He was installed pastor of the church in April, 1830. His ministry within it was of about five years in length. He seems to have labored faithfully. I judge, from what I can gather from the old records, that he had genuine love of his work. It seems as if it were overflowing from his pen, at times, as he was making some of the entries which we have in his handwriting. From what I hear about him and his family, from those who were personally acquainted with them, I should judge him to have been a good man with an excellent wife. He came here from Dundaff, Pa. He, too, has finished his work on earth. He died in March, 1855. Of those who united with the church while the Rev. Charles Thompson ministered to it, three are members now: Mrs. Maria Holbrook, Mrs. George Washburn, and Mrs. B. M. Durand.

The ministry of the Rev. Rollin S. Stone was also within this period. His arrangement with the church and society was a peculiar one. He engaged to be responsible for the weekly supply of the pulpit, with the understanding that the Rev. Mr. Swift, of Derby, should preach one half the time, by regular and stated exchange, Mr. Story spending the secular days of the week at New Haven, in the Theological Seminary. This arrangement was continued for fifteen months—from June 2, 1833, to Sept. 1, 1834, —the relation was then severed, according to his own record of the matter, " in peace and love."

The Rev. John E. Bray ministered to the church for about seven years and a half—from Sept, 1834, to April, 1842. Of those who united with the church within this time, two only are members now: Deacon David Johnson, and Mrs. Sarah Collins.

On the 26th of June, 1843, the Rev. William B. Curtiss was called by the church to become its pastor. His ministry was of somewhat over six years in length. He was a man who loved to work, and who always found work to do, if it was to be found—and it always was, and is.

When the Rev. Mr. Curtiss entered upon his ministry here, the house of worship on the other side of the river was not, by any means, an old one. But the fact had become very apparent that it was not centrally located. As business developed, the village grew away from it, instead of around it, and the company who had chosen to be called THE VILLAGE CHURCH decided that a new house ought to be built. And there was enterprise enough to do it. It is this house, within which we are now (one of the easiest houses to speak in I have ever used—of proportions conformed to acoustic law as fully as can be desired) which arose out of the energetic purpose formed at that time. The 20th day of April, 1847, was dedication day within it; a day of joy and gladness. The Rev. Mr. Curtiss remained pastor of the church and society for two and a half years longer—until Oct. 15, 1849. Of those who united with the church while he ministered to it, six are members now : Wm. Hull, Mrs. Emeline Bliss, Mrs. Emeline Steele, Mrs. Laura A. Culver, Mrs. Esther Canfield, and Chas. Durand.

Four years and nine days after this house was dedicated to the worship of God—on the 29th day of April, 1851—it was opened for the first installation service ever held within it. On that day the Rev. E. B. Chamberlain was constituted pastor of the church and society. The installation sermon was preached by the Rev. Mr. Harrison of Bethany. Mr. Chamberlain had been here for nearly a year before this day. The last record to which his name is signed, as pastor, is under date of March 21, 1852— nearly a year later. His request to have the pastoral relation dissolved was based on the ground of ill-health, and was acceded to by the church May 20, 1852—two and a half years after his name first appears on the records of the church. Of those who united with the church while he ministered the gospel to it, two are members now : Mr. and Mrs. Roswell Kinney.

The Rev. J. L. Willard, now, and for more than twenty years past the successful pastor of the Congregational church in Westville, commenced his ministry here Sept. 1, 1852, and continued it to May 1, 1855—two years and two-thirds. He left very warm friends here, and has made very warm friends elsewhere. Of those who united with the church while he ministered to it, two are members now: Mr. and Mrs. Sheldon C. Sanford.

About this time our village suffered the loss of a heavy manufacturing industry which involved the removal from the place of not far from thirty families connected with the congregation. Other disasters followed. A wave of financial embarrassment swept over the land. It was a time of dejection and discouragement, and this church and society felt the influence of it keenly.

On one of these days, a young man just out of college was passing through our village—Henry D. Northrop. He had never been ordained to the work of the ministry, but he had a soul aglow with the love of Christ — he had something to say for Christ, *and he could say it.* Mr. Wallace M. Tuttle was not deacon of the church at that time, but he was soon to become such, and he never did a wiser and better thing than when he sought out the young graduate of Amherst College and almost compelled him to stop and work for Christ here. It was the Lord's plan. The Lord ordained him first, and man ordained him afterwards. No such revival as the Lord gave him to see that winter, had, up to that point of time, been witnessed, in connection with the whole history of the church. The Lord set his own seal to the work faithfully and efficiently performed. The time which seemed so adverse proved to be a glorious time in which to nurture faith towards God. The ministry of the Rev. H. D. Northrop here was commenced in August, 1857, and continued through the larger part of the year 1858. Of those who united with the church at that time, twelve are members now : Henry P. Davis, Mrs. Hannah Canfield, Mrs. Harriet E. Denney, Mrs. Emeline Ricks, Mrs. Fidelia E. Holden, Miss Sarah L. Ormsbee, Mr. and Mrs. Geo. E. Lester, Mrs. William Losee, Miss Orilla E. Hurlburt, Miss Grace E. Botsford and Mrs. Mary Worth.

The ministry of the Rev. E. C. Baldwin

SEYMOUR AND VICINITY.

was of a year in length, from May, 1859, to May, 1860. The ministry of the Rev. Sylvester Hine was of about equal length. The ministry of the Rev. J. L. Mills, (now professor in Marietta College, Ohio,) was of about two years in length, from 1862 to 1864. The ministry of the Rev. George A. Dickerman was of a single year in length, from 1864 to 1865. Of those who united with the church within these years, seven are members now : Mr. and Mrs. James L. Spencer, Mrs. Augusta Lathrop, Mrs. H. A. Rider, Mrs. Lucy DeWolfe, Miss Huldah DeWolfe, Miss Harriet Hotchkiss and Mrs. Raymond French.

On the first day of February, 1866, this house was opened for another installation service. The Rev. A. J. Quick had accepted the call of the church and society, and on that day was constituted pastor. The Rev. J. L. Willard, of Westville, preached the installation sermon, and the installing prayer was offered by the Rev. C. S. Sherman, of Naugatuck. Mr. Quick's pastorate was a brief one. The exact length of it I have been unable to ascertain. The facts which I have found are—that he was engaged as stated supply for one year commencing April 30, 1865 ; that his name is to be found on the records, for the last time, as moderator of the church, under date of April 19, 1867; and that he was dismissed from membership on the 13th of June, 1868 ; a little less than two and a half years after his installation. Of those who were received within the time covered by his ministry, ten are members of the church now: Mr. and Mrs. James Swan, Mrs. S. J. Castle, Mr. and Mrs. John Whitney, Miss Francis Lounsbury, William Bell, Miss Catharine Bell, Miss Catharine C. Burwell and Mrs. Mary Lockwood.

On the 22d of May, 1868, this house was opened for an ordination service. The Rev. Allen Clark was on that day, ordained as an evangelist, by a council called by letters missive issued by this church, to which Mr. Clark was then ministering. The ordination sermon was preached by Dr. Churchill, of Woodbury, and the ordaining prayer was offered by Rev. C. Chamberlain, of Oxford. In connection with the ministry of the Rev. Mr. Clark, another glorious revival of religion occurred. It is of such recent date—only eight years ago—that there must be many very vivid recollections of it in the minds of many of you who are present. Of those who united with the church within the time covered by Mr. Clark's ministry, twenty are members now : Joshua Kendall, Mr. and Mrs. Charles F. Hard, Miss Emma Lockwood, Miss Hattie M. Ford, Mrs. James Richardson, Mrs. A. A. Harris, Mrs. Frank H. Russell, Mrs. William T. Fife, Mrs. Ella F. Reynolds, Mrs. E. A. Robinson, Miss Hortie V. Swift, Henry B. Lockwood, Charles Sherman, Mrs. E. C. Barr, Mrs. F. Boeker, William B. Nichols, Mr. and Mrs. Edwin C. Segears and Mrs. George Fowler.

The 25th of November, 1869, was another ordination day. The Rev. H. P. Collin was, at that time ordained to the work of an evangelist, by a council called by this church. The ordination sermon was preached by the Rev. Mr. Adamson, of Ansonia, and the ordaining prayer was offered by the Rev. Mr. Gray, of Derby. The scribe of the council was the Rev. Robert C. Bell.

I have not been able to ascertain the exact length of the ministry of Mr. Collin here. His hand writinng appears, on the records of the church, for the first time at date of July 18, 1869, and for the last time, as I judge, May 1, 1870. Of those who united with the church within the years 1869 and 1870, sixteen are members now : Mrs. Laura E. Northrop, David Williams, Mr. and Mrs. Roswell C. Canfield, Richard Evans, Mrs. Charles Bliss, Mrs. C. J. Olmstead, Mrs. Juliette B. Hull, William J. Barr, Mr. and Mrs. Noah Osborn, Mr. and Mrs. Rufus Spencer, Mr. and Mrs. George A. Benedict and Mrs. Elizabeth C. Pierson.

The ministry of the Rev. J. W. Fitch, here, seems to have been of from one to two years in length. His name appears on the records, for the first time under date of May 7, 1871, and for the last time, in his own hand writing, under date of May 28, 1872. Of those who united with the church within this time, two are members now: Mrs. Phebe A. Hubbell and T. B. Minor.

The Rev. William J. Thomson was installed pastor of the church and society on the 24th of January, 1873. The installation sermon was preached, and the installing prayer was offered by the Rev. J. L. Willard of Westville. The ministry of the Rev. Mr. Thomson here was closed on the 27th of October, 1874. Of those who united with the church within this period, six are members now: Mrs. W. J. Thomson, Mrs. D. Simpson, Miss Emma E. Beach, Miss Margaret Smith, Mrs. Benjamin B. Thayer and Miss Libbie O. Lockwood.

The ministry which has not yet terminated, was commenced on the 15th of November, 1874. Of those who have united with the church since that date, all—twenty-nine in number—are members now: Mrs. and Miss Leonard, Mr. and Mrs. Andrew Barr, Mrs. Isaac Losee, Charles Sheard, W. I. Warren, Charles J. Reynolds, Miss Jessie Swan, Miss Sarah S. Osborn, Miss Mattie Osborn, Miss Eliza M. Creelman, Mrs. Charlotte Hayman, Mr. and Mrs. Robert A. Weaver, Mrs. Mary A. Hurlbut, Miss Freddie Quiering, Miss Carrie L. Pickhardt, Miss Bertha E. Johnson, Miss Mary E. Spencer, Miss Mary E. French, Mrs. Annie E. Lyman, Frank H. Wyant, Walter W. Dorman, Miss Ellen C. Hard, Miss Lydia A. Hard, Miss Mary A. Hill, Frank A. Smith and Mrs. Sarah M. Lines. May the number be increased, and there be added to the church a multitude of such as shall be saved!

Of those who have ministered to the church as DEACONS, several have gone to their rest. The first deacon of the earliest church was Mr. Baldwin of Derby. When the church was reorganized in 1817, the two chosen to this service were, Bradford Steele and Nehemiah Botsford. They occupied the office for almost all that remained to them of life. Deacon Steele, in September, 1840—after nearly a quarter century of service, and a little more than a year before his death—asked to be released from the performance of further official duty, and, because of his age and infirmity, his request was granted. Deacon Botsford had, a little before, made a similar request, which had been granted also.

A hundred years ago to-day, Bradford Steele was a boy of not quite fifteen years of age. But there was a dark war-cloud coming up into view. It was seen from our hill sides and our valleys with very great distinctness. Many brave men and women looked upon it with the calmness of heroic courage. Boys saw it, and were ready to take their share in what it involved.

Bradford Steele was not quite sixteen when he enlisted in the army which represented the cause of freedom. Terrible scenes he passed through. There was one day memories of which seemed to lie gleaming in his mind through his whole long after life. It was the 22d day of August, 1777. He was taken prisoner and treated with a cruelty which was merciless, his very apppearance becoming so changed by what he endured, (and the boys of that time could endure a good deal of hardship without being greatly affected by it,) that his own father, when he met him did not at first know who he was. He died in peace, Dec. 23, 1841, at the ripe age of 80.

There have been very few firmer friends of the church than Deacon Sheldon Kinney, now among those who have gone before. It was out of a gift made by him to the society that our pleasant and convenient parsonage has come. He was a man, I judge from what I hear about him, of a clear head and a large heart. He was appointed deacon of the church on the 6th of September, 1840. The names of those who have served as deacons for a longer or shorter time I have tried to collect and arrange in the order in which they have performed the service: Capt. Timothy Baldwin, appointed in 1789; Bradford Steele and Nehemiah Botsford, appointed in 1817; Sheldon Kinney and Alfred Hull, 1840; Andrew W. DeForest, 1844; William Kinney, Miles Culver and J. L. Spencer, 1853; W. M. Tuttle, 1858; Charles Bradley, date of appointment not recorded; David Johnson and Levi Lounsbury, 1865; Joshua Kendall, 1868.

A very incomplete idea, (but still one of some value,) of the religious influences exerted here within the century of our existence as a nation, may be suggested by

SEYMOUR AND VICINITY.

an enumeration of the houses of worship which have been built.

What is now Seymour was, at first, a part of the old "jurisdiction of New Haven." For a little less than forty years (1639-1677) it was a part of Milford. For a hundred and seventy-three years (1677-1850), it was a part of Derby. For only twenty-six years has it had an existence as a township with its present name. And then we are wearing now our fourth local name—Naukotunk (meaning one great tree) the first; Chusetown, the second; Humphreysville, the third; Seymour, the fourth; each of the names, but the first, being personal in their reference; elevating into prominent view an individual; the first name bringing into prominence an object in nature. (They are all gone now.)

In the township of Milford—of which the land which is now covered by our village was then a part—a Congregational church was formed on the 16th day of August, 1639—the year after the beginning at New Haven, 237 years ago. As the basis of the plan on which this oldest church was organized, those who were to constitute it took the text Proverbs ix, 1: "Wisdom hath builded her house, she hath hewn out her seven pillars," and selected seven of their number to join together in covenant to be the church, and to be called the pillars, to whom the rest were afterwards added.

Thirty-seven years later, in 1677, the Congregational church in Derby was constituted. So it was two centuries ago, lacking one year, that this church, in what then became our town, was organized. It was long ago for this continent. It was only 93 years after the death of Luther, and it was 26 years before John Wesley was born, that this ancient church, only five miles away from us, was formed. It was after that church had been in existence and doing its work about a hundred and thirteen years that Jesse Lee, one of Wesley's followers, passed through, for the first time, the place where it had been standing until it had grown gray with age, and hired a bell man to ring the people out that he might preach to them.

A CENTURY AGO TO-DAY, the father of Gen. Humphreys had passed the middle of his pastorate, of more than half a century in length. A century ago to-day, the Rev. Daniel Humphreys had been doing the work of a pastor of the flock of Christ, five miles from where we are, for over forty years. Many times had he been over our hills and through our valleys, on errands for the Master. A century ago to-day, his son David, (whom he had named after the King of Israel, and whom he hoped would make something,) was a young man 24 years of age, looking up into the future to see what he could carve out of it. Those who were living in this part of the town—when they wanted to attend services of public worship—(and people in those days expected to, and *were* expected to)—went to what is now Derby, to hear Mr. Humphreys—it was *all* Derby then. There were families here a century ago who could have gained something by a steady going to meeting, and it is to be hoped they did go.

The Indian Sachem whom we know best as Chuse, (Joe Mauwehu,) was here a century ago, probably not far from where we are, only across the river; his wigwam standing on the south border of the flat, west of the residence of Mr. Raymond French, beautifully set among a grove of white oaks there. (He *may* have been, just then, in the vicinity of where Dr. Stoddard now lives.) A century ago his youngest child—Eunice—was an Indian girl 14 years old, her father an athletic, skillful hunter, with some knowledge such as civilization has to give, but with the instincts of his race strong within him. At some point of his long life (he died when about 80) he united with the church in Derby. But even after he came to *hope* that he loved the Lord, he *knew* that he loved—that which biteth like a serpent and stingeth like an adder.

The first house of worship—that built for the Rev. Benjamin Beach—was erected 86 years ago. The frame of it was probably raised in the month of April, 1791. The second house of worship ever erected at what is now our village is the pleasant and commodious one belonging to the

Protestant Episcopal Church. The Episcopal Society was organized Feb. 20, 1797. This house was originally built by two societies in union, but has been reconstructed at heavy expense, by the society owning it now, into its present attractive form. The third house of worship erected at our village was the second Congregational house, buit on the hill overlooking the river. This was commenced—or preparation was begun for it — in 1818. The fourth is this house in which we are—the third Congregational house—built in 1846. The fifth is the house owned by the Methodist Episcopal Church. The corner stone of this edifice was laid on Saturday, June 19, 1847. The sixth is the house built by the Baptist Church. The church was organized in 1848, and the house was erected in 1851. The house built by the congregation connected with the church of Rome, is of more recent date.

So there have been three years, not far apart, of the life of our village, which have been, characteristically church-building years. This temple-building work is of itself, on the surface, I know, but it traces away to something which lies deep down in human hearts—interest in the things of God's worship. It has self-denial underlying it—and mixed with it. There is prayer and faith back of it and below it. There has been a life lived within our village, invisible of itself, but which has come to view in these results. It has been quietly lived by many, It has been a blessing to us.

Within these sanctuaries which have arisen from the impulses and purposes of this life, (God aiding and blessing,) the gospel of our salvation has been preached, with earnestness and success. The healthful influences exerted by these different churches, through these 86 years of time past, has been, to our village, an advantage which cannot be estimated. These influences penetrate, to a greater or less extent, business and social life, encouraging integrity, and honesty, and honor, and discouraging evil. The more vigorous these churches of our village are, the better will be the village, as a place to have a home in—a place in which to spend, pleasantly and usefully, these days which bear us along to the end. Our days are all journey days—days of travel along our life-way.

These churches of Christ have been schools of the Master, from which a great many have been graduated and called up. These houses of worship have been centers from which have radiated invisible tendencies toward what is good and true—forces stimultive of elevating thought and feeling and action.

A church becomes localized, as it builds a house of worship around itself. It gains for itself a religious home. Then the home feeling has opportunity to act and react within the religious nature. A church is not infrequently moulded, to an extent—its daily and weekly life materially affected —by the house which belongs to it, and to which it belongs; not as it belongs to Christ, but as it can belong to earthly things.

The whole history of this church, taken in connection with the church out of which it came, most naturally divides itself into three periods, marked by the erection of its three different houses of worship.

The first period of 27 years in length, from the beginning in 1789 to the assembling of the Council of Five in 1817. This is the pioneer period, the period of struggle for the necessities of religious life. Of the church, as it lived through this period, we knew something, but much less than we should be glad to know. The 27 years of meeting within that house had sunshine and shadow within them, as years have now. There was trial bravely borne, and, probably, trial not bravely borne. They were years with days of weeping and days of rejoicing within them. The 26 men whose names are on this old paper—discolored by these 80 years and more through which it has come down to us—represented families, households, with young and old in them, and into which joy and sorrow came, as it comes into our dwellings now.

This earliest church gathers itself most naturally, in our thoughts, around the man who was, for 15 years its pastor; a man who honored God and sought to aid man to

SEYMOUR AND VICINITY. 19

find God; a man ready to do whatever his hands found to do, and whose hands, both of them, did find enough do.

The church, in this earliest period of its history, is sometimes spoken of as one of what were called the "separate" churches of the time.

The great awakening of 1740—of the time of Whitfield, and Edwards, and Bellamy—enkindled new zeal, and desire of larger liberty than the relation which then existed between the church and state allowed, and a number of churches arose as the result of this feeling, which were known as "separate" churches; some of them composed of the better elements, and some of the discordant ones. I do not, however, find this church in any list which has come to my knowledge thus far, of these churches. The fact that it was Congregational, and known as such, is not decisive, for the separate churches—some of them—claimed to be more truly Congregational than any others. The single fact which I do find, relating to the matter is that its first and only permanent pastor had been, before he came here, minister of a separate church in Prospect. I have found evidence enough that this early church was an earnest church. There was human nature in it, unquestionably. We find scars of misunderstanding and difficulty as we trace out its history; but this is not so strange a thing in churches of other times as I wish it was. After all the labor which I have given to the gathering of every item of information concerning it which I could find, in any quarter, I think of it as a praying, self-denying, earnest, energetic church of Christ; adjusted to its time, of course, as it needed to be in order to be most useful; but loving and serving the Master, and obeying God rather than man. I look back upon that first church of our place with a great deal of interest.

The second period is of 29 years in length; from the meeting of the Council of Five in 1817, to the dedication of this house in which we are assembled. This is the period of quiet, steady work and progress. The men whom we see ministering to it—going in and out of its house of worship, and of the dwellings of those who composed its congregation—sharing joys and sorrows with them—the Rev. Zephaniah Swift, the Rev. Bela Kellogg, the Rev. Ephraim G. Swift, the Rev. Charles Thompson, the Rev. Rollin S. Stone, the Rev. John E. Bray and the Rev. William B. Curtiss—form a company whom it is an honor to the church to have had within it. Among the laymen who come into prominent view, within this period—[among those who have gone home; of the living I will not speak] are Bradford Steele, Nehemiah Botsford, Sheldon Kinney, Alfred Hull, Ira Smith and Daniel White. Miles Culver, energetic, self denying, generous, prompt, serving the Master and loving to do it, and continuing to do it to the end, united with the church Jan. 5th, 1845, not far from the time when this house was built.

The third period is, up to this point of time, of just 30 years in length, but open for more to follow, of work for Christ, and of blessings coming—to the worker in the doing of the work, and to others through the work.

The merest sketch of the history of this church could not be, in anywise, complete, if it failed to include some notice of its vigorous SUNDAY SCHOOL, which has had life within it which has helped itself, and other good things around it.

The Sunday School can be traced back to the year 1828. The names of those who have been superintendents of it, so far as they can be collected, are: Joel White, George F. DeForest, Andrew DeForest, Sharon Y. Beach, W. M. Tuttle, P. B. Buckingham, George E. Lester, Robert C. Bell, Theodore S. Ladd, Andrew Y. Beach and James Swan. The present number of names on its roll is 222.

But it has what is better than mere members—vitality—vigor. The weekly teachers' meeting is a *very* live meeting; I never saw anybody asleep in that meeting; and teachers awake cannot easily help having a school awake. Both the school and the teachers' meeting breathe a little heavily just now, as we are suffering this excessive heat, but it is exhaustion only, not sleep.

In the revival of last winter almost all who came to Christ came from and through our Sunday School.

The superintendent is now an officer of the church, elected annually by ballot. This plan was adopted about four years ago, (May 28, 1872.) Up to that time no minute appears on the records of the church of the names of the officers of the Sunday School. Now they are put on distinct record every year.

There is one fact belonging to the origin of the church in its later form, which I have picked out of the old record with a good deal of interest. In less than two months after the church was organized, and when its first deacons were chosen, (at a meeting held May 9, 1817,) a librarian for the VILLAGE CHURCH LIBRARY was appointed. A committee of three also received appointment as a "Committee of Selection;" their duty evidently understood to be to select books for this library. Now to select books for a library involves money, furnished by somebody; and that three men were needed on this committee seems to indicate that there was something important for them to do. Now to do anything important in the way of selecting books, involves and implies a good deal, and more then than now.

I suppose this could not have been a Sunday-school library; if it was, the Sunday school originated a good deal earlier than the date which I have given. The library is called a church library. In either case the book power was recognized by the young church, and it was determined to make use of it. What a marvelous power has it become since that time!

This church has raised up, for service in the great field of christian labor, one minister and one missionary. The minster is the Rev. Ira Smith; and the missionary is the Rev. H. A. DeForest [class of 1832, Yale], who went to Syria, returned with the seeds of fatal disease in his system, and so ended his work on earth. I am glad to find that a missionary to that old land has had any connection with us. I am not quite certain what the connection was. I take the fact, as I have stated it, on trust, not having had opportunity to verify it. I have searched the old records for his name but have not, thus far, succeeded in finding it. I shall trace out the matter as fully as I can. It is certainly a benefit to us to have such a point of contact with the great missionary enterprise. To follow a missionary of the cross, who is a personal acquaintance, with prayer, and interest, and faith, is invigorating to the heart which does it, and is honorable to God, whose service the work is.

The Rev. Robert C. Bell, now the efficient pastor of the Congregational Church in Darien, in this state, was, for a time, before his entrance upon his ministry, a member of this church, and comes here to the family home. His name belongs to our history.

I designed to say more about the revivals which have occurred within the church, noticing not only its larger ingatherings, but also its other harvests. It ought to be *characterized* by them to be true to its origin, for the church in its later form was born in a revival. In the record left by the Council of Five, of the work which they performed on that 12th of March, 1817, they say:—"The meeting proceeded to consider this application, and the state of this village, especially the increase of godly people *in the present revival of religion*, and are of the opinion that a compliance with the above request may conduce to the prosperity of Zion."

I desired also to, at least, mention some of the lessons to be gathered from the facts which I have presented to you. But I will not. You are weary, and you can do this work for yourselves. I will only express the wish, which I find so distinctly in my heart that I cannot deny it some utterance, that this church of the Lord Jesus Christ may be ever true to the Master, earnest in the doing of his work, and receive of his blessing till it shall *overflow*. It has a PAST. May it have a FUTURE!

FIRST ORGANIZATION
OF THE
CONGREGATIONAL CHURCH,
IN 1789.

The following is a literal copy of an old MS., fixing the date of the formation of the first ecclesiastical society in Seymour:

DERBY, November 3d, A. D., 1789.

This may sertify all whom it may concern, that the subscribers have joined and paid towards the support of the Gospel at the Congregational Society, in Derby, near Bladen Brook, and mean for the future to support the Gospel there:

  Capt. Timothy Baldwin,
  Asahel Johnson,
  Gideon Johnson,
  Capt. Bradford Steel,
  Elisha Steel,
  Isaac Baldwin,
  Ebr. Turel Whitmore,
  Amos Hine,
  Bradford Steel, Jr.,
  Medad Keney,
  Hezekiah Wodin,
  John Adye,
  Ashbel Loveland,
  Truman Loveland,
  Ebenezer Warner,
  Leveret Pritchard,
  Levi Tomlinson,
  John Coe,
  Ebenezer Beacher Johnson,
  Nathan Wheler,
  Bezalel Peck,
  Frances Forque,
  Joseph Loines,
  Moses Clark,
  Philo Hinman,
  Thomas Hotchkis.

  Sertifyed by me,   LEVI TOMLINSON,
              Society Clerk.

COINS OF THE OLDEN TIME.

PINE TREE SHILLING.

One of the most interesting of the early coins is the variety known as the "Pine Tree Shilling," once known as the Boston or Bay Shillings, which was issued at intervals for more than twenty-five years, though these coins all bear the original date, 1652.

GRANBY COPPER.

The earliest Connecticut coin of which we have any record is the Granby Copper, issued in 1737, by a Mr. Higley of Granby and made of copper from Copper Hill, afterward the seat of the famous Newgate Prison. Within the exergue of the reverse are three sledge hammers crowned. Another variety with a similar obverse bears on the reverse the head of an ox, with the legend, ☞ I. CUT. MY. WAY. THROUGH. As these pieces were only private tokens and their issue quite limited, specimens are now rare and highly valued.

CONNECTICUT CENT.

The above, issued by authority of the colony of Connecticut, (Auctori Connec,) were struck only four years, viz: 1785–8, the further issue of money by the colonies being then prohibited by Congress. The motto, "Inde et Lib.," (Independence and Liberty,) was full of significence to the colonists, after the long war for liberty and independence in which they had suffered so much. Of the cents issued in these four years there are extant nearly a hundred types, distinguished by the bust of Liberty facing right or left, by the misspelling of the word AUCTORI, as AUCTOPI, AUCTOBI, AUCTOBE and AUCION, by variations in the punctuation, by correct obverses with a variety of reverses, &c. The cents of 1787 are the most common, and the varieties of this date the most numerous.

TRINITY CHURCH.
PROTESTANT EPISCOPAL.

At the request of Theophilos Miles, Jonathan Miles, and Benjamin Davis, a warrant was issued by Levi Tomlinson, a Justice of the Peace for New Haven County, directed to Benjamin Davis, an indifferent person, requesting him to give notice to all the inhabitants professing the religion of the Protestant Episcopal Church, residing within certain prescribed limits, to meet at the house of Dr. Samuel Sanford, on the 20th day of Feb., 1797; then and there to form an Episcopal Ecclesiastical Society.

This warrant was dated Feb. 12th, 1797, and was served on thirty-nine persons, viz: Reuben Lum, James Manville, Nathan Mansfield, William Tucker, Benjamin Hawley, Russell Tomlinson, Martin Beebe, Enos G. Nettleton, Ephraim Wooster, Nathaniel Holbrook, Jeremiah Gillette, Josiah Nettleton, Philo Holbrook, Edward Hayes, Nathan Stiles, Wilson Hurd, William Church, Abel Church, John Griffin, Daniel Davis, Bowers Washband, Alexander Johnson, Timothy Johnson, Joseph Johnson, Charles French, Israel Bostwick, Moses Riggs and John White. The persons met at the time and place named in the warning, (the house now owned by Mr. Henry Wheeler), when Benjamin Davis was appointed moderator, Samuel Sanford clerk, and Joel Chatfield, Israel French and Jonathan Miles Society's Committee. As there had been a union of the Parish of Great Hill with the Episcopalians of the new Parish it was concluded to call the new organization Union Church.

Beyond the organization of the Society no other business appears to have been transacted at this time, and the meeting adjourned to meet at the same place at the end of the week, Feb. 27th. At this meeting they began in earnest to lay the foundation of a house for the Lord; and Benjamin Davis, Edward Hayes, Nathaniel Johnson and John White were appointed a committee to furnish materials for the building of the Church. The land upon which the Church stands was purchased of Leverett Pritchard, and cost $60; the deed is dated March 23rd, 1797. The committee to whom was intrusted the provision of funds and materials for a church building immediately commenced their labors, and if their energy be judged by their success they are entitled to the award of industry and perseverance. Early in the spring the corner stone was laid by the Rev. Edward Blakeslee, then an assistant to Rev. Dr. Mansfield of Derby; during the summer the building was raised and before winter entirely enclosed. After the building had been inclosed the committee found the funds at their disposal exhausted, and not willing to involve the Society in debt, concluded to suspend their work, and the finishing of the building was reserved for a later day. Seats were however provided, benches made of slabs. To accomplish this much great sacrifices were made; for their number was not only small and limited in their worldly means, but they also had to contend against what was termed the "established order," viz: against the Presbyterian influence which had at that time complete power in the state, and which regarded every such effort as a direct attack upon itself.

Of this Church Dr. Richard Mansfield was the first pastor, and for his support the Society voted to pay him 3 pence on the pound on the grand list of 1797. He was at this time rector of the Church in Derby. This connection between the two parishes does not appear to have been harmonious; for early in the year 1800, a committee was appointed to devise some means for uniting Derby and this Society under one pastoral charge. How long Dr. Mansfield continued in the rectorship of the Parish can not be correctly ascertained; but probably not longer than 1802; for in that year a committee was appointed to employ a clergyman for one quarter of his time. But as he had been settled for life, this Society assisted in supporting Dr. Mansfield after his pastoral connection had terminated, and continued to do so for eighteen years, until the time of his death in the year 1820. Jonathan Miles was appointed the first delegate to the Convention of this Diocese. He was a member of the 13th annual convention, held in the year 1798.

In the year 1802 the Union Bank was established, out of which a fund was to be raised for the support of the ministry. Of this bank Abijah Hull was treasurer. The amount of subscriptions was about $2,000, by fifty-seven persons. This bank during its existence proved a bone of contention, and in 1811 action was taken for its dissolution, and subsequently the notes and money which constituted the bank were returned to the original proprietors, they paying interest on the same up to the year 1808. After the resignation of Dr. Mansfield in 1802, the church remained for a year unsupplied. In 1803 a committee was appointed to confer with committees from Oxford and Derby, in relation to employing a clergyman with power to agree with Derby and Oxford for one year, or to make proposals to the other committees, or either of them, to confer with a clergyman for a settlement and get his proposals, and report the same to a subsequent meeting. The clergyman about whom they were to confer was Rev. Samuel Griswold. These conferences were unsuccessful.

The next year they succeed in settling the Rev. Solomon Blakeslee; and yet he only remained three months, when the services of the Rev. Calvin White was secured for six months, at the end of which time he removed. In 1805 the Rev. Ammi Rodgers was engaged for one-third of his time for three months. At the expiration of three months the engagement was renewed and a resolution expressing the satisfaction of the Society with his services was adopted. This resolution was probably of his own proposal, and designed to varnish a character deeply stained with guilt. The Society subsequently became convinced of the charges made against him and he was dismissed. how long he continued in the Rectorship is not certainly known, but probably not more than one year; for in 1807 the services of the Rev. Ambrose Todd were secured for one-third of his time for one year. Who succeeded Rev. Mr. Todd the records do not show; but the Rev. Mr. Blakeslee was again rector in 1810, in which he continued nearly three years.

In 1812 an effort was made to unite this church and Oxford under one pastoral charge, but it failed. In 1813 the Rev. James Thompson became Rector, but he only remained one year. In 1814 the Rev. Mr. White was again employed. Like Mr. Thompson his connection with the parish was of short duration, and the following year, 1815, we find the Rev. Chauncy Prindle, Rector. In 1813 the Parish paid an assessment of $60 towards establishing a fund for the support of the Bishop.

At a meeting of the Parish, Jan. 29, 1816, measures were taken to complete the church, which up to this time had remained in an unfinished state. Abraham English, Josiah Nettleton, Theophilos Miles, Nathaniel Johnson and Josiah Swift were appointed a committee to obtain subscriptions towards this object; and in March of the same year they were authorized to expend the money thus raised. The amount subscribed was $1250, contributed by sixty-three persons. The Church when finished was consecrated Sept. 2nd, 1817, by the Right Reverend John Henry Hobart, D. D., Bishop of the Diocese of New York. After the consecration of the Church the Rev. Mr. Thompson again became the Rector and continued in that connection until 1819, when the Rev. Aaron Humphreys was elected.

In 1818 we find for the first time something of the condition of the Parish, so far as its strength was concerned, viz: number of communicants, 45; number of families, 63; number of persons, 279; grand levy, $7,420.95. In 1819 the Parish was drawn into a law suit by its first Rector, the Rev. Dr. Mansfield. The Parish became remiss in paying its portion for his support, and to quicken its energies this suit was brought. The Dr. gained his cause and the Parish was compelled to pay up all arrearages. The death of the Dr., April 11th, 1820, aged 96 years, relieved the Parish from this onerous charge. In 1821 a new roof was placed on the church at a cost of $60. In 1822 the slips were first rented at public sale, the proceeds of the sale amounting to $146.40. Up to this time the salary had been raised by a tax on the grand list. In the evening of the 1st of June of this year, 1822, the steeple of the church was struck by lightning; to repair the injury $182.88 was raised and $182.84 expended. In 1822 the Rev. Stephen Jewett became Rector of the Parish, and the following year made this report: number of communicants, 50; baptisms, 2; marriages, 4; funerals, 5; families, 55. Mr. Jewett continued in the Rectorship eleven years; and during his ministry there were baptised 127 infants and eighty adults; 51 marriages were solemnized and 88 persons were buried. In 1827 the Sunday School School was started, and "the Society's committee were appointed to superintend and regulate its affairs and procure such books as were required."

In the next year the bell was procured at a cost of $256.19. It was first used Aug. 12th, 1828, to toll the death of a son of Mr. John S. Moshier. In the summer of the same year a sum was raised by subscriptions for the purpose of painting the church and fencing the burying ground, amounting to $251, all of which was done at an expense of $247. In the same year Mr. Isaac Kinney presented the Parish with a stove. Before this time the church had not been warmed. The first organ was placed in the church about the year 1831. It was built by Mr. Whiting of New Haven, and in 1850 was enlarged and improved by Mr. Jardine of New York, at an expense of $505.

After the resignation of the Rev. Mr. Jewett in 1832, the Rev. Charles W. Bradlew became Rector of the Parish and remained in that connection one year, when he was succeeded by the Rev. John D. Smith at Easter, 1834. Mr. Smith continued in the Rectorship eleven years. In the first five years he officiated in this church every Sunday; the next two years he divided his services equally between this church and St. Peter's, Oxford. In 1841 this arrangement was discontinued, and Mr. Smith again confined his labors to this Parish. In 1841 the church underwent a complete repair at an expense of $150. The wood work in the interior was grained and the pulpit lowered about three feet; it would have added much more to the convenience of the hearers as well as the speaker, if it had been cut down five feet more; but the small reduction in height was looked upon as a great innovation by some of the older members of the Parish.

At Easter in 1845, Rev. Mr. Smith resigned the Rectorship of the Parish, and the Rev. John Purvis became the Rector. He remained two years and during his ministry he baptised six adults and twenty-six children, married three couple and attended sixteen funerals. At this time there were about one hundred communicants connected with the parish. In the summer of 1845 the church was painted on the outside at the cost of $120, which was defrayed by the ladies' sewing society. The next spring the ladies furnished the church with carpets, lamps and curtains for the windows. At the resignation of the Rev. Mr. Purvis the Rev. Abel Nichols officiated as a supply one year, until Easter, 1848. At the annual meeting in 1847 a report was made of the indebtedness of the Parish, which was $285.46. At the same time the committee were "instructed to procure from the grand list of the town the amount the several members of the Parish stand in said list and report the same to the next meeting." This action was taken with a view of taxing the members of the Parish sufficient to pay its indebtedness. Whether the prospect of a tax or dissatisfaction with the management of the affairs of the Parish or whether some other cause operated, is not recorded, but the records show that about this time a number of the members withdrew from its connection and left the burden which they had helped to create to be liquidated by the more faithful, though not more able, friends of the church. The report of the committee was not made as directed, and the debt was not paid. From Easter, 1848, until September of that year the church remained vacant, when the Rev. William F. Walker assumed the charge of the Parish. He was instituted into the Rectorship (the first and last institution in the Parish) Nov. 22nd, 1848, and continued in charge until January, 1851, when he removed to New York. He was subsequently tried by an ecclesiastical court and found guilty of immoralities for which he was degraded from the ministry, by Right Rev. Bishop Warnwright, at the General Convention of 1853. When he removed he took with him the Parish register, which has not yet, and probably never will be returned, as the last heard of it, it was being used for a scrap book. The loss of the register deprives the Parish of much valuable information in regard to the number of communicants, baptisms, marriages and deaths in the Parish for a long term of years. After his degradation from the ministry Walker lived a tragical life and died from the effect of an overdose of medicine prescribed for the relief of a nervous affection, in the early part of 1876.

At the Easter of 1851 the Rev. Charles G. Acly became Rector and remained two years. For several years previous to this a debt had been constantly increasing until it amounted to $850 at the Easter of 1853, which Mr. Acly succeeded in canceling before he left the Parish. The ladies' society contributed $170 of the amount paid. The Parish was now entirely free from debt. In June, 1853, the Rev. O. Evans Shannon became Rector of the Parish. At a meeting at Easter, 1856, the name of the Parish was changed from *Union* to Trinity. At this time the church needed considerable repairs; the timbers in the steeple were much decayed and it was considered unsafe by those who carefully examined it, the roof leaked badly, and the enlargement and repair of the church began to be seriously talked about. At Easter, 1857, a committee was appointed consisting of Thomas W. Holbrook, B. W. Smith and Sheldon Church, to see what could be done in regard to repairs, and to report at an adjourned meeting. Their report was made in the following June, that about $2,100 had been subscribed to defray the expense of the contemplated repairs, and it was resolved to begin the work. The plans of the alterations had been previously made by Mr. Austin of New Haven. A building committee was appointed, consisting of B. W. Smith, S. D. Russell and Sheldon Church, the two former only acted.

At the meeting which resolved to begin the work but four legal voters were present, viz: Harpin Riggs, S. D. Russell and Thomas W. Holbrook, Vestrymen, and B. W. Smith, Parish Clerk, three of which were in favor of the enterprise and one opposed it; but after the decision was made all acted in perfect harmony throughout. The last service was held in the old chhrch on the 5th of July, 1857. The expense of the work amounted to $6,000. The expense of furnishing the church with carpets, cushions, &c., and completing the steeple above the bell deck was defrayed by the ladies of the Parish, and amounted to over $800.

The church was consecrated by Right Rev. Bishop Williams, on the 11th of May, 1858. The building was almost entirely new, with the exception of the frame. The number of slips were increased from forty-two to seventy, and in doing the work a debt of $3,000 was contracted. To complete the church was no easy task with the limited amount of money at the disposal of the committee, and how the funds were furnished is known only to those who had the matter in charge. The collection of subscriptions or the loaning of money was made almost impossible by the financial crisis which commenced early in September after the work was begun, and caused financial ruin throughout the country. The committee received but little aid or encouragement from men connected with the Parish beyond its officers, and certainly they neither received or expected any from any other source; but on the contrary they were ridiculed in every possible manner, and it was prophesied that the undertaking would prove as disastrous as the "South Sea Bubble," that the church would never be completed, or if it was it never would be paid for. The workmen were advised to get their pay as they did their work or they never would get it; but to their credit they heeded not the advice. The lumber merchant was told more than once that he never would get pay for the lumber furnished for the building, and a leading merchant in the village refused to furnish the committee with *ten pounds of nails*, on the credit of the Parish. Acting under

SEYMOUR AND VICINITY. 29

these circumstances it is presumed that it would be an affectation for the committee to say that they were not considerably embarrassed; and yet, when the church was re-opened every bill of expense for the repairs had been paid with the exception of $30 for painting and about the same amount due to one of the joiners. In 1864 the debt contracted in rebuilding the church was reduced to less than four hundred dollars.

It has been said that the committee received but ltttle encouragement from the men connected with the Parish, but the same can not be said of the ladies, for they rendered most valuable aid, not only by the $800 which they contributed, but by the cheerful encouragement which was bestowed on every proper occasion. It will be doing no injustice to other ladies to mention in this connection the name of Mrs. M. P. Shannon, the wife of the Rector.

Rev. Mr. Shannon resigned the charge of the Parish the first of June, 1866. During his ministry here there were 185 baptisms performed, 105 persons were confirmed at nine visits of the Bishop; 166 were buried and 202 were joined in holy matrimony. On the 18th of May, 1864, the steeple of the church was again struck by lightning, but the damage done was but a few dollars. On the first of April, 1866, the Parish bought a house of Mrs. Lucy M. Beach for a Rectory, at a cost of $2,500. From the resignation of the Rev. Mr. Shannon to January, 1867, the Rectorship remained vacant. Regular services however were maintained by temporary supply. In the month of July, 1866, the church was painted on the outside at an expense of $290.53, of which sum $267.73 was paid by the ladies of the Parish.

The Rev. George Seabury entered upon the Rectorship of the Parish on the second Sunday in January, 1867. In the fall of the year 1867 the church was closed for two months; when the interior wood work was grained and the walls colored, at the cost of $800, over $600 of which was paid by the ladies of the Parish. The church was re-opened on the last Sunday in October. Before the re-opening of the church an altar had been placed in the chancel at the cost of 117.64, which was paid by the ladies of the Parish; and soon after a credence was placed at the left of the altar at the cost of $15.40, the gift of a female member of the Parish. At Christmas of this year a prayer desk and lecturn were placed in the chancel at the cost of $70.50, which was raised by subscriptions, and soon after prayer books for the altar and prayer desk at the cost of $29. In December, 1870, a cabinet organ was purchased for the Sunday School at the cost of $130, raised by subscriptions. In the summer of 1871 a new stone font was placed in the church. The cost of the same was $177.18, raised by the ladies of the Parish, the proceeds of a festival.

In 1872 hangings for the pulpit and lecturn were provided for by subscriptions at the cost of $26.50. In March, 1873, the Rectory property purchased in 1866 for $2,500, was sold for the same sum and the proceeds used to liquidate the debt incurred through the original purchase. About the same time subscriptions to the amount of about $1000 were secured to cancel the floating debt of the parish, (including the balance, $400, of the debt incurred in 1857 for rebuilding the church), this substantially freeing the Parish from debt.

The Rev. George Seabury resigned the Rectorship of the Parish on the 21st of April, 1875, after an encumbency of over eight years. During his Rectorship 132 persons were baptised, 74 persons received the rite of Confirmation, 169 persons were admitted to the Holy Communion, 46 marriages were solemnized, and the bodies of 128 were committed to the ground, "Earth to earth, ashes to ashes, dust to dust."

The present statistics of the Parish are nearly as follows: families, 135; baptised members of the church, 410; communicants, 157. The loss of the Parish register in 1851 rendes it impossible to state the statistics of the Parish with correctness previous to that time. On the 27th day of June, 1875, the steeple of the church was the third time struck by lightning; the damage done amounted to about $50.

Of the sixty-three persons who contributed to defray the expense of finishing the church in 1816, not one is now living. Mr. Isaac Kinney who died recently at the age of eighty-five was the last survivor. Of the slip holders in 1840, only two are slip holders at the present time, viz: Dr. S. C. Johnson and B. W. Smith, and only five of the whole number are now living. The subscription lists containing the names of the contributors and the amount contributed by each for church purposes, have in almost every instance been carefully preserved, and if now published, would probably prove more interesting to the public than to the living subscribers. During the first twenty-five years from the organization of the Parish eight clergymen were employed for a specified length of time, and in the next fifty-three years, nine, four of whom had charge of the Parish over forty-three years. On the 25th of September, 1875, the Rev. Edwin J. K. Lessel became Rector of the Parish. B. W. S.

THE INDIANS.

The Quinnipiac Indians, who mostly lived around New Haven Harbor, claimed the land to the north and northwest as far as the Naugatuck, but it was the Paugussetts who mostly occupied the valleys of the Housatonic and the Naugatuck. They were not numerous for a section so well adapted to yield liberal supplies to the hunter and the fisherman, for years before the merciless Mohawks from New York, of the warlike Iroquois race, had raided over this section, and the Connecticut Indians, who were of the peaceful Algonquin stock, had been greatly lessened in numbers.

The chief seat of the Paugussett Indians was at the mouth of the Naugatuck. On the triangular shaped tract of land which terminates at the junction of the two rivers, was their headquarters, and on the east bank of the Housatonic, about a mile above the confluence of the Housatonic and the Naugatuck, was their fortress, to which they retreated in times of danger. The last sachem at this place, Conquepotanah, died in 1731.

From the time of the first deeds from Indians to white men, in this vicinity, in 1662 and 1664, (see pp. 5 to 7), the Indians continued to dispose of their lands to the whites for probably about all they were worth at that time. The Indians were evidently satisfied with their renumeration and seem to have made no reprisals. Among those who sold the lands, and who were evidently sachems and chiefs, were Ansantaway, also written Ansantwan and Ansantawae, and his two sons Ockenuck, (Okenance, Akenanco and Ockenungo,) and Tountonemo, (Toutaemo); also Conquepotana, (Conchupatany, Conquepatana or Konkapotanauh, and Huntawah (Ahuntaway or Ahantaway). Cheshconeeg, who lived near Squantuck in 1693, is also identified with Chusqunnoog, who was in 1716 one of the grantors of a tract of land north of the Waterbury and Woodbury bounds, extending from the Naugatuck to the Shepang.

Referring to these sales of the lands, Dr. Anderson says: "It would be interesting to consider somewhat carefully the nature of this primitive proprietorship, for it has decided bearings upon the great modern question of the origin of property, and the significance of that 'institution' in the history of civilization. It was said by Sir Edmund Andross that Indian deeds were 'no better than the scratch of a bear's paw;' and there are those at the present day who, for different reasons from those which shaped the opinion of Andross, would deny that the aboriginal ownership of the soil was of any account whatever. Because their system was a kind of communism, their rights amount to nothing in the eyes of these modern thinkers. The early settlers, however, either from a sense of justice or out of regard to expediency, made it a rule to extinguish the titles of the natives by actual purchase. And when we consider the value of money at that day, the 'unimproved' condition of the lands, and the fact that in almost all cases the grantors reserved either large sections as hunting grounds, or else the right to hunt everywhere as before the sale, we can hardly say that the Indians were unfairly dealt with. The Indian usually reserved, or at least supposed that he was reserving, the right to hunt and fish everywhere, as before the lands were sold. In most of the towns, he remained harmless and unmolested in the neighborhood of the settlements, from generation to generation. The relations of the aboriginal inhabitants to the whites are well illustrated in the statement of an aged citizen of Farmington, who died within the present century, and who was born about 1730, 'that within his recollection the Indian children in the district school were not much fewer than those of the whites. In their snowballing parties the former used to take one side and the latter another, when they would be so equally balanced in numbers and prowess, as to render the battle a very tough one and the result doubtful.' But, however good the intentions of the white man may have been, the transformation of the wilderness into a fruitful field must go steadily on, and the Red Man must inevitably fall back, seeking new hunting grounds. For example, the Paugussets of the seacoast removed inland, as we have seen, and made their principal seat at the lower end of the Naugatuck Valley, which thus became practically a new settlement."

Joseph Mauwehu was the son of Gideon Mauwehu, a Pequot Indian, who lived for a time in or near Derby, and afterward removed to Scatacook and was chief of the Indians who collected there. Joseph was brought in his boyhood to Derby Neck to live with a Mr. Durand till he arrived at manhood, then was married to Sarah, of the Farmington Indians and settled in the south part of Derby near Turkey Hill, but afterward removed to Naukotunk, now Seymour. Joseph lived at first near the Falls, afterwards in a frame house built for him on the site where Dr. Thomas Stoddard now lives. De Forest, in his History of the Indians of Connecticut, gives the following account of Joseph Mauwehu:

THE INDIANS.

"Here a few followers gathered round him, and during forty or fifty years he played the part of a petty sachem. From his manner of pronouncing the word 'choose,' he was nick-named Chuce; and he is still well remembered in the village by the name of Old Chuce. He built his wigwam among a few oak trees near the falls, and supported himself, after the fashion of his race, by fishing and hunting and by the produce of a little patch of ground. When he took up his residence here, there were only two or three white families in the vicinity, but others followed, and gradually built up a village, which for many years was known by the name of Chuce-town. The sachem lived on the most amicable terms with his civilized neighbors, and I have heard him spoken of with feelings of evident kindness and sympathy by those who remembered him. Anecdotes are preserved of him which show that he was somewhat addicted to the use of ardent spirits, and considered rum or whisky essentially superior as a beverage to cold water. He used to come when he was thirsty to a fine spring bursting from a hollow rock at the foot of a hill, and there used to sit on the bank by the side of the spring, and drink the sweet water as it gushed from the rock, and praise it, and say that if there was only another spring, just such a spring, of rum, flowing by the side of it, he would ask for nothing more, but would be perfectly happy."

The spring referred to was a few rods east of where Davis' Block now stands, and the place is still marked by a well, the place having been gradually covered with earth to the depth of ten or twelve feet. There used to be a little lakelet south of the spring, three or four rods in length, abounding with small fish. This was drained about 1845, and afterward filled in.

Among the traditions of this period is one of a white man named Durand and an Indian who were hunting near the river about a mile below the bridge. Durand, seeing something moving in the bushes, which he supposed to be a deer, aimed at the place and fired. Hastening to the spot he found he had shot an Indian, who, in his last agonies, asked for water, which Durand brought for him from the river. The case was submitted to arbitration, and during the discussion one of the Indian witnesses remarked, referring to the Indian's bright leggings, that he never before knew of a deer wearing red stockings. The Indians were, however, satisfied that the homicide was accidental, and ever afterward treated the white hunter in the most friendly manner.

Mauwehu moved back to the falls for a while before he moved to Scatacook. He had eight children, two sons and six daughters. His oldest son, Joseph, enlisted as a soldier and went to Boston when hostilities commenced. After his term of service closed on his way home he was poisoned and died, probably by the opposers of the war. Three of his children died in childhood. Elihu, his youngest son, was an unusually intelligent Indian.

The tribe of which Mauwehu was a member, claimed the land as far north as Mattatuck or Waterbury. When the Indian census was taken by the colony in 1774, there were four of Chuse's band in Waterbury, where the first settlers were not particular to higgle with the Indians concerning the ownership of the land, but paid both the Farmington Tunxis and the Derby Paugussetts for it. They were paid in hard cash, not with the baubles sometimes used to cheat the Indians of their lands. The first deed was dated 1674, but the same land was bounded more definitely and again purchased in 1685, and the third time the Derby Indians were paid 25 shillings for "a small piece of land north of the Derby bounds, west of Naugatuck river and south of Toantick brook."

Of Eunice, a daughter of Mauwehu, and her children, De Forest said in 1850: "Old Eunice, as she was commonly called, died a number of years since. Her two children, Jim and Ruby, I have often seen coming into my native village, to sell parti-colored baskets and buy provisions and rum. Ruby was short and thick, and her face was coarse and stupid. Jim's huge form was bloated with liquor; his voice was coarse and hollow; and his steps, even when he was not intoxicated, were unsteady from the evil effects of ardent spirits. At present, I believe, they are all in their graves!"

"Knowing little of European modes of life, and judging of the colonists greatly by themselves, they supposed that the latter would cultivate but a little land, and support themselves for the rest by trading, fishing and hunting. Little did they think that in the course of years the white population would increase from scores to hundreds, and from hundreds to thousands; that the deep forests would be cut down; that the wild animals would disappear; that the fish would grow few in the rivers; and that a poor remnant....would eventually leave the graves of their forefathers, and wander away into another land. Could they have anticipated that a change so wonderful, and in their history so unprecedented, would of necessity follow the coming of the white man, they would have preferred the wampum tributes of the Pequots and the scalping parties of the Five Nations to the vicinity of a people so kind, so peaceable and yet so destructive." (De Forest, pp. 164, 165.)

"Chieftains of a vanished race,
In your ancient burial place,
By your fathers' ashes blest,
Now in peace securely rest.
Since on life you looked your last,
Changes o'er your land have passed;
Strangers came with iron sway,
And your tribes have passed away,
But your fate shall cherished be
In the strangers' memory;
Virtue long her watch shall keep,
Where the Red Men's ashes sleep."

HISTORY OF SEYMOUR. 35

In the early days of New England not only negroes, but Indians, were held as slaves to the whites. In the old records of Derby are occasional entries of Indian slaves. Following are deeds of this kind:

"Know all men by these presents that I, Joseph Gorham of Stratford, in the county of Fairfield, in the colony of Connecticut, for and in consideration of sixty pounds money in hand received, and well and truly paid by Col. Ebenezer Johnson of Derby, in the county of New Haven and colony aforesaid, to my full satisfaction and content, have sold and made over unto the said Ebenezer Johnson and to his heirs, executors and assigns forever, one Indian woman named Dinah, of about twenty-six years of age; for him, the said Johnson, his heirs, executors or assigns, to have, hold and enjoy the said Indian woman Dinah as his and their own proper estate from henceforth forever, during the said Dinah's life; affirming the said Dinah to be my own proper estate, and that I have in myself full power and lawful authority to sell and dispose of the said Dinah in manner as aforesaid, and that free and clear of all incumbrances whatsoever. In witness I set to my hand and seal in Stratford, this eight day of June in the year of our Lord God 1722. SAMUEL FRENCH,
Attorney for Capt. Gorham.

"Signed, sealed and delivered in presence of us,
JOHN CURTISS,
JOHN LEAVENWORTH."

"Know all men by these presents that I, Hannah Jonson, widow of the late deceased Colonel Ebenezer Jonson of Derby, in the county of New Haven, in the colony of Connecticut in New England, for the parently love and good will which I have towards my beloved son Timothy Jonson of Derby, in the county and colony aforesaid, and for divers other good and well-advised considerations me thereunto moving, have given and do by these presents fully, freely and absolutely give, grant and confirm unto my beloved son Timothy Johnson, him, his heirs and assigns forever: that is to say, one Indian woman called Dinah, and also a feather-bed that he hath now in possession; and by these presents I, the said Hannah Jonson, do give grant and confirm, and firmly make over the above-named Dinah and feather-bed with all their privileges and profits; and unto him, the said Timothy Jonson, his heirs and assigns forever, to have and to hold, to occupy, use and improve, as he, the said Timothy Jonson, his heirs and assigns, shall think fit, without any interruption, trouble or molestation any manner of way given by me, the said Hannah Jonson, or any of my heirs, executors or administrators, or any other person or persons from, by or under me. And furthermore I the said Hannah Jonson do by these presents for myself, my heirs, executors and administrators, covenant and promise to and with the said Timothy Jonson, his heirs and assigns, that we will forever warrant and defend him the said Timothy Jonson, his heirs and assigns, in the peaceable and quiet possession and enjoyment of the above-named Dinah and feather-bed against the lawful claims and demands of all persons whomsoever. In confirmation of all the above-mentioned pertikuarlyes [particulars], I the said Hannah Jonson have hereunto set my hand and seal this 22nd day of November, in the second year of the reign of our sovereign lord, King George the Second, and in the year one thousand seven hundred and twenty-eight. HANNAH JOHNSON,

"Signed, sealed and delivered in presence of
JOSEPH HULLS,
CHARLES JOHNSON.

"Derby, November 22, 1728.—This day Hannah Jonson, the subscriber of the above-written instrument, personally appeared and acknowledged this to be her own free act and deed, before me JOSEPH HULLS, Justice of the Peace."

The following entry is "verbatim et literatim":

"these may certifi whome it may consarn that tobee a Ingan that liv ed with me I had of a moheg Indian at new london 30 7 years agoo. he liv ed with me 12 year and is now and has bin a free man ever senc october the 6 1713

EBENEZER JOHNSON"

It is thought that Col. Johnson came in possession of Toby in 1688, the year of the beginning of King William's war, and perhaps Toby was one of the northern Indians in alliance with the French, taken prisoner in that war. A tradition has been handed down that Col. Johnson, with his forces, surrounded an Indian village, and cut down, as they supposed, every one in it, and that early the next morning as the Colonel was walking over the scene of the fight, a little Indian boy ran out of the bushes and clung to his leg with such a pleading look that the Colonel spared him, and brought him to his home by the Naugatuck. The manuscript quoted above seems to conflict with this interesting narrative.

Tobee's name is perpetuated by the appellation "Toby's Rocks," as applied to the rocky hills and cliffs south of High Rock, which, with the surrounding land, was given to him when he became a freeman.

The day of the Indian is passed, and that of the railroad and telegraph has come; yet we do not need to ride or walk far from our daily haunts to find a few mixed descendants of the aboriginees. These are mainly offshoots from the Pequots. They have lived for a long time in a narrow valley where a small stream and a large one unite, a spot which they have named, as Mr. Lossing tells us, *Pish-gach-ti-gock*—"the meeting of the waters." The name on white lips was changed to Scatacook, and the Indians became known as the Scatacook Indians. During a former generation these wards of civilization used to frequent the villages, peddling baskets and small wares to gain a livelihood.

At the beginning of the present century a remnant of the Paugussetts were still living in Woodbridge, bearing the name of Mack, and within a few years some, who were supposed to be their descendants, have frequently been seen in our streets offering for sale the baskets they had made.

Arrow heads of flint and quartz are still found in our fields, and occasionally an excavation reveals the resting place of some dusky warrior, distinguishable only by the relics which kindred hands had placed in his grave, hoping they might be of service to him in "the happy hunting grounds" to which they supposed his spirit had taken flight.

The last full blood Indian of this tribe, now reduced to a mere handful, mixed with negro and white blood—was the famous Eunice Mauwehu. She lived on a state reservation, as do now her dwindling descendants, and died in 1859, aged about 104 years. Her father was the last chief who ruled, and she was, consequently, of royal blood—a princess, in fact, as she would have been in name, had the tribal condition of her people continued. Until within a few weeks of her death, she often talked with freedom of the Indians and their habits. It was interesting to hear her pronunciation of the Indian words which have now become local property, and are attached to so many places. In almost every instance the modern use of them is merely a reduction of larger and more unmanageable ones—words which, as they are now used, have been shorn of a half or a third of their original syllables. She was intelligent, and accustomed to talk, and remembered, of course, many curious things. She made a striking statement that she saw, when a little girl, an old Indian who had seen King Philip. The Indian was telling her father of the personal traits and appearance of this doughty hero, and narrating, perhaps, some of his unrecorded exploits; and she was a wrapt listener to the conversation. To see an Indian who had seen King Philip was like putting your hand backward upon the vessel which landed on Plymouth Rock. When one sits down to think the matter seriously over, it does not seem so long as it did since Columbus discovered America, or since William the Conqueror set foot in England, or in fact, since anything ancient happened, when a few memories pasted together cover an arc of time."

The Early Settlers.

Benajah Johnson and Timothy, his brother, who settled in what is now Beacon Falls, came from Derby, but were natives of New Haven. Their father lived in a house which stood where the Exchange building now stands, and had eight sons. The wives of Timothy and Benajah Johnson were granddaughters of the Rev. Nathaniel Brewster, (son of Jonathan Brewster, who came to Plymouth in the Mayflower,) of Setauket Village, Brookhaven, Long Island, and great-granddaughters of Roger Ludlow, who was one of the four principal men who came over from England in 1630 with Gov. John Winthrop, and who began to settle the town of Dorchester, Mass. Mr. Ludlow was soon made deputy governor of Massachusetts. In 1636 he and seven others were invested by Massachusetts with all the powers of the government of the new colony of Connecticut. He removed to Windsor, where he lived till 1640, having been in the meantime appointed deputy governor of Connecticut and to other high offices of trust. In 1640 he and several others bought of the Indians Uncou, including the region now called Stratford, Bridgeport and Fairfield. The name belonged particularly to Fairfield, where Gov. Ludlow and his associates lived, and which was first discovered by Capt. Mason when pursuing the Pequot Indians westward after their memorable defeat in 1637. Thompson, in his history of Long Island, speaking of Mr. Brewster says: "He was a nephew of the Elder William Brewster of the Mayflower. He was a graduate in the first class of Harvard College in 1642, which consisted of nine young men.

During the Commonwealth, (from 1650 to 1660,) he was a minister in Norwalk, England, but on the restoration of monarchy, he returned, to America and was settled at Setauket, L. I., in 1665. His three sons, John, Daniel and Timothy, had resided there several years before his arrival from England. His wife was Sarah, daughter of Roger Ludlow, one of the most eminent men of New England. Mr. Ludlow was a member of the council and deputy governor of Massachusetts and Connecticut. He composed the first code of laws for the Connecticut colony, which was first published in 1650. Mr. Ludlow's daughter Sarah, the wife of Mr. Brewster, was represented as a person eminently distinguished for her genius and literary attainments. The three sons of Mr. Brewster were men of excellent character and highly useful during their lives. The wife of Benajah Johnson was first married to Joseph Hawkins of Derby, son of John Hawkins, Nov. 17, 1720, when she was 19 years old. He or his son Joseph, who was the ancestor of the Hawkinses of Derby, built the first house on Derby Point, where Birmingham now is, and a store for the purpose of importing and selling West India goods. This house and store were torn down not many years ago.

At this time the Housatonic below Derby was navigable for vessels which could come up to where now is the rolling mill of the iron works. This was the location of the store. There was no made land below the causeway, east of Birmingham. Where the two rivers met was a kind of triangular lake, deep and free from mud. Joseph Hawkins died about the year 1725. He had a daughter Mary, born Sept. 5th, 1721, who married Ebenezer Judd, of Waterbury, Nov. 17th, 1742, and was the mother of Brewster, Enoch, Ebenezer, Sarah, David, Benajah and Amos Judd, also a son Joseph, born April 30th, 1724, who carried on business in the store mentioned above. The widow Sarah (Brewster) Hawkins and Benajah Johnson were married Oct. 10th, 1728, and they soon occupied, as pioneers, the first house in Seymour, which was built at the foot of the first hill north of the house of Mr. Chatfield, posite the present house of William Gilyard. She took her name from her grandmother, Sarah Ludlow. About 1750 he built the house which was recently torn down to make room for Chatfield's present house. They had three children, Isaac, Zeviah and Sarah. Isaac was born in 1735 and died April 10th, 1813, aged 78 years. Zeviah was born in 1739 and died May 29th, 1816, aged 77 years. Isaac married Lois Hopkins, daughter of John Hopkins of Waterbury, and first cousin of the celebrated divine, Dr. Samuel Hopkins, who was the son of her uncle Timothy. The date of their marriage was January 21st, 1758, by Rev. Mark Leavenworth, the pastor of the church in Waterbury. Lois, his wife, was born in 1738, and died Oct. 16th, 1814, aged 76 years. Zeviah, sister of Isaac, was married to Abiel Fairchild, and their house was about three-fourths of a mile northwest of Pinesbridge. Mr. Fairchild was an excellent man. One of his neighbors said of him that he was an "Israelite indeed, in whom there was no guile." Sarah married John Hopkins of Waterbury. (Derby Records, vol. 9, p. 452.)

Benajah Johnson died April 13th, 1763, aged 59, and his remains were carried on a *horse litter* to the original burying ground of Derby. His widow, Sarah, died May 7th, 1773, at the house of her daughter, Mrs. Abiel Fairchild. Her remains were interred in a new burying ground which had been begun about five years previous to her death,—about 1768,—on a terrace above and west of the Naugatuck railroad, about a mile above the depot in Seymour. This place of burial was abandoned before the year 1800, when the present Pinesbridge cemetery was chosen and given by Alexander Johnson,

HISTORY OF SEYMOUR.

son of Timothy. This early burying ground of 1768 is now in the woods and overgrown with bushes and entirely neglected. The last burial in it was that of a mulatto by the name of Shubael, son of Pero, a pure-blooded African. When it was proposed to bury the remains of Shubael in the Pinesbridge ground, Mr. Alexander Johnson forbade it, and so they took them to the ground in the woods. The gravestones of Benajah Johnson and Sarah his wife were placed by their son Isaac, and are still standing.

Timothy Johnson and Abigail Brewster, sister of Sarah (Brewster) Hawkins, were married Feb. 21st, 1725. Their house was a little way below Pinesbridge, at a crossing-place on the Naugatuck, where a grandson, Elijah, died in 1847, aged 75. They were much annoyed by wild animals, especially by bears, which came down from Rock Rimmon and destroyed their crops, and by snakes which seemed to have a common rendezvous in that vicinity. After a while they went back to Derby, where they lived several years and then returned. They were both buried in the old burying ground in Derby. They had but one child, Alexander, who was born in 1730, and died in September, 1817, aged 87. The children of Capt. Alexander and Hannah Johnson were Timothy, born Jan. 21st, 1766, died Jan. 21st, 1836; David, Elijah, Nathaniel, Charles; Peter, born Oct. 9th, 1784; Alexander, born Feb. 22d, 1786; and Abigail Brewster, who married Moses Clark of Nyumphs.

Capt. James Wheeler of Derby, living in the section known as Turkey Hill, married Sarah Riggs, and had three daughters and seven sons—Samuel, Moses, John W., David, James, Joseph and Simeon. Capt. James Wheeler died in 1768. Samuel built the first house in Nyumphs, the eastern part of the town of Beacon Falls, and around him settled his brothers, Moses, David and James. Simeon built on Rimmon and had two sons, Nathan and Timothy, and a daughter who married Bradford Steele of Humphreysville. Samuel Wheeler was the father of Judge Abel Wheeler of Oxford, who built and lived in the house now occupied by S. P. Sanford. John W. Wheeler was the father of Mr. John Todd Wheeler, who recently died in Seymour at a great age. He was born at the house of his uncle, James Wheeler, which stood north of the woolen factory. Simeon's large two-story house stood opposite the auger factory north of the covered bridge.

What is called Lopus was first settled by Zadoc Sanford and Hezekiah Clark, grandfather of Sheldon Clark, about the year 1700. He and his brother David lost their lives in the Revolutionary war.

The dead were buried in Derby till about one hundred and ten years ago, when a few were interred in the burying ground opposite Rock Rimmon. The principal mode of carrying the dead to Derby was on a horse litter, which was extemporized as follows: Two horses with saddles were placed with their heads in the same direction, one forward of the other about seven or eight feet, and a long, stout linen bag turned or looped up at each end was put over each saddle to receive the ends of two long, smooth and strong poles, one on each side of the horses, and two or three cross pieces were put on the poles between the horses. On this litttter the coffin was placed lengthwise, and fastened to the cross pieces by cords. As the horses moved on, the bearers walked on each side and steadied the coffin. The mourners and their neighbors followed on foot and on horseback. The roads in those days were narrow and rough. When the distance from the house to the burying ground was not more than two or three miles, the coffin, placed on a bier, was usually borne on the shoulders of bearers, four and four. The coffin was often made of whitewood boards and colored with lamp black, but the most costly were made of cherry.

There were three principal ways to go from Derby to Waterbury in those old times. One way was on the east side of the Naugatuck by the house of Benajah Johnson and his son Isaac, on Skokorat, then up over Beacon Hill to Salem, &c. A second way was along the banks of the Naugatuck, crossing the stream sixteen times. This was often the way in summer, when the stream was low. A third way was over Great Hill, Rock'us (Rock-house) Hill, Quaker Farms, &c. When a man and his wife or daughter made the journey to Waterbury she rode behind him on a pillion.

The road across Great Hill was laid out previous to 1745, as appears incidentally in the following extract from the records:

To all whom it may concern, know ye, that we, the subscribers hereunto, at the desire of the selectmen of Derbey, were by the civil authority in Milford appointed and sworn to affix and sett up bounds between a certain highway within the bounds of Derbey aforesaid, on a place called the Great Hill, the land on the Northward side of the Highway claimed by Capt. Sam'l Bassitt on the rights of Saml. Hawley of Stratford, and on the Southward side of said highway claimed by Samuel Tomlinson, Abraham Wooster and Jonathan Lum. According to sd. appointment we on the second day of instant May did go upon the land, and considering the records and hearing the witnesses there present, set up, affix and renew the bounds on each side of sd. highway, and a heap of stones at the South west corner of said Bassitt's lying within the fence, and a heap of stones lying at the root of a great chestnut-tree that is blown down at the Southeast corner of said Bassitt's Claim, are the true original corners of Sd. Hawley's piece of land as laid out by a Committee December 21, 1698, and that a straight line from said Corners is the northward side of the Highway. And four rods Southward from said heap of stones at the root of said Chestnut tree there is a heap of stones at the root of a black oak tree in Sd. Jonathan Lum's fence, and another heap of stones by Woodbury road four rods Southward from a heap of stones at the corner of Sd. Bassitt's land, lying near to the corner of Sd. Tomlinson's land that was formerally Silvester Wooster's, and a straight line from said corners is the Southward side of said Highway. Done by us, Derbey, May 2d, 1745.

Entered July the 1st, A. D., 1745,
By me, Charles French, Regtr.

NATHANEL FAIRCHILD,
NATHAN BALDWIN, } Freeholders.
THOMAS CLARKE,

Joseph Mauwehu, or Chuse, about 1720, was presented by his father with a tract of land "near the falls of the Naugatuc," where a little band of Indians gathered around and recognized him as their chief. At first there were but two or three white families in the vicinity, but the number soon increased. Joe received the name Chuse from his manner of pronouncing *choose*, and from this the place was called Chusetown for more than fifty years. Chuse was a skillful hunter and captured not only small game, but occasionally a deer, wild turkey or bear. Finally the little tribe became scattered, and in 1763 Chuse and Houde sold a part of their land to Ebenezer Keeney, John Wooster and Joseph Hull, Jr. The following is a copy of the deed:

Know all men by these presents that we, Joseph Chuse, John Houde, Indians of Derbey, in the County of New Haven, and Colony of Connecticut in New England, with the advice of Samuel Baset, Esqr, Agent for the said Indians, according to the Allowance and Liberty Given to Ebenezer Keeney, John Wooster & Joseph Hull, Jr. of Derby in the county and colony aforesaid by the general assembly of the Colony of Connecticut on the first Thursday of May, A. D. 1760, & we the said Joseph Chuse, John Houde, Indians aforesd—with the Liberty and advice aforesd—do quit-claim and make over and confirm unto the said Ebenezer Keeney, John Wooster & Joseph Hull, Jnr., for the consideration of Eight Pounds Lawfull money to us paid by the said Ebenezer Keeney, John Wooster & Joseph Hull, Jr., which is to our full satisfaction, and we the said Joseph Chuse & John Houde do by these Presents Quitclaim, make over and Confirm to them the sd Ebenezer Keeney, John Wooster and Joseph Hull, Jr., a Certaine Parcell of Land Lying in sd Derby at the Falls, so called, Bounded as followeth, beginning at a heap of stones near the foot of the Great Bridge which is the original corner of the Falls Land, and run east four rods to a heap of stones on the edge of the hill by a walnut tree, then run north 46 degs. west eleven rods to a heap of stones on the edge of a knole, then West 14 Degs. north fourteen rods to a heap of stones four rods from the bank of the river, then run north 34 Degs. west fifteen rods to a heap of stones on the top of the high bank, then run west 45 Degs. north to a heap of stones by the river eighteen rods, and then its bounded southerly and westerly around to the first mentioned bounds near the foot of the Bridge all the way on the river, taking in the falls Rocks, Containing one acre against the falls and one acre and a half of land for highway to the said acre, with all the prevelidges and appurtenances belonging to said falls and land, and we the said Joseph Chuse, John Houde, Indians, as aforesaid do by these presents quitclaim, release and relinquish and make over to them, the said Ebenezer Keeney, John Wooster and Joseph Hull, Jr., and to their heirs and assigns forever without any molestation given by us or by our heirs or assigns. In Confirmation of the premises we have hereunto set our Hands and Seals this forth day of October, A. D., 1763.

Signed, Sealed and delivered
in presence of
CHARLES FRENCH,
JOHN HOLBROOK,

JOSEPH CHUSE | SEAL

JOHN HOUDE | SEAL

Derby, in the County of New Haven, on the day and date above said personally appeared Joseph Chuse and John Houde, signers and sealers to the above instrument and acknowledged the said instrument to be their free act and deed.
Before me, CHARLES FRENCH, Justice of the Peace.

It appears however, that some Indians remained in the vicinity long after this, as at a town meeting held Mar. 8, 1780, "Capt. Bradford Steel and Mr. Gideon Johnson were appointed a committee with full power to take care of the Indian Lands in Derby, and let out the same to the best advantage for the support of said Indians and to take care that there be no waste made on said land, and to render an account of their doings to said town of Derby."

Francis French, one of the original grantees of Derby, when it was set apart from the Milford plantation, came over in the ship "Defence" in 1635, being then but ten years of age. Savage, in his Dictionary of First Settlers of New England, says he came over with William, his * * * uncle, who settled at Cambridge, Mass. The English records of emigration of about that time record the departure of one Francis French, aged ten years, and his mother. This Francis French was one of the selectmen of the town in 1666, when the usual pay of town officials for their services was 2s. 6d. per day. His son Francis, born Feb. 11, 1677, was the father of Israel French, who built his house where now stands the house of William Gilyard, on Skocorat, in 1740, and so was a near neighbor of Benajah Johnson. This Israel French married Sarah Loveland Sept. 11, 1739. He was elected a Surveyor of Highway at a town meeting held Dec. 10th, 1764, and held the office several years. As the highway to Derby was then little better than a forest path, the office was probably no sinecure. His oldest son, David, born in 1741, lived in Bethany, then a parish of Woodbridge. He was familiarly known as King David, and the records mention him as a land holder of Nyumphs in 1766, and years afterward as prominent among the early Methodists. He died Aug. 4, 1821, aged 80 years. Another son of this pioneer,

Israel, was Charles, born Dec. 19, 1765, who was the father of Raymond French, Esq. Charles, brother of Israel French, was town clerk of Derby thirty-four years. The family were remarkable for their tenacious memories. It was said of Israel that after once hearing a sermon he could repeat it from memory with but little varation.

Richard Baldwin, one of the original grantees of the town of Derby, was a native of England, baptized there in 1622, and came over with his father Sylvanus on board ship Martin. Sylvanus was the son of Sylvester, from parish Ashton, Clinton, Bucks Co., Eng., who died in 1638 on ship Martin. Richard bought land Oct. 10th, 1669, in the south part of Derby, of Ockemunge, (written also Okenuch and Okenug,) "sole sachem of Paugussett," Chupps and Nehawkumme.

He was selected by the General Court as "Moderator of the new settlement of Paugussett, and he was one of the committee appointed on the part of the New Haven colony to effect the union with the Connecticut colony. Barnabas, son of Richard, was born in 1665. About six hundred acres in the south-west part of Woodbridge, which had been purchased of an Indian chief by his father, was conveyed to him by his brothers and sisters, and is largely in the possession of his descendants to the present day. He died in 1741. His son Timothy was born in 1695 and died in 1766. Capt. Timothy, son of the above mentioned, was born Dec. 13, 1722, in what was then Milford, near the Derby line, afterwards Woodbridge. Jan. 15, 1744, he was married to Sarah Beecher, who died in 1794. He was in 1779 one of the committee to facilitate the arrangements to strengthen the patriot army. He lived in what is now Seymour, and in 1789 was the first signer of the petition for the establishment of the first religious society formed in this place. See page 17. He had a slave Peter, baptized Dec. 23rd, 1790. He died Dec. 22, 1800. His children were Sarah, b. Apr. 11, 1746, m. Simeon Wheeler of Derby, Oct. 10, 1764: Timothy, b. 1749, lived in Derby, d. Aug. 30, 1822: Thaddeus, b. June 22, 1751: Anne, b. Feb. 24, 1757, m. Edmund Clark of Derby.

Occasionally the records of public proceedings seem to indicate a large proportion of the public men as residing in this part of old Derby. At the town meeting held Dec. 10, 1764, Daniel Holbrook was chosen moderator; Charles French, town clerk; Ashbel Loveland and Abiel Fairchild, grand jurors; John Howd, one of the tything men; and John Washband, surveyor of highways. In 1765, (Dec. 9th,) Daniel Holbrook is again mentioned as moderator of the town meeting, and Gideon and Nathaniel Johnson and John Basit were chosen surveyors of highway. Daniel Holbrook lived on Skocorat.

The practice of allowing cattle and swine to run at large on the common lands made necessary some method of marking, and each proprietor had his "earmark" duly recorded. Dr. Josiah Canfield's earmark was a swallow fork in the end of the left ear. (Entered Mar. 27, 1769.) Jonathan Miles' earmark was a swallow fork in each ear and a half penny cut in the upper side of the right ear. (Entered May 9, 1766.)

OXFORD.

As an adjoining town, carved, like Seymour, from what was once Derby, and whose boundary line has been changed from time to time, so as to include more or less of what is now Seymour, some account of the early history of Oxford may properly be inserted here. The first petition looking to the setting apart of Oxford as a separate parish was made to the General Assembly in May, 1740. A committee was appointed to investigate the case, and in May, 1741, the petition was granted in the following words:

"Whereas upon the memorial of Timothy Worster, John Twitchel and John Towner, &c., dwelling in the north and northwest part of the township of Derby, Isaac Trowbridge, John Weed, Jonas Weed, Joseph Weed, Thomas and Joseph Osborn, dwelling in the southwest part of Waterbury woods, in the old society in said Waterbury, and Isaac Knowles, Joseph Towner, Eliphalet Bristol, John Tift and Aaron Bristol, dwelling in the southeast part of the township of Woodberry woods in the parish of Southberry, moving to the General Assembly holden at Hartford, May, *anno Dom.* 1740, that they might become one entire, distinct ecclesiastical society, and praying for a committee, &c.; the said General Assembly did appoint a committee, who accordingly making their report to the General Assembly at New Haven in October last, and the same not being accepted; and the said General Assembly in October last appointing another committee, Colo. Benjamin Hall, Capt. Isaac Dickerman and Capt. John Fowler, to view and report, &c.: And whereas the said last mentioned committee have to this Assembly made their report, that according to the direction of said Assembly they have repaired to the abovesaid places, &c., and find and are of opinion, that it is necessary and best that the said inhabitants be made a distinct, separate ecclesiatical society, and that their bounds and limits be as followeth: Beginning at the mouth of the four mile brook in Derby bounds, where the brook emptieth itself into the great river, and to run as said brook runneth by said brook unto the bridge that is between the dwelling houses of Abel Gun and John Holbrook; and from said bridge by the highway that runneth between the land commonly called the Camp's Mortgage and the land called Quakers Farm Purchase, unto the river called the Little river; and thence as the Little river runneth to Naugatuck river; and thence northerly, by said Naugatuck river, that being the east bounds of said society, until it comes to the dividing line between the towns of Derby and Waterbury; thence turning westerly and running as the line runneth between the towns of Derby and Waterbury, as aforesaid, until it comes to the southeasterly boundary of Thomas and Joseph Osborn's farm in the bounds of Derby; and from thence to run northerly to the northeast corner boundary of Jos. Weed's farm in Waterbury town bounds; and from thence a northwesterly line to the northeast corner boundary of Isaac Trowbridge's farm in said Waterbury town bounds; and from thence to run westerly, in the line of said Trowbridge's farm, about sixty rods, to Woodberry town line; and thence to the northwest corner of Isaac Knowles's farm in the township of Woodberry; and from the northwest corner of said Knowles's farm a west line to the eight mile brook in the bounds of Woodberry; and then by the said brook, until it comes to the dividing line between the towns of Woodberry and Derby; and thence to run westerly in the line that divideth between the said towns of Woodberry and Derby, unto the great river; thence by the river southerly to the first mentioned boundary, the mouth of four mile brook; as by said report on file, dated May the 7th, *anno Dom.* 1741."

"*It is thereupon resolved by this Assembly*, That the above said memorialists, inhabitants of Derby, Waterbury and Woodberry, situate and living within the bounds and limits above described, be and become together one entire, separate and distinct ecclesiastical society or parish, subsisting and known by the name of the parish of Oxford, and endowed with all powers and privileges wherewith other parishes within this government are by law endowed."

The members of the "Society of Oxford," as they termed themselves, met for the first time and organized June 30, 1841. On the 6th of October, 1741, in meeting lawfully warned, it was voted, "by a two-thirds part of the inhabitants by law qualified to vote and present in meeting, to build a meeting house, and to meet the assembly in their next session at New Haven, to pray for a commission to appoint, order and fix the place whereon their meeting house shall be erected and built." Mr. Ebenezer Riggs was appointed agent to the General Assembly. The following is the order of the Assembly:

"Upon the report of Capt. Isaac Dickerman, Mr. James Talmadge and Mr. John Hitchcock, appointed by this Assembly to affix the place for the inhabitants of the parish of Oxford to build their meeting house upon, &c., the said committee having viewed their circumstances, and have set down a stake and laid stones to the same, at the south end of the hill, commonly called Jack's Hill, and near the highway that runs on the east side the Little river, on land belonging to Ephraim Washbourn, which said place the said committee report to be the most convenient place for the said inhabitants to build a meeting house upon: Resolved by this Assembly, that the abovesaid place be the place for the said inhabitants to build their meeting house upon; and the said inhabitants are hereby ordered to build a meeting house at the said place accordingly."

In May, 1743, "upon the prayer of Isaac Trowbridge, of Oxford parish, in behalf of himself and the rest of the inhabitants of said parish, praying this Assembly that they may be allowed to imbody into a church estate and be impowered and enabled to settle a minister according to the establishment of the churches in this government, &c.: Whereupon it is granted by this Assembly, that the said parish of Oxford, by and wiih the consent and approbation of the neighbouring churches, may imbody into church estate, and are hereby allowed and impowered to proceed to and settle a minister according to the establishment of the churches in this government."

Rev. Johnathan Lyman was ordained minister of the parish Oct. 4, 1745, and received a settlement of £500, to be paid in four yearly installments, and a salary of £125 per year. The next minister was Rev. David Bronson, from Milford, called Mar. 3rd, 1764, with a settlement of £200 and a salary of £60. He served the parish forty years, dying in 1806.

The Episcopal parish of St. Peter's was organized in 1764 by Rev. Richard Mansfield, the rector of the Derby church. The first settled clergyman of this parish was Rev. Mr. Prindle.

Although a separate parish since 1741, Oxford was not incorporated as a town until 1798. Father mention will be made in connection with contemporary events.

The Period of the Revolution.

The hardy pioneers who had made their homes among these hills and vales, of good old English stock, and, in part, descendants of the puritans who came over in the Mayflower, had grown stronger in their love of freedom, and were prompt to second the resistance to the encroachments upon their liberty. Meetings were held and arrangements made to send men, provisions and clothing, to the extent of their ability, to the patriot army. Of necessity the business was done in town meetings, but the records show that those living in this section did their duty nobly.

As early as Nov. 29th, 1774, a special town meeting was called to consider "the doings of the Reputable Continental Congress held at Philadelphia, Sept. 5th 1774," Daniel Holbrook, moderator. They agreed that the proposal of Congress was "a wise and judicious plan," and resolved that they would "faithfully adhere to and abide by the association entered into by said Congress." The meeting also voted as follows: "That the Gentlemen hereafter named be a Committee to see the same carried into execution, viz: Capt. John Holbrook, Mr Henry Tomlinson, Maj. Jabez Thompson, Mr John Pickit, Capt Thomas Clark, Mr Abraham Smith, Henry Whitney, Capt Joseph Riggs, Lieu^t Bradford Steel & Lieu^t Ebenezer Buckingham. In case a county Congress should be agreed upon in this county, then the aforesaid committee shall chuse and appoint two out of their number to attend such congress. Again the town have taken into their consideration the needy & distressed circumstances of the poor of the Town Boston, by the operation of a late act of Parliament blocking up their Harbour, this Town is opinion that it is necessary and their duty to contribute for their help."

In 1777 all male citizens of lawful age were required to take an oath of fidelity. Among those who took this oath appear the following familiar names. Rev. Daniel Humphrey, Charles French, Esqr, John Davis, Esqr, Thomas Clark, Esqr, Capt John Holbrook,* Agur Tomlinson, Joseph Durand, Benjamin Tomlinson, Capt Joseph Riggs, Abraham Basit, David DeForest, Philo Johnson, John Coe, Daniel Chatfield, Ruben Baldwin, Gideon Johnson, Nathan Mansfield, Bradford Steel, Eleazer Lewis,* Ebenezer Keeney, Henry Tomlinson,* Turel Whittemore, Abraham Beacher, Enos Bradley, Johnathan Hitchcock, Noah French, Nathaniel French, Samuel French, John Howd, David Johnson, Deacon Daniel Holbrook, Jn^r, Capt Nathaniel Johnson, Abraham Hawkins, Isaac Smith, Capt John Tomlinson, Capt William Clark, John Botchford, Ashbel Loveland, Asahel Johnson, Capt Joseph Lum, Joseph Loveland, Jehiel Spencer, Ebenezer Johnson, Samuel Russell, Zachariah Fairchild, Freegift Hawkins, Edward Howd, Joseph Canfield, Silas Baldwin,

Abijah Hull, Lewis Hubbell, Philo Holbrook, Eleazer Wooster. (*Specified in records as living on Great Hill.)

At a town meeting held Feb. 10th, 1777, the following action was taken: "Whereas the General Assembly of this state at their sessions at Middletown on the 18th day of December last past, by an act did regulate the prices of a number of articles in s^d act enumerated; and whereas it appears to this town that it is of the utmost consequence to the Community in general and to this town in particular that said act should be immediately carried into execution——Voted therefore that this town will by every legal measure endeavour to have the directions of said act strictly complyed with, this town being fully sensible that it is the duty of every friend to his country to sell & dispose of the articles enumerated in the act of assembly fixing the price of labour, provisions, &c., at the prices at which they are therein stated. Therefore,

Voted, that those of us who have any of them beyond what we want for our own consumption will readily and cheerfully sell them either for money or produce at the price in said act stated: and that we will esteem all persons who shall not do the same, enemies to their country, and treat them accordingly: Provided such person is properly convicted thereof before the Committee of Inspection of this Town: whom we impower to take cognizance of such offense."

That those who were serving their country on the field of battle were provided for by those who remained at home, as far as their means would permit, is shown by frequent votes of supplies and appointment of special committees to see that the supplies were furnished. On the 8th of Dec., 1777, John Coe, David DeForest and Capt Thomas Clark were appointed such a committee. In Dec., 1778, Saml Hull, David DeForest, Abraham Beecher, Capt John Tomlinson, Capt Timothy Baldwin, Capt John Riggs, Lieu^t Samuel Wheler, Saml Basit, Danl Holbrook, Junr, Capt Joseph Riggs, Ruben Tucker, Capt Nathaniel Johnson, Jos Russell, Noah Tomlinson, Thomas Clark, Esqr, John Howd, Capt John Holbrook, Edward Howd, Thadeus Baldwin and others were appointed a committee to provide clothing for the soldiers.

At a town meeting held Dec. 28th, 1778, it was voted to "give to each soldier in the Continental Army that counts for the town of Derby Ten Pounds money each in lew of the linnin overhawls, linnin shirts, and shoes that was voted to them last year as a bounty," and a town tax was laid of one shilling nine pence on the pound. Ensign John Humphrey was appointed to receive the money and to pay it to the soldiers.

Notwithstanding the excitement caused by the war and the heavy taxes upon the resources of the people, the schools were not forgotten, as the following documents show. The first seems to define a district in the western part of what is now Beacon Falls. The petition was granted in a town meeting Dec. 13th, 1779.

"Considering the distance that a considerable number of the inhabitants of the 4th & 5th districts live from the center of said districts and the inconvenience it is attended with, we therefore whose names are under written, desire to be set off to be an entire District. Signed and approved by us, Joseph Davis, Abraham Basit, Saml Smith, Jr., David Person, John Davis, John Church, Isaac Beecher, Abraham Beecher, Ebenezer Riggs, John Riggs, Bradford Steel, Committee. Beginning at the Stone Bridge at the lower end of Mr. Abraham Basit's Little river meadow, from thence running East to the top of the hill South of said Basit's, then running north with the high-way to Capt. Joseph Davis' including said Capt Davis, and from thence running East to the high way that runs west of Tobey's rock, then running

SEYMOUR AND VICINITY. 47

north to the head of the bounds between Derby & Waterbury, including Mrs Abigail Gunn's farm, then running West with the line to Waterbury road, then running South with the road down to Mr. Miles' barn, then running West to Touantick brook, then running South with the brook to the bridge over said Brook Southeast of David Twitchel's, and from thence southerly down to the road to the first mentioned bounds, including widow Ruth Bunnell."

The following seems to describe what now constitutes the sub-districts of Shrub Oak and Bungay, Seymour. Petition granted in a town meeting Dec. 27th, 1779.

"We the Subscribers whose names are underwritten desire the town of Derby would permit us to be formed into a school district, to take in part of the north district in the old society, and part of the Great Hill, and part of the Rimmon District, bounded as followeth, beginning at the mouth of Hassekee meadow brook, running northerly by Naugatuck river till it comes to the upper end of Long Plain, so called, then running westerly to the north side of the Park, then running southerly to the west side of John Botchford's farm, then running southerly to Mr. Joseph Canfield's barn, then running southerly to the highway twenty rods north of Nehemiah Botchford's house, then running with the highway to Hassekee meadow brook, then running by said brook to the first mentioned corner."

Bradford Steel,	Eunis Pritchard,	Abra^m Wooster,
Ashbel Steel,	James Pritchard, Jr.,	Daniel Davis,
Hezekiah Woodin,	Samuel Wooster,	Benjn Davis,
Ruben Perkins,	William Gordin,	Eben^r Keeney,
Ranford Whitney,	John Botchford,	Wm. Keeney,
Lowis Riggs,	Edward Harger,	Theo^{us} Miles,
John Wooster,	Josiah Washband,	Jona^n Miles.

JOHN RIGGS, } Committee.
JOHN TOMLINSON,

The following is from the minutes of a town meeting held Mar. 8th, 1780. "The town by their voate appoint Capt. Bradford Steel and Mr. Gideon Johnson a committe with full power to take care of the Indians' Lands in Derby, and let out the same to the best advantage for the support of said Indians, and to take care that there be no wast made on said land, and to render an account of their doings to said town of Derby." At the same meeting it was "voted that Abraham Hawkins, James Beard, Esq., Mr. John Humphrey, Capt. Nathan Person, Mr. Noah Tomlinson, Major Nathan Smith, David Tomlinson, Lieut. Levi Hotchkiss, Walter Wooster and Ebenezer Warner be a committee to assist the officers of the several companies in the town of Derby in raising their quota of men that shall be requested in this town for the continental and state service, at the expense of the town, with discretionary orders to give such premiums as said com^{tte} in their wisdom shall judge reasonable."

At a town meeting held June 27th, 1780, a rate of sixpence was voted "to pay the bounty to the Contenental soldiers and to defray town charges," and Capt. John Riggs, Capt. Daniel Holbrook and Capt. Bradford Steel were "appointed a com^{tte} to enlist contenental soldiers and to pay them their bounty."

It was also voted "that the town shall give each man that shall enlist himself as a soldier into the Contenental army during the war shall receive of the town as a bounty the sum of £20, to be paid in bills of credit of this state at the time the muster, and £20 pounds at the commencement of the second year of their service, and twenty pounds at the commencement of the 3^d year of their service. And all such as shall list for three years into the contenental army shall receive in bills of credit of this state £20 at the time of passing muster, & £15 at the commencement of the 2nd year of their service, and £10 at the commencement of the 3^d year of their service. And also all such persons as have or shall enlist into the contenental service for one year and seven months from the date of these presents shall receive £10 at passing muster, and £5 at the commencement of the 2nd canpaign.

By a vote at a town meeting held Nov. 13, 1780, it was provided that two shirts, two pair stockings, one pair shoes, and 1 pair mittens should be sent to each soldier.

In accordance with an act of the Assembly for collecting and storing a quantity of provisions, in the winter of 1780-81, the following prices were allowed for produce received as taxes, in lieu of money; beef of the best quality 5p. per pound, merchantable 4½p., pork 5 and 6p. per pound, wheat flour 24p. per hundred.

In Nov., 1780, "Johnathan Hitchcock, Capt. Thos Clark, John Howd, Capt John Tomlinson, Mr Johnathan Lum, Jn^r, and Lieu^t John Basit were appointed a committee to class the people agreeable to a late act of Assembly for filling up & compleating the state's Quotas of the Contenental Army," and measures were taken to provide clothing for those already in the field. At a town meeting held Dec. 11th, 1780, the following committee was appointed to take care of the soldiers' families; Peter Johnson, Joseph Russell, Thadeus Baldwin, Daniel Holbrook, Isaac Smith, Benj. Basit, Jabez Thompson, Christopher Smith, Andrew Smith, Johnathan Lum, Jn^r, John Basit, Josiah Strong, Robert Wheler, Isaac Beecher, Ebenezer Johnson, Abiel Fairchild, Jn^r and Noah Tomlinson.

Emancipation. At the same meeting it was "Voted that the authority and selectmen be impowered and directed to give certificates to Capt. Daniel Holbrook and Capt. John Wooster to free and emancipate their servants, Negro men, on the condition that the said negro men inlist into the State Rig^t to be raised for the defense of this state, for the town, one year." At a town meeting held in 1781 it was voted that the selectmen give to the Revd David Humphreys a certificate or liberty to manumit his servants, Cambridge and Cate his wife.

In April, 1781, the town was called on for men for the post of Horseneck, and the selectmen were empowered to provide horses and accoutrements for the service.

In March, 1782, some who had been called on for service in the army were released on payment of Fifty pounds and the required number of soldiers for one year were obtained by the offer of bounties. A tax of two pence on the pound was laid to pay the bounties. George Beard was chosen collector for the Great Hill Society, and with Micah Pool was to be a committee to enlist the number of soldiers required. Capt Nathaniel Johnson was appointed collector for the old Society and with Capt Daniel Holbrook constituted the committee of enlistment. Abraham Beecher was appointed collector in Oxford Society and Capt Ebenezer Riggs was associated with him as enlisting committee. At a later meeting Ebenezer Plant was appointed to assist in the Oxford Society. There were, here as elsewhere throughout the colonies, some who believed that they owed first and indissoluble allegiance to King George III. Except these "loyalists," those who could best leave home had freely volunteered early in the contest, and now those who re-

GEN. DAVID HUMPHREYS.

mained, as freely contributed of their scanty means to fill the quota needed to secure the final victory.

The names of those who served their country on the field of battle are not all now to be found, but so many as can be gleaned from old manuscripts and records are given below.

Gen. *David Humphreys*, son of Rev. Daniel Humphreys, was born in Derby in 1752. As a boy he was passionately fond of books, and in 1767 he entered college at the early age of fifteen, graduating with distinguished honor. During his college course he earned the title of "the young bard of Yale." As a poet he graced the progress of freedom and the pathways of liberty with the flowers of his pen, and in this way helped to fire the hearts of patriots and hasten the growth of that public opinion which culminated in the establishment of our republic. After a short residence in New York he returned to New Haven county, and before joining the army in 1778, he wrote many poetic effusions, one of which was addressed to his friends in Yale College, of which the following lines are a specimen.

> "Adieu, then, Yale! where youthful poets dwell,
> No more I linger by thy classic stream—
> Inglorious ease and sportive songs, Farewell!
> Thou startling clarion, break the sleeper's dream."

He entered the army as captain and in 1778 had been promoted as aid to Gen. Putnam with the rank of Major. Two years later he was appointed aid to General Washington, which position he retained during the war, enjoying the full confidence of the Commander-in-chief, and sharing his toil and danger. When the army of Cornwallis laid down their arms at Yorktown, Oct. 19th, 1781, Humphreys had the honor to receive the English colors and as a mark of approbation was dispatched to Congress "with copies of the returns of prisoners, arms, ordnance, etc., and twenty-five stands of colors, surrendered," with a letter from Washington warmly commending Col. Humphreys to the thanks and consideration of the government for his valor, fidelity and signal services. In November following he was voted an elegant sword in the "name of the United States in Congress assembled," and in 1786 it was presented by Gen. Knox, then Secretary of War, with imposing ceremonies. Congress also commissioned him Lieut. Colonel, dating back his commission to his appointment as aid to Washington. In 1784 he embarked for France in company with the brave but unfortunate Kosciusko; having on the appointment of Mr. Jefferson as ambassador to France, been appointed Secretary of Legation. In 1786 he returned to America and revisited the scenes of his youth.

Soon after his return, he was elected by his fellow citizens to be their representative in the legislature of the State, and continued to be elected for two years, when he was appointed to the command of a regiment raised for the western service. During the period that he held his office, he remained most of the time in Hartford; and, with Hopkins, Barlow and Trumbull, assisted in the publication of the Anarchiad. On the reduction of his regiment, he repaired to Mount Vernon, and continued with Gen. Washington until 1790, when he received the appointment of Minister to the court of Portugal, where he resided seven years. He was then appointed Minister to Spain, in which position he continued until 1802. He married a Spanish lady and thus added to his influence and rendered easier a project he had formed for the benefit of his native land. Knowing the superiority of Spanish wool, he planned to export some of the unrivalled Merino sheep to the United States, and in this he succeeded, though at great risk and cost, inasmuch as the Spanish laws forbade the exportation by stringent laws. He obtained permission to purchase four hundred Merinos in the mountain pastures of Estremadura and employing shepherds, drove them to the coast by night, remaining secreted by day. During this trip and the voyage to America the number was rapidly reduced, so that when landed at Derby dock they numbered only about one hundred. This was the first importation of Merino sheep into the United States. Gen. Humphreys then erected the first woolen factory in the United States in the village which took his name—Humphreysville—and in connection with which the labor of his later years will be spoken of at length.

Capt. Ebenezer Dayton was one of the brave privateersmen of the Sound, who annoyed the transports and boats of the tories and the British admiral offered a large bounty for his head and that of Caleb Brewster, his cousin. Fearing to leave his family at their home in Brookhaven, L. I., he brought them across the Sound to Milford. After remaining there a while, as a further precaution, he removed them to Bethany hill in Woodbridge. The robbery of the house occupied by Mrs. Dayton at that place by a British company and a band of tories is well described at length by Rev. Israel Warren in the book entitled "Chauncey Judd." Soon after the Revolution Capt. Dayton removed to Chusetown, where he opened a tavern, afterward the home for a time of Gen. Humphreys while he was establishing his woolen factory. Capt. Dayton, early seeing the advantage to his public house of a more direct communication with Waterbury and the towns above, set about the project of opening the Dug Road, which was finished about the beginning of the present century. Being of a restless disposition, he, after a while, undertook an enterprise in Louisiana, where he spent the latter part of his life.

Capt. Raymond Sanford, died in March, 1805, aged 53 years. *E.*

Lieut. Jabez Pritchard, who enlisted in July, 1777, under Capt. Corris, in the regiment of Col. Enos, was in command of the guard at Horseneck and afterward under the command of Major Humphreys near Fort Independence. In the conflict which occurred there, Lieut. Pritchard, with others, was taken prisoner and confined, first at King's Bridge, then in New York, and afterward on a prison-ship in the North River. His commission was taken from him by his inhuman captors and he was so ill treated that—like most of the other prisoners on that infamous ship—he survived but a short time. His generous character may be inferred from the fact that he might have escaped being taken prisoner but that he would not abandon a wounded comrade, and that he afterward divided his funds with a fellow prisoner, to which act of liberality Bradford Steel ascribed his own recovery by means of the decent provision and comforts which he was thus enabled to purchase.

Bradford Steel, son of Capt. Bradford Steel, born in 1761, enlisted July 10, 1777, at the age of sixteen, under Capt. Corris, regiment of Col. Enos. Tho company was at first stationed at Horseneck, but was soon after ordered to join a branch of the continental army under the command of Maj. Humphreys. They marched to Peekskill and there joined the army and marched to West Chester, about 2,000 strong and having two pieces of artillery. At the battle near Fort Independence, (General Varnum, commanding officer,) Steel, with Lieut. Pritchard and others, were taken prisoners. One of the number becoming deranged under his sufferings, the British soldiers beat him with their muskets, then tied him on a horse, took him to King's Bridge and threw him over, leaving him with his head and shoulders buried in the mud. At night Steel and thirteen companions were placed in a small tent guarded by Hessian soldiers, and if any one pressed out the tent cloth he was sure to feel the prick of a bayonet. Next day they were taken

SEYMOUR AND VICINITY.

to the Sugar House, where most of the prisoners had nothing to eat for three or four days. They were then allowed four ounces each of wormy sea biscuit and four ounces of Irish pork daily.

About the 1st of December they were put on board a ship in the North River. After fifteen days the small pox broke out. Steel and twenty-five others were taken to the hospital, where they had so little care that only four of the number survived. Steel saw one man with his feet so frozen that after a time they dropped off at the ankles. One day while Steel was imprisoned at the Sugar House, a well known tory came along and was all allowed by the guard to pass in. The prisoners seized him, dragged him to the pump, and the old pump handle went up and down in fine style until he was thoroughly drenched. He was then allowed to run, the prisoners saying good-bye to him with a shower of brickbats. Aug. 8, 1778, the few survivors received tidings that they were to be exchanged. Said Steel, "On the next day we were called out and paraded in the prison yard. To behold such a company of living skeletons, one might almost imagine that the prophecy concerning the dry bones had been fulfilled in us." Aug. 16th, they landed at Elizabethtown Point, and were marched to the meeting house where the exchange was effected. Steel and three others who were too much reduced by their sickness and sufferings to be capable of farther military service, were discharged and returned home. Steel recovered his health after some months and was for many years a highly respected citizen of Humphreysville, and deacon of the Congregational Society, dying Dec. 24, 1841, aged 80 years.

John White, son of Daniel White, died Feb. 19th, 1830, aged 73. *C.*

—— *Leach*, fought under Washington seven years, was several times badly wounded. *M.*

Abram Bassett, died Nov. 17th, 1853, aged 81 years. *E.*

Theophilus Miles, died 1822, aged 83 years. *E.*

Truman Loveland. E.

Sergt. James Baldwin.

Jesse Baldwin, brother to above.

Isaac Johnson, son of Benajah, died April 10th, 1813, aged 78. *M.*

Ezra Butler, afterward lived in the house now standing in the rear of the house of Sheldon Tucker.

—— *Ball.*

Jethro Martin, colored, Gen. Humphrey's servant, died in North Haven. Received a pension from the government until his death.

Joseph Mauwehu, (Chuse.)

Phineas Johnson, from Pinesbridge.

Nathaniel Johnson, from Pinesbridge, drafted, served till the close of the war.

Linus Lounsbury, of Nyumphs, was a soldier in the last French War and in the Revolution.

C—Buried in the Congregational Cemetery ; *E*—Episcopal Cemetery ; *M*—Methodist Cemetery.

SEYMOUR AND VICINITY.

The memorandum of Lieut. Jabez Pritchard, who was taken prisoner with Bradford Steel and others, and died on board the prison ship, was brought home by Steel, and contains the list of guards detailed at Horseneck from Sept. 15th to 21st. Most of the company were probably from this immediate vicinity. The names are

Gideon Alling,
Samuel Andress,
Abraham Barns,
Nathaniel Black,
Edward Bassett,
David Blakesley,
Corp. Bristol,
Corp. Candee,
Oliver Chatfield,
Caleb Chatfield,
Reuben Canfield,
Martin Clark,
George Clark,
Chauncey Clark,
Amos Collins,
Johnathan Cartright,
Jairus Congdon,
Joseph Deremore,
George Dachester,
Samuel Durand,
Ebenezer Durand,

Isaac Durand,
Vespation Eastman,
Corp. Foot,
Amos Fox,
Joseph Hulse,
Johnathan Lyman,
James Leech,
James Lines,
Nathan Mallory,
Major Morriss,
Abraham Murray,
Asahel Newel,
Ensign Osborn,
Lieut. Pierson,
Noah Peck,
John Prindle,
Jabez Pritchard,
John Priestly,
Oliver Root,
Joseph Sanford,

Philo Sperry,
Jabin Sperry,
Job Sperry,
Alexander Sperry,
Johnathan Sperry,
Corp. Smith,
Wm. Smith,
Lieut. Steel,
John Swift,
Wm. Tomlinson,
Thomas Torrance,
Adam Vose,
David Whittemore,
Samuel Wood,
Hezekiah Wooding,
Eli Washband,
Aaron Webster,
Bowers Washburn,
married the widow of David Wheeler, who died in the revolutionary service.
James Yatman.

That those who had sacrificed so much for freedom were prompt in more peaceful times to frame aright the new government may be seen from the following resolution, adopted Oct. 8th, 1787:

"Resolved that this Town will instruct, and that it does hereby instruct its representatives in the General assembly to use their influence to have a Convention called as speedily as possible for the purpose of taking into consideration the Constitution proposed by the Federal Convention, agreeable to the recommendation of Congress; in hopes that the business may be entered upon at an early period by the Legislature. Voted and passed unanimously."

Capt Daniel Holbrook and Capt John Holbrook were appointed the delegates to the State Convention.

A lottery was established in 1782 by authority of the Town of Derby to defray the expense of a highway from Derby to Woodbury, by the Housetunnock river and Wesquantuc or Rock House Hill Purchase, the cost not to exceed £500. Capt. Thomas Clark and Daniel Holbrook were to petition the General Assembly for its consent and approval. John Humphrey and Lieut Joseph Riggs were appointed to lay out the road. The same year Ashbel Loveland was appointed to build a bridge over the Naugatuck "below the falls."

Amity, embracing the present towns of Woodbridge and Bethany, was constituted a parish in October, 1739, in the following words:

Whereas upon the memorial of Ebenezer Beecher, Jasper Gunn, and the rest of the inhabitants of that part of the town of New Haven called Chestnut Hill, and also of Barnabas Baldwin, Joel Northrop and others, to the number of fifteen, living on the northerly bounds of Milford, moving to the General Assembly at New Haven in October last that they might become one entire distinct parish, and praying for a committee, &c., the said General Assembly did appoint a committee, who accordingly making their report to the General Assembly at Hartford in May last, and the same not being accepted; and the said General Assembly in May last appointing another committee, (*viz.*) Messrs. William Gould, William Ward and Joseph Thompson, to view and report, &c.: And whereas the said last mentioned committee have to this Assembly made their report, that according to the direction of the said Assembly they have repaired to the above said places, &c., and find and are of opinion that they, the above said inhabitants and farms, are able and sufficient to support parish charges, and that their bounds and limits ought to be as follows, *viz:* The north bounds in part upon the line between New Haven and Wallingford, so far as from New Haven north-west bounds easterly to the West Rocks till it comes down to the south side of Samuel Baldwin's land; thence westerly to the highway at the end of Sperry's Farms; thence southerly, keeping said highway that leads up the great hill to Darby road; then southerly at the rear of Westfield lots or second division lots; then southerly till it comes to the south side of Capt. Isaac Johnson's farm; then westwardly, between said Johnsons and that which was formerly Jeremiah Osborn's farm, to Milford east line; then westwardly to a cross highway; then keeping said highway to the south-east corner of Hogs Meadow Purchase, so called, in Milford; then westerly with the south line of Hogs Meadow Purchase, to the partition line between Milford and Derby; then northerly, in said partition line, to Lebanon brook, so called; then easterly by said Lebanon brook to New Haven line; then northerly in said line between New Haven and Milford till it comes to New Haven north-west corner bounds aforesaid; excluding the lands in said Milford on the race between New Haven line and Hogs Meadow Purchase from the aforesaid south bounds of the same, north to Derby road; and the lands of Fletcher Newton and John Hind in said Hogs Meadow Purchase, and Ephraim Gillett and his estate; and also exclusive of Samuel Sperry, Joshua Sperry and Jonathan Sperry, with their estates in New Haven bounds; as per said report on file, dated October sixth, 1738, doth appear:

It is thereupon resolved by this Assembly, That the above said memorialists, inhabitants of New Haven and Milford situated and living within the bounds and limits above described, exclusive of the persons and estates above in said committee's report exempted and excluded, as also exclusive of the lands of Capt. John Riggs, Samuel Riggs and Joseph Riggs, lying within the bounds of Milford, be and become together one entire, separate and distinct society or parish, subsisting and known by the name of the Parish of Amity, and endowed with all powers and privileges wherewith other parishes within this government are by law endowed." Col. Records, Vol. 8, pages 201–2.

Woodbridge was incorporated as a town in 1784, and was named from Rev. Benjamin Woodbridge, the first clergyman, who was ordained in 1742. This town has a fund of about five thousand dollars, given by Mr. Stephen

Sanford, who it appears was a firm friend to the American cause during the Revolution. His will read thus: "I also give to the society of Amity, in the town of New Haven, for the support of a Presbyterian or Congregational minister, in said society, *he being a friend to this, and the United States of America,* after my wife's estate therein shall be ended," &c.

Rev. Daniel Humphreys, the father of General David Humphreys, for fifty-four years the established minister of the First Society, died in 1787. The follwing is a copy of the inscription on his monument in the old Derby burying ground:

The Revd. Daniel Humphreys died Sept. 2d, 1787, in the 81st year of his age. For more than half a century he was the established minister of the first Society in this town. Mrs. Sarah Humphreys, the affectionate wife of his youth, and the tender companion of his advanced age, died July 29th, 1787, just five weeks before him.

> The seasons thus
> As ceaseless round a jarring world they roll,
> Still find them happy; and consenting spring
> Sheds her own rosy garlands on their heads:
> Till evening comes at last serene and mild,
> When after the long vernal day of Life
> Enamour'd more as more remembrance swells
> With many a proof of recollected love,
> Together down they sink in social sleep,
> Together freed their gentle spirits fly,
> To scenes where love and bliss immortal reign.

In 1789 the Congregational Society was formed by the withdrawal of twenty-six persons from the Congregational church in Derby, as narrated in the account of the Congregational church of Seymour, on pages 10 and 17 of this book. Capt. Timothy Baldwin was the first deacon of the new society and Levi Tomlinson the next. The latter lived in the house on the Ansonia road now owned by Judge Bronson. After losing three children he moved to Ohio. The third deacon was Bradford Steel, Jun.

The first mention on record of any action leading to the incorporation of the parish of Oxford as a separate town is in the record of a town meeting held Dec. 28th, 1789:—Doct^r Edward Carrington and Mr Shadrac Osborn were appointed a com^{tte} to take into consideration all the circumstances of the town respecting Oxford being made into a town.

In 1791 the first Methodist sermon in this vicinity was preached by Rev. Jesse Lee and from that time meetings continued to be held in the open air, in school-houses, and in dwelling houses, until 1818.

At this time there was a gristmill at the mouth of Little River, known as "Baldwin's Mill." The owner was Isaac Baldwin, a man of strong religious opinions and an unwearying student of the Scriptures. The Bible was kept near at hand and when the mill did not require his attention he improved his leisure in conning the sacred pages. William Kelly, of Litchfield, who was then a boy of eight or nine, living with his parents above Pinesbridge, said that when he came on horseback to the mill he would frequently find Mr. Baldwin reading his bible. One day in the winter of 179– he went down in the wheelpit to chop away the ice and was killed by the sudden starting of the wheel. His remains were interred in Milton Parish, Litchfield. His children were named Isaac, Esther, Sarah, and Eunice.

Bezaleel Peck owned the farm where Naaman Peck's house was since built. He was one of the early Methodists.

Samuel Sanford, from Bethany, was the first physician who located here. The following petition, in which he represented Chusetown, was granted at a town meeting held Jan. 7th, 1793:

"To the Inhabitants of the Town of Derby in Town Meeting assembled, sir^s, we the subscribers, of s^d Derby, Physicians, humbly beg liberty of said town that we may have liberty to set up the Enoculation of the Small Pox in s^d Town, as there is many of the inhabitants of said Town that have and now are going into other towns for s^d purpose, and the, yongue people much exposed to have it the natural way if not enoculated, & we beg leave to suggest whether it be not for the advantage of this town to save as much of the money in the town as may be, and your Petitioners are willing to be under any restrictions as shall be thought reasonable, and are likewise of opinion that they can enoculate as cheap if not cheaper than is done by other Physicians in other Towns.

EDWARD CRAFTS,
SAMUEL SANFORD,
Derby, Dec. 10th, 1792.   LIBERTY KIMBERLY.

The following is a copy of a report relative to the incorporation of the town of Oxford accepted in a town meeting held Feb. 4th, 1793. Pages 203-204, Derby Records, B., M., D. & T. P.

To the inhabitants of the town of Derby to be assembled in a meeting of s^d town to be held at the town house in s^d Derby, on Monday, the 4th day of Feby instant—we the subscribers, com^{tte} appointed at a meeting of s^d town on Monday, the 7th day of Jany last, to go out and view the circumstances and situation of s^d town respecting a division thereof, and to ascertain certain boundaries and lines for s^d division, and also to to take into consideration the expense or burden of s^d town, and all matters relating to s^d division, and to report our opinion thereon, beg leave to report;—That we have attended to s^d business and mutually agreed on the following boundaries and lines of a division of s^d town, viz:—beginning fifty rods above the mouth of Eight Mile Brook by Ousatonic River, from thence running north-easterly to the bend in Five Mile Brook at the foot of the hill, from thence running by s^d Brook to the bridge over s^d Brook in Woodbury old road, from thence to the south-east corner of Timothy Johnson's—formerly Abner Johnson's—dwelling house, from thence a due east course to the Little River, from thence by said River to the mouth where it empties into Naugatuck River, from thence crossing s^d Naugatuck River to the eastern shore, from thence running up by said River on the east side of s^d River to the mouth of the brook at the lower end of old Rimmon Plain, from thence to the end of the hill on the north-easterly side of s^d brook at the lower end of s^d Plain called Pessemire Hill, from thence on the ridge of s^d Rock to the upper end of s^d brook, from thence a due east course to the Woodbridge line. Also agreed that all land on either side of s^d line where lands are divided by s^d lines shall be put into the List in either of the towns where the owner thereof resides so long as the present owners shall possess the same. And it is further agreed that Oxford or the new proposed town shall support one-half of the Falls Bridge, so long as the present bridge shall stand; and when the present bridge will not answer to repair and it is necessary that a new bridge to be built, then Oxford or the s^d new town shall at their own expense, build a good and sufficient new bridge where s^d bridge now stands, to the acceptance of s^d town of Derby. And it is further agreed that any persons living near said line on either side where the line divided their land shall have their choice on which town they will belong, provided they make their choice in one year after s^d division, and shall belong where they enter ther List the first year after s^d division. And it is further agreed that when a division of s^d town shall be completed, the poor of s^d town of Derby shall be divided to each town, and all other burdens which may arise in consequence of any existing circumstances, shall be equally borne by each of said towns if divided according to the List of each town. All of which is submitted by your most humble servants.

Dated, Derby, Feby 4th, A. D., 1793.

SAM^l HULL,
DANIEL HOLBROOK,
THOMAS CLARK,
CALEB CANDE,
JOSIAH STRONG,
LEMAN STRONG,
} Com^tte

Leveret Pritchard, son of Sergt. Leveret Pritchard, who perished in the war of the revolution, was a sergeant of the 8th Company of the 32nd Regiment of Connecticut militia in 1793. Following is a copy of his commission.

Daniel Holbrook, Esqr, Lieu^t Col^o Commandant of the Thirty Second Regiment of Militia in the State of Connecticut in America.

To Leveret Pritchard, Greeting: You being nominated by the Eighth Company or train band in said Reg^t to be a Serg^t in S^d Company; Reposing special trust and confidence in your fidelity, courage and good conduct, I do by virtue of the Laws of this State me thereunto enabling, appoint and impower you to take S^d Company into your care as one of their Serg^ts and carefully and diligently to discharge that trust, exercising your inferior officers and soldiers in the use of their arms according to the discipline of war ordained by this State, keeping them in good order and commanding them to obey you as their Serg^t, and you are to observe all orders and directions as from time to time you shall receive from one or other your superior officers pursuant to the trust hereby reposed in you, and this shall be your sufficient warrant. Given under my Hand in Derby, the 2nd day of May, A. D., 1793.

DANIEL HOLBROOK.

Following is the roll of the company from the list left by Lieut. Pritchard. The marked ✕ were crossed off on account of death, removal to other towns, etc.

Ahira Anderson, ✕
Isaac Baldwin, ✕
Elias Baldwin,
Jesse Baldwin,
Silas Baldwin,
Samuel Bartist,
David Beach, ✕
William Beard,
Rubin Blake, ✕
Henry Carpenter,
John Church Caftrin,
John Churchel,
Timothy Churchel, ✕
Amos Clark,
Elias Clark,
Levy Clark,
Rufus Clark, ✕
Hezekiah Clark, Jun.,
Abel Church,
William Church,
Worrin Cridenton,
Sheldon Davis,
Asey French,
Enoch French,
Jeremiah Grissell,

Simeon Gunn,
Jonah Harden,
Joseph Hawkings,
Samuel B. Hine,
William Hine,
Chancy Johnson,
David Johnson,
Elijah Johnson,
Levy Johnson, ✕
Timothy Johnson,
Seley Judd,
John Kelley, ✕
Thomas Leavinsworth,
Zebulon Lines,
Ethel Lounsbury,
Samuel W. Mitchell,
Sebra Molthrop,
Ebenezer Orsborn, ✕
Philo Page,
Salmon Parker,
Eleazer Patchen, ✕
John Perry, ✕
Thomas Pitcher, ✕
Asher Rheylee,
James Riggs,

John Riggs, 4th,
Samuel Riggs,
John Sanford,
Moses Sanford, ✕
Abial Skeals, ✕
Elijah Smith,
Jesse Smith,
Lyman Smith,
John Spenser, ✕
George Steel,
Nathan Stiles, Jun.,
Oliver Stoddard,
Josiah Swift,
Thadias Thomas,
Cyrus Tomlinson,
William Tomlinson, ✕
Benjamin Tuttle,
Abel Wheeler,
Moses Wheeler, Jun.,
Thomas Wooding,
Jacob Warner, ✕
William Warner,
Josiah Worshburn, Jun.,
Henry Wooster, Jun.

SEYMOUR AND VICINITY.

In a town meeting held Sept. 21st, 1795, it was voted that to facilitate the division of the town, Derby would divide its representation with Oxford, if set off, each to have one representative.

At the same meeting it was "voted unanimously that this Town (Derby) Remonstrate ag^t the petition of Thad^s Burr & his associates praying for leave to build a bridge over Ousatonnack River near Stratford ferry, and do hereby app^t Mes^{rs} Leman Stone & John Howd our agents to Prefer a Remonstrance to the General Assembly & to prepare all Needful Evidence & Information to oppose Said Petition at the General Assembly."

Small Pox continued to be subject of legislation, and Dec. 11th, 1797, it was voted that "twenty-six persons and no more be granted liberty to receive the small pox, they to receive it by the evening of the 12th, and give bonds that they remain at the dwelling house of Mr. Benj. Davis in Derby and not depart the house until liberty be obtained from the authority and selectmen, and that the physician who inoculates them shall give bonds not to spread the small pox, and that the bonds be made payable to the selectmen, and that the selectmen and civil authority or their committee shall set limits to said house and have the superintending of the Physician and Patients, and that those who receive the small pox shall pay all expenses and save the town harmless."

At this meeting Dr. Sanford of Chusetown, with Dr. Crafts, petitioned for liberty to "inoculate at some suitable place." At an adjourned meeting held Dec. 17th permission was given to inoculate in separate hospitals, under the restrictions before established. The hospital established by Dr. Sanford was on the hill a little north of Castle Rock, convenient of access from his house, which stood on the northwest corner of West and Church streets.

In 1797 Rev. Michael Coate, circuit preacher, organized the Methodist Society, including in its membership Jesse Johnson, Isaac Baldwin, Esther Baldwin, Sarah Baldwin, Eunice Baldwin, George Clark, Lucy Hitchcock, Silas Johnson and Olive Johnson. Trinity church was built the same year. Vide page 25.

In 1798 an attempt was made to get a more direct road from Chusetown to New Haven, the town of Derby opposing it and appointing a committee to "the General Court to oppose the granting of liberty to a turnpike company to make a road from New Haven to Rimmon Falls, near Mrs. Dayton's, unless the turnpike company will agree and become obliged to be at all the expense of purchasing, making and repairing said road." Notwithstanding this the arrangement was finally made, the road to terminate at the lower bridge, then known as the bridge "at the falls of the Naugatuck" or Rimmon Falls.

At first the road ran down what is now Pearl and Main streets, but in 1802 purchases of land were made from Edmund Page, Lydia Keeney and Moses Riggs of a right of way direct to the bridge. The purchases were made by "Henry Daggett and Thomas Punderson of New Haven, and Levi Tomlinson of Chusetown, committee of the proprietors of the Turnpike Road from Thompson's Bridge in New Haven to the Falls Bridge in Chusetown." Page sold 45 rods of land 3 rods wide, 18 rods on the northeasterly line and 12 rods on the southwesterly line; bounded southerly on highway, easterly on grantor's land, northwesterly on land deeded to said committee, and westerly on grantor's land. D. R. Vol. 16, p. 197. Lydia Keeney sold "a part of her home lot containing sixty rods, being three rods wide and about twenty-five rods in length, for the purpose of extending the turnpike road from the highway between the dwellinghouse and blacksmith shop of Edwin Page, in a direct line to the Falls Bridge, running angling through the land of s^d Lydia in a direct line with the s^d turnpike extending southerly of s^d Blacksmith Shop," for $70, Feb. 16th. D. R., Vol. 16, p. 198.

On the 22d of February Moses Riggs of Oxford sold to the same parties "about one acre and thirty-five rods on the east side of the Naugatuck river, running on the Southwesterly line a straight line from the northeast corner of said bridge to about two feet easterly of the northeast corner of Edmund Page's Blacksmith Shop, from said bridge about fifty rods to Lydia Keeney's land, bounded southerly on said grantor's land then easterly on land, deeded by s^d Keeney to the grantees and their associates, then northeasterly on the grantor's land, and is three rods wide where it leaves s^d Keeney's land on the northerly line and on the top of the hill four rods wide, and four rods opposite said corner of said bridge, and is bounded northwesterly on highway. Said land is for the purpose of extending the Turnpike Road from the highway near s^d Blacksmith shop to said Bridge, D. R., Vol. 16, p. 199. The names—Thompson's Bridge Turnpike and Rimmon Falls Turnpike, were both used to designate this road.

These deeds make the old blacksmith shop, corner Maple and Pearl streets, quite an important landmark. There was never any deed of the land, the shop having been built on "proprietor's land," *i. e.* undivided land. When the right of location was questioned, it was defended on the ground of a vote of the town in 1798 which gave a title to any such land occupied by buildings standing at that time, at the same time forbidding any farther unauthorized appropriation of the public lands. It was claimed that the blacksmith shop was there in 1798, and that the title was therefore good. To make sure that the building, or some portion of it should continue to mark the spot, the north side of the building was cut out and the stone wall built, and under such circumstances it is probable that the exact location was preserved.

In making the turnpike, the cut on Maple street, below Washington avenue, was made in part by ponding the brook crossing the intersection of Maple and Pearl streets, and turning the water down the cut, carrying the sand and gravel into the river.

In April, 1798, John Riggs, Caleb Candee and Charles Bunnell on the part of the Parish of Oxford, and James Lewis, David Hitchcock and Canfield Gillett on the part of "the old town," as a joint committee, reported in addition to previous arrangements, that Oxford should pay £170 to the old town in three annual installments, as a condition of the division of the town.

The Falls Bridge seems to have been a continued source of discussion and expense, either for repairs or rebuilding. In March, 1802 arrangements were commenced for building a new bridge, the expense to be borne principally by Oxford Turnpike Co. and Rimmon Turnpike Co., assisted by the town of Derby on condition that citizens of the town may pass toll free. A toll gate was to be put up at the end of the bridge. In this year John Wooster sold his third of the Falls property to Bradford Steel for $167, and Oct. 8th, 1803, Steel purchased of Nathan Stiles his share of the Falls property and also a separate tract of land near by. Stiles came from Southbury and married a daughter of Capt. Ebenezer Dayton. He had carried on business here a number of years previous to 1802.

Bradford Steel had been carrying on business at the mouth of Little River, having his fulling mill and dye shop at the foot of the hill, and his finishing shop at the top of the hill east of the church. He lived in the old house (still standing in 1879,) until he sold it to Abial Canfield.

Up to this time the spinning wheel for flax and wool had been a necessary article in a well-ordered farm-house, and it was often accompanied by

SEYMOUR AND VICINITY.

the hand loom, reel, and cards,—soon superseded by carding machines. Mothers and daughters were skilled in making stout and durable cloth, as well as in the preparation of woolen yarn for mittens and stockings. Plainness of apparel was the rule and garments which had cost so many days of tiresome labor by members of the household were not likely to be thrown by for trifles. Steel made no cloth, the cloth dressed and finished by him being woven on hand looms in the homes of the industrious weavers.

In 1803, Col. David Humphrey, afterward known as General Humphrey, who was to be so closely identified with the interests of the place, came and purchased the Falls property, as appears by the deed in Derby Records, Vol. 17, page 30. The deed was given Dec. 13th and recites that "Col. David Humphreys, now of Boston, in the commonwealth of Massachusetts," purchased of Bradford Steel, Bradford Steel, Jr., and George Steel, for the sum of $2,647.92, "one certain piece of land lying in said Derby at a place called Rimmon Falls, it being the same tract of land formerly deeded by John Howd and Joseph Chuse, Indians, to John Wooster, Ebenezer Kinney and Joseph Hull, Jr., as may appear on Derby Records; for a particular description, refer to said Records; together with all the privileges, together with the saw mlll, two fulling mills, clothier's shop, and all the utensils, implements and apparatus belonging to and used in, and appendant and appurtenant in and to the said mills and clothier's shop standing on said land, together with the buildings thereon standing, together with the whole mill-dam across said Rimmon Falls."

The merino sheep had been introduced into the country and their great superiority being immediately manifest, farmers were everywhere glad to avail themselves of the opportunity to improve their stock. Gen. Humphrey did not encourage speculation but distributed his sheep judiciously among the farmers at $100 each, a price said to be less than the original cost. When the price rose to $400 he refused to sell, saying that he believed such sales would lead to ruinous speculation. But soon the price of merino bucks went up to $1,500 and a few were even sold as high as $3,000, and ewes sold from $1,000 to $1,500, John Bassett was offered $1,000 by Philo Bassett for a full blooded merino ewe lamb eight days old and refused to take less than $1,500. A few days after it was killed by a fox. Two young farmers united in buying a buck at $1,500 and the same day it died by being choked with an apple. But such mishaps checked the speculation but little, and it rapidly extended throughout New England, Vermont in particular being quickly supplied with some of the merinos.

Gen. Humphrey considered it of great importance to the interests of the country that manufactures, especially that of woolen cloths, should be introduced, and with the nucleus of the "mills and clothiers' shop" purchased of Stiles he immediately set about it. In 1806 he had the factory built which still stands on Factory street, near the race. The frame was raised on the fifth and sixth of June.

The name "Chusetown" appears on the town records as late as 1804, but it was soon changed to Humphreysville in honor of Gen. Humphrey, and this name was retained until 1850.

That he might the better carry out his plans Gen. Humphrey made several other purchases of land, among others the two following April 25, 1804. Of Nathan and Experience Wheeler, for $600, "one piece of land at a place called Northend, * * * lying on the west side of the highway, bounded northerly on John Swift's land, westerly on the Naugatuck River, southerly on land of Daniel Tucker, Jr., then easterly on s^d Tucker's land, then southerly on s^d

Tucker's land to the highway, then bounded easterly on highway to said Swift's land, containing about 117 acres, more or less; also one other piece of land, lying on the hill, bounded westerly on highway, northerly on land of Henry Wooster, Jr., then westerly on land of s^d Wooster, then again northerly on land of s^d Wooster, to the O'Cain land, then easterly on the O'Cain land, then again easterly on highway to land of Zephaniah Tucker, then southerly on s^d Tucker's land, then again easterly on s^d Tucker's land, then running westerly to the highway, as the fence now stands, containing about thirty-five acres of land, more or less, with the buildings belonging to s^d pieces of land."

Witnessed by John Humphreys, and John Humphreys, Jr.

He also purchased of Nathan Wheeler, a tract of 131 acres, adjoining lands of John Swift, Daniel Tucker, David Treat, Levi Hotchkiss, Fitch Smith, Capt. Reuben Tucker, "common land," and highway, with another piece of eight acres, for the consideration of $4,500.

Cattle sheep and hogs still roamed at large on the common lands. One item of the record says:—"David Humphrey's ear mark is a square half penny the upper side the right ear. Entered May 15th, 1804. Per John Humphreys, Reg^r."

A road from Shrub Oak to Derby Narrows was demanded by the people of Woodbury and adjoining towns, and laid out in 1805. The following resolution in regard to it was passed June 11th, "Voted that the selectmen of the town of Derby be directed, and they are hereby directed to take such measures as in their judgment shall appear most prudent and proper to procure the making of the Road they have lately laid out on the west side of Naugatuck River, Shruboak to Derby Landing, and cause the same to be well made at the expense of said town, and they are directed to collect and apply to that use any or all the monies due to said Town as they may find themselves needful."

President Dwight, of Yale College, wrote an interesting sketch of Humphreysville as he found it in the fall of 1811, which is here given:

"Within the limits of Derby, four miles and a half from the mouth of the Naugatuc, is a settlement named by the Legislature *Humphreysville*, from the Hon. David Humphreys, formerly Minister Plenipotentiary at the Court of Madrid. At this place a ridge of rocks, twenty feet in height crosses the river, and forms a perfect dam about two thirds of the distance. The remaining third is closed by an artificial dam. The stream is so large as to furnish an abundance of water at all times for any works which will probably ever be erected on the spot. Those already existing are a grist-mill, a saw-mill, a paper-mill, woolen manufactory, and a cotton manufactory, with all their proper appendages, and a considerable number of other buildings, destined to be the residences of the manufacturers, and for various other purposes.

A strong current of water in a channel, cut through the rock on the Eastern side, sets in motion all the machinery employed in these buildings. By this current are moved the grist-mill; two newly invented shearing machines; a breaker and finisher for carding sheep's wool; a machine for making ravellings; two jennies for spinning sheep's wool, under the roof of the grist-mill; the works in the paper-mill; a picker; two more carding machines for sheep's wool; and a billy with forty spindles in a third building; a fulling-mill ; a saw-mill, employed to cut the square timber, boards, laths, &c., for the different edifices, and to shape many of the wooden materials for the machinery ; two more fulling-mills on improved principles, immediately

SEYMOUR AND VICINITY.

connected with the clothier's shop; and the various machinery in a cotton manufactory, a building about one hundred feet long, thirty-six wide, and of four stories, capable of containing two thousand spindles with all their necessary apparatus.

The houses can accommodate with a comfortable residence about one hundred and fifty persons. Ten others in the neighbourhood will furnish comfortable residences for upwards of one hundred and fifty more. Gardens on a beautiful plat in the rear of the manufactories, furnish all the vegetables, necessary for the establishment.

The institution contains four broad and eight narrow looms, and eighteen stocking-frames.

The principal part of the labour in attending the machinery, in the cotton and woolen manufactories, is done by women and children; the former hired at from fifty cents to one dollar per week; the latter, apprentices, who are regularly instructed in reading, writing, and arithmetic.

The wages of the men are from five to twenty-one dollars, per month.

In Europe great complaints have been made of manufacturing establishments, as having been very commonly seats of vice, and disease. General Humphreys began this, with a determination either to prevent these evils, or if this could not be done, to give up the design. With regard to the health of his people it is sufficient to observe, that from the year 1804 to the year 1810, not an individual, belonging to the institution, died; and it is believed, that among no other equal number of persons there has been less disease.

With respect to vice it may be remarked, that every person, who is discovered to be openly immoral, is discharged.

At the commencement of the institution, discreet parents were reluctant to place their children in it, from unfavourable apprehensions concerning the tendency of such establishments. Since that time they have been offered in more than sufficient numbers.

In 1813, the Legislature, at the instance of Gen. Humphreys, passed a law, constituting the select-men and magistracy of the several towns in which manufactories had been or should be established, visitors of these institutions. This law required the proprietors to controul in a manner specified, the morals of all their workmen, and to educate the children, as other children in plain families throughout the State are educated. The visitors were directed to enquire annually, into the manner in which the proprietors conformed to this law. The reports of the visitors in Derby, concerning the establishment at Humphreysville, have been in a high degree honourable both to the proprietor and his people.

The manufactures at Humphreysville are esteemed excellent. The best broadcloth made here, is considered as inferiour to none which is imported.

Americans make all the machinery; and have invented several kinds of machines, which are considered as superior to such as have been devised in Europe for the same purposes.

Most of the weaving has been done in private families.

The scenery at this spot is delightfully romantic. The Fall is a fine object. The river, the buildings belonging to the institution, the valley, the bordering hills, farms, and houses, groves, and forests, united, form a landscape, in a high degree interesting.

The people of this country are, at least in my opinion, indebted not a little to Gen. Humphreys, both for erecting this manufacturing establishment, and for introducing into the United States the invaluable breed of Spanish sheep, known by the name of Merinos. One hundred of these animals he procured to be brought by the connivance of the Spanish Court, from the interiour of Spain to Lisbon ; and thence transported to Derby under his own eye. A few of them died in consequence of the voyage. The rest speedily regained their strength and flesh, and from that time the breed, instead of declining, has sensibly improved. For some years strong prejudices existed in the minds of the farmers throughout our country against this breed of sheep. Gen. Humphreys has done more than any other man, perhaps than all others, to remove this prejudice, and to spread them through the country.

In this manufactory he has, I think, fairly established three points of great importance. One is, that these manufactures can be carried on with success ; another, that the workmen can be preserved in good health, as that, enjoyed by any other class of men in the country ; and the third, that the deterioration of morals in such institutions, which is often complained of, is not necessary, but incidental, not inherent in the institution itself, but the fault of the proprietor.

Derby, then including Oxford, contained in 1756, 1,000 inhabitants; in 1774, 1,889; in 1790, 2,994. Derby alone contained in 1800, 1,878 inhabitants ; and, in 1810, 2,051."

The employes of the works were mostly Americans, but it was necessary to send to England at great expense for men who were skilled in some branches of the work which were entirely new in this country. Among them were John Winterbottom, father of Mrs. Ann S. Stevens, and Thomas Gilyard, son of Edmund and Nancy Gilyard, born in Leeds, England, March 20, 1786. He came to New York in the "Commerce" in the summer of 1807, having had a very fine passage of 45 days, and by packet to New Haven in three days sail, a quick trip for those times. He immediately commenced work for Humphreys and worked for him until March 28th, 1810. In this year the manufacture of stockings was carried on here on a considerable scale. This was new work for Gilyard, but he soon learned it. He was an active member of the Methodist Society for many years. His very interesting journal has furnished many dates and incidents for these pages.

In 1802 Canfield Gillett was appointed a committee to make application to the General Assembly for permission to sell the land near Rimmon Falls still belonging to the Indians, (D. R., B. M. D., p. 419,) but the permission was not granted until 1810. The land was sold in 1812. Following is a copy of the deed to Gen. Humphreys.

"*Whereas the General Assembly at their Session in May*, 1810, *authorized the Subscriber, Joseph Riggs of Derby, in New Haven County, to sell and convey certain lands lying in said Derby, Humpreysville, the property of Philip, Hestor and Mary, ando other certain Indian Proprietors, under the direction of the judge of Probate for New Haven District, who has ordered the subscriber to proceed in the sale thereof, now thereupon, in pursuaiance of said authority and in consideration of three hundred and forty-six dollars and twenty-five cents received to my full satisfaction of David Humphreys, Esq., of Derby aforesaid, I, the said Joseph Riggs, have remised, released and quitclaimed, and do by these presents remise, release and quitclaim to said Humphrey, his heirs and assigns forever, the following described two pieces of land, part of said lands directed to be sold as aforesaid, one piece bounded southerly and easterly on highways, northerly and westerly on said Humphreys' land, the other piece southerly and westerly on highways, northerly on part of said Indian lands I have sold to Phebe Styles, and easterly on said Humphreys and said Styles, containing by estimation in both pieces six acres and one half, the whole lying easterly of said Humphrey's Factorys, and comprehending the whole Indian Land excepting those contained in the conveyance to said*

SEYMOUR AND VICINITY.   63

Phebe Stiles, to have and to hold said remised and quitclaimed premises to him, the said David, his heirs and assigns forever, so that said Indians and no persons under them shall hereafter make claim to said remised premises, and I hereby covenant that I have full right to sell and convey in manner aforesaid. In testimony whereof I have hereto set my hand and seal this 7th day of Sept., 1812.

JOSEPH RIGGS { SEAL }

Signed, sealed and delivered
in presence of
ELIZUR GOODRICH,
BENJAMIN BULL.
Recorded March 9th 1813.
JOHN L. LOUNSBURY.

New Haven County ss. New Haven, Sept. 7, 1812, Personally appeared JOSEPH RIGGS, signer and sealer of the foregoing instrument, and acknowledged the same to be his free act and deed before me.

ELIZUR GOODRICH, Assistant.

The land referred to in above deed as sold to Phebe Stiles consisted of 2 acres and 20 rods, "beginning five rods and three feet from the northwest corner of Col. Humphrey's new cellar, and running northerly by highway to Col. David Humphreys' land, thence easterly to said Phebe's land, thence southerly by her lands to lands this day conveyed to said Humphreys, and thence by said land to place of beginning."

From the following extracts from the town records it appears that another tract of land was purchased for the Indians with the proceeds of the above sales. "Whereas the General assembly, June 7th, 1813, authorized Joseph Riggs to sell certain lands the property of Philip, Moses, Hester, Frank and Mary Seymour, which lay in Derby and which descended to them from John Howder (Howd), an Indian, and to lay out the avails in other real estate," a tract of land was purchased "for $230 for and in behalf of said Moses, Hester and the children of said Mary Seymour, the said Mary being deceased,"—four acres, three quarters and eleven rods bounded north on James Lewis, easterly and northerly on the lands of Isaac Short, and easterly on Isaac Thompson, southerly on land of Peter Johnson, and westerly on highway, "the children of said Mary Seymour (evidently Moses, Frank and Mary) to have one undivided third. To Phillip, Hester and representatives of said Mary, by Lewis and Betsey Prindle." Deed executed June 15th, 1813.

The War of 1812, calling for men and means from every section of the country, though it could but interrupt to some extent the progress of the peaceful arts, did not prevent a continued growth of the manufacturing industries in Humphreysville. The busy hum of machinery and the sound of preparations for war were alike heard in our peaceful valley. A company of artillery was formed in Humphreysville, including a few from Oxford, and sent to New London and stationed at the fort at the mouth of the river Thames. The following names of the members of the company have been obtained from inscriptions in our cemeteries and elderly people of the vicinity:

Col. Ira Smith, died Nov. 19th, 1822, aged 44 years.
Capt. Daniel Holbrook, d. Dec. 28th, 1828, æ 59.
Capt. Amadeus Dibble, d. Sept. 25th, 1843, æ 65.
Anson Baldwin.
Jesse Baldwin.
Abel Bassett, d. March 23rd, 1863, æ 78.
Samuel Bassett, d. Sept. 28th, 1851, æ 67.
William Bassett.
James Bowman.
Lewis Broadwell, d. Sept. 6th, 1844, æ 53.
Thomas Gilyard, d. Nov. 12th, 1853.
Jesse Hartshorn.
Chauncey Hatch, from Oxford.

Daniel Holbrook, 2nd.
William Kinney, d. Jan. 7th, 1847, æ 87.
Calvin Leavenworth, from Pines Bridge.
Isaac Leavenworth.
Isaac Losee.
Theophilus Miles, Jr., d. March 15th, 1840, æ 70.
John Moshier.
Ebenezer Northrop, d. Jan. 11th, 1835, æ 49.
Sheldon Tucker, d. Jan. 5th, 1843, æ 57.
Isaac White, d. Feb. 6th, 1862, æ 72.
Nathan Wooster.

The company was completed by a draft and Samuel Canfield was one of those who were drafted. He was then apprentice to Elias Gilbert, a machinist who worked in a shop which he had built near the corner of Hill and Pearl streets, next to the blacksmith shop, now occupied by William J. Roberts as a dwelling. Canfield was then eighteen years of age and had become so skillful a machinist that his employer, rather than lose his services, hired a substitute in his place. Gilbert did the machine work for Gen. Humphreys. William Humphreys, brother of Squire John Humphreys and nephew of Gen. Humphreys invented several useful machines to facilitate the manufacture of broadcloth, and the machines were built by Gilbert.

Gen. Humphreys was always ready to honor the memory of his brave com-patriots. At a town meeting held April 12th, 1813, he introduced and the following resolutions, which were passed unanimously:

Resolved, that Isaac Hull, Esq., a native of this town, Captain in the Navy of the U. S., and lately Commander of their Frigate Constitution, with the aid of his gallant officers and ships company and the smiles of Providence, having led the van in the career of our naval glory, capturing his Britanic Majesty's Frigate Guerriere commanded by Captain Dacres, has in our opinion deserved well of his country and is an ornament to the place of his nativity.

Resolved, that joining cordially in the universal applause, bestowed by our countrymen on Hull, Jones, Decatur, Bainbridge and Lawrence, and their brave and skillful associates in perils and triumphs, for their glorious naval achievements, we judge we have a right in our corporate capacity without showing an undue partiality to the first mentioned officer or stepping aside from our municipal duties, to notice more particularly his exemplary merits from having better opportunities of becoming acquainted with them.

Resolved, that Messrs. John L. Tomlinson, William Humphreys and Pearl Crafts be a committee to collect and digest such distinguishing and illustrative facts on the subject matter now before us as may be attainable and that they will cause the result to be communicated to the public in such manner as they shall deem most proper.

Resolved, that from the interruption of our Fisheries and navigation by war, silver and gold we have not, to offer in costly demonstrations of respect and esteem in imitation of richer towns, yet what we have we freely give, to wit, a tribute of gratitude.

Therefore, voted that Isaac Hull, Esq., being already constitutionally entitled to the freedom of this corporation, the thanks of this town be presented to him in a box made of heart of oak, the congenial growth of his native hills.

Voted, that the committee take order from the Selectmen for the performance of this service and report their proceedings to a future meeting for the express purpose that a town Record be made for the perpetual remembrance of these transactions.

Voted, that the committee above named be directed to transmit to Capt. Hull a certified copy of the foregoing resolutions.

SEYMOUR AND VICINITY.

While the fathers were intent on raising sheep the boys had their department in the new industry, and busied themselves to raise the teasels used in dressing the cloth. Gen. Humphreys organized the boys of the factory into a trainband, and furnished them with the articles necessary for drill. The silk flag, beautifully embroidered by Lady Humphreys, is now in the possession of Carlos French, Esq. The inscription is as follows:

PERSEVERANDO.

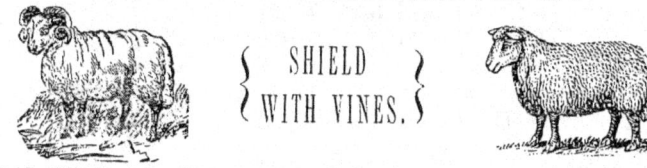

{ SHIELD }
{ WITH VINES. }

PACTA SEMPER SERVANDA.

MDCCCX.

Reverse: Semi-circle of 16 stars, "HUMPHREYS VILLE," eagle, arrows and state emblems.

Gen. Humphreys died in 1818. His remains were interred in New Haven Cemetery. Upon the monument is the following inscription on two tablets of copper inserted in the pedestal:

David Humphreys, LL. D. Acad. Scient. Philad. Mass. et Connect. et in Anglia Aquæ Solis et Regiæ Societat. socius. Patriæ et libertatis amore accensus, juvenis vitam reipub. integram consecravit. Patriam armis tuebatur, consiliis auxit, literis exornavit, apud exteras gentes concordia stabilivit.——In bello gerendo maximi ducis Washington administer et adjutor; in exercitu patrio Chiliarchus; in republica Connecticutensi, militum evocatorum imperator; ad aulam Lusitan. et Hispan. legatus. Iberia reversus natale solu n vellere vere aureo ditavit. In Historia et Poesi scriptor eximius; in artibus et scientiis excolendis, quæ vel decori vel usui inserviunt, optimus ipse et patronus et exemplar Omnibus demum officiis expletis, cursuq; vitæ feliciter peracto, fato cessit, Die XXI Febr nar. Anno Domini MDCCCXVIII, cum annos vixisset LXV.

This may be rendered as follows:

DAVID HUMPHREYS, Doctor of Laws, Member of the Academy of Science of Philadelphia, Massachusetts, and Connecticut; of the Bath [Agricultural] Society, and of the Royal Society of London.——Fired with the love of country and of liberty, he consecrated his youth wholly to the service of the Republic, which he defended by his arms, aided by his counsels, adorned by his learning, and preserved in harmony with foreign nations. In the field, he was the companion and aid of the great Washington, a Colonel in the army of his country, and commander of the Veteran Volunteers of Connecticut. He went Ambassador to the courts of Portugal and Spain, and returning, enriched his native land with the true golden fleece. He was a distinguished Historian and Poet;—a model and Patron of Science, and of the ornamental and useful arts. After a full discharge of every duty, and a life well spent, he died on the 21st day of February, 1818, aged 65 years.

Mrs. Mills, the wife of the pastor of Fairfield, and sister of General Humphrey, died in 1815. When the British burned Fairfield, July 7th, 1779, she fled on horseback, having put her best feather bed across the horse, and came to old Derby. The parsonage and the church in which her husband had preached were burned to the ground. She afterward had built for her the house in the rear of that now occupied by Dr. J. Kendall, and there remained until her death.

The representation of Humphreysville on the opposite page is from a woodcut made either by Abial Canfield or by an English engraver in his employ, for use as a trade mark in the papermill, which may be distinguished in the woodcut by the water wheel outside the mill. Between the papermill and the dam was the gristmill, previously occupied by Nathan Stiles as a woolen mill. At the right of the papermill was the sawmill. The large building at the right of the sawmill was the woolen factory in which General Humphreys made the first broadcloth ever manufactured in the United States. At the right of the factory was the "Long House," built by General Humphreys for dwellings for his employes. The building on the right and the smaller one adjoining were used by Gen. H. as an office and storehouse. The little building at the foot of the hill was a machine shop connected with the woolen factory. The barn on the hill beyond the office spire belonged to Abel Bassett.

There was a great revival in the fall and winter of 1816 among the Methodists. "Uncle Timothy" Hitchcock was one of the converts. Reuben Harris was in charge. He lived in the house with Stiles Johnson. The summer of 1816 was known as "the cold summer." There was frost every month in the year. In this year Worrull & Hudson sold out the papermill to Ebenezer Fisher and Henry LeForge.

In 1817 the Congregational Society was organized. Vide page 9. In connection with the sale of the old church to the Methodists the following from the records is of interest:

"*Humphreysville, Oct. 31, 1817. At a meeting of the Brethren of the Methodist Society, convened at the house of Timothy Hitchcock, for the purpose of transacting business for the benefit of sd. society, Voted that Robert Lees, Bezaleel Peck, Timothy Hitchcock and Stiles Johnson be appointed a Committee to arrange business with a committee appointed by the Congregationalists relative to the old Meeting House in Humphreys Ville.*

Robert Lees, Moderator.

☞*2nd, Voted, Newel Johnson—Secretary.*

☞*3rd, Voted, Stiles Johnson, Bezaleel Peck, Robert Lees, Thomas Gilyard, Timothy Hitchcock, Trustees for the said Methodist Society.*"

"*Copy of the Deed of the old Presbyterian Meeting-house in Humphreys Ville:*

To all people to whom these presents shall come, greeting: Know ye that we, Bradford Steele, Sarah Steele, William Kenney, Ira Smith, Phebe Stiles, & Philena Baldwin, of Derby in New Haven County, for the consideration of forty Dollars, rec'd to our full satisfaction of Stiles Johnson, Bezaleel Peck, Thomas Gilyard, Robert Lees and Timothy Hitchcock, do remise and release and forever quitclaim unto the said Johnson, Peck, Gilyard, Lees, and Hitchcock, for the use of the said Methodist Society, and unto their heirs and assigns forever, all the right, title and interest, claim & demand whatsoever, as we the said releasors have or ought to have in or to one certain House in Humphreys Ville, adjoining the burying ground

built for a House of Public Worship, to have and to hold the said premises, with all their appurtenances, unto the said Releasees & their heirs & Assigns forever, so that neither we the releasors, nor our heirs, nor any other person under us or them shall hereafter have any right or title in or to the premises or any part thereof, but therefrom we, and they are by these presents forever debarred & secluded.

In witness whereof we have hereunto set our hands & seals this 22nd day of Sept^r, Anno Domini, 1818.

       BRADFORD STEELE, [seal]
       SARAH STEELE, [seal]
       IRA SMITH, [seal]
       PHEBE STILES, [seal]
       WM. KENNEY, [seal]
       PHILENA BALDWIN. [seal]

Signed, sealed & delivered in presence of   John Humphreys, Jr.,
                 Phebe Stiles,
                 Elias Baldwin.

New Haven Co. S. S., Derby, Sept. 22, 1818, personally appeared B. S., S. S., I. S., P. S., W. K. & P. B., signers and sealers of the foregoing instrument, and acknowledged the same to be their free act & deed before me. John Humphreys, Jun'r, Justice of the Peace."

In 1818, Stiles Johnson gave by will to the Methodist Society the ground on which the church stands, with the green in front, also $334 in money, of which $134 was to be applied to repairs on the church, the $200 to be kept as a perpetual fund, the interest only to be applied for the support of "regular Sabbath preaching." Following is a copy of the clause of his will making the bequest to the church:

2nd.—*I will and bequeath to the Methodist Society in Humphreys Ville the land on which the meeting house now stands, together with the Green in front of said House, to be in the care of the Trustees of said house, for the benefit of said Society, and I also give three Hundred and thirty-four dollars of my Estate to be applied to the support of the Methodist traveling Preachers as long as there shall be regular Sabbath preaching in the aforesaid Meeting House, which money shall be raised and paid out of my Estate as though it was a Debt to the Trustees of said House and the Interest annually applied as aforesaid. But if it should be thought by the aforesaid Trustees more for the benefit of said Society, they may apply any sum not exceeding one Hundred and thirty-four dollars to making further repairs on said House, and the remainder to be applied as aforesaid. But if the Traveling Connection should neglect or refuse to supply said House as aforesaid then the Interest of said money shall be given to such local preachers as shall for the time being supply their place according to the discretion of the Trustees.*

In May, 1822, the Humphreysville Manufacturing Company was incorporated by act of the Legislature and organized with a capital of $50,000. John H. DeForest was the first president and J. Fisher Leaming, secretary. D. R., Vol. 22, p. 439. The falls property was purchased of Lewis Wahn of Philadelphia Aug. 1st, for $10,000; being described in D. R., Vol. 22, p. 432, as follows:

Beginning "*a few rods north of the east abutment of the Rimmon Falls bridge, at the corner of the highway, thence bounded northerly on said DeForest, thence easterly and southerly on said DeForest, thence easterly on highway to Bladen's Brook, thence northerly on Bladen's Brook to Naugatuck River, thence on said River to the dam, including the whole of the dam and all the water privileges appertaining thereto, then bounded southerly on said Naugatuck River to a point where the highway strikes said river, thence easterly on highway* to said first mentioned bounds, with all the mills, manufactories, & buildings standing thereon, (one piece of land—north of "Promised Land" to Bladen's Brook,) * * * one other piece of land on the west side of Naugatuck River, opposite the manufactory, bounded westerly on highway, southerly on highway to the channel, where the stream sometimes crosses the road, then bounded easterly on said channel to the Rimmon falls rock, thence running on said Fall rocks, bounded easterly on said Naugatuck River to the north side of the pathway leading from the river up the hill to the road bounded northeasterly on John, William and Elijah Humphreys' land, to the bars on the top of the hill at the highway, reserving a passway to the said John, William & Elijah Humphreys' land & to the burying ground, * * * containing about Sixteen acres, more or less, with the full, absolute & exclusive water privileges on both sides the river," &c.

The dam was soon rebuilt, the watercourse to the mills widened and cotton machinery put in. There was then one store in the valley and one on the hill near the Episcopal Church, DeForest lived at first in the Roth house, on west side of south Main street, opposite Pearl street, till he built the house now occupied by Raymond French, Esq., in which he lived until his death in 1839.

The shop in the fork of the road near the M. E. Church was built in 1825 by Newel Johnson, Isaac Kenney and Jesse Smith owning a portion of the building. The upper part of the building was used by Johnson for a carpenter and cabinet shop and what coffins were required in the village were made there. Newel Johnson built the houses of Denzel Hitchcock and others. Johnson's father lived in the house now occupied by Jeremiah Durand.

In 1828, Samuel R. Hickox, a local preacher from Southbury, moved into Humphreysville and took charge of the grist mill near the falls. Rev. Amos Pettengill was the pastor of the Congregational church, Rev. Stephen Jewett of the Episcopal church, and Rev. A. H. Sanford of the Methodist church. In this year a bell was first procured for the Episcopal church and a stove put up in the church. Previous to this, foot stoves were the only means of producing artificial warmth in the churches. About this time Judson English came from Hotchkisstown, now Westville, and bought out the tannery on the premises now owned by Arthur Rider, previously run by Benham. The bark mill was further south on the brook just below the railroad crossing. About ten years later English sold out to George Kirtland and removed to Great Hill. The father of Judson was one of the early Methodists, and Judson was a class-leader when living in Hotchkisstown. Always a very hard working man and strictly temperate, few men could beat him in the field until he was nearly seventy years of age. He was always a working member of the church of his choice, and a trustee and steward of the Great Hill Society until his death.

In 1830, Leveret Pritchard was living on the knoll opposite the saw-mill still standing near the upper end of Maple street. Previous to that time he lived in the house in the rear of Dr. J. Kendall's.

Chester Jones, a paper maker, built the north "Kirtland house," and kept a store in it. He afterward moved to Ohio, returning in a year or two, and was for several years superintendent of the Humphreysville Manufacturing Co's Papermill, living in the house close by. His wife was a daughter of Dea. Bradford Steele. The house afterward owned by William Kinney, was built by Jones. He afterward moved to Erie and died there. Ezekiel Gilbert had kept a store below Squantuck on the river road, but about this time he came to Humphreysville and kept the tavern on Broad street about two years, when he built the store now kept by H. W. Randall. Moshier then moved back into the hotel and occupied it until his death. While Gilbert was in the hotel Moshier lived in Mrs. Bliss' house, corner of north Main and Day streets, and built the paper mill.

In 1831, George Kirtland on behalf of the Methodist Society paid $110 for the land for the parsonage, including the place now owned by Evan Llewellyn, corner of Pearl and Grand streets, and the lot on the opposite corner now owned by Edwin Smith, Grand street not having been opened until many years after. The parsonage was built the following year.

The Humphreysville Manufacturing Co. commenced the work of paper-making in May with four employes, Chester Jones, Wm. Bates, Jane Patchen and Lois Thomson; but increased the number during the month to sixteen.

In 1832 business was prosperous and local industries remunerative. The Humphreysville Manufacturing Co. employed 18 hands and the 16th of April commenced running night and day, making paper for the New Haven Palladium and other papers. The mill produced not only news but tissue and colored papers.

Bethany was incorporated as a town in this year, having previously been a parish of Woodbridge.

At this time the store and house, corner of Pearl and Hill streets were occupied by David Sanford, and Lyman Smith kept the store across the road, in a building since removed. Sanford was called "Pitchfork Sanford." Years before he kept the blacksmith shop on the Woodbridge road, and one day in an altercation he killed a man with a pitchfork. Sanford was tried, branded and made to wear a cord around his neck the remainder of his life.

Butter sold at fourteen cents a pound and oak wood at three dollars a cord. Factory girls paid $1.12½ per week for board. A horse and wagon could be hired to go to New Haven for one dollar. These were fair samples of the prices of those times and illustrate the comparative purchasing value of a dollar then and now.

A "Caravan of Wild Beasts" exhibited near Moshier's tavern, in the summer of 1834 and excited considerable interest, being probably the first exhibition of the kind which ever passed through the village.

There was a great flood Jan. 31st, 1835, overflowing the lowlands, but doing no great damage. May 4th was the annual training day and a general holiday in the village.

The hard times of 1837, following years of prosperity and undue specu-lation, when the banks of New York and New Orleans alone failed to the amount of a hundred and fifty million of dollars, could but seriously affect the fortunes of Humphreysville, though far less in proportion than larger places generally, which had launched more deeply into the tide of inflation. Most of the factories and shops continued their work, though compelled for a time by a lack of a reliable circulating medium to do business principally by barter. The Humphreysville Manufacturing Co. however reduced its em-ployes to seven, and May 6th stopped entirely until the 9th of October, and the Cotton Factory shut down and remained idle until January 16th, 1838.

At this time there were three auger factories in the village, as follows: Raymond French, Blueville, where Rubber factory now stands.

Gilbert & Wooster, forges in Bennett Wooster's blacksmith shop, east of row of maples shown in cut on page 67, filing room in the south part of Gilbert's building on the corner of Main and Hill streets, and finishing room under the sawmill shown in cut of Humphreysville.

Walter French, near house now occupied by Warren French.

Wm. Burritt, now living in Waterbury, carried on the stove and tinware

VIEW OF THE CENTER IN 1838.

FROM BARBER'S HISTORICAL COLLECTIONS.

business in the Lyman Smith Building, as successor to Burritt & Lewis, whose store and shop was in the Wheeler Building, at the foot of Falls Hill. The firm had been dissolved in the fall of 1836, Edward Lewis going to Birmingham, where he still continues in the same business. In the spring of 1839 Burritt removed to Norwalk. Henry Bradley was then learning his trade with Burritt, and went with him to Norwalk to complete his engagement, returning a few years later to pursue the same business with M. Bradley, now in Westville, under the firm name of H. & M. Bradley.

The merchants of the place were—Ezekiel Gilbert, store adjoining his house, corner of Main and Hill streets; Wakeman & Stoddard, (Uri and Thomas,) store in Kinney's Building; and Andrew DeForest, store in the building now kept by Mr. Randall. Ezekiel Gilbert afterward sold out to Humphrey & Wooster.

Jeremiah Coggswell, an Indian, was shot on Great Hill Jan. 30th, 1838, by James Driver, in the house of the latter. From the evidence at the examination held at Moshier's tavern three days after it appeared that Coggswell was drunk and quarrelsome, and was killed in self-defence.

There was a great flood Jan. 7th, and considerable damage done to the paper-mill and other property.

Raymond French's auger factory was burned on the night of the 15th of July, 1841, but with characteristic energy he soon rebuilt.

Miles Culver built a house on the upper plains. He was a valuable member of the Congregational Church and also opened his doors to the Methodist ministers, services being frequently held in his house by Revs. Oliver Sykes and Sylvester Smith.

The Humphreysville Graveyard Association was organized in 1842. Anything relating to the last resting places of so many of our deceased relatives and friends must always be an object of mournful interest and no apology is needed for copying here the concise preamble and articles of association from the Derby Records, Vol. 32, page 51.

"Whereas, B. W. Smith, Samuel Bassett and 93 others formed an Association for the purpose of establishing a Village Grave Yard, and through Clark Wooster, Joshua Kendall and Wales French, a committee of trust, did purchase on the 26th day of Sept. 1842, one certain tract of land situated in Derby at Humphreysville bounded and described as follows, viz: Westerly on highway, southerly on land of Sarah Holbrook and John Lindley, easterly on the Naugatuck River, northerly on land of John Lindley, containing two and a half acres—now therefore for the well ordering of the affairs of said Association, and acting under the original articles of agreement, and in accordance with an act of the General Assembly of this state entitled an act concerning Burying Grounds and places of Sepulture, approved June 2, 1842, do for ourselves and successors form a body politic and corporate under the following articles of Association, viz:—

Art. 1st. This Association shall be called and known by the name of the Humphreysville Grave Yard Association.

Art. 2nd. The tract of Land described in the foregoing preamble is hereby appropriated to be forever used and occupied as a graveyard, and for no other purpose, and each original proprietor thereof in consideration of three dollars paid by him or her shall be entitled to one family lot in said Grave Yard 12 by 21 feet, and the surplus of ground shall be held in common by this Association and may be disposed of in such manner as the Association shall from time to time direct.

Art. 3rd. No Proprietor shall at any one and the same time hold in his own right more than five family lots in s^d Grave Yard.

Art. 4th. This Association shall at any meeting called for that purpose have power to lay taxes and order the collection thereof for the purpose of defraying all needful expenses for repairs and improvements, provided that each proprietor shall be taxed according to his right title and interest in said Grave Yard.

B. W. SMITH,
SAMUEL BASSETT,
BURITT HITCHCOCK.

Humphreysville, Dec. 14th, 1842.

Curtis Randall, who died Oct. 2nd, 1842, was the first to be buried in the new grave yard.

The Humphreysville Manufacturing Co. sold their paper-mill to Hodge & Co. Aug. 17th, 1843. The firm consisted of G. L. Hodge, S. Y. Beach and Samuel Roselle. Rev. Moses Blydenburg, pastor of the M. E. Church, lived on Great Hill, the Great Hill M. E. Church being then in a prosperous condition. The son of this zealous laborer in his Master's vineyard is now a prosperous lawyer in New Haven.

In '42 and '43 Anson G. Phelps and others talked of building a dam at Bryant's Plain and taking the water on the west side to Birmingham. Parties along the line of the proposed canal generally were willing to sell at fair prices, but one, a Mr. Booth, who owned considerable land in the proposed line, demanded such an exhorbitant price that the project was dropped for the time. Mr. Phelps, however, made considerable purchases on the east side of the river in and above what is now Ansonia, evidently preparing in a very quiet way for the execution of some important undertaking which he was not fully prepared to announce.

In 1844, Raymond French, John Dwight and Timothy Dwight, under the firm name of Raymond French & Co., were manufacturing augers, chisels, plane irons, &c., in their mill at Blueville, and finding their business increasing beyond the capacity of the mill, they put up additional machinery in the building at the mouth of Little River. Looking about for increased facilities Mr. French went to "Kinneytown" and called on Sheldon Church, who owned considerable land along the river, and together they rowed up and down the stream, noticing the surroundings and capacity of the stream. Returning down the stream he noticed a ledge of rocks in the bed of the river. Stepping out of the boat into the water, which, was perhaps three feet in depth, he walked across, to ascertain the extent of the ledge. Finding it afforded a rock bottom nearly the whole width of the stream he immediately determined that he would build a dam there. Mr. F. immediately bought a large tract of land on both sides of the river and work commenced without delay, to the great surprise of the people in the village below, who thus saw the fruit plucked while they were talking about it. In a few days Mr. Phelps came up and in his blandest manner congratulated Mr. French on his enterprise, and wished him success. After that not a week elapsed during the building of the dam but that Mr. Phelps came up to note the progress made. As the work progressed Mr. French found that the rock extended the whole width of the river, making a sure foundation ready for the superstructure. The bend at the west end was made to follow a turn of the rock. When the dam neared completion Mr. Phelps claimed a portion of the power on the ground of his owning so much land on either side where there was a fall below the dam. Mr. F. had however acquired sufficint land on the west side, as he supposed, to answer his purpose, either by actual deed or promise. Capt. Philo Holbrook had not yet given a deed, and probably without thinking of the effect, was induced to sell to Mr. Phelps for a trifling sum the right to flow a small stream back on his land. Mr. F. hearing of this went below Holbrook and made a purchase of William Church, from the river to the hill, and Phelps was checkmated. The result was that Phelps finally purchased the dam and appurtenances Dec. 5th, 1844, (D. R., Vol. 32, p. 53-55,) and R. French & Co. built the brick shops on the west side of Main street.

William Buffum purchased the cotton mill from the Humphreysville Manufacturing Co. July 1st, 1845, for $12,000 and the payment of $300 annually. The purchase included land 100 by 132 feet, being 50 feet on the front and rear, and 10 feet at each end of the mill, "with sufficient water to drive the water wheel in a reasonable manner for the purpose of propelling machinery to an amount suitable to the capacity of the wheel, using the water advantageously and economically," &c. D. R., Vol. 32, p. 98. He carried on the business until R. French & Co. sold their mill in Blueville to DeForest & Hodge, Oct. 31st, 1845, for $5,000. D. R., Vol. 33, p. 87. Portions of this property had been purchased by French & Upson of J. C. Wheeler, Nov. 21st, 1839, and Nov. 12th, 1840; and of Bassett & Smith Oct. 27th, 1843.

Some of the tradesmen of the place were—Robert J. Abbott, Apothecary and Druggist; David B. Clark, tavernkeepeer; John S. Moshier, tavernkeeper; Harrison Tomlinson, general country store; Ransom Tomlinson, dealer in meat, &c.

The first number of the Derby Journal appeared Dec. 25th, 1846, and contained the following appeal to the people of the Naugatuck Valley to aid in the construction of the Naugatuck railroad.

"The New York and New Haven Railroad Co. have contracted for the construction of their road, which is to be completed within the coming year.
This road will cross the Housatonic river a short distance above the present Washington Bridge, and from this point to Waterbury is probably from 25 to 28 miles. By following the Valley of the Naugatuck from Waterbury, or some point above, to where that stream unites with the Housatonic, and thence on the bank of that river to where the line intersects the New York road, a very easy grade would be obtained, and at a very moderate expenditure. An act of incorporation for this road was obtained in 1845, with power to commence at Plymouth or Waterbury, and to terminate at New Haven, Milford or Bridgeport, after passing through Derby.
* * * *   Much more might be said of the wants of the Naugatuck Valley, as well as of its resources, its business, its large amount of yet unused water-power, and its enterprise, but my present object is to direct attention to the subject, hoping that those more conversant with it will engage in the cause, and especially our northern friends." Humphreysville responded by subscribing $40,000.

The Mexican War created quite an excitement here and the Humphreysville Greys volunteered their services to the government to aid Gen. Taylor. The official document to muster them into service was received on the evening of Jan. 27th and read in the armory of the Humphreysville Greys, amidst much enthusiasm. The principal officers of the company were G. W. Divine, Captain ; Charles W. Storrs, 1st Lieutenant; Wilson Wyant, 2nd Lieutenant; W. W. Smith, Orderly Sergeant. The armory was over Ezekiel Gilbert's store and Mr. Gilbert came out and said,—"Zach. was whipped at one time, but he didn't know it and went on and conquered, and he will be our next president." And he was, but for some reason the company did not go to Mexico. Capt. Divine had served in the Florida War, and Capts. Wyant and Smith afterward did efficient service in the war of the rebellion. Clark Ford, now a resident of Seymour, was in the 9th New England Regiment, (Thomas H. Seymour, Col.) and is said to have pulled down the Mexican colors at Chapultepec. George N. Shelton, who was for many years a resident of Seymour and engaged in various enterprises here, was appointed Adjutant General by the Governor in May, 1847. Ransom Gaylord, a lawyer from Massachusetts, who had been teaching the Shrub Oak school, went to Waterbury and there enlisted as a private.

The Congregational Church was commenced in 1846, (vide, page 13,) and dedicated April 20th, 1847.

Daniel White represented Humphreysville this year in the board of selectmen of the town of Derby.

There were three heavy freshets in the spring of 1847, viz: Feb. 3rd and 8th, and March 20th.

The firm of French, Swift & Co. was formed in 1847, and April 5th, they bought the property on Little River, now owned by Henry B. Beecher, of James L. Spencer for $1,800. The firm consisted of Warren French, Charles Swift, John F. Marshall, Lemuel Bliss, H. B. Beecher and H. A. Radford, who were spoken of as the "six partners." A farther purchase was made from Clark Wooster Dec. 17th.

A union Sunday school celebration of the Congregational, Episcopal and Methodist churches was held the first Thursday in September. The Westville and Bethany Sunday schools were also invited and a grand holiday was the result.

The upper dam was commenced this year by French & Dwight, and the west abutment and wall were built.

The works of French, Swift & Co. caught fire Dec. 6th, in the finishing room, and the flames spread rapidly but were subdued after considerable damage had been done.

Albert J. Steele sold his furniture and undertaking business Dec. 20th, 1847, to Johnson & Bassett, David Johnson selling out to E. F. Bassett a year later. The salesroom was in the building in the south angle of Main and Hill streets, with a shop on the west side of Hill street, a little above, and another with power in the rear of the sawmill, near the falls. Five years later Mr. Bassett put up the building on the east side of Hill street for a shop and salesroom.

Phonography and phonotopy was taught by Charles Randall and the study was quite popular among the young folks.

Among the members of the Humphreysville Lyceum which met in the basement of the Congregational Church in the winter of 1847-8, was Dr. Yale, a botanic physician, who went to California in the time of the gold excitement, and died there. The name of the Lyceum was changed to the Humphreysville Literary Association. Luzon P. Morris was the president. Among the leading members were J. Kendall, John W. Storrs, John L. Daniels, Clement A. Sargent, George W. Divine and Henry Russell.

The cornerstone of the M. E. Church was laid June 19th, 1847, and the church was dedicated Jan. 18th, 1848. The following description of the church was published in the Derby Journal of Feb. 3rd:

The house is Gothic in design, 40 by 60 feet in dimensions, with a basement almost entirely above ground containing a commodious lecture-room and two classrooms. It has an excellent toned bell of 1,150 pounds weight. The slips, the ceiling, the altar and the galleries are grained; the scrolls on the slips are of black walnut. The base on the pulpit is painted in imitation of Egyptian marble, and the pulpit Sienua marble. The walls, above and below, are frescoed. The ascent from the basement to the vestibule, and from thence to the galleries, is by a spiral stairs in the steeple and turret. The windows in front, as also those in the steeple and turret, are of stained glass. The sofa, chairs and table, together with the columns for the pulpit

F. H. BEECHER'S AUGER AND BIT WORKS.

lamps are of black walnut. The cost of the building is about five thousand dollars. In the afternoon of the day of dedication the slips were rented, and the Trustees will realize about $600 therefrom.

Mr. Hotchkiss, of Birmingham, was the architect; and he is justly deserving of credit for the plan of the building—the proper proportion and beautiful symmetry of which, favorably impress almost every beholder. The writer of this is authorized to say that the building committee and trustees of the church take great pleasure in giving publicity to the feeling of entire satisfaction which they entertain in reference to those who have been employed in erecting the house—by the manner in which they have acquitted themselves.

To the Builder, Mr. Amos Hine, of Woodbridge, who has shown himself to be both competent and faithful. While engaged in the construction of the house, he has apparently identified himself with the interests of those by whom he was employed.

To the Masons, Mr. Jerry Bassett and Mr. Isaac Davis, both of this village, the former for the neat and substantial wall of the basement, together with the steps, both of which are pronounced second to none in this region; the latter, who has done himself great credit by the manner in which the walls were finished, in the plastering and frescoing, above and below.

To the Painter, Mr. Martin, also of this village, who in the external painting and sanding of the house, together with the internal work, has shown himself master of his business.—The work upon the pulpit was done at his own suggestion and expense, and is considered to be in excellent taste, presenting a beautiful contrast with the base, as well as the other parts of the house.

The trustees and members of the church take great pleasure in acknowledging the donation of the beautiful black walnut table, valued at twenty-six dollars, presented by Mr. Albert J. Steele, of this village, the workmanship of Mr. David Johnson, also of this village.

Great praise is also due to the ladies connected with the "Female Aid Society" of this church, and others who have assisted in the work, for the neat and tasteful manner in which they have furnished the church.—The carpets, the trimmings of the pulpit, the sofa, the chairs for the altar; together with the lamps, are the result of their labors, and speak much for their zeal and diligence in the cause.

While the members connected with this church congratulate themselves in having by the good hand of God, so comfortable a place in which to worship the God of their fathers, they are not insensible to the feeling of kindness and good will which has prompted members of the sister church to lend a helping hand in this enterprise. May the good Lord reward them an hundred fold, in spiritual blessings.   C. S.

The strip of land west of the church, now surrounded by rows of elms and maples, was deeded to the Society, Oct. 31st, 1848, by Rev. Sylvester Smith. D. R., Vol. 35, page 215.

"*Commencing at a point on the line of the highway at the corner of the land this day deeded to Medad K. Tucker, and running easterly on sd highway line $3\frac{28}{100}$ rods to the line of this grantee, thence southerly on sd grantee's line $14\frac{20}{100}$ rods to a point on Bennett Wooster's line close by a maple tree, thence running the south side of sd tree on sd Bennett Wooster's line $3\frac{20}{100}$ rods, thence northerly on Medad K. Tucker's line to the place of beginning, said last mentioned line being $14\frac{24}{100}$ rods, containing an area of 43 rods, hereby saving and reserving to myself the fee simple of sd land after the sd church shall fail to sustain a meeting house where their house now stands, hereby only granting the use of sd land to sd church so long as the same shall remain in the control and direction of the trustees of sd church during the time aforesaid solely for the accommodation of the Methodist E. Society of Humphreysville, and when the sd Society ceases to maintain sd church in the place where it now stands, then sd land is to revert to this Grantor, his heirs and assigns.*"

The subject of temperance was prominent at this time and the Humphreysville Total Abstinence Society had been organized for the purpose of holding temperance meetings and in various ways advancing the temperance cause. Mr. Isaac Losee, Sen., was the President of the Society in 1847. There were at this time five liquor-selling establishments in the place. In April of this year the officers of the Total Abstinence Society were John L. Daniels, President; Joshua Kendall and Julius Bassett, Vice-presidents; John W. Storrs, Secretary and Treasurer; William Tuthill, James L. Spencer and Charles Swift, Standing Committee.

The other Temperance Association, Rock Spring Division, No. 12, S. of T., was in a flourishing condition. In January its officers were:—John W. Storrs, W. P.; Daniel I. Putnam, W. A.; William W. Steele, R. S.; John Adams, A. R. S.; William B. Curtiss, F. S.; James A. Stephens, C.; David Tucker, A. C.; Charles Swift, I. S.; Perry Cadwell, O. S. In the fall they were—John W. Storrs, P. W. P.; D. J. Putnam, W. P.; J. A. Stevens, W. A.; John Adams, R. S.; James L. Spencer, A. R. S.; W. B. Curtiss, F. S.; Wilson Wyant, T.; David Tucker, C.; Austin R. Pardee, A. C.; Wilson Hendryx, I. S.; Edwin Wheeler, O. S.

The New Haven Courier in February contained the following in regard to the proposed Naugatuck Railroad, the building of which was commenced in April:

No business man can doubt but that the trade of 20 or 30,000 people is worth obtaining, or that it would be desirable to have this city a depot for the five millions worth of manufactured goods annually produced in that region. But the present trade of that valley is nothing, absolutely nothing, to what it will, and must, be when communication is opened by means of a railroad. We have the authority of the State Surveyor for saying, that the facilities for manufacturing on the Naugatuck are greater than on any other stream in the State, and these facilities are not as yet half or quarter improved. Besides the Naugatuck, there is an unimproved power on the Housatonic, at Birmingham, more than twice as great as all the power at Lowell, and capitalists already have their eyes upon this, and it will be improved.

The Saturday before May 25th, there was a tremendous hailstorm accompanied by terrific thunder and lightning and torrents of rain. The ground was literally covered with hailstones, many of which were as large as pigeons eggs. As described by a writer of the scene, "It seemed for a few moments as if all Iceland had been broken up and was being showered down on our devoted heads." One horse was so frightened that he ran, throwing out its driver, who was seriously injured. Other horses were so stupefied with fear that it was with great difficulty that their drivers could urge them to places of shelter.

Leverett Pritchard died June 4th, in the 83rd year of his age. He had "been an inhabitant of the town from his infancy, and his character ever remained unspotted, so much so that his morality had become proverbial. From his door the friendless were never spurned, and from his bounty the hungry were fed and the naked clothed. In him the needy and destitute found a friend."—(Derby Journal.)

The Thursday before June 15th two men were covered by a landslide about a mile above the village, where workmen were engaged in making excavations for the railroad. One of them was not found until life was extinct. The railroad bridge across the Naugatuck was built under contract by Dwight & French.

The new hall of Rock Spring Division, at the west end of the Naugatuck Bridge, was dedicated on the Friday evening before the 16th of October.

George W. Bungay was the principal speaker and a poem was read by John W. Storrs.

On Tuesday evening, Aug. 1st, 1848, Gough made a powerful temperance speech in the M. E. Church, and on Monday and Wednesday evenings of the same week he lectured in the Congregational Church.

The telegraph came following close upon the railroad, and in November was in operation.

In this year Mr. Hyde from Oxford, N. Y., called to see his native place after an absence of thirty-four years. His father had been drowned in the Housatonic River. His mother was buried in the Methodist cemetery. His brother Abijah Hyde was then living in Quaker Farms. Orson Hyde, the Mormon, was a brother of these. The old homestead was in the corner of the lot opposite Cedar Ridge school house, now owned by Judge Munson. The Hydes were remarkable for their good memories. Abijah and his brother from York state were Methodists, and the York state man has sons who have been noted as scholars in the M. E. Church.

A young man named Pitt was killed Nov. 11th, 1848, near the Bell school house, by the bursting of a cannon which was being fired in honor of the election of General Taylor to the presidency.

Most of the maples near the M. E. Church were set out Oct. 28th, 1848, by Rev. Sylvester Smith and his son. Two had been set out on the west side of the church some years before by Alva Davis.

Lewis Bunce lost about $4,000 by the burning of his papermill, Dec. 23, 1848. Stock to the amount of $675 was saved and he received $1,325 insurance.

The Rimmon paper Co. seems then to have been organized, as the D. R., Vol. 32, page 306, under date of Jan. 27th, 1849, refers to machinery of the mill which was destroyed by fire and states that the Company has a paid in capital of $5,100. The stock was taken as follows: Andrew W. DeForest, 66 shares; Burritt Hitchcock, 66 shares; Eli Hayes, 36 shares; Horace Riley, 12 shares; James H. Bidwell, 30 shares; James Wallace, 20 shares; A. W. DeForest, Agt., 10 shares; total, 240 shares. Burritt Hitchcock, president; A. W. DeForest, secretary. Bunce continued in charge of the mill which was located near the mouth of Little River, where the Douglass Manufacturing Co's lower shop now is.

The establishment of Humphreysville Academy is best recorded by quoting from the prospectus issued at the time.

HUMPHREYSVILLE ACADEMY,
HUMPHREYSVILLE. CONN.,
GEORGE B. GLENDINING, A. M., AND MRS. NANCY H. GLENDINING, PRINCIPALS.

The selection of Humphreysville for an Academic Institution, has been made not more with reference to the place itself than to a wide tract of the surrounding country, for which there have seemed to be educational demands.

Located in the romantic valley of the Naugatuck, Humphreysville is peculiarly healthy; and distant only ten miles from New Haven, sixteen from Bridgeport, and eighty from New York—with all of which places it is connected by a railroad soon to be in operation, it is most easily accessible.

For the youth of the place and the country around it, a higher institution of learning has appeared to be needed; at the same time regard has been had youth of the cities, for whom there may be here furnished, in connection with educational facilities at the most moderate rates, the safest guarantees for health and morals. The course of instruction to be pursued in Academy is designed to meet the wants of pupils of both sexes, and of various ages and destination. Whatever the pupils shall *profess to learn* they will be required *to learn thoroughly*—superficial attainments being regarded as of little worth. * * * Instruction will be given in all the branches of an English education; in the Classics—Latin and Greek; in French and Music. * * *

The Principals trust to the fruits of their labors so to commend them as to gain for their Academy an extended patronage. At their commencement they offer their qualifications, experience in teaching and devotion to the work, as pledges to satisfy such as may commit pupils to their charge. In addition they may refer to the Rev. W. F. Walker, Rector of Union Church, Humphreysville, who has known them for many years in their office as teachers; to the principal inhabitants of Troy, N. Y., where for nine years they taught successfully; to the trustees of Cayuga Academy, Aurora, New York, of which Mr. G. was more than two years Principal; to Professor Mills of New York city, and to Professor Berteau of Brooklyn, L. I., in whose institution Mr. G. was more than two years professor of Belles Lettres. Humphreysville, Feb. 22nd, 1849.

Speaking of Glendining's Academy the Derby Journal said, "The natural and picturesque scenery with which Humphreysville abounds, and the quietness of the village, render it exceedingly well adapted for the location of an institution of the kind."

The new comers were immediately received with favor. In May the Academy had already forty-seven pupils.

Buffum's Cotton Factory took fire Feb. 22nd, but the flames were suppressed before any great damage was done. Loss about $200. Insured. A portable fire engine which was kept in the building was made to render good service, the water being carried from the "canal" to the reservoir of the engine in pails and then forced in a stream against the building.

In March Nathan White made an engraving of the village, which was spoken of by the Derby Journal as "very prettily gotten up and giving an accurate idea of the place."

There were in operation one cotton factory, three paper mills, French & Dwight's large establishment for the manufacture of augers, plane irons and other edge tools; also three other auger factories and one ax factory. A large building was being erected for the construction of cars.

Thursday evening, Mar. 15th, about 9 o'clock, French & Dwight's machine shop was found to be on fire and was burned with all its contents. The shop was an old wooden one and was well stocked with tools, patterns, &c. Loss from $2,000 to $3,000. It stood on the east side of the canal where is now the tinning shop of the N. H. Copper Co.

John J. Rider was licensed as taverner and all licenses to sell spirituous liquors were refused. Jacob Carter lectured on temperance Feb. 12th. Julius Bassett sailed for California Jan. 23rd.

Joshua Kendall, D. G. W. P., installed the officers of Rock Spring Division Jan. 13th, as follows: William B. Curtiss, W. P.; John Adams, W. A.; John W. Storrs, R. S.; William Hughes, A. R. S.; Edward F. Bassett, F. S.; Henry Patterson, C.; Alonzo T. Smith, A. C.; Edward Hotchkiss, I. S.; E. Gainsby, O. S.

In April, Joshua Kendall was elected representative for the town of Derby.

The first locomotive came to Humphreysville on Thursday afternoon, May 10th, 1849; and the first passenger train on the following Monday, May, 14th.

Wilson Weston had his left hand and arm severely mangled June 28th, by the shears for cutting iron and steel, in the works of the Humphreysville Manufacturing Co.

The Rimmon dam was commenced this summer by Dwight & French.

The society of the "Daughters of Temperance" was instituted in August.

Friday, Dec. 14th, William B. Watson's horse was killed by a locomotive and his stage broken up.

In June the small pox was prevalent in Blueville, the dreaded disease having been brought in rags to the papermill.

VILLAGE DIRECTORY IN 1849.

Alopathic Physicians, Joshua Kendall, S. C. Johnson, Thomas Stoddard.
Attorney, H. B. Munson.
Augers and bit manufacturers, Dwight & French; French, Swift & Co.; and Hiram Upson.
Ax manufacturer, Clark Wooster.
Boot and shoe dealer, William Hull.
Botanic Physician, J. D. A. Yale.
Clergymen, Congregational, William B. Curtiss; Episcopal, William F. Walker; Methodist, Charles Stearns; Baptist, William Dennison.
Cotton manufacturers, William Buffum, shirtings, 500,000 yds. yearly, consuming fifty tons of cotton, and running 54 looms. Forty-one persons employed. Sherman & Beardsley were manufacturing stocking yarn, batting twine and carpet warp.
Druggists, James Davis, Robert J. Abbott.
Furniture manufacturers and dealers, Johnson & Bassett.
Harness maker, Isaac N. Martin.
Justice of the Peace, Albert J. Steele.
John Moshier kept the only livery stable, in connection with the tavern.
Merchants, Lyman Smith, Lucius Blackman, Downs & Sanford, Harrison Tomlinson, Elias Hotchkiss, Humphrey & Wooster, Tuttle & Bassett, and Lucius Tuttle.
Paper makers, DeForest & Hodge, manufactured 480,000 ℔s. printing paper yearly; Lewis Bunce, manufactured printing paper, clothiers' boards and press paper; Smith & Bassett, manufactured wrapping, straw and button boards.
Stove and tinware dealers, E. Lewis & Co.
Tailors, J. A. Stevens, Charles W. Storrs.

The Humphreysville Copper Co. was organized in 1849 with a capital stock of $40,000. The first issue of stock was forty shares to S. C. Johnson, Jan. 23rd. The proposal to establish a coppermill here was first made by Isaac Nathans to Raymond French. Mr. F. went to New York and made inquiries in regard to the manufacture of copper, prices of stock and manufactured goods, etc., and becoming satisfied that the business was then a profitable one, returned and organized the company. J. W. Dwight was the first president of the company. The directors, Feb. 8th, were—Raymond French, Harrison Tomlinson, George Rice and Sheldon Kinney. D. R., Vol. 32, page 309.

In the spring of 1850 there was quite an exciting time over the election. The postmaster, Mr. Lum, had recently died and Rev. Samuel Hickox was talked of as successor, but John W. Storrs was finally appointed. The decision being partly a party matter, aided by religious preferences and prejudices, it became evident in March that the matter would considerably affect the spring election. Thomas Burlock of Ansonia was nominated by the whigs and Rev. Sylvester Smith of Humphreysville by the democrats. The election was held in the basement of the Congregational Church in Humphreysville. The friends of the defeated candidate for postmaster rallied for Rev. Sylvester Smith, and while Mr. Burlock confidently expected a majority of 125, Mr. S. received a majority of 26. Burlock was a great politician, and to be beaten by a local preacher and a papermaker, was no less a surprise than the success of the democratic ticket in a strong whig town.

The subject of dividing the town had not been agitated until after this election, but now it quickly became prominent. Messrs. Dwight and French led in the movement and Judge Munson was active in its advocacy. Why no one proposed the name of Humphrey for the new town, we have been unable to learn. The bill to grant the petition was prepared and printed with the name "Richmond," but before it was put on its passage Judge Munson came to Mr. Smith and suggested the name "Seymour." Mr. S. replied, "It is short, our Governor and the Speaker of the House have that name, and it is an eminent name in Connecticut, and we will have it the name of our town." The bill was so amended and passed. Following is a copy of the

Charter of the Town of Seymour,

General Assembly, May Session, A. D., 1850.

Upon the petition of Leman Chatfield and others praying for the incorporation of a new town, as will fully and at large appear by their petition on file, dated the   th day of April, 1850, which petition has been duly served upon the town of Derby and was duly returned to and entered in the office of the Secretary of this State according to law.

RESOLVED BY THIS ASSEMBLY. That all that part of the town of Derby lying northerly of the following described line, to wit: commencing at the Housatonic River, thence running easterly in a straight line touching the most northerly point of Martin B. Bassett's stone building on the east bank of said river, thence running easterly in the same straight line to the north side of the dwelling house now occupied by said Martin B. Bassett, thence in a straight line easterly to the stone bridge in the highway, about twenty-five rods westerly of the house occupied by Pearl Carpenter, thence from said bridge following down the brook that runs under said bridge, till it empties into the Naugatuck River, thence from the mouth of said brook easterly, in a straight line to the intersection of the line dividing the town of Woodbridge from the town of Derby with the centre line of the Rimmon Falls Turnpike road; with all the inhabitants residing therein, be, and the same hereby are incorporated into a distinct town by the name of *Seymour*, and the inhabitants aforesaid, and their successors forever, residing within said limits shall have and enjoy all the powers, privileges and immunities which are enjoyed by other towns in this State, with the privilege of sending one representative to the General Assembly of this State.

Said new town shall support all bridges within their bounds, (except such as belong to turnpike companies or other corporations or individuals to support) and be released from supporting any bridges without the limits of said new town; shall pay and perform their proportion of the present debts and liabilities of Derby, and be allowed the same proportion of its credits, including the like proportion of the town deposit fund, and the same proportion of interest in the almshouse land; and shall take and support their proportion of the present town poor of said town of Derby; the proportion of the said new town in all the respects aforesaid being as the list of that part of the new town taken from the town of Derby for the year 1849, bears to the whole list of Derby, in the same year; and the selectmen of the said town of Derby and Seymour are hereby empowered to apportion and divide the present town poor, the debts, credits, town funds and alms house land aforesaid, according to the rule aforesaid; and in case they should not be able to agree, then such apportionment shall be made by Samuel Meigs, Esquire, of Oxford, whose decision shall be final. And said town poor when so apportioned, shall be settled inhabitants for all purposes in the respective towns to which they are set and said new town shall be liable to maintain all such poor of the town from which it is taken, as are or may be absent therefrom; provided, such poor person or persons at the time of their departure belonged to the portion of said town of Derby hereby incorporated, or were residents therein as settled inhabitants at the time of such departure therefrom.

Resolved further, That the collector of town and state taxes of said Derby, be hereby authorized to collect the several taxes already laid, in the same manner as though this act had not passed.

Resolved further, That it shall be the duty of said new town to assume and perform the contracts and liabilities now subsisting between the town of Derby and any other person or persons for keeping in repair such portion of the roads of the old town of Derby as lie within the limits of said new town, and to save the said old town from all expense therefrom.

Resolved further, That the mileage of the said town of Seymour to Hartford be forty-five miles, and to New Haven be eleven miles.

Resolved further, That the first meeting of said town of Seymour shall be held on the fourth Monday of June, 1850, at the basement of the Methodist Episcopal Church at Humphreys Ville, in said town of Seymour; and Leman Chatfield, Esquire, (and in case of his failure to attend the same, Harris B. Munson, Esquire,) shall be moderator of said meeting; and said meeting shall be warned by setting up a notification of the same on a sign post hereby established at the east end of the bridge over Naugatuck River, at said Humphreys Ville, and at such other place or places as said persons or either of them deem proper, at least five days before said meeting. And said town of Seymour shall at said first meeting, have all the powers incident to other towns in the State, and full right to act accordingly, to elect town officers; and the officers so elected at such meeting shall hold their offices until others are chosen and sworn in their stead.

STATE OF CONNECTICUT, ss. } I hereby certify that the foregoing
Office of Secretary of State, } is a true copy of record in this office.
In testimony whereof I have hereunto set my hand and affixed the Seal of said State, at Hartford, this 12th day of September, A. D., 1850.

{ SEAL } JNO. P. C. MATHER, SECRETARY OF STATE.

January, 1850, was a remarkably warm month, and in the following month the snows were followed by heavy rains, raising the streams and causing considerable damage. In the freshet of Feb. 10th and 11th the lower bridge was considerably damaged and narrowly escaped being carried away. There was also a high flood March 1st.

The water lease of S. Y. Beach's papermill expiring in this year, it was pulled down and removed to its present location on Bladen's brook. Papermaking was discontinued June 15th and resumed Sept. 2nd.

A town meeting was held June 24th in the basement of the M. E. Church, as provided by the charter, Leman Chatfield presiding as moderator. The principal officers of the new town were as follows:

Selectmen, Leman Chatfield, Daniel L. Holbrook, Thomas Cochran.

Town Clerk, Charles B. Wooster; *Town Treasurer*, Sylvester Smith.
Grand Jurors, Burton W. Smith, Thomas Stoddard, George L. Hodge, Abel Holbrook, Charles L. Hyde, Walter B. Clark.
Constables, George H. Merrick, Philo Beecher, Oliver H. Stoddard, Hiram P. Johnson, Roswell Humaston, John J. Rider.
Committee on Roads, Sheldon Kinney, Daniel L. Holbrook.
Tithingmen, Church Society—Burton W. Smith, Sheldon Hurd, Isaac Lindley; Methodist Society—John L. Hartson, Jarvis Polly; Congregational Society—Medad K. Tucker, William H. Tuthill; Baptist Society—Sharon Y. Beach, George L. Hodge; Great Hill Methodist Society—William C. Smith, Roswell Humaston.

The second town meeting was held in the basement of the Congregational Church, Oct. 30th, 1850. Leman Chatfield, Daniel L. Holbrook and Thomas Cochran were elected selectmen; Charles B. Wooster, town clerk; and Burton W. Smith, town treasurer.

At the electors' meeting held Mar. 31st, 1851, Bennett Wooster was elected the first representative of the Town of Seymour to the General Assembly.

The Baptist Society was organized in March, 1848, Rev. William Dennison, from White Hills, in charge. The church on Maple street was built in 1851. Tythingmen were last elected for the church in October, 1859.

A union Sunday school festival was held Aug. 28th by the Baptist, Congregational, Episcopal and Methodist Sunday schools.

At the annual town meeting held Oct. 6th, the selectmen, town clerk and treasurer were re-elected.

At a special town meeting held in January, 1852, it was voted to build a new bridge over the Naugatuck, near Moshier's tavern, and Isaac B. Davis, Philo Holbrook and Raymond French were appointed building committee.

At the spring election, Rev. Sylvester Smith was elected representative, receiving 217 of the 354 votes cast. The following persons were elected justices of the peace:—Harris B. Munson, Leman Chatfield, Sharon Y. Beach, Isaac B. Davis, Charles B. Wooster, Philo Holbrook, George P. Shelton, Daniel L. Holbrook, Samuel R. Hickox, Eli S. Cornwall.

At the town meeting in the basement of the Congregational Church in October, Daniel Holbrook was elected first selectman but declined to serve another year. Isaac B. Davis, Sharon Y. Beach and Harpin Riggs were then elected and Burton W. Smith was elected treasurer. A resolution was passed authorizing the layout of a street past the house Denzel Hitchcock, now known as High Street, also accepting Humphrey street as highway. The following resolution was adopted:

Voted, that all Horses and Cattle be restrained from going at large upon the highways and commons in Seymour (except that any man owning one cow only can by permission from any one selectman, let her run at large provided she has a strap on her neck with the owners name on) and if so found going at large shall be liable to be impounded and that the penalty for each animal so impounded shall be seventy-five cents, two thirds of which sum to be paid to the person or persons so impounding the same, by the owner or owners of the animal or animals so impounded, and one-third to the pound keeper.

Voted, that Sheep and Swine be restrained from going at large upon the highways and commons in said town, and if so found going at large shall be liable to be impounded, and the penalty for each Sheep or Swine so impounded shall be twenty-five cents, to be paid to the person or persons so impounding the same by the owner or owner of the Sheep or Swine so impounded eighteen cents, and to the pound-keeper seven cents.

Voted, that Geese be restrained from going at large upon the highways or commons in said town.

and if so found going at large shall be liable to be impounded, and the penalty for each Goose so impounded shall be eight cents, one-half of which shall be paid to the person impounding the same and the other half to the pound-keeper, by the owner or owners of the geese so impounded.

Voted that any inhabitant of said town may lawfully impound all such creatures found going at large as aforesaid, and it shall be the duty of the person or persons impounding the same to give notice thereof to the owner or owners of such creatures, if known, within twenty-four hours after impounding the same, and in case the owner or owners of such impounded creatures be not known by the impounder, to inform forthwith one of the Constables of said town, whose duty it shall be to proceed in the same manner as is by law prescribed for Constables when they are informed that creatures are impounded for doing damage upon land, and the owners thereof is not known, and said Constable shall be entitled to his lawful fees in the same manner as for creatures doing damage upon land, provided that nothing in this vote or By-Law shall be so construed as to prevent the owner or owners of such creatures from redeeming them from the person or persons while driving them to pound, by paying the drivers fees.

Voted, that the foregoing By-Law be effectual from and after the 26th day of November, 1852, until the first Monday in October, 1853.

Voted, that the town clerk be directed to cause the foregoing By-Law to be published four weeks successively in the Columbian Register printed in New Haven, also in the New Haven Palladium.

This by-law was re-enacted in 1853 and the penalties increased one-fourth. In 1854 it was repealed.

The vote of the town for presidential electors, Nov. 2nd, 1852, was—democratic, 258; whig, 105; free soil, 4.

The Humphreysville Copper Co. was re-organized in 1852 and the capital increased from $100,000 to $200,000 by the addition of 4,000 shares of $25 each. S. R., Vol. 3, p. 123. The President of the company certified that the whole amount had been paid in Feb. 2nd. A large part of the stock was taken in Humphreysville, the bank taking 700 shares. The directors of the company then were—William Cornwall, Timothy Dwight, George F. DeForest, Charles Durand and Harrison Tomlinson. In February, 1853, the directors were=John W. Dwight, William Cornwall, Timothy Dwight, Charles Durand, Nathan Peck, Jr., of New Haven, Raymond French, George F. DeForest, Harrison Tomlinson and Sheldon Kenney of Seymour. The works were greatly enlarged and the business increased. Up to this time the business had proved very lucrative, but after the enlargement the profits decreased and the stock finally went down.

At the electors' meeting in April, 1853, H. B. Munson was elected representative by a majority of 82 in a total vote of 329.

Prof. Gay, a graduate of Yale, opened a "high school" in Glendinning Hall in August.

At the October town meeting Leman Chatfield, Harpin Riggs and Jabez E. Pritchard were elected selectmen, and B. W. Smith, town treasurer.

On Sunday, Nov. 13th, there was a heavy rain all day, and during the afternoon the river rose rapidly, until it was seventeen feet and three inches above low water mark at Derby. Such a flood had not been known for many years, the water was said to have been four feet deep in the coppermill. The south half of the railroad bridge was carried away, with the south abutment, and many other bridges above and below Seymour, including those at Pines bridge, Beacon Falls and Ansonia. In the evening the Ansonia bridge was carried away, and with it a young couple whose cries were heard far down the river, but all attempts to rescue them in the darkness were unavailing.

On Wednesday evening, Jan. 8th, 1854, there was another freshet which again swept off the railroad bridge and also the dam of French, Swift & Co. The next forenoon the dam which stood a little above where the rubbermill dam now is was carried away. It continued to be an unusually rainy season for two months, and the July and August following were as exceptionally dry. At the elector's meeting in April, H. B. Munson was elected representative by a majority of 65 in a total vote of 293, and S. Y. Beach, Leman Chatfield, Isaac B. Davis, Samuel B. Hickox, Daniel L. Holbrook, Philo Holbrook, H. B. Munson, Luzon B. Morris, George P. Shelton and Charles B. Wooster, justices of the peace.

From Thursday, April 22nd, to the following Sunday morning there was heavy and continuous rain, resulting in a flood on Sunday, when the water rose eight or ten inches higher than in the November freshet. Great damage was done throughout the valley. Derby Avenue was washed out from Broad street to Pine to the depth of three feet. The water at Derby was 19 feet 8½ inches above low water mark. A special town meeting was called and a vote passed to build a breakwater at the west end of Broad street and to fill Derby Avenue where washed out. The work was done immediately and so substantially that there has been no farther trouble at that point.

Feb. 6th, 1855, the mercury stood 12° below zero, and the 11th, 10° below. At the April election Luzon B. Morris was elected representative by a majority of 45 in a total vote of 315. In October Jabez B. Pritchard, Henry Bradley and Philo Holbrook were elected selectmen, and B. W. Smith, treasurer. Charles B. Wooster was town clerk from the first election after the incorporation of the town until he removed to New Haven in the winter of 1862-63.

The winter of 1855-6 was remarkably severe. The snow lay from eighteen inches to two feet in depth all through January, '56. The mercury stood 13° below zero Jan. 9th at 7 a. m., 8° below Mar. 4th, and 10° below Mar. 14th. The next summer was unusually warm. June 23rd the mercury stood at 100° in the shade, and the 17th of July at 102°.

At the April election Luzon B. Morris was elected representative by a majority of 58 votes. The justices elected were H. B. Munson, Henry Bradley, C. B. Wooster, Philo Holbrook, D. L. Holbrook, Sheldon Church, L. B. Morris, David Beach, B. W. Smith and Joseph Chipman.

A vote was taken upon the proposition to change the name of the town from Seymour to Humphrey, the change being defeated by a vote of 117 to 81.

At the October election of 1856, Sheldon Church, Miles Culver and Daniel L. Holbrook were elected selectmen; Hiram W. Randall, town treasurer; and George F. DeForest, Philo B. Buckingham and Luzon B. Morris, school visitors. This was the first election of school visitors by the town. Previous to this time they had been elected by the School Societies, of which there were two, the first comprising the school districts on the east side of the river, and the second the districts on the west side.

Land was purchased of Alfred Blackman by Rev. James Lynch of Birmingham, Sept. 24th, 1854, for a Roman Catholic Church. The land was deeded to Rt. Rev. Bernard O'Riley of Providence, R. I., June 5th, 1855. Work was commenced in the fall of 1855, and the edifice completed and dedicated in the fall of 1856.

A vote for presidential electors, Nov. 4th, 1856, was—democratic, 192; republican, 129; et al, 6.

Jan. 22nd, 1857, at 7 a. m., the mercury was 4° below zero; 23rd,—13°; 24th, 23°; 25th,—10°; 26th,—20°.

There was a great freshet Feb. 7th, the water at Derby being 22 feet 3 inches above low water mark. The Housatonic bridge at Birmingham was carried away. Henry C. Johnson was elected representative in April by a majority of 41. The "Bank of North America," corner of Main and Maple streets, had been incorporated in 1851 with a capital of $100,000. In 1854 the General Assembly authorized an increase of the capital stock to $200,000, but the increase seems not to have been made, as on the 1st of January, 1856, George F. DeForest, the president of the bank, reported the stock worth only $116,775. In June, 1859, an addition of $100,000 to the stock was authorized, and in June, 1860, permission was given to remove the bank to Ansonia. The name was changed to Ansonia Bank in 1861.

The Naugatuck Railroad Company was incorporated in 1845. Timothy Dwight, William DeForest and and Anson G. Phelps being among the petitioners for the charter. The capital stock was at first $600,000 with the privilege of increasing to one million dollars. The time in which the road was to be built was extended in 1848 and 1853, and the stock increased to $2,000,000.

The Eagle Manufacturing Co. was organized June 27th, 1850, with a stock of $50,000, for the manufacture of goods from silk, wool and cotton. Geo. Rice was the first president of the company. The stock was increased to $100,000 Oct. 28, 1852; Geo. F. DeForest, president. In January, 1855, Geo. P. Shelton, pres., and Harrison Tomlinson, sec., certified to estimated losses of $27,000 and assetts of $42,000, the indebtedness of the company being about $60,000.

In 1851 the capital stock of the Humphreysville Manufacturing Co. was estimated at $300,000, and the estimate was approved by a committee of the Legislature. Pr. Acts, Vol. 4, p. 803. In 1859 the stock was reduced to $150,000 by the distribution of property to the stockholders.

The Humphreysville High School Association was incorporated in 1851, as follows:

SEC. 1. *Resolved by this Assembly,* That Raymond French, Harrison Tomlinson, George F. DeForest, Lucius Tuttle, Eli S. Cornwall, Samuel Bassett. Philo B. Buckingham, E. F. Bassett, George H. Merick, Nehemiah Robbins, Oliver H. Stoddard, Clark Wooster, and all others, who now are, or shall hereafter become associated with them, and their successors and assigns, be, and they are hereby constituted a body politic and corporate, by the name of "The Seymour High School Association," and by that name they are hereby authorized and empowered to purchase, take, hold, occupy and enjoy, notes, bonds, mortgages and estate, real and personal, to an amount not exceeding twenty thousand dollars; and the same to sell, transfer and convey at their pleasure; and shall also be capable of suing and being sued, pleading and being impleaded, defending and being defended in any lawful court; to have perpetual succession, and to have a common seal, and the same to alter at pleasure.

SEC. 2. The stock of said corporation, consisting of the building or buildings, for the use of said high school, such as may be from time to time erected, together with the lands which now are, or may hereafter be owned by said corporation; and all moneys, funds, notes, bonds, mortgages, real and personal estate of any description, which now belong, or may hereafter belong to said corporation, excepting donations, legacies. devises and bequests, shall be divided into shares of twenty-five dollars each; and each share shall entitle the holder thereof to one vote at all meetings of said corporation; and said shares shall be deemed and held to be personal estate, and shall be transferable in such manner as shall be prescribed by the by-laws, rules and regulations of said corporation.

SEC. 3. For the management of the affairs of said corporation, the members thereof shall, at their first meeting, elect five trustees, who shall hold their office for the term of one year, at least, from the time of their election, and until others may and shall be chosen by said corporation, to supply their places; said trustees shall have power to fill any vacancies which may occur in their number, during the time of holding their office; they shall have the immediate management and control of the funds, property, and general concerns of said corporation, receive and disburse all moneys belonging to said institution; regulate the course of instruction and the price of tuition, and if they think proper, prescribe the terms of admission of scholars; they shall have the power of enacting such rules and regulations concerning the conduct of students while members of said high school, as they may deem proper; and a majority of them may, at any time, expel or dismiss, or suspend, as the case may require, such students as, for any reasonable cause, they may consider it improper to retain in the school; *always provided*, that the by-laws, rules and regulations shall not be repugnant to the laws of this state, or of the United States.

SEC. 4. That in all meetings of the trustees, a majority of the whole number shall be necessary to form a quorum for transacting business of any kind; and a vote of the majority of those present shall be necessary to render any act done by them binding on said corporation.

SEC. 5. All meetings of the trustees shall be called at such times, in such manner, and on such notice, as the trustees by their by-laws shall prescribe. And a meeting of the corporation may at any time be called by vote of the trustees, or by a written request presented to the secretary or the trustees or corporation, and signed by members of the corporation, who are owners of at least one-third of the stock of said corporation; and each meeting of the corporation shall be warned in such manner as the trustees shall direct.

SEC. 6. In all meetings of the corporation, all the stockholders may vote in person, or by proxy, and one vote shall be allowed for each share.

SEC. 7. The books and records of said corporation shall be always open to the inspection of any of its stockholders.

SEC. 8. The use of such buildings as may belong to said corporation, shall be under the direction of the trustees, and shall be appropriated to no other purposes than that of a school, unless by the consent of a majority of the trustees expressed in writing under their hands, and prescribing the terms on which, and the purposes for which, they are to be used.

SEC. 9. The members of this corporation shall have the power of appointing a committee to consist of at least two, to procure such instructors as may be necessary, and agree with them in relation to the terms; and in case they shall neglect to do so, it shall be the duty of the trustees to procure such itstructors as may be required.

SEC. 10. The first meeting of the corporation shall be called by George F. DeForest, Esquire, or in case of his inability or neglect, by Raymond French, of the town of Seymour, at such time and place, and with such notice as he shall direct; *provided always*, that this act may be altered, amended or repealed at the pleasure of the general assembly.   (Pr. Acts, Vol. 3, p. 20.

In 1852, Geo. P. Shelton, Raymond French, Philo Holbrook, Henry S. Mygatt, Sheldon Kinney, George F. DeForest, Harrison Tomlinson, John W. Dwight, John Clark and Sylvester Smith were incorporated under the style and title of the Seymour Savings Bank.

The Union Mercantile Co., was established Jan. 6th, 1852, with a capital stock of $4,000, in shares of $25. There were sixty-four stock-holders, taking from one to eight shares each. B. W. Smith was the first president of the company, and John J. Rider the second. The store was in the building on the north side of Broad street, at the west end of the Naugatuck bridge.

The American Car Co. was organized in the spring of 1852, with a stock of $150,000, one half of which was certified to be paid in May 14th, by I. H. Lyman, Pres., and T. Dwight, R. French and J. W. Dwight, a majority of the directors. Sey. Town Rec., Vol. 3, p. 76. The stock was increased Sept. 1st, to $200,000. Of the additional shares J. W. and Timothy Dwight each took 800 and J. H. Lyman 400. S. R., Vol. 3, p. 82. Five large shops were built on the "flat," with track laid to each, and a large business was done for a time, until the business was moved west.

The Humphreysville and Salem Turnpike Co., organized in 1825 and incorporated in 1832, was discontinued in 1856.

The New Haven and Seymour Plank road company was incorporated in 1852. The parties named in the act were William H. Ellis, Zelotes Day and William Hull of New Haven, Bevil P. Smith and Thomas Sanford of Woodbridge, William A. Clark of Bethany, and Sylvester Smith and Sharon

SEYMOUR AND VICINITY.

Y. Beach of Seymour. The capital was not to exceed $100,000, and the road to run from Seymour through Woodbridge and Bethany to Westville bridge.

The Woodbury and Seymour Plank Road Company was incorporated in 1852. Lewis B. Candee, Norman Parker, Charles B. Phelps, Reuben H. Hotchkiss, Lewis Judd and William Gaylord were among the first stockholders. The road from Seymour through Oxford and Southbury to Woodbury is now the only road from Seymour on which toll is collected.

The Upson Manufacturing Co. was organized in 1852 with a capital of $6,000, by Hiram Upson, Horace A. Radford and Lucius Tuttle, for the manufacture of augers, bits, &c. The business was carried on where the Douglass Manufacturing Co's lower shop now is, at the mouth of Little River, The property was sold by H. A. Radford to Charles Douglass, in 1859. The first auger shop on this site was built by Timothy Dwight, Sr., son of Pres. Dwight, in 1837, and by his heirs sold to H. A. Radford.

The Humphreysville Copper Co., in addition to their works in Seymour, had a wharf and mill in East Haven, and were in 1853 authorized by the General Assembly to build a breakwater for the protection of their vessels from the surf and winds while loading and unloading. Pr. Acts, Vol. 4, p. 798. The stock was increased Feb. 3rd, 1854, from 12,000 to 16,000 shares. The stock was certified Jan. 30th, 1855, to have been paid in to the amount of $390,000, the property to be worth $525,000, and the bills receivable $75,000; while the liabilities were $350,000. A new Humphreysville Copper Co. was incorporated in 1855, (Pr. Acts, Vol. 4, p. 799,) the stock being placed at $750,000, with liberty to increase to any amount not exceeding $1,000,000, and to purchase the stock of the old company. The parties named in the act of incorporation were John W. Dwight, Wm. Cornwall, George F. DeForest, Henry Bronson, Chas. Durand, Sheldon Kinney, Saml. K. Satterlee, Geo. R. A. Ricketts and Henchman S. Soule. The New Haven Copper Co. was organized Nov. 21st, 1855, with a capital stock of $400,000. John W. Dwight, president; George R. A. Ricketts, secretary. Mar. 12, 1856, J. W. Dwight and Wm. Cornwall certified that the stock amounted to $300,000, all paid in, Dwight having 4,080 shares, Cornwall 3,920, and Wm. W. Goddard 4,000. S. R., Vol. 3, p. 226. The statement of the New Haven Copper Co., Jan. 20th, 1857, claimed assets to the amount of $615,000 with $295,000 liabilities. 7,900 shares of the stock were in the name of the Humphreysville Copper Co., 4,000 were held by Wm. W. Goddard, and the remaining 100 by Dwight Cornwall, DeForest and Ricketts. After various changes the company was reorganized in 1874, and Thomas James was elected president, vice Lazarus Lissberger, resigned, and F. Farrell, secretary, vice Samuel Holmes, resigned. C. W. James is the agent of the company, with office in New York City. Under the present able management this is one of the heaviest (both literally and financially,) and most reliable industries of the town.

The Humphreysville Library Company was incorporated in 1854. The following is the act of incorporation from Pr. Acts, Vol. 4, p. 1193-4.

Resolved by this Assembly, SEC. 1. That P. B. Buckingham, B. W. Smith, G. H. Merrick, Raymond French, Sylvester Smith, Samuel Bassett, Henry S. Mygatt, Ransom Tomlinson, Ashbel Storrs, L. B. Morris and Andrew Bassett, and their associates and such other persons as shall hereafter be admitted members of said company, be, and they hereby are made a body politic and corporate, by the name of the Humphreysville Library Company, and by that name may sue and be sued, and have perpetual succession, and may have a common seal, and may alter the same at pleasure, and may hold real estate to the amount of one thousand dollars, and may increase their stock in books to the amount and value of five thousand dollars; and the stock of said company shall be divided into such shares as by the by-laws of said company shall be ordained and established. And the first meeting of said company shall be held on the third Monday of July next, at such hour and place as shall be designated for that purpose, by notice signed by the said P. B. Buckingham and B. W. Smith, which shall be served by reading to each petitioner, or by copy left at his usual place of abode three days previous to said meeting; and thereafter the annual and special meetings of said company shall be held at such time and place and on such notice as the by-laws of said company shall prescribe.

SEC. 2. The company at their annual meeting shall choose a secretary, a president, a vice-president, a treasurer, and seven persons to be a board of directors, who shall continue in office until others are chosen to fill their places; and if the company shall hereafter increase, the board of directors shall be increased, but shall at no time exceed eleven persons, exclusive of the president and vice-president, who shall *ex officio* be members of the board of directors.

SEC. 3. The board of directors shall have a general superintendence of the library; direct in what manner it shall be kept, appoint a librarian and grant him such compensation as they shall judge necessary, adjust all accounts and exhibit the same once in every year to the company, select and purchase books for the use of the company, and regulate from time to time the manner in which books shall be drawn from the library.

SEC. 4. The board of directors shall have the sole power of making by-laws relative to the use of the company's books, and the fines, penalties and forfeitures to be inflicted for any injury to, or loss, obstructions or undue detention of the same; but no such by-law shall be of any force until it has been engrossed and posted up fourteen days in the library room. *Provided*, that no fine, penalty or forfeiture shall exceed the assessed value of the book or books so injured, lost, detained or destroyed.

SEC. 5. No person shall become a member of the company by purchase, without the consent and approbation of the board of directors.

SEC. 6. The proprietor of each share of said stock shall pay annually into the treasury of said company one dollar on each share held by him; and if the proprietor of any share or shares of said stock shall neglect or refuse to make such payment for the space of thirty days after the same shall be due, and after having been notified of such neglect in a manner to be provided by the board of directors, each proprietor neglecting or refusing shall forfeit all his right, title and interest in said company, and shall cease to be a member of the same.

SEC. 7. These resolves may be altered, amended or repealed at the pleasure of the legislature.

The foregoing outline of the joint stock speculations of 1850—60, made from the records with very little comment, includes companies that have since prospered and been largely instrumental in building up the place, and others which, by the heavy losses inflicted upon the stockholders, have since intimidated capital and sometimes hindered the development of meritorious enterprises.

A portion of the town of Oxford was annexed to the town of Seymour in 1854, as follows:

Resolved by this Assembly, That all that part of the town of Oxford lying southerly of a line drawn from the town bounds, standing between the towns of Seymour and Oxford in New Haven county, near the dwelling house of Mrs. Sabra Lindley; thence running in an easterly direction about one hundred and thirty-four rods to a pile of stones on Diamond Rock, so called; thence running easterly about one hundred and twenty rods from the Naugatuck railroad; thence running easterly to a pile of stones with a stake standing therein, on the town line between said Seymour and Oxford, easterly of the dwelling house of Miles Culver, and southerly of the south end of Rock Rimmon, so called, be, and hereby is incorporated in and made part of the said town of Seymour, and that the aforesaid lines and boundaries be the boundaries between said towns. [Pr. Acts, Vol. 4, p. 1265.

From Conn. Private Acts, Vol. 4, p. 1314:—

Upon the petition of the Humphreysville and Salem Turnpike Company, showing that heretofore, to wit, at a general assembly of the state of Connecticut, holden at Hartford on the first Wednesday of May, A. D. 1832, the said Humphreysville and Salem Turnpike Company was by a resolve of the general assembly duly incorporated by the name of the "Humphreysville Turnpike Company," with power to construct a turnpike road from the Falls bridge, so called, then in the town of Derby, but now the town of Seymour, to Salem bridge, in the then town of Waterbury, now Naugatuck, and that said turnpike road was afterwards during the said year last mentioned laid out and constructed by said company, and has ever since been kept open for public travel by said company, until on or about the 1st day of January, A. D., 1853, when the same became useless and valueless to said company, and has ever since been abandoned by them, and praying that the said charter and resolve of incorporation may be repealed, as per petition on file :

Resolved by this Assembly, That the charter of the Humphreysville and Salem Turnpike Company, granted by a resolve of the general assembly, at its May session, A. D., 1825, and all powers and privileges therein conferred, be and the same hereby is revoked and repealed.

The following resolution was adopted by the General Assembly in 1856, and made of no avail by the vote before mentioned :

Resolved by this Assembly, That the name of the town of *Seymour* be and the same is hereby changed to that of *Humphrey*, and by said name of Humphrey, the said town shall hereafter be called and known. *Provided*, that this resolution shall not take effect until the same shall be approved by a majority of the voters of said town, present at the next annual town meeting of said town, or at some special meeting of said town duly warned and held for that purpose.

At the October election Henry Bradley, Edwin Smith and Abel Holbrook were re-elected selectmen; and B. W. Smith, town treasurer; Martin Kelley, James E. Fisher and John W. Bassett, tythingmen for the Episcopal Society; Methodist, Smith Botsford, W. N. Storrs, John E. Blackman; Congregational, David Tucker, Philo B. Buckingham, Joshua Kendall; Baptist, S. Y. Beach; Roman Catholic, Patrick Tracey, James Robinson; Great Hill Methodist Society, Eli Gillett, Clark Hull. S. Y. Beach and Joshua Kendall were elected school visitors.

January, 1858, was noted as being remarkably warm, the mercury averaging nearly fifty degrees higher than in January, '57.

At the spring election Charles B. Wooster was elected representative by a majority of fifty-three, and B. W. Smith, Harpin Riggs, J. J. Wilcoxen, S. L. Bronson, Abel Holbrook, C. B. Wooster, Joshua Kendall, Ebenezer Fairchild, N. R. Wooster and Samuel Roselle, justices of the peace. When the announcement of the completion of the first Atlantic cable was received the people of Seymour, like the people of New England generally, united in a general rejoicing by ringing of bells and firing of cannon.

At the town meeting held Oct. 4th, the selectmen, town clerk and town treasurer of the previous year were all re-elected; the "poke by-law" was passed, and it was voted to lay a tax of 20c. on the dollar. P. B. Buckingham was elected school visitor for three years.

On Tuesday, Jan. 4th, 1859, the snow fell to the depth of two and a half feet. On Wednesday, Aug. 31st, a strong wind, passing over the place, threw down the steeple of the Baptist church and caused considerable damage in the vicinity. At the April election Samuel L. Bronson was elected representative by a majority of 61. At the October election Henry Bradley, Edwin Smith and Abel Holbrook were elected selectmen, Henry S. Johnson, town treasurer; and S. Y. Beach, school visitor.

The waters of the Naugatuck rose very high Feb. 22nd, 1860, and the ice broke up and was in many places piled high on the banks.

At the electors' meeting held April 2nd Carlos French was elected representative to the General Assembly by a majority of 179 over all other candidates. The justices elected were—B. W. Smith, H. B. Munson, Sheldon Church, David Beach, J. J. Wilcoxen, Thomas James, Jr., C. B. Wooster, S. L. Bronson, Elliott Bassett, John A. Cochran.

At the annual town meeting held in Glendining hall, Oct. 1st, Henry Bradley, Edwin Smith and Stephen D. Russell were re-elected selectmen; Henry S. Johnson town treasurer; and Joshua Kendall, school visitor. A tax was laid of $5\frac{1}{2}$ mills.

The vote for president Nov. 6th was—for Douglass electors, 98; Breckenridge, 98; Lincoln, 134, *et al*, 4.

In April, 1861, Clark Wooster was elected representative by a majority of twenty-nine.

At the annual town meeting held Oct. 7th, Henry Bradley, John Davis and Stephen D. Russell were elected selectmen; David Betts, Jr., treasurer; C. B. Wooster, school visitor.

Abel Holbrook was elected representative April 7th, by a majority of 34 votes. The following were elected justices of the peace: C. B. Wooster, B. W. Smith, H. B. Munson, Sheldon Church, E. R. Bassett, J. J. Wilcoxen, Smith Botsford, John Chatfield, Edward Hoadley, James Baker.

SEYMOUR IN THE GREAT REBELLION.

At the first call of the President for volunteers there had been a prompt response, many patriotic young men going forth in the first regiments to devote their lives, if it should so be, to their country, leaving home and family to face the peril of a destructive war. As the war progressed and call after call was made for more men, it became necessary to make greater efforts to fill the quotas, and those who remained at home contributed liberally to assist those who went to the front.

At a special town meeting held Aug. 25th, 1862, the following resolutions were adopted:—

Resolved, That the sum of one hundred dollars be and hereby is appointed to each volunteer soldier who has enlisted in any company forming in this town for the military service of the United States since July 1st, 1862, or who may hereafter enlist in such company for said service before the 3rd day of September 1862, until the quota of men required of this town under the orders of the President of the United States, or as apportioned by the Adjutant General or Governor of this State, shall be filled, and said sum herein before appropriated shall be paid to each and every volunteer so enlisting immediately after such volunteer or volunteers shall have been mustered into the military service of the United States.

Resolved, That the sum of five thousand dollars, or so much thereof as may be required, be and is hereby appropriated for the purpose of carrying the foregoing resolutions into effect, and the selectmen or town agent of this town are hereby authorized and instructed to procure a loan or loans on the credit of this town of such sum or sums of money not exceeding in the whole the amount appropriated under these resolutions as may be required to pay the aforesaid appropriations.

Resolved, That the selectmen of this town be and hereby are empowered and instructed to draw their order on the treasurer of this town for the sum of one hundred dollars in favor of each and every volunteer enlisted as aforesaid, when such volunteer or volunteers shall have been mustered into the service of the United States.

Resolved, That a tax of three mills on the dollar be and hereby is laid and assessed upon the Grand List of this town next to be completed for the purpose of defraying the expense of the foregoing appropriations.

SEYMOUR AND VICINITY.

The following additional resolutions were adopted at a special meeting held Sept. 8th.

Resolved, That in addition to bounties heretofore voted by this town in legal town meeting, a bounty of one hundred dollars be paid to each and every person who has or may hereafter volunteer from this town, and has been or may hereafter be mustered into the military service of this State or the United States since July 1, 1862, previous to the draft ordered by the Governor or Adjutant General of this State dated the 26th day of August 1862, until the quota assigned to this town shall be completed, unless such volunteer or volunteers shall have already received a bounty in accordance with a previous legal vote of this town, and that the selectmen be instructed to draw an order on the town treasurer for the sum of one hundred dollars in favor of each person who has or may so volunteer, when he shall be accepted and mustered into the military service of this State or the United States.

Resolved, That to carry out the intent of the foregoing resolutions the sum of twenty-five hundred dollars or so much thereof as may be required is hereby appropriated, and the selectmen are hereby authorized to loan on the credit of this town the sum of two thousand five hundred dollars.

At a special town meeting held Aug. 3rd, 1863, a resolution was adopted authorizing the selectmen to pay a bounty of $300 to any citizen of this town who had enlisted or might enlist into the service of the United States under the provisions of the Act of Congress approved March 3rd, 1863, or who might be drafted and accepted, and the town treasurer was authorized to borrow upon the faith and credit of the town such sums as might be necessary, not exceeding in all $9,500.

In December an additional appropriation was made of $105 to each man who would enlist under the call of the President dated Oct. 17th, 1863, and for this and also the consolidation of the previous debt, the town treasurer was authorized to issue six per cent bonds to the amount of $16,000.

At a special town meeting held Sept. 15th, ('64,) a tax of thirteen mills, was voted for the purpose of defraying the expense of filling the quota of the town under the last call of the President for volunteers. The money was to be kept in a separate fund called the Soldiers' Bounty Fund, and to be drawn upon for no other purpose. The selectmen were authorized to draw an order on the fund for $300 in favor of each person who had or should enter the military service of the United States, and be counted on the quota of the town, until the quota should be filled. The selectmen were also instructed to use all reasonable diligence to fill the quota of the town.

At a special meeting held Dec. 19th, it was voted that $3,500 be appropriated for the purpose of procuring volunteers to enlist into the service of the United States.

LIST OF SEYMOUR SOLDIERS

OF THE

WAR OF THE REBELLION.

It is but an act of simple justice to keep in affectionate and lasting remembrance the name and fame of those who from amongst us have given their lives that the nation might live. It is not for us to honor them, but it is they who have honored us.—COL. A. H. FENN.

Ichabod E. Alling, Corporal, Co. H, 20th Conn. Vols. Mustered in Aug. 20th, 1862. Mustered out June 13th, 1865.

John Baldwin, Third Ind. Battery. Mustered in Sept. 24th, 1864. Mustered out June 23rd, 1865.

Julius Bassett, mustered as Capt. Co. A, Fifteenth Conn. Vols., at Meriden, July 10th, 1862. Killed in action March 8th, 1865, near Kinston, S. C.

Lorenzo M. Bassett, Co. A, First Artillery. Mustered in Nov. 23rd, 1863. Discharged, disability, June 17th, 1865.

Samuel Bassett, Co. H, 20th Conn. Vols. Mustered in Dec. 16th, 1863; transfered to the Fifth Regiment. Mustered out July 19th, 1865.

Sheldon Bassett, Co. B, Fifteenth Conn. Vols. Mustered in Mar. 13th, 1864; transfered to 7th Conn. Vols. Mustered out July 14th, 1865.

Samuel A. Beach, Sergeant, Co. H, Twentieth Conn. Vols. Mustered in Aug. 8th, 1862. Discharged, disability, Sept. 9th, 1862.

Henry B. Beers, Co. K, Tenth Conn. Vols. Mustered in Oct. 5th, 1861. Discharged, disability, Feb. 22d, 1863.

Bennett Benham, Co. H, 20th Conn. Vols. Mustered in Aug. 9th, 1862. Mustered out June 13th, 1865, at Washington, D. C.

Howard Bliss, Co. H, 20th Conn. Vols. Mustered in Aug. 20th, 1862. Mustered out June 13th, 1865, at Washington, D. C.

Andrew Bodge, Co. F, First Heavy Artillery. Mustered in May 23rd, 1861. Wounded at Battle of Malvern Hill. Discharged May 22nd, 1864.

George E. Bodge, Co. F, Sixth Conn. Vols. Mustered in Sept. 7th, 1861. Killed at the charge on Fort Wagner, on Morris Island, S. C., July 18th, 1863.

SEYMOUR AND VICINITY. 93

Noyes E. Bassett, Co. I, Twentieth Conn. Vols. Mustered in Mar. 7th, 1864. Transferred to Fifth C. V. Mustered out July 19th, 1865.

Henry I. Booth, Co. H, 20th Conn. Vols. Mustered in Aug. 6th, 1862. Died in Washington, D. C., Jan. 4th, 1863.

Edward Botsford, Third Ind. Battery. Mustered in Sept. 19th, 1864. Mustered out June 23rd, 1865.

Edward Botsford, Co. E, Fifth Conn. Vols. Mustered in July 22nd, 1861. Discharged for disability Dec. 17th, 1862.

Harvey L. Botsford, Co. H, 20th Conn. Vols. Mustered in Aug. 5th, 1862. Discharged, disability, Feb. 21st, 1863, at Stafford Court House.

Henry I. Bradley, Co. B, Twelfth Conn. Vols. Mustered in Dec. 19th, 1861. Re-enlisted Jan. 1, 1864.

Matthew Brassil, Third Ind. Battery. Mustered in Sept. 16th, 1864. Mustered out June 22d, 1865.

Wm. H. Bray, Sergeant, Co. G, Eleventh Conn. Vols. Mustered in Dec. 1st, 1861. Discharged, disability, Nov. 29th, 1862.

Royal L. Bronson, Co. H, 20th Conn. Vols. Mustered in Aug. 25th, 1862. Died May 4th, 1863, of wounds received at Chancellorsville, Va., May 3rd.

Rodney O. Bronson, Co. D., First Conn. Cavalry. Mustered in Nov. 27th, 1863. Mustered out Aug. 2nd, 1865.

Charles Brown, Third Ind. Battery. Mustered in Sept. 19th, 1864. Mustered out June 23rd, 1865.

Philo B. Buckingham, mustered in as Major of Twentieth Conn. Vols. Aug. 29th, 1862. Taken prisoner at Chancellorsville, and sent to Libby Prison. Exchanged and returned to service. Promoted Lieut. Col. Mar. 22d, 1864. Made Brevet-Colonel by the President, by and with the advice of the Senate, to date from March 13th, 1865, for gallant and meritorious services during the campaign in Georgia and the Carolinas. Mustered out June 13th, 1865.

James E. Buckley, Corporal, Co. B, Twentieth Conn. Vols. Mustered in Aug. 4th, 1862. Wounded Mar. 19th, 1865. Mustered out June 13th, 1865.

Owen Buckley, Third Ind. Battery. Mustered in Sept. 19th, 1864. Deserted Nov. 21st, 1864.

Geo. B. Candee, Third Ind. Battery. Mustered in Sept. 23rd, 1864. Mustered out June 23rd, 1865.

Wm. Carroll, 1st Vol. Battery. Mustered in Sept. 15th, 1864. Mustered out June 23rd, 1865.

Nicholas Cass, Co. C, First C. V. Heavy Artillery. Mustered in Dec. 8th, 1863. Mustered out Sept. 5th, 1865.

Thomas Chadwick, Co. F, Twelfth Conn. Vols. Mustered in Nov. 25th, 1861. Re-enlisted Jan. 1, 1864. Mustered out Aug. 12, 1865.

SEYMOUR AND VICINITY.

Eli Clement, Co. B, First C. V. Heavy Artillery. Mustered in May 22d, 1861. Discharged May 21st, 1864; term expired.

Abraham Collins, Co. A. Tenth Conn. Vols. Mustered in Oct. 29th, 1861. Discharged, disability, Feb. 22d, 1863.

Richard Condon, Co. E, First Conn. Vols. Mustered in July 22d, 1861. Re-enlisted Dec. 21st, 1863. Wounded. Mustered out July 19th, 1865.

Richard Conway, Co. B, First C. V. Heavy Artillery. Mustered in May 22d, 1861. Discharged May 21st, 1864; term expired.

Reuben Cox, Co. C, First C. V. Heavy Artillery. Mustered in Dec. 3rd, 1863. Deserted Aug. 5th, 1865.

Frederick Cross, Third Ind. Battery. Mustered in Sept. 24th, 1864. Mustered out June 23rd, 1865.

Dennis Crummey, Co. I, Twenty-Seventh Conn. Vols. Mustered in Sept. 9th, 1862. Lost an arm in front of Mary's Heights, Dec. 13th, 1862. Discharged Feb. 12th, 1863.

Wm. E. Curtiss, Third Ind. Battery. Mustered in Sept. 15th, 1864. Mustered out June 23rd, 1865.

Charles H. Davis, Co. C, First Heavy Artillery. Mustered in Dec. 4th, 1863. Mustered out Sept. 25th, 1865.

Harry W. Davis, Rifle Co. C, Third Conn. Vols. Mustered in May 14th, 1861. Honorably discharged Aug. 12th, 1861.

Zerah B. Davis, Co. H, Twentieth Conn. Vols. Mustered in Aug. 6th, 1862. Mustered out June 13th, 1865.

Charles Domingo, colored, Co. H, Twenty-ninth Conn. Vols. Mustered in Mar. 2nd, 1864. Killed at Petersburg, Va., Sept. 3rd, 1864.

Patrick Donahue, Third Independent Battery. Mustered in Sept. 15th, 1864. Mustered out June 23rd, 1865.

Loren J. Farrell, Co. E, First Heavy Artillery. Mustered in April 8th, 1862. Died Aug. 8th, 1862, at Harrison's Landing, Va.

Hugh Fitzpatrick, mustered in Co. H, Twentieth Conn. Vols., August 13th, 1862. Discharged for disability, Feb. 8th, 1863. Mustered in Co. B, Seventh Conn. Vols., Dec. 21st, 1863. Died at David's Island, N. Y., Aug. 5th, 1864.

De Grasse Fowler, Second Lieut., Co. E, Fifth Conn. Vols. Mustered in July 22nd, 1861. Resigned Sept. 23rd, 1864.

Charles French, Co. H, Twentieth Conn. Vols. Mustered in Aug. 5th, 1862. Wounded July 20th, 1864. Mustered out June 13th, 1865.

Harpin R. French, Co. K, Tenth Conn. Vols. Mustered in Oct. 14th, 1861. Discharged Oct. 7th, 1864; term expired.

Herman B. French, Corporal, Co. F. First Heavy Artillery. Mustered in May 23rd, 1861. Discharged, disability, Nov. 18th, 1861.

SEYMOUR AND VICINITY. 95

Hobart French, Co. A, Tenth Conn. Vols. Mustered in Sept. 21st, 1861. Discharged, disability, Dec. 21st, 1861.

John W. French, Musician, Co. H, 20th Conn. Vols. Mustered in Aug. 20th, 1862. Mustered out June 13th, 1865.

Robert H. Geissler, Sergeant, Co. C, Eleventh Conn. Vols. Mustered in October 25th, 1861. Discharged, disability, June 25th, 1862.

Hyatt Gregory, Third Ind. Battery. Mustered in Sept. 21st, 1864. Mustered out June 23rd, 1865.

Wm. Grogan, Co. C, Eleventh Conn. Vols. Mustered in Nov. 14th, 1861. Enlisted in U. S. Army Nov. 1st, 1862.

John Hanley, Co. C, First Heavy Artillery. Mustered in Dec. 8th, 1863. Mustered out Oct. 9th, 1865.

Wm. Hawley, Third Ind. Battery. Mustered in Sept. 24th, 1864. Mus- out June 23, 1865.

Richard E. Hayden, Co. B, First Heavy Artillery. Mustered in May 22nd, 1861. Discharged May 21st 1864; term expired.

James W. Hendryx, Co. H, Twentieth Conn. Vols. Mustered in Aug. 6th, 1862. Killed at the battle of Chancellorsville, May 3rd, 1863.

John W. Holcomb, Co. E, First Conn. Vols. Mustered in July 22nd, 1861. Re-enlisted Dec. 21st, 1863. Mustered out July 19th, 1865.

Charles B. Holland, Corporal, Co. H, Twentieth Conn. Vols. Mustered in Aug. 5th, 1862. Transferred to Invalid Corps. Mustered out Aug. 4th, 1865.

James Holeren, Co. F, Fifth Conn. Vols. Mustered in July 22nd, 1861, Re-enlisted Dec. 21st, 1863. Mustered out July 19th, 1865.

Geo. W. Homan, Orderly-Sergeant, Co. H, Twentieth Conn. Vols. Mustered in Aug. 6th, 1862. Taken prisoner at Chancellorsville and confined in Richmond prison. Exchanged and returned to service. Promoted Second-Lieut. June 6th, 1865. Mustered out June 13th, 1865.

Calvin A. Hubbard, Co. E, First Conn. Vols. Mustered in July 22nd, 1861. Re-enlisted Dec. 21st, 1863. Wounded. Mustered out July 19th, 1865.

Thomas Hurlburt, Co. B, First Conn. Cavalry. Mustered in Nov. 19th, 1861, re-enlisted Jan. 1st, 1864. Imprisoned at Andersonville. Mustered out Aug. 2nd, 1865.

Charles Isles, Third Ind. Battery. Mustered in Sept. 19th, 1864. Mustered out June 23rd, 1865.

Andrew Jackson, Third Ind. Battery. Mustered in Sept. 17th, 1864. Mustered out June 23rd, 1865.

Wm. B. Johnson, Sergeant, Co. B, Fifteenth Conn. Vols. Mustered in July 22nd 1862. Mustered out June 27th, 1865.

SEYMOUR AND VICINITY.

Ralph Judd, Third Ind. Battery. Mustered in June 22nd, 1864. Deserted Nov. 17th, 1864.

Simon Lathrop, Co. A, Tenth Conn. Vols. Mustered in Oct. 2nd, 1861. Killed at Kinston, N. C., Dec. 14th, 1862.

William Lee, Co. C, First Heavy Artillery. Mustered in Dec. 3rd, 1863. Mustered out Sept. 25th, 1865.

Lewis E. Leigh, Co. B, First Heavy Artillery. Mustered in May 22d, 1861. Re-enlisted Jan. 1, 1864.

Albert W. Lounsbury, Co. H, 20th Conn. Vols. Mustered in Aug. 9th, 1862. Taken prisoner at the battle of Chancellorsville, and sent to Libby Prison. Exchanged and returned to service. Mustered out June 13th, 1865.

Henry W. Lounsbury, Co. A, Tenth Conn. Vols. Mustered in Oct. 2d, 1861. Died Aug. 14th, 1862, at Newbern, N. C.

Duane M. Lynde, Co. D, First Conn. Cavalry. Mustered in Nov. 28th, 1863. Mustered out June 28th, 1865.

Charles B. Lyons, Co. C, First Heavy Artillery. Mustered in Dec. 3rd, 1863. Mustered out Sept. 25th. 1865.

David Luckett, colored, Corporal, Co. C, Thirtieth Conn. Vols. Mustered in Feb. 22d, 1864. Mustered out Nov. 7th, 1865.

Albert McArthur, Co. C, First Heavy Artillery. Mustered in Dec. 3rd, 1863. Mustered out Sept. 25th, 1865.

John McCormick, Co. E, First Artillery. Mustered in Sept. 23rd, 1864. Deserted Aug. 10th, 1865.

Byron W. Munson, Co. G, First Conn. Cavalry. Mustered in Dec. 3rd, 1863. Mustered out Aug. 2nd, 1865.

Marcus E. Munson, Co. R, First Conn. Cavalry. Mustered in Dec. 21st, 1863. Died in Baltimore, Md., Mar. 11, 1864.

William Nicholas, colored, Co. A, Thirtieth Conn. Vols. Mustered in Feb. 22nd, 1864. Mustered out Nov. 7th, 1865.

George O'Brien, Co. H, Twentieth Conn. Vols. Mustered in Aug. 20th, 1862. Killed at Chancellorsville, Va., May 3rd, 1863.

David O'Claughessy, Third Ind. Battery. Mustered in Sept. 23rd, 1864. Mustered out June 23rd, 1865.

Martin Perry, Third Ind. Battery. Mustered in Sept. 24th, 1864. Mustered out June 23rd, 1865.

Edward D. Phelps, Co. F, Seventh Conn. Vols. Mustered in Sept. 9th, 1861. Re-enlisted Dec. 22d, 1863. Mustered out July 20th, 1865.

Charles Prince, Co. B, First Heavy Artillery. Mustered in May 22d, 1861. Discharged May 21st, 1864; term expired.

SEYMOUR AND VICINITY.

John Y. Reynolds, Co. B, First Heavy Artillery. Enlisted May 22nd, 1861. Discharged May 21st, 1864; term expired.

John H. Riggs, Co. F, Seventh Conn. Vols. Mustered in Sept. 9th, 1863. Re-enlisted Jan. 2nd, 1864. Mustered out July 20th, 1865.

Henry C. Rogers, Co. I, Second Artillery. Mustered in Aug. 13th, 1862. Severely wounded in the hand at the battle of Fort Fisher, Mar. 25th, 1865. Mustered out July 7th, 1865.

Henry Rose, Co. H, Twentieth Conn, Vols. Mustered in Aug. 8th, 1862. Wounded March 19th, 1865. Mustered out June 23rd, 1865.

John Ryan, Co. H, 20th Conn. Vols. Mustered in Aug. 20th, 1862. Wounded May 3rd, 1863. Discharged, disability, June 31st, 1865.

Patrick Ryan, Co. I, Twenty-third Conn. Vols. Mustered in Oct. 9th, 1862. Honorably discharged July 27th, 1863. Mustered in Third Ind. Battery, Sept. 19th, 1864. Mustered out June 23rd, 1865.

Wm. E. Ryan, Co. H, Twentieth Conn. Vols. Mustered in Aug. 20th, 1862. Deserted Sept. 11th, 1862.

David W. Sharpe, Co. B. First Heavy Artillery. Enlisted May 22d, 1861. Re-enlisted Jan. 1st, 1864. Highly commended by his superior officers and recommended for promotion. Mustered out Sept. 25th, 1865.

Cornelius Shehan, Third Ind. Battery. Mustered in Sept. 23rd, 1864. Mustered out June 23rd, 1865.

Francis Sheldon, Third Ind. Battery. Mustered in Sept. 17th, 1864. Mustered out June 23rd, 1865.

Sylvester Short, Co. F, Twenty-Third Conn. Vols. Mustered in Sept. 8th, 1862. Honorably discharged at expiration of term of enlistment, Aug. 31st, 1863.

Anson Smith, Co. E, First Conn. Vols. Mustered in July 22nd, 1861.

Geo. A. Smith, Co. E, First Conn. Vols. Mustered in July 22nd, 1861. Discharged July 22nd, 1864; term expired.

Wilbur W. Smith, Co. H, Twentieth Conn. Vols. Mustered in as First Lieut. Aug. 15th, 1862. Taken prisoner at Chancellorsville and confined in Libby prison. Paroled and exchanged. Promoted Captain Jan. 28th, 1863. Mustered out June 13th, 1865.

Jacob L. Still, Co. H, Twentieth Conn. Vols. Mustered in Aug. 20th, 1862. Wounded July 3rd, 1863. Transferred to invalid corps Mar. 15th, 1864.

Charles W. Swift, Co. H, Twentieth Conn. Vols. Mustered in Aug. 20th, 1862. Mustered out June 13th, 1865.

Reuben W. Thayer, Co. E, Fifth Conn. Vols. Mustered in July 22nd, 1861. Re-enlisted Dec. 21st, 1863. Wounded. Mustered out July 19th, 1865.

Wm. Thayer, Co. A, Tenth Conn. Vols. Mustered in Oct. 2nd, 1861. Transferred to Signal Corps, Sept. 26th, 1863.

Ransom P. Tomlinson, Co. B, First Heavy Artillery. Mustered in May 22nd, 1861. Deserted July 8th, 1861. Enlisted in Co. B, First Regiment Cavalry, Nov. 2nd, 1861. Taken prisoner at the battle of the Wilderness, confined at Libby and Andersonville. Exchanged and promoted First Sergeant. Re-enlisted Jan. 4th, 1864. Mustered out Aug. 2nd 1865.

Lucius B. Truesdell, Co. D, First Heavy Artillery. Mustered in Nov. 27th, 1863. Killed in action Sept. 12th, 1864, near Petersburg. Aged 19.

Byron Tucker, Co. B, First Heavy Artillery. Mustered in Sept. 13th, 1864. Died at Broadway Landing, Va., Nov. 27th, 1864.

Frederick Tucker, Third Ind. Battery. Mustered in Sept. 17th, 1864. Mustered out June 23rd, 1865.

Wm. Uminger, Co. C, Eleventh Conn. Vols. Mustered in Nov. 14th, 1861. Wounded Sept. 17th, 1862. Discharged, disability, April 3rd, 1863.

Hiram Upson, Jr., Sergeant, Co. F, Seventh Conn. Vols. Mustered in Sept. 9th, 1861. Died June 18th, 1862, of wounds received at James Island, S. C.

Aaron Walker, colored, Co. H, Twentieth Conn. Vols. Mustered in Dec. 28th, 1863. Mustered out Oct. 24th, 1865.

Wm. S. Ward, Musician, Co. H, Twentieth Conn. Vols. Mustered in Aug. 15th, 1862. Mustered out June 18th, 1865.

Augustus White, Musician, Co. B, First Heavy Artillery. Mustered in May 22nd, 1861. Re-enlisted Jan. 1st, 1864.

James White, Co. H, Twentieth Conn. Vols. Mustered in Aug. 6th, 1862. Killed at Peach Pine Creek, Ga., July 20th, 1864.

Leslie B. Wooster, Co. C, First Conn. Vols. Mustered in Nov. 21st, 1861. Discharged, disability, June 23rd, 1862.

Geo. S. Wyant, Sergeant, Co. H, Twentieth Conn. Vols. Mustered in Aug. 7th, 1862. Died Dec. 15th, 1862.

Wilson Wyant, Captain, Co. E, Fifth Conn. Vols. Enlisted April 22nd, 1861; mustered in July 22nd. Resigned on account of disability, Jan. 31st, 1863.

It will thus be seen that notwithstanding differences of opinion which here, as throughout the north generally, sometimes gave rise to dissension and bitterness, the town contributed liberally of men and means to suppress the rebellion and sustain the Union, and our representatives in the terrible contest acquitted themselves bravely in the defence of the "Red, White and Blue."

Soldiers of the Rebellion

Enlisted Elsewhere, but Buried in Seymour, or now Residents of the Town.

James K. Adams, Co. R, 15th Conn. Vols. Mustered in Aug. 6th, 1862. Mustered out June 27th, 1865, at Newbern, S. C.

T. P. Aylesworth, Sergeant, Co. E, 5th Vermont Vols. Enlisted Aug. 27th, 1861. Lost a leg at Fairfax, Va. Honorably discharged Feb. 27th, 1862.

Geo. H. Bartlett, Co. B, 128th New York Vols. Mustered in Sept. 4th, 1862, at Hudson, N. Y. Mustered out July 12th, 1865, at Savannah, Ga.

Edgar Beecher, Co. K, 10th C. V. Mustered in Oct. 5th, 1861, from Bethany. Died, Aug. 3rd, 1864, from wounds received at Deep Bottom, Va. Buried in the Union Cemetery.

William Blake, Co. L, First Conn. Cavalry. Mustered in from Hartford, Dec. 16th, 1863. Mustered out Aug. 2nd, 1865.

John H. Bradley, Co. I, 20th Conn. Vols. Mustered in from Hamden, Aug. 14th, 1862. Wounded. Mustered out June 13th, 1865.

Geo. W. Burroughs, Co. D, 15th W. Va. Vols. Mustered in Sept. 8th, 1862. Wounded at Winchester and Laurel Hill. Mustered out May 12th, 1865.

Henry R. Chamberlain, Co. F, 7th Conn. Vols. Mustered in from Redding, Nov. 4th, 1863. Mustered out July 20th, 1865, at Goldsboro, N. C.

Horatio S. Chamberlain, Co. A, 150th N. Y. Vols. Mustered in Sept. 6th, 1862. Mustered out June 8th, 1865; at Washington.

F. M. Clemons, corporal, Co. D., 23rd C. V. Mustered in from Huntington, Aug. 30th, 1862. Honorably discharged Aug. 31st, 1863.

William S. Cooper, from Winchester, Co. E, 2nd Conn. Vol. Artillery. Enrolled July 31st, 1862. Promoted Corporal Oct. 4th, 1862; promoted Sergeant Mar. 22nd 1863; promoted First Sergeant Jan. 13th, 1864; wounded at the battle of Winchester, Va., Sept. 19th, 1864; promoted Second Lieutenant Feb. 4th, 1864, and assigned to Co. D. Discharged Sept. 6th, 1865.

SEYMOUR AND VICINITY.

Clark Ford, Co. I, 1st C. V. Heavy Artillery. Mustered in from Woodbridge, Feb. 10th, 1864. Mustered out Sept. 25th, 1865.

F. C. Gerard, corporal, Co. H, 23rd C. V. Mustered in from Naugatuck, Sept. 2nd, 1862. Honorably discharged Aug. 31st, 1863.

William Halligan, Co. E, 52nd Mass., Vol.

Robert Healey, Corporal, Co. E, 22nd Ind. Vols. Mustered in Sept. 15th, 1861. Wounded at Perryville, Ken., Oct. 8th, 1862. Re-enlisted December, 1864. Discharged Aug. 1st, 1865.

Joseph Hitchcock, corporal, Co. D, 22nd Conn. Vols. Mustered in from Bloomfield, Aug. 23rd, 1862. Honorably discharged July 7th, 1863.

Joseph Ineson, Co. B, 20th Conn. Vols. Mustered in from Derby, Aug. 2nd, 1862. Wounded July 20th, 1864. Discharged, disability, Feb. 20th, 1865.

Martin O. Judson, Co. D, 20th C. V. Killed at the battle of Gettysburgh, July 3rd, 1863. Buried in Union Cemetery.

Charles D. Kelsey, Co. E, 5th Vermont Vols. Mustered in Aug 14th, 1861. Honorably discharged Sept. 16th, 1864.

G. F. Kelsey, Co. C, 115th Ill. Vols., died in '77. Buried in Union Cemetery.

James R. Mathews, Co. I, 27th C. V. Mustered in Sept. 1st, 1862, from New Haven. Honorably discharged July 27th, 1863.

William Morris, Co. F, 12th Conn. Vols. Mustered in from Danbury, Nov. 23rd, 1861. Re-enlisted Jan. 1st, 1864. Mustered out Aug. 12th, 1865.

Richard Pearson, Co. K, 6th U. S. Cavalry. Mustered in Sept. 1st, 1861. Transferred from 3rd Md. in October, 1862. Mustered out Sept. 3rd, 1864.

Benjamin B. Thayer, Co. E, 2nd C. V. Heavy Artillery. Mustered in from Canton, Aug. 6th, 1862. Mustered out July 7th, 1865, at Washington, D. C.

John Wooster, Mass. Battalion, Cal. Cavalry. Buried in Union Cemetery.

Notes, 1862 to 1870.

——:o:——

There was an extraordinarily heavy rain June 4th and 5th, 1862, followed by a high flood. June was remarkable as a very rainy month and the July following as a very dry one.

At the annual town meeting held Oct. 6th, 1862, Henry Bradley, John Davis and Stephen D. Russell were re-elected selectmen; David Betts, Jr., treasurer; Owen Shannon, school visitor.

An old resident of the vicinity of Bladen's Brook says that the greatest freshet ever known on that stream occurred Feb. 7th, 1863.

At the annual town meeting in October, Harvey Hotchkiss, Stephen R. Rider and Nathan Holbrook, were elected selectmen; B. W. Smith, town clerk; David Betts, Jr., treasurer; and John Chatfield, school visitor.

A teachers' institute was held in the Congregational Church Jan. 7th, 8th and 9th, 1864, at which thirty-two teachers were present from Ansonia, Birmingham, Seymour, Oxford, Naugatuck and Waterbury. Hon. N. D. Camp of New Britain, lectured on Common Schools in the evening.

The Day Brothers' Rubbermill was burned on the night of March 18th, but was immediately rebuilt.

The name of the "Stone Schoolhouse" district was changed to "Cedar Ridge."

At the electors' meeting held April 4th, 1864, H. B. Munson was elected representative, and the following named persons were elected justices of the peace: H. B. Munson, B. W. Smith, J. J. Wilcoxen, C. W. James, Wm. B. Stoddard, E. R. Bassett, Israel French, John Chatfield, Adonijah French, Leonard Wyant.

At the annual town meeting held Oct. 3rd, Stephen R. Rider, Charles A. Wooster and Nathan Holbrook were elected selectmen; B. W. Smith, town clerk; C. W. James, treasurer; and Frederick Durand, school visitor.

A resolution was adopted instructing the selectmen and school visitors to inquire into the expediency of establishing a graded school, to ascertain if a suitable building could be rented for the purpose, the probable expense of such school, and to report at an adjourned meeting to be held the following Saturday. The report was duly made and accepted, and it was voted that a school of a higher grade be established. Burton W. Smith, Harvey Hotchkiss and G. W. Divine were appointed a committee to establish and superintend the school, and to fix a rate of tuition sufficient to defray the expense. Glendinning Hall was leased for a schoolroom, and Miss Hermance was engaged as teacher.

At the electors' meeting held Nov. 8th there were 222 votes cast for the democratic presidential electors, and 124 for the republican.

At the annual town meeting held Oct. 2nd, 1865, Henry Bradley, Philo Holbrook and Stephen D. Russell were elected selectmen; B. W. Smith, town clerk; C. W. James, treasurer; and O. Evans Shannon, school visitor.

At the spring election, H. B. Munson was elected representative to the General Assembly.

The house of Capt. James Baker on Great Hill, was burned on the night of Nov. 16th.

H. B. Munson was elected representative April 2nd, 1866. The justices elected were J. J. Wilcoxen, H. B. Munson, Israel French, Leonard Wyant, Norman Sperry, B. W. Smith, C. W. James, E. R. Bassett, John Chatfield, Elbert A. Peck.

At a special meeting held April 3rd, action was taken relative to building a town-house with suitable provision for a high school-hoom, and at a subsequent meeting it was voted to build, not to exceed 40x70 feet; but at a meeting held May 18th, to act on a report of the committee as to plan and specifications, the whole matter was indefinitely postponed.

The Fengot Coal Co. was organized in 1866, for the preparation of compressed fuel from peat. A large swamp near the Woodbridge line was purchased, building erected, machinery obtained, and some of the fuel prepared for use. The venture proved unprofitable and the business was closed up at great loss to the stockholders, one of whom stated that his patent fuel had cost him one thousand dollars per ton.

The Rimmon Water Company was organized July 2nd, 1866, and soon after commenced building a dam at the place where an abutment had been built in 1850. The work was vigorously pushed forward under the direction of Raymond French, and finally completed and the gates closed Oct. 27th, 1867, at a cost of $65,000. The plate or overflow is about 300 feet long and the fall nineteen feet.

The selectmen elected Oct. 1st, were Wm. A. Fairchild, Samuel P. Davis and Charles A. Wooster; town clerk, Edward F. Bassett; treasurer, Nathan R. Wooster; school visitors, Joshua Kendall and C. W. James; high school committee, G. W. Divine, Sylvester Smith and S. Y. Beach.

On the 15th of March, 1867, the Naugatuck rose rapidly until at the mouth of the river it was fourteen feet and five inches above low water mark.

At the April election H. B. Munson was again elected representative to the General Assembly.

In October Wm. F. Betts was elected town clerk; Henry G. Hurd, Stephen R. Rider and Adonijah French, selectmen; Henry Davis, town treasurer and school visitor.

A series of revival meetings were commenced in the M. E. Church, Rev. Joseph Pullman, pastor, December, 1867, and continued through January and February, 1868, resulting in quite a number of conversions. A series of similar meetings were commenced in the Congregational Church Feb. 9th, under the direction of Rev. Allan Clark.

On the 10th of February, 1868, the Naugatuck rose to thirteen feet and three inches above low water mark at Derby.

At the electors' meeting held April 6th, Carlos French was again elected to representative, and H. B. Munson, Adam Newheim, E. R. Bassett, James Howard, Israel French, Lewis Judd, Matthias Bunyan, C. W. James, Leman Whitlock and Philo Holbrook were elected justices of the peace.

On the 4th of October, 1868, the Naugatuck rose to the highest point reached in fifteen years, while Little river and Bladen's brook were foaming torrents. Two bridges on Bladen's Brook were carried away and the new stone bridge by Ames' factory was much damaged. About thirty feet of the wall of the raceway below Kalmia Mills, was also carried away, stopping all the factories on the main stream.

At the annual meeting held Oct. 5th, 1868, Stephen H. Culver, Samuel P. Davis and Geo. W. Divine were elected selectmen; S. H. Canfield, town clerk; Henry Davis, treasurer; Joshua Kendall, school visitor; Joshua Kendall and Henry B. Beecher, assessors; Joshua Kendall and Henry Bradley, registrars of electors; Joseph J. Wilcoxen, S. H. Canfield, G. W. Divine, Ashbel Storrs, Henry P. Davis, Israel French, grand jurors; Sylvester Smith and Sharon Y. Beach, board of relief. The total vote was 359; average republican majority, 30.

At an adjourned town meeting held Oct. 12th, the following resolutions were adopted:

Resolved, That the selectmen be instructed to cause their annual report to be printed, and have at least five hundred copies, to be left at the town clerk's office on or before the 28th of September in each year, for distribution among the voters of the town. Such report shall contain the amount of each bill and to whom paid, the amount paid for the support of the poor out of the Alms House, and for whom the expense was incurred, the amount paid to each town officer for services, and any other information which they may deem necessary to show the expenses and indebtedness of the town; to which shall be added the report of the town treasurer.

Resolved, That the school districts of this town be consolidated into one school district, to be known as the Seymour School District, and that chapter 87 of the laws passed May session, 1867, are hereby referred to and made part of this regulation.

At an adjourned town meeting held Oct. 15th, the following named persons were elected a committee of the Seymour School District: Eli Gillette, C. W. Storrs, J. W. Bassett, Joshua Kendall, C. W. James, Harpin Riggs, Joel R. Chatfield, Peter Worth, Henry Davis. At the first meeting of the school board J. Kendall was chosen chairman; Henry Davis, Secretary and treasurer; and J. Kendall and Henry Davis, school visitors.

The funeral of Carl Zurcher, junior agent of the Kalmia Mills, Dec. 10th, was attended by a large concourse of his friends. He had resided in Seymour four and a half years, and was highly esteemed by those who knew him best.

The rebuilding of Smith's papermill, which was burned Jan. 11th, 1869, was completed in March. The Kalmia Mills Co. contracted for three dwelling houses of four tenements each to be erected on Third street. Business was thriving and the place grew rapidly, the grand list of the town exceeding $1,000,000. Messrs. Hendryx & Peck purchased the old car shop north of the depot and remodelled it into a store and several tenements.

At the April election Philo Holbrook was elected representative to the General Assembly of 1869.

The second meeting of the Seymour School District for the election of members of the board, was held in the High School room Sept. 25th, and Elliott R. Bassett, Samuel A. Beach and Henry Davis were elected for three years.

In October the town clerk and selectmen were re-elected: S. H. Canfield was elected treasurer; Joshua Kendall and Henry Bradley, registrars of voters; Joshua Kendall and W. W. Smith, assessors; Ashbel Storrs, G. W. Divine, N. R. Wooster, Eli Gillette, J. W. Smith and Norman Sperry, grand jurors; and John W. Bassett, registrar of births, marriages and deaths.

Kalmia Mills were closed the following winter, and in its failure seemed to betoken decreased prosperity for the ensuing decade; yet the place has continued to grow, and in 1877 the population was at least five hundred more than in 1870. The debt of the town, which in 1869, was over twenty-three thousand dollars, has virtually been paid, only two bonds, not yet due, being outstanding, and these more than balanced by the assets of the town. The various industries of the town are now improving and there seems to be no reason why the season of depression through which we have just passed should not be followed by prosperity and renewed growth.

TOWN CLERKS, TREASURERS AND REPRESENTATIVES.

	TOWN CLERKS.	TREASURERS.	REPRESENTATIVES.
1850—	Charles B. Wooster.	Sylvester Smith.	*Sylvester Smith.
1851	" "	Burton W. Smith.	Bennett Wooster.
1852	" "	" "	Sylvester Smith.
1853	" "	" "	Harris B. Munson.
1854	" "	" "	" "
1855	" "	" "	Luzon B. Morris.
1856	" "	Hiram W. Randall.	" "
1857	" "	Burton W. Smith.	Henry C. Johnson.
1858	" "	" "	Charles B. Wooster.
1859	" "	Henry S. Johnson.	Samuel L. Bronson.
1860	" "	" "	Carlos French.
1861	" "	David Betts, Jr.	Clark Wooster.
1862	" "	" " "	Abel Holbrook.
1863—	Burton W. Smith.	" " "	Harris B. Munson.
1864	" "	Cornelius W. James.	" "
1865	" "	" "	" "
1866—	Edward F. Bassett.	Nathan R. Wooster.	" "
1867—	William F. Betts.	Henry Davis.	
1868—	Samuel H. Canfield.	" "	Carlos French.
1869	" "	Samuel H. Canfield.	Philo Holbrook.
1870	" "	" "	Virgil H. McEwen.
1871	" "	" "	Smith Botsford.
1872	" "	" "	James Swan.
1873	" "	" "	Horatio N. Eggleston.
1874	" "	. " "	Edmund Day.
1875	" "	" "	Lewis A. Camp.
1876	" "	" "	Henry P. Day.
1877	" "	" . "	Samuel A. Beach.
1878	" "	" "	Albert B. Dunham.

* For Town of Derby. Joshua Kendall represented the town of Derby in 1849.

SELECTMEN OF THE TOWN OF SEYMOUR.

1850-51, Leman Chatfield, Daniel L. Holbrook, Thomas Cochran.
1852, Isaac B. Davis, Sharon Y. Beach, Harpin Riggs.
1853, Leman Chatfield, Harpin Riggs, Jabez E. Pritchard.
1854, Harpin Riggs, Jabez E. Pritchard, Henry Bradley,
1855, Jabez E. Pritchard, Henry Bradley, Philo Holbrook.
1856, Sheldon Church, Miles Culver, Daniel L. Holbrook.
1857-8, Henry Bradley. Edwin Smith, Abel Holbrook.
1859-60, Henry Bradley, Edwin Smith, Stephen D. Russell.
1861-2, Henry Bradley, John Davis, Stephen D. Russell.
1863, Harvey Hotchkiss, Stephen R. Rider, Nathan Holbrook.
1864, Stephen R. Rider, Charles A. Wooster, Nathan Holbrook.
1865, Henry Bradley, Philo Holbrook, Stephen D. Russell.
1866, Wm. A. Fairchild, Samuel P. Davis, Charles A. Wooster.
1867, Henry G. Hurd, Stephen R. Rider, Adonijah French.
1868-9, Stephen H. Culver, Samuel P. Davis, George W. Divine.
1870, Sharon Y. Beach, Nathan R. Wooster, Samuel P. Davis.
1871, Edwin Smith, Frank C. Gerard, Edwin Buckingham.
1872, Edwin Smith, Frank C. Gerard, Roswell N. Kinney.
1873, Lewis A. Camp, Frank C. Gerard, Roswell N. Kinney.
1874, Lewis A. Camp, Cornelius W. James, Samuel P. Davis.
1875, Lewis A. Camp, Cornelius W. James, Frederick M. Clemons.
1876, Lewis A. Camp, Frank E. Steele, Frederick M. Clemons.
1877, Lewis A. Camp, Frank E. Steele, Edward L. Hoadley.
1878, Horace A. Radford, Frank E. Steele, Edward L. Hoadley.

JUSTICES OF THE PEACE.
For lists previous to 1870 see foregoing pages.

1870, H. B. Munson, J. J. Wilcoxen, B. W. Smith, Israel French, Nathan Holbrook, Matthias Bunyan, Samuel Roselle, David Betts, Jr., Adam Newheim, S. Y. Beach.

1872, H. B. Munson, Geo. A. Rogers, Wm. S. Cooper, Henry P. Davis, Edwin Tomlinson, Geo. W. Divine, Wilson Wyant, Henry B. Beecher, C. W. James, Sheldon Tucker.

1874, G. W. Divine, James Swan, L. A. Camp, Ebenezer Fairchild, W. N. Storrs, S. Y. Beach, S. P. Davis, W. S. Cooper, F. M. Clemons, C. W. James.

1876, F. M. Clemons, Wm. R. Tomlinson, G. W. Divine, W. S. Cooper, H. S. Chamberlin, J. W. Rogers, Samuel Butler, S. Y. Beach, Ashbel Storrs, Theodore S. Ladd.

1878, Edwin Buckingham, Gustave Becker, John W. Rogers, Frederick M. Clemons, William R. Tomlinson, James Buckley, Horatio S. Chamberlin, Ashbel Storrs, John Smith, William S. Cooper.

THE SCHOOLS

UNTIL 1856 the schools were managed by districts and school societies. The districts on the east side of the river constituted the First School Society, and those on the west side the Second School Society. The meetings of the latter were held in the meeting house on Great Hill from 1824 to 1851, when the whole of the districts of Seymour were united in one Society. The Naugatuck river was made the division line between the two societies by an act of the Assembly in 1832. (Pr. Acts, Vol. 2, p. 1086.) In 1841 the boundaries were defined as follows :

We the School Committee of the Second School Society in the Town of Derby have laid and established the fourth Day of June, A. D., 1842, the following described bounds and limits to the 2d School Society in Derby, viz., commencing at the Town bounds between Derby and Oxford, on the west side of the highway a few rods ——— of the House now occupied by Oliver Nettleton, thence proceeding in a direct line south-westerly to the former site of the old District School House at the center of which site we have laid bounds; thence proceeding in a direct line a little south of west to bounds laid by us near an old cellar about three rods south of a large pine tree, said bounds on the highway near the fence, thence proceeding in a direct line a little south of east to a large rock a little off the road near the house of Jube Weston, by a spring, on which rock we have laid bounds ; thence proceeding in a direct line south easterly to bounds laid by us on the highway about two rods ——— of small house now occupied by the widow of Ephraim Allen and James Harding; thence proceeding in the same direction until the line strikes Naugatuck river; from thence said district is bounded on the east and separated from the first society by Naugatuck river until it meets the line between Derby and Oxford, when it strikes the west side of the said river; from thence said district is bounded on the north by said town line, running west until it strikes the bounds on the highway first commenced at. Said boundaries of the above named district, so far as they have not been legally settled and defined before, are hereby settled and defined by us.

ANSON DAVIS,   } SOCIETY
JAMES C. TOMLINSON, } COMMITTEE.

At each annual meeting of the Second Society were elected a moderator, clerk, treasurer, a society's committee of three, a visiting committee of nine, and until 1840 the district committees were elected at the Society's meetings.

The Shrub Oak district appears to have been first included in the Second Society in 1831.

At a special meeting of the voters of the Great Hill School Society held Sept. 30th, 1851, it was voted that the fund of the Great Hill School Society be divided equally between the four districts, and that the first meeting of the

SEYMOUR AND VICINITY.

School Society of Seymour be held in the Congregational Church in Humphreysville. At the said first meeting Daniel L. Holbrook was elected chairman; B. W. Smith, clerk; G. F. DeForest, treasurer; Sylvester Smith, S. Y. Beach and Harpin Riggs, society's committee; John B. Steel, collector; and Joshua Kendall, visiting and examining committee. The numbers of the districts were continued the same except that the Falls district, now the Center district, which had been known as the eighth, was made the sixth.

At a special meeting of the Seymour School District held Feb 1st, 1869, it was voted to purchase a lot in the Pines and to build thereon a school-house of sufficient capacity to accomodate 160 scholars. A tax was to be laid sufficient to raise the sum of $6,000 to defray the expenses. The lot was purchased at a cost of $700 and is still held by the town, but on account of objections to the location the school-house has not been built.

SCHOOL VISITORS OF THE TOWN OF SEYMOUR.

ELECTED IN SCHOOL SOCIETY MEETINGS.

1850 to 1855, Joshua Kendall.

1855-6, Sylvester Smith.

ELECTED IN TOWN MEETING, FOR THREE YEARS EACH.

The stars indicate those elected each year.

1856-7, George F. DeForest,* Philo B. Buckingham,* Luzon B. Morris,*

1857-8, Joshua Kendall,* Sharon Y. Beach.*

1858-9, Joshua Kendall, Sharon Y. Beach, Philo B. Buckingham,*

1859-60, Joshua Kendall, Sharon Y. Beach,* Philo B. Buckingham.

1860-1, Joshua Kendall,* Sharon Y. Beach, Philo B. Buckingham.

1861-2, Joshua Kendall, Sharon Y. Beach, Charles B. Wooster.*

1862-3, Joshua Kendall, Charles B. Wooster, Rev. Owen E. Shannon.*

1863-4, Rev. Owen E. Shannon, Frederick Durand, John Chatfield.*

F. Durand elected by the other visitors to fill vacancy caused by the resignation of C. B. Wooster.

1364-5, Rev. Owen E. Shannon, Frederick Durand,* John Chatfield.

1865-6, Rev. O. Evans Shannon,* Frederick Durand, John Chatfield.

1866-7, Rev. O. Evans Shannon, Frederick Durand, Cornelius W. James.*

F. Durand resigned May 21, 1867, and J. Kendall was elected to fill the vacancy.

1867-8, Joshua Kendall, Cornelius W. James, Henry Davis.*

ELECTED BY THE BOARD OF EDUCATION.

1868-9, Joshua Kendall, Cornelius W. James, Henry Davis.

1869-70, Joshua Kendall, Cornelius W. James, Henry Davis.

1870-1, Joshua Kendall.

1871-2, Joshua Kendall, Edmund Day, Harpin Riggs.

1872-3, Joshua Kendall, Samuel P. Davis.

1873-4, Joshua Kendall, Norman Sperry.

1874-5, Joshua Kendall, Virgil H. McEwen, Norman Sperry.

1875-6, Joshua Kendall, Virgil H. McEwen, William C. Sharpe.

1876-7, Joshua Kendall, Virgil H. McEwen, William C. Sharpe.

1877-8, Joshua Kendall, William C. Sharpe.

1878-9, Joshua Kendall, William C. Sharpe.

MEMBERS OF THE BOARD OF EDUCATION.

ELECTED IN UNION SCHOOL MEETING.

1868, *elected for one year*—Cornelius James, Henry Davis, Eli Gillette.
For two years—Harpin Riggs, John W. Bassett, John R. Chatfield.
For three years—Joshua Kendall, Peter Worth, C. W. Storrs.
1869, Elliott R. Bassett, Samuel A. Beach, Henry Davis.
    Carlos French was elected by the board June 6th, 1870, to fill the vacancy caused by the removal of Henry Davis.
1870, Harpin Riggs, Wilbur W. Smith, John W. Bassett.
1871, Joshua Kendall, Edmund Day, Thomas James.

ELECTED IN TOWN MEETING.

1872, Carlos French, A. Y. Beach, Samuel P. Davis.
    A. Y. Beach resigned Nov. 12th and S. H. Canfield was appointed by the Board to fill the vacancy.
1873, Sharon Y. Beach, Norman Sperry, H. N. Eggleston.
1874, V. H. McEwen, Joshua Kendall, Edmund Day.
1875, S. H. Canfield, Carlos French, William C. Sharpe.
1876, Sharon Y. Beach, Frederick M. Clemons, Nathan Holbrook.
1877, Edmund Day, Joshua Kendall, Norman Sperry.
    V. H. McEwen elected to fill vacancy caused by resignation of Norman Sperry, until the next town election.
1878, S. H. Canfield, W. C. Sharpe, David Tucker, James Howard.
    James Howard to fill vacancy for two years.

GREAT HILL SCHOOL, No. 1.

This is probably the oldest school in the town. An abstract of a volume of the earlier records is given on pages 19 and 20.

At a meeting of the Second Society held Nov. 7th, 1831, Wm. Smith, Samuel Wire and Samuel Meigs were appointed a committee to designate a location for a new school-house in the First or Great Hill District, and decided upon the north-east angle of the roads below the present location of the church.

The district line was changed by vote of the school society Oct. 12, 1843, as follows:

Resolved, That so much of the 1st school district, 2d society in Derby, be and hereby is, set off to the 5th school district in Oxford, as lies north and west of a line beginning at the Oxford line, by the dwelling-house of Andrew S. Graham, running southeasterly to the corner of road leading to Rock-house Hill; thence by said road to the corner of land of Abel and Benjamin English, near the house of Christopher Smith; thence northwesterly to Oxford line, including the house of Abel and Benjamin English.

The lines were laid out anew Nov. 1st, 1843, as follows:

Whereas, The record defining the lines of the Great Hill School District in the second school society in Derby being lost, and the undersigned committee being empowered by an act of the legislature of the State of Connecticut, passed 1841, to lay out new and establish old lines, do make and establish the following lines, which shall constitute the school district of Great Hill, viz: Beginning eighty rods from the mouth of Toby Brook on 2d brook; thence in a straight line to the north-east corner of Monroe Scranton's farm; thence in a straight line to Josiah Bassett's saw mill; thence in a straight line to the west side of the highway, running by the dwelling-house formerly belonging to Truman Hawkins, now Anson Davis; thence on the west side of said highway until opposite a pine tree standing near the Rowe place, so-called; thence in a straight line to the town bounds lying in the highway some thirty or forty rods south of Stephen Baldwin's dwelling-house; thence on the town line until it comes in a parallel line with the road south of Abel and Benjamin English; thence following the lines of that part of said English farm lying north of said road to the town line; thence

SEYMOUR AND VICINITY. 109

on town line to a stone bridge near the dwelling-house of widow Ammon Tomlinson; thence on the town line to the northwest corner of Bennet Lum's farm, adjoining Simeon Hinman's land; thence in a straight line to the place of beginning. The above lines shall constitute and define the school district of the Great Hill.

Done in Derby, Nov. 1st, 1843.

LUTHER FOWLER,
EPHRAIM SMITH, } Society Committee.
WM. D. LUM,

In 1852, by joint action of the School Society and the 1st and 4th districts, the Squantuck district was consolidated with the Great Hill district, and the lines were defined as follows:

Whereas, The legal voters of the school society in the town of Seymour, at a meeting warned and held on the 3rd day of July, 1852, voted to annex the Squantuck School District to the First School District in said school society; *Therefore*, We, the undersigned Society's Committee, hereby establish the following described lines, and boundaries annexed, viz: Beginning at the Ousatonic river, at the mouth of the Old Field brook at the boundary of the school society line between Derby and Seymour, running easterly on said line to the late dwelling-house of Philo Lum, deceased, leaving said dwelling-house in the North District in Derby School Society; thence running easterly on school society line to a heap of stones on a rock at the west corner of Asa Bassett's land, about thirty rods southerly of the house occupied by Miles Bronson; thence running northerly by the Bunga School District to Josiah Bassett's saw mill; thence northerly in a straight line to the west side of the highway at the east side of the Beard land, so called, southerly of the dwelling-house of Marcus Davis; thence on the west side of said highway till opposite a pine tree standing near the Rowe place, so called; thence north-westerly to the old town bounds in the highway, about thirty rods south of the house of Stephen Baldwin; thence west on society line between Oxford and Seymour to the west side of highway in front of the dwelling-house of Andrew S. Graham; thence southwesterly to the corner of the road leading to Rock-house Hill; thence by said road to the corner of land of Abel and Benjamin English, near the house of Christopher Smith; thence north-westerly to the school society line between Oxford and Seymour; thence on said line to stone bridge on Rockhouse Hill road, north of the Ammon Tomlinson place, so called; thence on society line to the north-west corner of Bennet Lum's farm, adjoining Simeon Hinman's land; thence straight line to the south end of Otter Rocks on the Ousatonic river; thenceby the east side of the Ousatonic river to the first-mentioned bounds; and the above-described lines and boundaries hereby constitute the boundaries of the First School District in Seymour.

Dated at Seymour, Feb. 22d, 1855.

SYLVESTER SMITH, } Society's Committee.
HIRAM UPSON,

The above is a true record. Attest:

B. W. SMITH, Clerk.

At a town meeting held Oct. 1st, 1877, it was voted that a new schoolhouse be built at an expense of $700 and that the location be changed to the angle of the roads on the Hill near the house of Wm. R. Tomlinson. The building was completed about the first of January, 1878.

TEACHERS.

1826, Henry Scott.
1827, Eliza Russell, Henry Burton.
1828, Maria Wattles, Simon Curtiss, Jr.
1829, Jane Tomlinson, Simon Curtiss, Jr.
1830, Catherine Umberfield, S. Curtiss, Jr.
1831, Jane Fowler, Simon Curtiss, Jr.

1832, Betsey Tomlinson, John Riggs, Jr.
1833, Jane Fowler, Simon Curtiss, Jr.
1834, Lilly Wakeley, John Lindley.
1835, Jane Fowler, Silas Hurd.
1836, Sarah A. Benham, Simon Curtiss, Jr.
1837, Mary A. Smith, David Hawes.

1838, Sarah Lindley.
1839, Miss Davis, John Lindley.
1840, Sarah E. Gilbert, Judson Candee.
1841, Sarah M. Osborn, John Lindley.
1842, Eliza. A. Mansfield, Merwin Bowen.
1843, Ann Eliza Shelton, Abel Holbrook.
1844, C. A. Fowler, A. T. Hotchkiss.
1845, Elizabeth Durand, Merwin Bowen.
1846, Maria Chatfield, William Bristol.
1847, Jane M. Wooster, Albert E. Smith.
1848, Jane M. Wooster.
1849, Frances E. Wooster, Gid. H. Candee.
1850, Eliza Lum, Betsey Cable.
1851, Rossetta Bassett, Henry Harger.
1852, Mary Bradley, Charles Gillette.
1853, Augusta Sanford.
1854, Juliette Wooster, John Allen.
1855, Augusta Sanford, Clark E. Lum.
1856, Julia A. Fairchild, John Smith.
1857, Julia A. Fairchild, Marcus E. Hyde.

1858, Nancy Sutton, R. S. Hinman.
1859, Mary F. Meacham, Clark E. Lum.
1860, Elvira W. Somers, Eben G. Wheeler.
1861, Elvira W. Somers, Jane E. Tyrrell.
1862, Jane E. Tyrell.
1863, Frances E. Wheeler, H. A. Tomlinson
1864, Martha E. Davis, John Killon.
1865, Martha E. Davis, C. C. Burwell.
1866, C. C. Burwell, Martha E. Davis.
1867-8, Martha E. Davis.
1869, Sophia Davis.
1870, Virginia Davis.
1871, Emily A. Smith, Emmarette Sperry.
1872, C. E. Lum, E. Sperry, C. E. Lum.
1873, C. E. Lum, 2 t; Matilda Smith.
1874, Rufus Spencer, Lottie E. Booth.
1875, Rufus Spencer, Clara S. Rider.
1876, Clara S. Rider, Hattie Riggs.
1877, Josie E. Ladd.
1878, Rufus Spencer, Phoebe Tomlinson.

SHRUB OAK SCHOOL, No. 2.

The records of the Shrub Oak District not having been handed over to the town clerk, are not now available, and but little account can be given of it. The district seem to have been set off Dec. 27th, 1779. See page 47. The names of the teachers, so far as ascertained, are:

Winter terms of 1846-7, 1847-8, 1848-9, Frederick Durand.
Oct., 1861, to April, 1863, Rhoda Kendall.
Summer of 1866, Sarah Swift.
Fall of 1866 to Dec., 1876, C. C. Burwell.
Jan., 1877, to July, 1878, Harriet Riggs.
Sept., 1878, Josie E. Ladd.

BUNGAY SCHOOL, No. 3.

Records not filed in town clerk's office.

TEACHERS.

May, 1867 to Oct., 1868, Emma S. Tomlinson.
Oct., 1868, to July, 1869, Sarah M. Riggs.
Sept., 1869, to April, 1870, Alice Northrop.
April, 1870, to July, 1872, Sarah M. Riggs.
Sept., 1872, to July, 1873, L. Davis.
Sept., 1873, to July, 1874, Ellen C. Hard.
Sept., 1874, to July, 1875, Hattie J. Riggs.
Sept., 1875, to 1878, Hattie Bassett.

CEDAR RIDGE SCHOOL, No. 4.

The fifth district was divided in 1837, the new district, called the seventh, being bounded southerly by a line from the mouth of Bladen's brook, easterly to the Woodbridge line, passing south of the house of Samuel R. Hickox. The first meeting of the new district was held Aug. 30th, and arrangements commenced for building a school-house. The location was selected by Joel White, Isaac White and Joel R. Chatfield, and at a meeting held Sept. 20th it was voted to accept the proposals of Solomon Terrell to build a stone school-house, 18 x 25 feet, 7½ feet clear, with six windows of 24 lights and one of 9 lights, to be plastered inside and out, with a hall of five feet in width at one end, and two doors from the hall; the whole to be completed for $175. Terrell was afterward allowed $8 for extra work, and some slab benches and sloping boards for writing-desks, with a stove and desk and chair for teacher, completed this "temple of science" in time for the winter school. It was found necessary to remove the partition in 1843 to enlarge the school-room. The teacher was then paid $2.25 per week and required to "board around." Board being then estimated at $1.75, the teacher's services were valued at $4 per week, teaching five and one-half days. The next year the price was raised one dollar per week. In 1852 it became evident that a larger school-house was needed, and in July it was voted to build 26 x 40 feet, but at a subsequent meeting the matter was indefinitely postponed.

January 31st, 1868, it was voted to build a new school-house, and Smith Botsford, Ashbel Storrs and Joel R. Chatfield were appointed building committee. The size finally determined upon was 27½ x 34 feet, to cost $1,700, including furniture of the best patterns. The school-house was well built, by Ashbel Storrs, and is a credit to the district. Up to 1863 the building had been known as the "Stone School-house." The name, "Cedar Ridge," was then given to the school and has since been retained.

Charles Oatman was clerk of the district from 1837 to 1849, and Sylvester Smith from 1849 until the schools of the town were consolidated in 1868.

The old stone building, small, inconvenient and antiquated, is yet the subject of many pleasant reminiscences by teachers and scholars, now scattered among the scenes of busy life, to whom the following list of teachers will recall pleasant memories of by-gone days.

TEACHERS.

1841, A. T. Hotchkiss, winter term.
1842, Frances N. Thomas, two terms.
1843, Laura Tomlinson, George Bassett.
1844, Laura Tomlinson, H. B. Munson.
1845, Miss Fairchild, H. B. Munson.
1846, Charlotte M. Smith, Jane E. Terrell.
1847, Annie Holcomb, Wm. E. Holbrook.
1848, Henry Warren.
1849, Rosetta Bassett, Mrs. P. E. Clark.
1850, Rosetta Bassett, Mary A. Wooster.
1851, Miss Fairchild, Frederick Durand.
1852, M. A. Wooster, Frederick Durand.
1853, Miss Hull, Frederick Durand.
1854, M. A. Wooster, Thomas Munson.
1855, Eliza Clark, Thomas Munson.
1856, Charles T. Hotchkiss, Miss Upson.
1857, Eliza J. Tuttle, two terms.
1858, Jane Doolittle, Clark Lum.
1859, Marietta Benham, David Hawley.
1860, Laura M. French, Joel F. Selleck.
1861, Kate McKay, Clark E. Lum.
1862, Lucy A. Atwood, two terms.
1863, Julia Leavenworth, W. C. Sharpe.
1864, Mrs. M. A. Gleason, Miss Swift.
1865, Josephine A. Walker.
1866, Minerva Bassett, Miss Bradley.
1867, Mary Chatfield, three terms.
1868, Mary Chatfield.

1869, Mary Chatfield, Josephine Walker.
1870, J. Walker, 2 t; L. C. Chatfield.
1871, L. Cornelia Chatfield.
1872, L. Cornelia Chatfield.
1873, L. Cornelia Chatfield.
1874, L. Cornelia Chatfield, C. F. Abbott Libbie O. Lockwood.
1875, Libbie O. Lockwood.
1876, Clara F. Abbott, E. O. Lockwood.
1877-8, Libbie O. Lockwood.

DISTRICT COMMITTEES.

1837, Isaac White.
1838, Jared Bassett.
1839, Sylvester Smith.
1840, Oliver Stoddard.
1841, Samuel Bassett.
1842, Hiram Upson.
1843, Joel R. Chatfield,
1844, Smith Botsford.
1845, Israel French.
1846, Julius Bassett.
1847, Wm. B. Watson.
1848, David Johnson.
1849, Stephen H. Culver.
1850, George Merrick.
1851, Ashbel Storrs.
1852, Samuel Hickox.
1853, Henry W. Benedict.
1854, Smith Terrell.
1855, Wm. B. Watson.
1856, David Johnson.
1857, Wm. F. Gilyard.
1858, Wilson Wyant.
1859, Wm. W. Dibble.
1860, Lorenzo M. Bassett,
1861-2, Smith Terrell.
1863-6, Ashbel Storrs.
1867, Joel R. Chatfield, (app. by Sch. Vis.)
1868, David Johnson.

THE BELL SCHOOL, No. 5.

In 1769 Joseph Johnson deeded a piece of land on the east side of Pearl street, a little south of the house of Smith Terrell, for a location for a school house, as follows:

KNOW ALL MEN BY THESE PRESENTS, *that I, JOSEPH JOHNSON of Derby in the County of New Haven, Collony of Connecticut, New England, do firmly set, remit & releas unto the proprietors of the third Destrict for Schooling in Derby, one certain piece of land pitch upon by the proprietors of the third Destrict, to set up a School House upon for the benefit of Said Destrict, containing twenty feet square, for the term of Ninety Nine years Next Coming the Date hereof, to have & to hold it for the use said schoolhouse.*

Furthermore I the said Johnson do promis for myself, my heirs, Executors & Administrators, to defend the Same from all Claims and demands whatsoever. In witness whereof I have hereunto set my hand and seal this 5th Day of may in the year of our Lord, one thousand Seven hundred Sixty Nine.

Signed, sealed and delivered in presents of
   Benjamin Crawford.
   Hezekiah Johnson.   *JOSEPH JOHNSON.*

This school-house seems to have been occupied about forty years. In that time the number of the district was changed to six, and in 1799 it was known as the Chusetown District.

At a school meeting held in the school-house September, 27th, 1799, Lieut. E. Beecher Johnson was chosen moderator and Bradford Steele, Jr., clerk. At this meeting Calvin Lines was engaged to teach the school six months at $11 per month, or, if he should continue a year, he was to teach at $10.50 per month. At an adjourned meeting, held October 7th at the house of Joseph Johnson, Leroy Tomlinson and Bezaleel Peck were chosen a committee "to pitch a stake for a school-house."

On the 21st of November, 1803, it was voted that Daniel Holbrook and Amadeus Dibble be a committee to repair the school-house and build an

SEYMOUR AND VICINITY. 113

addition 14 feet long with two chimneys, the whole to be completed by Oct. 4, 1804, and painted Spanish brown. Chauncey Johnson was elected district committee.

On the 8th day of February, 1804, the following persons were recorded as residents of the district: "Levi Tomlinson, Esq., Joel Chatfield, Jesse Johnson, Ebenezer B. Johnson, Amadeus Dibel, Daniel Holbrook, Jn^r., Enoch French, Gibson Smith, Isaac Johnson, Amos Dorman, Bezaleel Peck, Isaac Chais, Ebenezer Peck, Charles French, John Wheler, Samuel Smith, Jarvis Downs, Elephas Bradley, John White, Isaac Bostick, Joseph Johnson, Benjamin Beach, Simeon Beach, Hezekiah Johnson, Erazmass Sperry, Ashbell Steel, John Crawford, Lydia Keney, Phebe Dayton, Hanah Stodard, Nathan Stiles, Silas Baldwin, Elezer Patchen, James Leach, Charles Deal, Mary Bartis, Sebrie Molthroop, Bradford Steele, John Shenson, Hezekiah Tomson, Josiah Swift, Lydia Cowel, Oliver Clark, Richard Freeman, Isrel French, Reuben Davis. SERGT. CHAUNCEY JOHNSON, Clerk."

At a meeting held Oct. 17th, 1805, the valuation of "good wood brought to the school-house" was estimated at "$2 a chord, the Master to be the judge of the size of the loads." Special committees were appointed to repair the school-house nearly every year from 1802 until 1812.

In 1810 John Ward was hired for the winter at $20 per month, he to be his own collector, and John T. Wheeler was appointed clerk. At an adjourned meeting, held Nov. 22nd, the last vote to repair was rescinded, and it was voted to have the school kept in Silas Baldwin's room until the first of May, 1811.

In October, 1811, Chester Jones was chosen clerk and another repair committee appointed. On the 9th of December it was "Voted that there should be 2 schools kept in s^d District."

"Voted, 2nd, that Col. Ira Smith & Capt. Josiah Swift be a Committee for the south part of the District, & Amadeus Dibble & E. B. Johnson be a Committee for the north part, to employ teachers."

April 6th, 1812, it was "Voted that there should be two schools kept in the District, one Man school & one Woman school, & the Free Money be equally divided according to the time the school is kept." Stiles Johnson was elected a committee "to employ a school Dame."

On the 15th of the same month Levi Tomlinson, Esqr, Ira Smith, Josiah Swift, Elias Gilbert and Bradford Steele were appointed a committee to look for a place to build a school-house and to draw a plan. Several meetings were called and adjourned without transacting any business, except employing a male teacher in the south part of the district in the winter of 1812-13, and a teacher for three months in the winter of 1813-14.

On the 7th of March, 1814, at a school meeting held at the store of Jones & Keeney, it was "Voted that all needlework should be prohibited from school." At a meeting held the 25th of the same month the above vote was rescinded and declared "null & void." The name Humphreysville first appears on the record in 1814. The next winter it was voted to employ a female teacher and to divide the money equally between the two schools of the district.

The school-house first built on the location of the present Bell school-house was long owned as joint stock property, as shown in the following deed given June 1st, 1816:

Know Ye, That I, Newel Johnson of Derby, in New Haven County and State of Connecticut, for the the consideration of Ten Dollars received to my full satisfaction of John Wheeler, Newel Johnson, Elias Gilbert, Bradford Steele, John Humphreys, Jr., Genl. David Humphreys, Chester Jones, Seba Moulthrop, Stiles Johnson, Jesse Johnson, Edmund Steele, John Riggs, Silas Baldwin, Samuel B. Hine, Joseph Johnson, Josiah Swift & Danl. Thompson, Do give, grant, bargain, sell and confirm unto the said Grantee, one certain piece or tract of land situated in said Derby at Humphreysville, containing about six acres of land, bounded Southerly on highway, Easterly and Northerly on sd Newel Johnson, Westerly on Seba Moulthrop. The said piece of land has a School-House erected thereon and divided into one hundred shares, and is owned by the above named Grantees in the following proportion, viz: to the said John Wheeler twenty nine shares; Newel Johnson, thirteen; Elias Gilbert, thirteen shares; Bradford Steele, seven; John Humphreys, Junr, five; Gen. David Humphreys, five; Chester Jones, seven; Seba Moulthrop, four; Stiles Johnson, three; Jesse Johnson, two; Edmund Steele, two; John Riggs, two; Silas Baldwin, two; Samuel B. Hine, two; Joseph Johnson, one; Josiah Swift, one; Daniel Thompson, one.

In October, 1815, Chester Jones was elected committee and Newel Johnson clerk.

"At a Legal Meeting of the Inhabitants of the 5th School District at the School House in Humphreysville, held Oct. 30th, 1816, Newel Johnson was appointed a special committee to obtain from Mr. Samuel Riggs his terms for teaching a winter school," apparently without success, as a few days later Bradford Steele and Johnathan Beement were added to the committee.

On the 10th of December it was voted to employ Isaac Rowe as teacher at $18 per month. April 13th, 1819, it was voted to employ Anna C. Martin as teacher for the summer, "provided she can be had on reasonable terms not to exceed one dollar and fifty cents per week."

Ebenezer Fisher was appointed collector Nov. 20th, 1820, and it was voted that board be $1.25 per week. Smith & Sanford then kept the store on the southeast corner of Pearl and Hill streets. On the 4th of December, 1820, it was "Voted that there be a stove purchased for the benefit of the destrict and made up in the school bill." Until that time the school-room had been warmed by a fire in the large old-fashioned fire-place.

On the 12th of April, 1822, it was "Voted that Mr. Isaac Sperry be employed to teach this school for one year if he can be obtained for ten dollars per month," and "that the district hire the school-house of the proprietors at the rate of seven dollars a quarter."

From Nov. 9th, 1818, to Oct. 10th, 1825, Lyman Smith was clerk of the district, and during this time the book was kept with a neatness and precision seldom found in the old records.

At a meeting held Dec. 11th, 1822, David Beach was appointed district committee and Newel Johnson and Daniel White were appointed a committee to confer with the proprietors of the school-house for the purpose of seeing what the shares of the school-house can be purchased for. Provision was made for wood for the stove *and fireplace.*

In the fall of 1823 the price of board was fixed at eight (Yankee) shillings ($1.33½) per week, and it was voted to hire Mr. Sperry, provided that not more than $15 per month should be paid. If any scholars came from out of the district, they were to pay two dollars per quarter. Ebenezer Fisher, committee.

On the 29th of March, 1824, it was voted to hire Isaac J. Sperry for a year at $15 per month, and that he have an assistant for six months at $5 per month. The school-house was hired as before.

It was voted, Aug. 16th, to release Mr. Sperry, to hire Aaron Pierson in his place, and to continue Miss Tuttle as assistant teacher.

Oct. 12th, 1824, Russel Clark was elected committee; David Beach, Jr., collector; and Sheldon Tucker, treasurer. It was voted not to hire a teacher unless he will board with the district. The committee was instructed to hire Mr. Parsons (or Pierson) or Harlow P. Sage, wages not to exceed $15 per month. Dec. 6th it was voted to employ an assistant teacher.

April 12th, 1825, voted to hire Harlow P. Sage at $19 per month, he to board himself, provided that should any choose to board him at $1 per week, they might do so. An assistant to be hired if necessary.

Up to this time the business seems to have been wholly directed in district meetings, and the names most frequently occurring on the record are "Chusetown Destrict" and 5th School District of the school society, but at a meeting held Oct. 10th, 1825, Thomas Gilyard was "recommended to the School Society to be appointed committee," and Isaac Losee was elected asst. committee. Mr. Persons was to be hired. Wm. Humphreys, John De Forest and Ebenezer Fisher were "recommended to the School Society as visitors."

In the spring of 1826 the committee were authorized to employ Mr. Persons (Aaron C.?) at $16 per month, and it was voted that each proprietor draw his rent from the treasurer.

Sept. 29th, 1826. Recommendations to school scoiety: Sheldon Tucker, committee; John H. De Forest, Wm. Humphrey, Ebenezer Fisher and John Wheeler, school visitors. Voted to give Mr. Persons the preference for teacher.

Sept. 27th, 1827. Ebenezer Fisher, district committee; Edmund Steele, school society's committee; Newel Johnson, clerk; J. H. De Forest, J. T. Wheeler and Wm. Humphreys recommended to school society as visitors. Voted to try to hire the lower story of the school-house for $18 per year.

April 8th, 1829, voted to give Mr. Hubbell the preference as teacher.

At a meeting held March 29th, 1830, it was voted to purchase from fifty to one hundred shares of the Bell school-house of the proprietors at one dollar per share. It was voted (April 15th) to rescind the previous motion and to purchase a lot and build a school-house. The latter vote was rescinded May 15th, and the former motion re-enacted. A tax of $200 was voted for the purchasing and repairing the school-house. Geo. Kirtland acted as moderator Oct. 17th, 1831. Apr. 16, '32, the Committee had permission to employ a teacher for each of the two rooms if they thought best.

Oct. 18th, 1836. Chester Jones, treasurer; Denzel Hitchcock, clerk; Isaac Losee, asst. com.; Chas. Oatman, collector. Mr. Northrop was engaged to teach the winter school.

Mar. 7th, 1837. Thomas Ellis, moderator. Voted to divide the district and to run the line from the mouth of Bladen's Brook, and go south so far as to take in the house of Isaac White, and then a straight line to Woodbridge.

At a meeting held April 15th, 1837, it was voted "to run the line beginning at the bank south of the mouth of Bladen's Brook, so called, and run straight to Woodbridge line, running far enough south to take in the house of Samuel R. Heacox," and "to apply to the school society's committee for division."

The following description of the District limits, from the minutes of the First School Society, was certified to by Almon Smith, Society's Clerk.

"Fourth District begins at the Dam across Naugatuck River, running up the east side of said river until you come to the brook emptying into said river, through the land formerly belonging to Henry Wooster; then an easterly coarse to Woodbridge line so as to take Isaac Blake and David Hotchkiss' dwelling-houses into the Fourth School District."

"Fifth District begins at the Henry Wooster Brook, so called, by Naugatuck River, running up northerly the east side of said river to Oxford line; then easterly by said Oxford line to Woodbridge line; then southerly by said Woodbridge line until it strikes the northerly line of the Fourth District; then westerly by said Fourth District to the place of beginning at the mouth of the Henry Wooster Brook at the Naugatuck River."

"Voted, that the society divide the said Fifth District, and that the bounds commence on the Naugatuck River at a high bluff or bank about twenty rods south of the mouth of Bladen's Brook; from thence to run easterly to Woodbridge line, passing by the south side of the house of Samuel R. Hickcok; and the north part of the said Fifth School District shall constitute the Seventh District."

At a school meeting held Sept. 22d, 1840, it was voted "that a building committee be appointed and that they be instructed to make a contract for repairing the school-house by cutting it down to one story high, putting on new shingles and new pine clapboards, laying a new floor, painting the outside with two coats of good paint and making such other repairs as they shall deem necessary for a thorough repair in every respect." Bennet Wooster, George W. De Forest and Walter B. Clark were appointed committee on repairs.

At a meeting held Oct. 1st, 1841, it was voted to buy Harrison Tomlinson's lot on the Promised Land, on west side of the highway, and build a good school-house thereon, and a 15c. tax was laid Dec. 10th. Feb. 7th, 1842, the tax was raised 5 cents. On the 15th of February it was voted not to sell or dispose of the old school-house.

On the 4th of September, 1842, it was voted "that the committee hire a room on the Falls known as the Conference Room for a school this winter;" but the vote was rescinded the 11th. On the 10th of May, 1843, it was voted not to rent the upper story for a workshop, and the vote laying a tax of 20c. for building purposes were rescinded June 22nd; also, the vote fixing location of new school-house. The old school-house was cut down and repaired in the summer of 1843. In August the committee were directed to sell the old bell and pay the proceeds to the treasurer. In the summer of 1844 board was estimated at eight shillings ($1.33⅓) per week, and the following winter at $1.75 per week.

The school-house was appraised Jan. 13th, 1847, by Isaac J. Gilbert, Ephraim Birdsey and Wm. M. Hull, at $360, and at a school meeting, held Nov. 21st, it was voted that the 5th district pay to the 8th district $112.50 as their share of the district. The offer not being accepted by the district the matter was left to the society's committee, who named $175 as the amount to be paid. The new district was the one since known as District No. 8, and now as the Center sub-district, No. 6.

A meeting was held June 10th, 1852, for the purpose of uniting with the other districts in forming a union high school, without any successful action resulting.

DISTRICT COMMITTEES.

1838, Walter B. Clark.
1839, Walter B. Clark, Isaac Kinney and Chester Jones.
1840, Amos Smith, Bennet Wooster and Sharon Y. Beach.

1841, Jeremiah Durand, Sharon Y. Beach.
1842, Thomas Cochran, Daniel White and John W. Bassett.
1843, B. Wooster. (G. F. DeForest, clerk.
1844, Ezekiel Gilbert,   "   "

SEYMOUR AND VICINITY. 117

1845, Daniel White. (W. B. Clark, clerk.)
1846, A. J. Steele. (H. Tomlinson, clerk.)
1847, David B. Clark. (S. Y. Beach, clerk.)
1848, Smith Clark. (H. B. Munson, clerk.)
1849, Medad K. Tucker. (J. B. Steele, "
1850-51, Thomas Stoddard.
1852-3, Joseph Chipman. (L. Sharpe,
1854, William S. Mallory. collector.)
1855, Stephen H. Culver.
1856, E. F. Bassett.

1857, David Beach. (H. B. Beecher, clerk
1858, H. B. Beecher. 1857 to 1859.)
1859, Edwin Smith. (L. Sharpe, collector
1860-61, John Davis. 1858 to 1861.)
1862, J. W. Bassett.
1863, Henry P. Davis.
1864, J. Armstrong.
1865-7, W. E. Hendryx.
1868, A. W. Lounsbury.

TEACHERS.

1843, Mr. Lum, two terms.
1844, Miss Lindley, summer term.
1846, Mr. Stuart, two terms.
1852, Miss Chatfield from Quaker farms.
1855, Leverett Mallory, Fred'k Durand.
1857, Leverett Mallory.
1859, Miss Wilcox, summer term.
1863, Ellen M. Clark.

April, 1864, to Mar., 1865, Mary Tomlinson,
April to Sept., 1867, Mary Tomlinson.
Jan. to April, 1869, Ella Davis.
April, 1869, to April, 1870, Lydia Payne.
April, 1870, to July, 1873, M. A. Hotchkiss.
Sept., 1873, to July, 1874, Emma J. Downs.
Sept., 1874, to Dec., 1875, M. A. Hotchkiss.
Jan., 1876, to 1878, Lottie E. Booth.

CENTER SCHOOL, No. 6.

This was set off from No. 5 in 1847. A "select school" had been kept by Mrs. Hodge in a building which stood near where the south end of the pin-shop now is. The building was taken for the district school and removed above the cotton factory, to where the wool-room of Kalmia Mills now is, then to where Second street terminates, above Maple street, and when the car-shops were built it was removed to its present location.

TEACHERS.

1852, Charles W. Sharpe.
1867, Miss Coltingham.
1869 to July, 1875, Jessie O. Perkins.
Sept., 1875, to 1878, Maria M. Tucker.

SECOND INTERMEDIATE SCHOOL.

Established in September, 1878. Arthur L. Candee, teacher.

FIRST INTERMEDIATE SCHOOL.

TEACHERS.

April, 1869, to April, 1870, Mary A. Swift.
April to July, 1870, Cornelia A. Chatfield.
Sept., 1870, to July, 1872, H. A. Woodford.
Sept., 1872, to July, 1873, E. J. Downs.
Sept., 1873, to April, 1875, Sarah M. Riggs.
April to Dec., 1875, Clara F. Abbott.
Jan., 1876, to 1878, Emma S. Tomlinson.

THE HIGH SCHOOL.

Humphreysville Academy, established in 1849, during its continuance, satisfied the demand for a school of higher grade, and perhaps for this reason the High School Association, incorporated in 1851, failed of its purpose. The Humphreysville Academy was very popular under the direction of Geo. B. Glendining, and deservedly so. He was an efficient instructor, and drew many pupils from neighboring towns as well as from distant cities. In 1853 he removed to a larger town towards New York and was succeeded by Frederick Durand, who taught two years in Union Hall. Mr. Gay, a graduate of Yale, came in August, 1855, but continued only a few months. The subject of a Union High School was agitated, but the meetings called to consider the subject were no avail until after the passage of a law authorizing the establishment of such a school by the town, independent of school societies and school districts. The school was permanently established in 1864. Martha J. Morris was employed as assistant from September, 1867, to December, 1868. Since then no assistant has been employed in the High School, but the establishment of the two intermediate departments has practically made a high school of three grades, and only a new and commodious school building is especially needed to place Seymour in the first rank as regards the facilities for common school education.

TEACHERS.

1864 to July, 1866, Miss Hermance.
Sept., 1866, to July, 1867, Frederick Durand.
Sept., 1867, to Dec., 1868, Prof. A. F. Reynolds.
Jan. to April, 1869, Martha J. Morris.
April, 1869, to April, 1870, Celia A. Stanley.
April to July, 1870, Miss S. A. Atwater.
Sept., 1870, to July, 1871, Mrs. Lottie E. Bigelow.
Sept., 1871, to July, 1872, Lucy S. Merwin.
Sept. to Dec., 1872, Mary R. Deery.
Jan., 1873, to July, 1874, Arthur Kilgore.
Sept., 1874, to April, 1875, Frank H. Brewer.
April, 1875, to July, 1878, William H. Warner.
Sept., 1878, Rev. C. W. Sharpe.

Great Hill M. E. Church.

THIS is one of the oldest Methodist societies in Connecticut and at one time ranked highest in strength and numbers in the Derby Circuit, which then included the towns of the Naugatuck Valley as far as Waterbury. Rev. Heman Bangs, who was presiding elder about sixty years ago, said Great Hill was his main stay, and Rev. Elijah Woolsey, circuit preacher in 1814, in his book called "The Lights and Shadows of the Itinerancy," gives space to incidents of his experience on Great Hill. It had been an old Presbyterian parish, the church standing near the Davis place. Abner Smith was the pastor of the Presbyterian Society in 1814 and for many years preceding, but moved west soon after, and the pulpit was by general consent occupied by Methodist clergymen. From the time when Rev. Jesse Lee proclaimed the "Glad Tidings" through the valley of the Naugatuck, service was held here by his successors from time to time, and a prosperous church grew up. For a number of years, between 1810 and 1820, Cyrus Botsford was chorister and was considered an excellent music teacher. The choirs in those days were large and some humorous anecdotes are told of corrections made by Mr. B. when discordant notes were heard, when his words were more emphatic than appropriate to the place. Mr. B. was four times married and had seventeen children. Capt. Isaac Bassett and wife, grand parents of Capt. Elliott Bassett, were among the first Methodists on the Hill. The late Judson English was closely identified with the Great Hill church for half a century. The eccentric George L. Fuller, pastor in 1845 and 1846, is still remembered by many residents of the Hill. Fearless and untiring in his Master's service, he labored with great success and many were the anecdotes told of his labors. At one time in a revival meeting he preached from the parable of the swine, (Matt., viii: 30-32), and afterward passed around among the congregation urging them to repentance. A young man, T—— W——, replied to him very discourteously that there was no need of it, since, according to the sermon, all the devils were drowned. The eccentric clergyman knelt in prayer and remembered the young man as follows: "Oh Lord, we read in Thy blessed word that the swine rushed down into the sea and were drowned; but oh, Lord, one hog swam ashore, and here he is right before us. Drive the devil out of him and make a man of him," etc. It is said that if the logic was not convincing, the whole-souled earnestness of the preacher was, and apparently the prayer was answered. A man, at whose house a prayer-meeting was to be held one Saturday evening, sent an invitation to a neighbor, a staunch Presbyterian, to attend. He sent back word that he wished to be excused as he "kept Saturday night," but he soon began to attend the meetings and continued to be a regular attendant for more than thirty years. Anson Gillette was the first class-leader, over sixty-five years ago. The present church edifice was built by subscription in 1853-4. Almost the only preaching on the hill for the forty years preceding had been by the Methodists, to whom the old Presbyterian church had been given up. The church was dedicated on Wednesday, October 25th, 1854. The subscriptions that day were $580, leaving a debt of only $300, which has since been paid. Though the society is smaller now by reason of the draught upon it by the flourishing manufacturing centers around, yet considerable improvements have been made in and about the church in the past few years, and the services of the sanctuary are well sustained.

PAPER MAKING IN SEYMOUR.

THE first to establish the manufacture of paper in this place was General Humphreys. He built the first paper mill in 1805, but soon sold it to Worrull & Hudson. At this time the paper was made by hand. An engine for preparing the pulp was in use, but from this it was dipped out into fine sieves, the size the sheet of paper was to be made, shaken about to pack the fiber, a felt or flannel laid on, and the paper tipped out on it. 125 sheets were so piled up, making, with the felts, a pile about 15 inches high. This was pressed in a screw press, then taken out of the felts and hung on poles to dry, then pressed in $1\frac{1}{4}$ ream bunches. The next day the sheets were "stripped" or separated and pressed in the dry press. Writing paper was laid sheet by sheet between press boards with occasional iron plates and pressed again. In 1816 Worrull & Hudson sold out to Ebenezer Fisher and Henry LeForge. In 1817 Samuel Roselle, afterwards a partner, came to the place and commenced work in the paper mill.

The mill was raised a story in 1825, and paper then first made altogether by machinery. The mill was sold to the Humphreysville Manufacturing Company January 27th, 1831. This company commenced the manufacture of paper in May, 1831, with but four employees—Chester Jones, Wm. Bates, Jane Patchen and Lois Thompson, but during the month the number was increased to 16, and afterward to 18. The 16th of April, 1832, they commenced running night and day. They were then making paper for the New Haven Palladium and other papers. Not only news but tissue and colored papers were produced. It is evident that the circulation of the papers was not very large from the fact that 500 pounds of paper was considered a good day's work at the time they were supplying several printing offices besides making other kinds of paper.

The establishment was taken by George L. Hodge, Sharon Y. Beach and Samuel Roselle August 17th, 1843, under the firm name of Hodge & Co., this partnership continuing two years.

In 1845 the Humphreysville Manufacturing Company, by their special agent, Timothy Dwight, sold the paper mill with a five years' lease of the water to Ezekiel Gilbert, Sharon Y. Beach and Samuel Roselle, who carried on the business five years under the firm name of Gilbert, Beach & Co. The water lease expired in 1850, and as the Humphreysville Manufacturing Company declined all offers for a renewal, Mr. Beach bought out the other two partners, pulled down the mill, and put it up again in "Blueville," on Bladen's Brook, about a mile east of the old location, where it has since remained. Among the numerous publications for which Mr. B. has furnished more or less paper is Barber's History of Connecticut, New Haven Palladium, Register, Journal and Courier, the Waterbury American, and the Seymour Record.

In February and March of 1859 a large addition was built to the mill. In September of 1860 the wooden flume was taken out and an iron one put in. New machinery has been added from time to time, engines, boilers, calenders, &c., reservoirs built on the hill near by to insure a full supply of pure water, so much needed in the manufacture of paper, and other improvements made, until Mr. B. has about $20,000 invested in the business, making a large mill, furnished with the most approved machinery and turning out large quantities of superior colored papers, that having been made a specialty of the mill for a number of years past.

SEYMOUR AND VICINITY.

The first mill on the site of Smith's paper mill was built in 1831 under the direction of John Riggs for John S. Moshier. The machinery was designed and built by Cyrus Lee, millwright, in whose employ were Smith Botsford and Sheldon Hurd. Mr. Moshier purchased the land from the Capt. Merrick farm, once owned by Rev. Jesse Johnson, including the upper mill site, now occupied by the rubber mill. Newel Johnson purchased the latter and paid Moshier in work on the paper mill. Johnson built a small dam near the upper end of the present rubber mill dam, and built a small machine shop. The paper mill was completed and commenced running in the spring of 1832. William Bates was employed as superintendent and Samuel Bassett run the paper machine. John Bodge was also employed in the mill, and so continued until his death in 1868, a period of thirty-nine years. At this time the wages paid for work in paper mills varied from one dollar for sixteen hours' work to five shillings for twelve hours.

Early in 1833 the paper mill passed into the hands of John C. Wheeler, and in April was leased to Daniel White for three years at an annual rent of $600. Mr. White was then in the paper business at the Falls, and his lease of that mill had one year longer to run. Sylvester Smith, who had been in Mr. White's employ one year in the old mill, was now transferred to the superintendency of the new mill. During the year the most of the paper made in the mill was of a fine quality, for books and periodicals. All paper was then sold on six and nine months' credit. For about four years this mill furnished the paper for reprinting Blackwood's Magazine and other foreign periodicals by T. Foster in New York.

Mr. White, being unsuccessful in business, gave up the mill in the spring of 1834, and his successor (John C. Wheeler) gave Sylvester Smith a one-quarter interest in the business, Wheeler furnishing the capital. Their partnership lasted three years. But from 1834 the times were hard and the price of paper fell off almost one-fourth. Wheeler, who was also in company with Raymond French in the auger business, met with heavy losses in the hard times of 1837. The dam was carried away in April, 1837, but rebuilt before July, and Wheeler then rented the mill to Smith & Bassett for fifty dollars a month, to be paid in wrapping paper. This was the commencement of a partnership which lasted nineteen years. Feb. 10th, 1840, Smith & Bassett bought the mill of John C. Wheeler for $4,220, payable in wrapping paper—$200 every three months.

Straw was made into paper in this mill in 1837, and was the first paper made from straw in Connecticut. Money was very scarce and for several years barter was more common than cash; paper and augers being extensively used as a circulating medium in this vicinity. In January, 1841, an addition of twenty feet was built on the south end of the mill. Other improvements were made in 1846, but on the 29th of January, 1847, the paper mill was entirely consumed by fire. The loss was about $9,000 and the insurance was $3,500. With improved times and better facilities for making paper, all seemed ready for increased profit when this fire occurred. On Saturday, March 13th, 1847, the frame of the new mill was raised, about 100 men being present. Daniel White had charge of the carpenter work and Smith Botsford superintended the mill work. On Saturday, July 17th, paper making was resumed.

In January, 1856, Mr. Bassett sold his half of the mill to Mr. Smith. During the time of their partnership a large proportion of the paper made in the mill was straw boards and button boards. When they commenced the price of straw delivered at the mill was $5 per ton. In the last twelve years of their partnership the mill was much used in grinding and cleaning rubber, which added much to the profit of the mill. But in 1855 this branch of the business was closed up. The paper business was then poor for several years. The panic of 1857 came and the prospects were gloomy. Then came the sound of war and the tramp of armies, and everything was uncertain. But in the spring of 1863 the paper business revived, and the sun of prosperity arose on the old paper works. Prices improved, orders increased and the dream of profits was upon the mill owner. But another unlucky Friday came and the paper mill was again burnt down, about noon of March 13th, 1863. The loss was about $10,000 and the insurance $5,000. Fourteen tons of old iron was sold from the ruins. In two weeks the timber for the new mill was on the ground. The main building was raised the last week in April. It was 46 by 70 feet, and three stories high. The machinery was all put on the lower floor, and two turbine wheels took the place of the large wooden ones. On the 4th of July the mill was so far completed that a festival was held in it for the benefit of sick and wounded soldiers. About five hundred people attended, and with the music and speaking it was a pleasant affair. About the 15th of August the mill was in running order.

A large bleach-house was added to the main building, and in the same year an ell was added to the east side, 60 by 27 feet, two stories high. Ashbel Storrs planned and superintended the building, and Smith Botsford was the master millwright. Perhaps it was the most complete mill for the work for which it was designed that had been built in the country up to that time. During the next two years the mill did a successful business.

In 1866 W. W. Smith took charge of the mill on a salary, and his father retired from the business. In 1867 an addition was made to the south end of the mill, a steam engine put in, and the manufacture of manilla paper commenced.

On Monday evening, January 11th, 1869, a fire broke out in the second story of the ell part of the mill, and in a short time the whole building was destroyed. The loss was about $30,000 and the insurance $14,000. Mr. Amasa Trowbridge perished in the flames. At the cry of fire he left his home and lost his life in the effort to save his neighbor's property. In three months another mill was running in part, and at the end of five months from the date of the fire it was completed. The cost of this mill was nearly double that which was built in 1863, so great had been the increase in the price of labor and material.

In May, 1870, the mill was sold to Mr. W. W. Smith. This year was remarkable for the long-continued drought. Nothing like it had ever been known. In the summer of 1871 the dam was carried away, and Capt. Smith, at great expense, brought the water down from Rimmon Pond in Naugatuck River, put in a wheel opposite the mill, and applied that power, underneath the highway, to his mill, the new power going into operation in the first week in November. But another black Friday came November 10th, and in the rainy afternoon the cruel fire made short work of the mill. There were ten policies of insurance of $2,000 each on the property, but the then recent disastrous fire in Chicago had so damaged several of the companies that a large part of the insurance was lost. The whole loss by this fire was estimated at $30,000. The mill was again rebuilt and has since been confined to the manufacture of a superior quality of manilla paper.

De Dorest and Hodge purchased the water privilege and buildings where the rubber works now are and changed it to a paper mill, running partly by steam, making fine calendered book paper. They soon sold out to Smith &

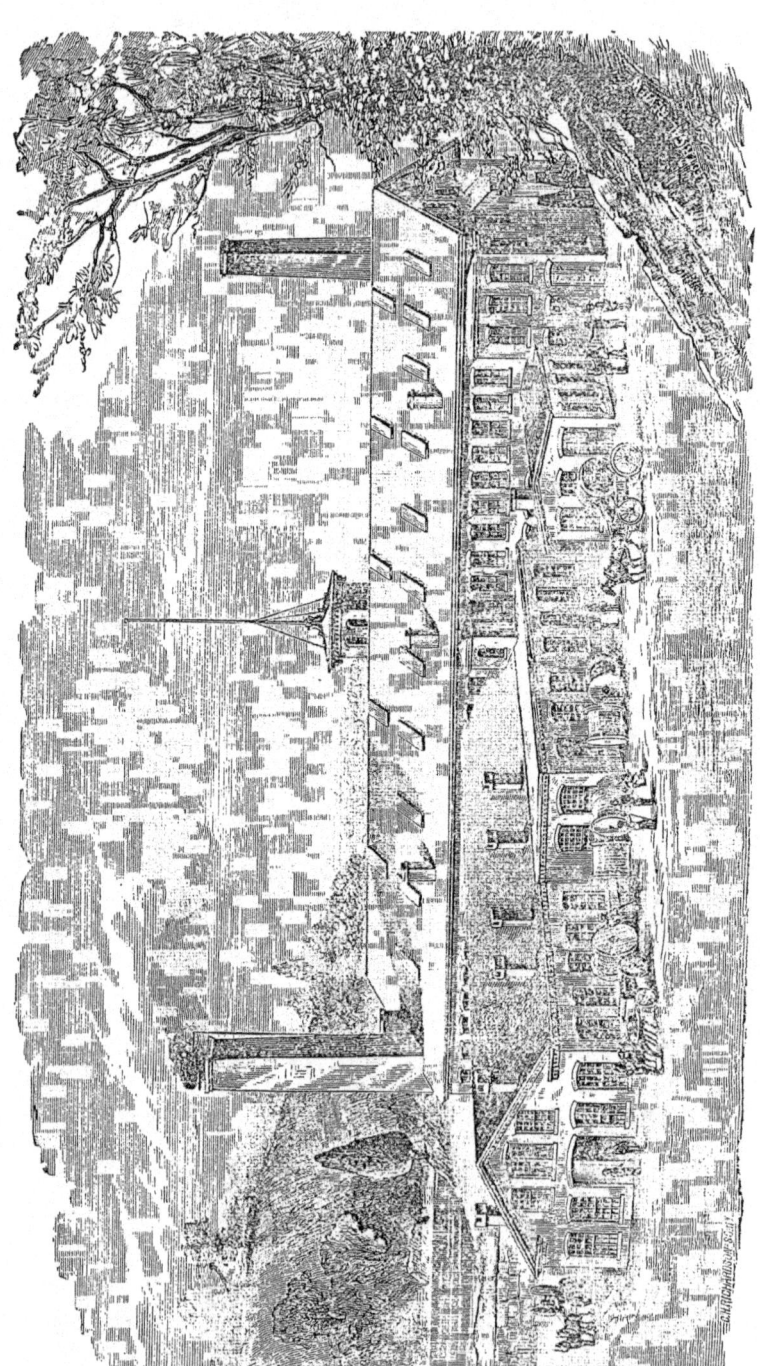

A. G. DAY'S TELEGRAPH CABLE WORKS.

Bassett, who continued the paper business, but added the grinding of rubber. They also hired the mill at the mouth of Little River to grind rubber in, and even then were unable to do the work as fast as wanted. This mill at the mouth of Little River had been run as a paper mill by Lewis Bunce, and afterward by the Rimmon Paper Company. In 1854 Smith & Bassett sold the upper mill to Austin G. Day, and it has since been occupied by the Day Brothers in the rubber business exclusively.

SUFFERINGS OF REVOLUTIONARY SOLDIERS.

THE following extract from Ramsay's History of the Revolution, published in Trenton in 1811, gives a good representation of the sufferings of patriots of the Revolution who were captured by the British, among whom were Bradford Steele, Jabez Pritchard and others mentioned in this book in the account of the Revolutionary period.

The prisoners captured by Sir William Howe in 1776, amounted to many hundreds. The officers were admitted to parole, and had some waste houses assigned to them as quarters; but the privates were shut up in the coldest season of the year, in churches, sugar houses, and such like large open buildings. The severity of the weather, and the rigor of their treatment, occasioned the death of many hundreds of these unfortunate men. The filth of the places of their confinement, in consequence of fluxes which prevailed among them, was both offensive and dangerous. Seven dead bodies have been seen in one building, at one time, and all lying in a situation shocking to humanity. The provisions served out to them were deficient in quantity, and of an unwholesome quality. These suffering prisoners were generally pressed to enter into the British service, but hundreds submitted to death, rather than procure a melioration of their circumstances by enlisting with the enemies of their country. After General Washington's successes at Trenton and Princeton, the American prisoners fared somewhat better. Those who survived were ordered to be sent out for exchange, but some of them fell down dead in the streets, while attempting to walk to the vessels. Others were so emaciated that their appearance was horrible. A speedy death closed the scene with many.

The American board of war, after conferring (December 1, 1777) with Mr. Boudinot, the commissary-general of prisoners, and examining evidences produced by him, reported among other things, "That there were 900 privates and 300 officers of the American army, prisoners in the city of New York, and about 500 privates and 50 officers prisoners in Philadelphia. That since the beginning of October, all these prisoners, both officers and privates, had been confined in prison ships or the Provost: That from the best evidence the subject could admit of, the general allowance of prisoners, at most, did not exceed four ounces of meat per day, and often so damaged as not to be eatable: That it had been a common practice with the British, on a prisoner's being first captured, to keep him three, four or five days, without a morsel of meat, and then to tempt him to enlist to save his life: That there were numerous instances of prisoners of war perishing in all the agonies of hunger."

About this time (Dec. 24, 1777) there was a meeting of merchants in London, for the purpose of raising a sum of money to relieve the distresses of American prisoners then in England. The sum subscribed for that purpose amounted in two months to 4647*l* 15*s*. Thus while human nature was dishonoured by the cruelties of some of the British in America, there was a laudable display of the benevolence of others of the same nation in Europe. The American sailors, when captured by the British, suffered more than even the soldiers which fell into their hands. The former were confined on board prison ships. They were there crouded together in such numbers, and their accommodations were so wretched, that diseases broke out and swept them off, in a manner that was sufficient to excite compassion in breasts of the least sensibility. It has been asserted, on as good evidence as the case will admit, that in the last six years of the war upwards of eleven thousand persons died on board the Jersey, one of these prison ships, which was stationed in East river near New-York. On many of these, the rites of sepulture were never or very imperfectly conferred. For some time after the war was ended, their bones lay whitening in the sun, on the shores of Long-Island.

STREETS OF SEYMOUR.

BIRCH, from Washington avenue to Day street.
BROAD, from Main street to Derby avenue.
CEDAR, from River street, along foot of Castle Rock, to West street.
CHURCH, from West street, east, past Trinity church, to Mill street.
CULVER, from First avenue to Grand street.
DAY, from North Main street to Pearl street.
DERBY AVENUE, from intersection of Broad and West streets, southward.
ELM, from Pearl street to house of Edwin Smith.
FACTORY, from Main street to Kalmia Mills.
FIRST, from Factory street to Maple street.
FIRST AVENUE, from Grand street to Culver street.
GRAND, from Washington avenue to Pearl street.
GROVE, from Derby avenue to Cedar street, past house of B. W. Smith.
HIGH, from Pearl street, opposite M. E. Church, to Culver street.
HILL, from Main street, southward, formerly Rimmon turnpike.
HUMPHREY, from Pearl street to house of Isaac Losee.
JAMES, from Main street to Washington avenue.
MAIN, running north towards Pinesbridge and south towards Ansonia.
MAPLE, from Main street to West street, near house of E. L. Hoadley.
MILL, from River street, northwest, to West street.
MONSON, from Grand street to Culver street.
NORTH, from Day street, north, to North Main street.
OAK, from Derby avenue to Cedar street, past house of Frederick Emery.
PEARL, from South Main street to Day street.
PINE, from Broad street to Derby avenue.
RAYMOND, from Factory street to foot of Third street.
RIMMON, from Maple street, north, over Rimmon Hill.
RIVER, from West street to Maple street.
ROSE, from Derby avenue to Cedar street, past house of S. C. Ford.
SECOND, from Raymond street, north, to the river.
THIRD, from Maple street, south, to Raymond street.
THIRD AVENUE, from Grand street, south, to Culver street.
WALNUT, from Hill street, near house of S. C. Ford, to Pearl street.
WASHINGTON AVENUE, (Promised Land,) from Hill street to Main street.
WEST, from intersection of Broad street and Derby avenue, towards Oxford.
VINE, from Derby avenue to Cedar street, south of house of C. W. Storrs.

NOTES FROM DWIGHT'S TRAVELS.

Published in 1822.

From Derby the road crosses Naugatuc river; and thence proceeds by the side of the Hooestennuc to the near neighbourhood of its fountains in New-Ashford. From Derby to Kent the course is nearly North-West; and throughout the whole distance to New-Milford is almost literally on the bank. The valley is every where narrow; and the prospect limited on both sides by hills of considerable height. A few of these are bold, masculine bluffs, with rude precipices, which may be called magnificent. Almost all of them present declivities, too steep for convenient cultivation, covered with a soil too unpromising to tempt the labours of the husbandman. At times it is sandy; at others rocky; and at others cold. Hence this region is more thinly populated than any other, of equal extent, within the limits of Connecticut. The houses, also, are few; and most of them indifferent buildings. In the parish of South-Britain, eighteen miles from Derby, and twenty-six from New-Haven, there is a small exception to these remarks. The rest of the tract is solitary; and, with the aid of a road generally sandy and heavy, is far from inviting excursions of pleasure.

You will remember, that these observations are applied only to the narrow valley of the Hooestennuc, through which we passed; extending rarely more than a mile in breadth; and generally not more than one fourth of a mile. As soon as these steep hills are ascended, their surface presents a good soil, and sprightlier scenery, had numerous population and flourishing settlements.

The first township, along the skirt of which we passed after we had left Derby, is Oxford; formerly a part of that township. Oxford is a collection of hills and vallies, generally covered with a strong soil. The inhabitants are universally farmers. It includes two Congregations;. a Presbyterian and an Episcopal plurality; and, in 1800, contained 1,410 inhabitants; in 1810, 1,413.

Immediately North of Oxford lies the township of Southbury, along a tributary stream of the Hooestennuc. Its surface is pleasant: and the soil, excellent. It is divided into two parishes; the Town, and South-Britain. The town is a pretty collection of houses, chiefly on a single street, running from North to South. The parish of South-Britain is small. That part of it, which borders upon the Hooestennuc, presents the only specimen of soft scenery on our road, until we reached New-Milford. The expansion here was wider, the hills more handsomely shaped, and the river adorned with several intervals. The soil was better than in the parts through which we have passed before. Here, also, was a scattered hamlet, the inhabitants of which appeared to be in better circumstances. Southbury contains two Presbyterian congregations. In the year 1774, it was a part of Woodbury. In 1790, it contained 1,738 inhabitants: in 1800, 1,757; and in 1810, (a part of it having been taken off to form the township of Middlebury,) 1,413.—[Vol. III, pp. 396-7.]

New-Haven is the shire town of the County of New-Haven, in a State distinguished for the rigid execution of its laws. Of course all the capital punishments in the County have been inflicted here. The whole number of these in one hundred and seventy-five years, has been thirteen. Of these, five were whites; five were Indians: and three were blacks. Of the whites, one was a stranger taken up as a spy, as he was passing through this town, and executed, pursuant to a sentence of a court martial. Three of the remaining four were natives of England. It does not appear, that any inhabitant of this town, or County, ever suffered death by the hand of law. There is no reason to conclude, that the people of this County are more distinguished for their morals than most of the other settlements, which have been established for any length of time. In this respect, (the paucity of capital punishments,) New-England may be compared with Scotland, and Switzerland; and will suffer no disadvantage by the comparison.—[Vol. IV, p. 334.]

There is not a spot on the globe, where so little is done to govern the inhabitants; nor a spot, where the inhabitants are so well governed, or, perhaps, in more appropriate terms, where the state of society is so peaceable, orderly, and happy. A recurrence to the manner, in which elections are carried on here, as described in a former part of these letters, will enable you to compare them with your own. Those in your country have been described to me on various occasions, by authority which cannot be questioned. They are scenes of riot, tumult, and violence. Ours are scarcely less decent than religious assemblies.—[Vol. IV, p. 335.]

The people of New-England have always had, and have by law always been required to have, arms in their hands. Every man is, or ought to be, in the possession of a musket. The great body of our citizens, also, are trained with a good degree of skill, and success, to military discipline. Yet I know not a single instance, in which arms have been the instruments of carrying on a private quarrel. * * * On a country, more peaceful and quiet, it is presumed, the sun never shone. * * * In Connecticut, the government, whether of the Colony or the State, has never met with a single serious attempt at resistance to the execution of its laws. * * * Our laws provide effectually for the comfortable maintenance of all the poor; who are inhabitants; and, so long as they are with us, of poor strangers, in what country soever they are born; and, when they are sick, supply them with physicians, nurses, and medicines. The children of the poor are furnished with education and apprenticeships, at the public expense.—[Vol. IV, p. 336-7.]

BIOGRAPHICAL SKETCHES.

ABIEL CANFIELD,

A soldier of the Revolution, was born April 6th, 1753. He enlisted in the company of Capt. Pierson as piper, May 8th, 1777, and marched to New Haven the same day, where he remained with the forces for the protection of the city and harbor during the term of his service. He married Mary Barlow of Stratford Dec. 23d, 1779, and lived in West street, the second house on the left from Church street, still standing. He had a shop in the rear, where he manufactured brass and pewter buttons, buckles, sleigh bells, metal tags, &c. The pewter buttons were cast in moulds. He employed an English engineer to cut the dies used in making the figures upon the buttons, for military and other uses. He afterward purchased of Bradford Steele the house east of the Episcopal church and built a shop near by. He died Dec. 6th, 1812, aged 59 years and 7 months.

REV. ALONZO B. PULLING,

Pastor of the Methodist Episcopal church a portion of 1876 and 1877, laboring zealously and efficiently for the good of those under his pastoral care. "A good minister of the Lord Jesus Christ, put in trust with the Gospel." He became superannuated at the end of his pastorate and continued to reside at East Village, with the exception of his pastorate in Seymour, until his death. He united with his conference in the spring of 1846, and filled important charges with marked fidelity and acceptability, remaining almost without exception the full term allowed by the church. He served in the New Milford charge twice, the first term of two years and the second three years. He leaves a good record, and has been called from labor to his reward. "Well done good and faithful servant."

MRS. ANN S. STEPHENS,

The gifted writer, was the daughter of John Winterbottom, junior partner of T. Vose & Co., successors to General Humphreys in the manufacture of broadcloth. She went to school in Sheffield, Canaan and other places, and wrote her first composition - an epigram upon a boy in her father's employ— at the age of seven. The first composition she published was an address to a

LUGRAND SHARP.

friend, a student in Yale College, printed in the New Haven Post. In 1832 she married Mr. Edward Stephens of Plymouth, Mass., and in 1834 published the "Polish Boy." Two years later she started a literary magazine in Portland, Maine, and in it wrote her first story and published "The Tradesman's Daughter." In 1838 she became editress of the Ladies' Companion, in New York, and published "Mary Derwent," "The Deluded," and other serials. Later she was with George R. Graham and Edgar A. Poe on Graham Magazine in Philadelphia, at the same time acting as co-editress with Charles J. Peterson, of Peterson's Magazine. Mrs. Stephens and Mr. Peterson have been associated for over thirty years. About twenty years ago Mrs. Stephens published the original of "Fashion and Famine" in Peterson's Magazine, which was afterwards printed in book form, being the first book she ever published. Her published works now include about thirty novels, a "History of the War" in two volumes, and two humorous works. The opening scenes of "Bertha's Engagement" are laid here, and also the story of "Malvina Gray." She is now a regular contributor to Peterson's Magazine and other publications. Her story of "Fashion and Famine" had a circulation of over 80,000 copies.

SQUIRE DAVID FRENCH,

The oldest son of Israel French, was a patriot of the Revolution, going to Boston after the battle of Bunker Hill to assist in resisting the encroachments of despotism. He was trial justice of the north part of the town of Woodbridge for many years, and tried more cases than any other justice in Woodbridge. The late Judge David Dagget of New Haven said that he had pleaded a great many cases before 'Squire David. He represented the town of Woodbridge in the General Assembly twenty successive semi-annual terms. He first built his log-house in Nyumphs, at a place which he afterwards gave to his son Luther. He was for many years a deacon of the First Congregational Church of Bethathy under the Rev. Samuel Hawley, but when Rev. George Whitfield visted this country he became a convert to his views of experimental religion, and afterwards was a regular member of the new sect of Methodists, which soon spread over the country like a great tidal wave. He was never one of the enthusiastic kind, but earnest and strongly sincere. All his public life he was much accustomed to public speaking, and used often in the General Assembly to encounter the celebrated Pierpont Edwards. He had a strong voice and expressed his opinions with energy and confidence. These opinions, whether religious or political, were always such as to command respect. He died Aug. 4th, 1821, aged 80 years.

LUGRAND SHARP,

Son of Thomas and Mary Sharp, was born in Ridgefield, Ct., June 1st, 1797. He was a great-grandson of Thomas Sharp of Newtown, who emigrated from England to Stratford in 1700, and was one of the original thirty-six proprietors and a surveyor of the the town of Newtown. Thomas Sharp, 3rd, purchased lands in Oxford, near Zoar Bridge in 1804 and settled there, but died in 1805, Lugrand being then but eight years of age. In 1821 he purchased the place in Southford on which the Abbott mansion now stands. In 1823 he married Olive M., daughter of Ebenezer Booth, cabinet maker, who built the house, dam and factory since owned by Rev. William Cutts, knife manufacturer. He was an earnest and efficient laborer in the Methodist society formed at Southford, of which Rev. Samuel Hickox of Seymour was the first pastor. It was to a great extent due to his efforts that a union meeting-house was soon built at Southford, and a class formed at Quaker Farms, of which he was the first leader. His house was always open to the hard-working itinerant preachers of those days, and he continued to be one of the most active members of the Southford church until 1843, when he sold out and came to Humphreysville, now Seymour. In 1849 he built the house on Hill street, which he afterwards occupied until his death. He was for several years superintendent of the Sunday school, and afterwards an active member of it until within two or three years of his death. He contributed liberally to such religious and benevolent causes as received his approval, giving over $1,500 to the missionary cause during the last nine years of his life. He died May 1st, 1876, aged 78 years. His last years were literally and fully devoted to the service of the Lord, and when his last sickness came he felt that his work was done and he waited in patience for the Master's call.

SAMUEL WIRE

Was born at Greenfield Hills, Fairfield, Feb. 8th, 1789. He came to Humphreysville when thirteen years of age to learn the clothing business under General Humphreys. At the age of twenty-three he married the sister of the late General Clark Wooster, who died after several years of happy married life, without children. Mr. Wire soon afterwards commenced the manufacture of satinet warps in the south part of Oxford, and married his second wife, who was the daughter of David Candee. He represented the town at several sessions of the General Assembly and held other important offices of trust, being at one time the most influential politician in town. In 1847 he removed to New Haven, where he was a constable for several years and then city sheriff. He was one of the oldest Freemasons in the State, and a member of Franklin Chapter and Harmony Council. He was a man of genial disposition, faithful and upright. He died May 3rd, 1874, aged 86 years.

IN MEMORIAM.

In the Rimmon burying-ground, on a bluff on the west side of the Naugatuck, are seven gravestones with the following inscriptions:

Susanna, wife of Lieut. Thomas Clark, died Apr. 1, 1768, aged 29 years.
Phœbe, wife of David Johnson, Aug. 6, 1777, in the 47th year of her age.
In memory of Joseph Riggs, son of Mr. Joseph and Mistress Anna Riggs, who departed this life March 22, 1794, in the 8th year of his age.
Joseph Riggs died Mar. 19, 1791, in the 38th year of his age, who was a pattern of industry, a friend to virtue, and a pillar of society.
In memory of David Johnson Riggs, son of Mr. Joseph and Mistress Anna Riggs, who departed this life March 24th, 1794, in the 15th year of his age.
In memory of Mrs. Sarah, relict of Mr. Benajah Johnson, who departed this life May 7, 1773, aged 72 years.
Thomas Clark, died Oct. 11, 1797, aged 33 years.

DEATHS, ARRANGED ALPHABETICALLY.

Abram Bassett, Nov. 17th, 1853, aged 81 years.
Samuel Bassett, Sept. 28th, 1851, aged 67 years.
Betsey, wife of David Beach, Oct. 9th, 1822, aged 21 years.
Mrs. Beebe, Nov. 15th, 1822, aged 70 years.
Mrs. Charles Benham, June 1st, 1822, aged 27 years.
Dorcas Bradley, Dec. 3rd, 1814, aged 92 years.

SEYMOUR AND VICINITY.

Betsey Broadwell, March 10th, 1821, aged 33 years.
Lewis Broadwell, Sept. 6th, 1844, aged 53 years.
Huldah, wife of Stephen Booth, Feb. 2nd, 1848, aged 70 years.
Annie Case, Nov. 10th, 1821, aged 68 years. Residence, Skokorat.
Joel Chatfield, June 14th, 1836, aged 79 years.
    Ruth, wife of Joel Chatfield, Nov. 2nd, 1831, aged 62 years 6 months.
Sheldon Church, Nov. 8th, 1873, aged 76 years.
    Laura, wife of Sheldon Church, Feb. 10th, 1871, aged 73 years.
William Clark, Oct. 24th, 1834, aged 70 years.
Miles Culver, July 28th, 1857.
Phebe Dayton, widow of Capt. Eben[r] Dayton, March 18th, 1827, aged 77 yrs.
John H. DeForest, Feb. 12th, 1839.
Capt. Amadeus Dibble, Sept. 25th, 1827, aged 65 yrs. Residence, Skokorat.
    Mary, wife of Capt. Amadeus Dibble, March 7th, 1826, aged 29 years.
Raymond Dibble, Nov. 17th, 1826, aged 29 years.
Joseph Durand, Aug. 6th, 1792, aged 84 years.
    Anna, wife of Joseph Durand, Feb. 14th, 1778, aged 64 years.
Samuel Durand, Feb. 18th, 1852, aged 68 years.
Nathaniel French, Nov. 13th, 1780, aged 64 years.
Samuel French, Feb. 2nd, 1883, aged 78 years.
Charles French, Esq., Nov. 9th, 1783, aged 79 years.
Enoch French, May 21st, 1824, aged 64 years.
Hannah, wife of David French, Esq., Aug. 19th, 1823, aged 19 years.
William French, Oct. 16th, 1823, aged 37 years.
    Nancy, wife of William French, July 13th, 1823, aged 19 years.
William Gerling, Nov. 25th, 1814, aged 60 years. From England.
Ezekiel Gilbert, July 6th, 1848, aged 55 years.
    Sarah Hurd, wife of Ezekiel Gilbert, Nov. 16th, 1870, aged 76 years.
Thomas Gilyard, Nov. 12th, 1853, aged 67 years.
Annie Gilyard, Jan. 11th, 1821, aged 61. Born at Hightown, Yorkshire, Eng.
Mrs. Jona. Harden, April 10th, 1822, aged 51 years. Residence, Skokorat.
Matilda Hatte, Nov., 1814, 15th daughter of Stephen Hatte.
Elizabeth, wife of Samuel Hickox, Dec. 9th, 1841, aged 26 years.
Timothy Hitchcock, Aug. 5th, 1820, aged 72 years.
Capt. Daniel Holbrook, Dec. 28th, 1828, aged 59 years. Residence, Skokorat.
    Lois, wife of Capt. Daniel Holbrook, March 10th, 1827, aged 63 years.
David Humphreys, 2nd, March 21st, 1814, aged 28 years.
David Humphreys, 3rd, Dec. 2nd, 1814, aged 3 years.
George, son of William Humphreys, Esq., July 8th, 1828.
Hon. John Humphreys, Jr., June 29th, 1826, aged 53 years.
Alexander Johnson, Sept., 1817, aged 87 years.
Benajah Johnson, April 13th, 1763, aged 59 years.
    Sarah, wife of Benajah Johnson, March 7th, 1773, aged 72 years.
Chauncey Johnson, Dec. 26th, 1814, aged 37 years.
Ebenezer Johnson, Sept. 25th, 1792, aged 31 years.
Ebenezer Johnson, Feb. 11th, 1830, aged 38 years.
    Eleanor Allen, wife of Ebenezer Johnson, July 3rd, 1870, aged 76 years.
Elijah Johnson, 1847, aged 75 years.
Hepsibah Johnson, April 13th, 1823, aged 43 years.
Hezekiah Johnson, Nov. 15th, 1826, aged 70 years.
Isaac Johnson, April 10th, 1813, aged 78 years. Residence, Skokorat.
    Lois, wife of Isaac Johnson, Oct. 16th, 1814, aged 76 years.
Rev. Jesse Johnson, Oct. 21st, 1829, aged 56 years.

SEYMOUR AND VICINITY.

Jesse Johnson, Jr., Feb. 9th, 1826, aged 25 years.
Joseph Johnson, June 26th, 1818, aged 59 years.
Stiles Johnson, Oct. 4th, 1818, aged 36 years. Residence, Skokorat.
Timothy Johnson, Jan. 21st, 1836, aged 70 years. Residence, Pinesbridge.
Zeviah Johnson, May 29th, 1816, aged 77 years.
Abraham Kenney, Oct. 29th, 1822, aged 30 years.
Isaac Kinney, Aug. 18th, 1875, aged 85 years and 6 months.
  Anna Church, wife of Isaac Kinney, Jan. 24th, 1868, aged 64 years.
Wife of William Kenney, Sr., March 9th, 1827, aged 70 years.
William Kinney, Jan. 7th, 1847, aged 87 years.
Elijah Kirtland, May 25th, 1831, aged 31 years.
John Lane, July 6th, 1834, aged 26 years.
Jonathan Miles, Feb. 25th, 1830, aged 85 years.
  Mrs. Jonathan Miles, Oct. 5th, 1822, aged 70 years.
Theophilus Miles, Nov. 11th, 1822, aged 83 years.
Theophilus Miles, Jr., March 15th, 1840, aged 70 years.
Ebenezer Northrop, Jan. 11th, 1835, aged 49 years.
Miss Lucy Norton, Dec. 31st, 1809, aged 30 years.
John Pitt, Nov. 11th, 1848, killed by the bursting of a cannon.
Ebenezer Peck, Sept. 20th, 1813, aged 70 years.
Hiram Randall, Dec. 14th, 1833.
Betsey, wife of Moses Riggs, Sept. 12th, 1828, aged 40 years.
John Riggs, Nov. 14th, 1855, aged 84 years.
  Mary, wife of John Riggs, Dec. 15th. 1827, aged 53 years.
David Sanford, March 7th, 1842.
Dr. Samuel Sanford, Jan. 25th, 1803, aged 38 years.
Jason Skeels, Nov. 1st, 1855, aged 40 years.
Col. Ira Smith, Nov. 19th, 1822, aged 44 years.
Jesse Smith, 1831, aged 65 years.
  Sarah, wife of Jesse Smith, Feb. 1820, aged 55 years.
James Spencer, May 30th, 1827, aged 30 years.
Capt. Bradford Steele, April 18th, 1804, aged 69 years.
  Mary, wife of Capt. Bradford Steele, Oct. 16th, 1788, aged 57 years.
Deacon Bradford Steele, Dec. 23rd, 1841, aged 80 years.
Norman Steele, July 9th, 1822, aged 40 years.
Abiram Stoddard, Nov. 23rd, 1855, aged 79 years.
  Eunice, wife of Abiram Stoddard, Aug. 23rd, 1855, aged 69 years.
John Storrs, March 18th, 1841, aged 42 years.
Mark Tomlinson, Oct. 2nd, 1822, aged 36 years.
Sheldon Tucker, Jan. 5th, 1843, aged 57 years.
Zephaniah Tucker, Sept. 18th, 1848, aged 89 years.
Smith Washburn, May 21st, 1823, aged 28 years.
John Todd Wheeler, (born May 4th, 1777), died Sept. 3rd, 1868, Æ. 91 yrs. 4 m.
  Sarah Clark Wheeler, Aug. 14th, 1823, aged 47 years.
  Almira Chatfield Wheeler, Dec. 12th, 1873, aged 82 years and 6 months.
Sally Wheeler, Aug. 14th, 1823, aged 47 years.
Simon Wheeler, Sept. 22nd, 1794, aged 24 years.
Daniel White, May 6th, 1854, aged 76 years.
Isaac White, Feb. 6th, 1862, aged 72 years.
John White, Nov. 17th, 1830, aged 73 years.
Abigail, wife of Marchant Wooster, Dec. 18th, 1832, aged 78 years.
Grace, wife of Clark Wooster, Jan. 1st, 1826, aged 27 years.
Henry Wooster, May 30th, 1815, aged 79 years.

SEYMOUR AND VICINITY.   131

Elizabeth, wife of Henry Wooster, Sept. 7th, 1786, aged 44 years.
John Wooster, Aug. 2nd 1804, aged 84 years.
Eunice, wife of John Wooster, Nov. 17th, 1799, aged 74 years.
John Wooster, Oct. 27th, 1823, Æ. 60. Arrived from England Sept. 5th, 1819.

MORNING STAR LODGE, No. 47, F. & A. M.

The time-honored order of Free Masonry is represented in this town by a lodge which has reached the venerable age of seventy-four years. Morning Star Lodge was constituted under a charter from the M. W. Stephen Titus Hosmer, Esq., Grand Master of the Ancient and Honorable Society of Free and Accepted Masons for the State of Connecticut, bearing date, or rather granted the 18th day of October, A.D. 1804. The petitioners to whom the charter was granted were Adam Lum, Veren Dike, Silas Sperry, Geo. W. Thomas, Benjamin Candee, Lewis Wakelee, E. C. Candee, Joel Finch, Arnold Loveland, William Hurd, Wm. Bronson, Daniel Candee, Abel Wheeler, Samuel Riggs, William Morris, Levi Candee, Nathan Davis, Charles Monson, Jessie Scott and Moses Candee, "Brethren of the Honorable Society of Masons residing in the town of Oxford."

Abel Wheeler is named in the charter as first Master, Levi Candee as Senior Warden and William Morris as Junior Warden.

In 1832, so much had the principles of the order been misrepresented that the following declaration was prepared by the Grand Lodge, signed by members of the order generally throughout the State, and published, not only in the Masonic proceedings, but in the newspapers of the day, and helped to a great extent to allay the prejudices against the order. Appended is the declaration and the names of signers who lived in this vicinity.

PREAMBLE.

WHEREAS, charges have been made against the Institution of Freemasonry, accusing the whole Fraternity with having adopted and cherished principles dangerous to the community and repugnant to morality and religion; and from the silence of the members of our Institution concerning these accusations, many persons have supposed or may suppose that we admit the truth of these charges, or that we cannot conscientiously deny them:

We, the officers and members of the *Grand Lodge of the State of Connecticut*, and of the subordinate Lodges under its jurisdiction, have come to the conclusion that justice to ourselves and a decent regard for the opinions of our fellow-citizens, demand from us a public avowal of the principles of the Order, and of the nature and tendency of the Institution. A declaration on this subject, dated December 31st, 1831, having been made and published by our brethren of the Masonic Fraternity in the State of Massachusetts, to which we fully assent, as it is strictly true in all respects, we have adopted the same, and now beg leave to present it to the public.

THE DECLARATION.

WHEREAS, it has been frequently asserted and published to the world, that in the several degrees of FREEMASONRY, as they are conferred in the United States, the candidate, on his initiation and subsequent advancement, binds himself by oath, to sustain his Masonic brethren in acts which are at variance with the fundamental principles of morality, and incompatible with his duty as a good and faithful citizen. In justice, therefore, to themselves, and with a view to establish TRUTH and expose IMPOSITION, the undersigned, members of the Masonic Fraternity, and many of us the recipients of every degree of Freemasonry known and acknowledged in this country, do MOST SOLEMNLY DENY the existence of any such obligation in the MASONIC INSTITUTION, as far as our

SEYMOUR AND VICINITY.

knowledge respectively extends. And we do also solemnly aver, that no person is admitted to the Institution, without first being made acquainted with the nature of the obligations which he will be required to incur and assume.

Freemasonry secures its members in the freedom of thought and of speech, and permits each and every one to act according to the dictates of his own conscience in matters of religion, and of his personal preferences in matters of politics. It neither knows, nor does it assume to inflict upon its erring members, however wide may be their aberations from duty, any penalties or punishments other than *Admonition, Suspension* and *Expulsion*.

The obligations of the Institution require of its members a strict obedience to the laws of God and man. So far from being bound by any engagements inconsistent with the happiness and prosperity of the nation, every citizen, who becomes a Mason, is doubly bound to be true to his God, his country, and his fellow-men. In the language of the "Ancient Constitutions" of the Order, which are printed and open for public inspection, and which are used as text-books in all our Lodges, he is "required to keep and obey the moral law, to be a quiet and peaceable citizen, true to his government and just to his country."

Masonry disdains the making of proselytes. She opens the portals of her asylum to those only who *seek* admission, with the recommendation of a character unspotted by immorality and vice. She simply requires of the candidate his assent to one great fundamental religious truth,—THE EXISTENCE AND PROVIDENCE OF GOD, and a practical acknowledgement of those infallible doctrines for the government of life, which are written by the finger of God on the heart of man.

Entertaining such sentiments, as Masons, as Citizens, as Christians, and as moral men, and deeply impressed with the conviction that the Masonic Institution has been, and may continue to be, productive of great good to their fellow-men; and having "received the laws of the Society, and its accumulated funds, in sacred trust for charitable purposes," the undersigned can neither renounce nor abandon it.

We most cordially unite with our brethren of Massachusetts, in the declaration and hope, that, "should the people of this country become so infatuated as to deprive Masons of their civil rights, in violation of the written constitutions and the wholesome spirit of just laws and free government, a vast majority of the Fraternity will still remain firm, confiding in God and the rectitude of their intentions for consolation under the trials to which they may be exposed."

Newel Johnson,	Lyman Riggs,	Seth Green,
John L. Daniels,	Gad Hitchcock,	Sheldon Beebe,
Ebenezer Fisher,	Smith Clark,	George Gunn,
John S. Moshier,	John Smith,	Jacob Rockwell,
Josiah Nettleton,	Sidney R. Wildman,	Thomas M. Hedden,
Henry Leforge,	Charles Ransom,	David Candee,
David Sanford,	Chauncey Haines,	David McEwen,
Hiram Upson,	Daniel Hyatt,	Noah Stone,
Daniel Hitchcock,	Samuel Riggs,	Nathan B. Fairchild,
Leman Chatfield,	Chauncey M. Hatch,	Isaiah Candee,
Sheldon Canfield,	John M. Hart,	Willis Smith,
Henry Wooster,	David M. Clark,	Harry Osborn,
Oliver H. Stoddard,	Samuel Wire,	Ethel Blackman,
J. H. De Forest,	Minot Barnes,	John Storrs,
Chester Jones,	Edward Booty,	Roswell Cable,
Isaac White,	Levi Candee,	Nathan J. Wilcoxon,
Henry C. Atwood,	Thomas A. Dutton,	William Morris,
Seth Crosby,	Samuel Meigs,	Jesse Joy,
Thomas Buxton,	James W. Hurd,	Alfred Harger,
Henry Buxton,	Daniel Smith,	Philo Wooster,
Garry Riggs,	Joseph Clark,	Ashbel Baldwin,
Henry A. McGary,	Charles Morgan,	George B. Platt.

The Lodge met in Masonic Hall, Oxford, until 1844, when owing to decreased numbers from removals and other causes, the sessions were suspended. It was re-organized May 14th, 1851, with George B. Glendining as

SEYMOUR AND VICINITY.

Master, David J. McEwen Senior Warden, and Alfred French Junior Warden, and removed to Seymour. E. G. Storer was then Grand Secretary. Since this time the lodge has prospered and its total membership, from the date of the charter until now, has been about three hundred and seventy-five.

MASTERS OF THE LODGE.

1804, Abel Wheeler.
1805, Abel Wheeler.
1806, Abel Wheeler.
1807, Levi Candee.
1808, Abel Wheeler.
1809, William Morris.
1810, David J. McEwen.
1811, William Morris,
1812, Chauncey M. Hatch.
1813, Levi Candee.
1814, David J. McEwen.
1815, Levi Candee.
1816, David J. McEwen.
1817, Chauncey M. Hatch.
1818, David J. McEwen.
1819, Merrit Bradley.
1820, Merrit Bradley.
1821, Merrit Bradley.
1822, Samuel Wire.
1823, Chauncey M. Hatch.
1824, David M. Clark.
1825, Cyrus Humphreys.
1826, Jesse Joy.
1827, Jesse Joy.
1828, John M. Hart.
1829, John M. Hart.
1830, Henry C. Atwood.
1831, Henry C. Atwood.
1832, Henry C. Atwood.
1833, John M. Hart.
1834, John M. Hart.
1835, John M. Hart.
1836, David M. Clark.
1837, David M. Clark.
1838, William Hinman.
1839, John M. Hart.
1840, David M. Clark.
1841, Garry Riggs.
1842, John M. Hart.
1843, Charles Ransom.
1851, George B. Glendining.
1852, David J. McEwen.
1853, Harris B. Munson.
1854, Joseph Chipman.
1855, Joseph Chipman.
1856, Stephen D. Russell.
1857, Ashbel Storrs.
1858, Stephen D. Russell.
1859, Elihu D. Foote.
1860, Israel French.
1861, Philo Buckingham.
1862, George W. Divine.
1863, Ashbel Storrs.
1864, Samuel P. Davis.
1865, Samuel P. Davis.
1866, Samuel P. Davis.
1867, Samuel P. Davis.
1868, Samuel P. Davis.
1869, Stephen R. Rider.
1870, Stephen R. Rider.
1871, Stephen R. Rider.
1872, Henry A. Rider.
1873, William S. Cooper.
1874, William S. Cooper.
1875, William K. Holmes.
1876, William K. Holmes.
1877, William K. Holmes.
1878, William Halligan.

MECHANICS' LODGE, No. 73, I. O. O. F.

INSTITUED MAY 27TH, 1851.

CHARTER MEMBERS.

Horace A. Radford, Julius Bassett, John Scott, W. W. White,
Martin Kelly, John Hilton, Charles Newton, John Davis,
Daniel J. Putman, H. P. Davis, John L. Hartson, J. A. Stevens,
W. J. Merrick.

Geo. E. Lester and Wm. A. Hughes were the first candidates for initiation.

NOBLE GRANDS.

Julius Bassett, R. W. Scott, Peter Ward, Harvey Rugg,
Daniel J. Putman, A. G. White, F. H. Beecher, E. C. Brown,
Martin Kelly, David Tucker, W. D. Bissell, J. W. Smith,
W. J. Merrick, H. T. Booth, John W. Woodruff, Samuel Butler,
John A. Hartson, Mitchell Vincent, W. S. Cooper, Robert Healy,
Harpin Davis, Charles Newton, John Whiting, S. A. Beach,
W. W. White, George Upson, Sylvester Smith, James E. Buckley,
Wm. A. Hughes, John Hilton, W. D. Dibble, Charles Edwards,
George E. Lester, H. A. Radford, Ed. D. Phelps, W. H. Williams,
Henry Bradley, A. J. Beers. James K. Adams, Charles P. White.
John Davis, 2nd, W. E. Hendryx,

SECRETARIES.

W. J. Merrick, H. T. Booth, M. K. Tucker, E. C. Brown,
H. Davis, George E. Lester, James K. Adams, J. W. Smith,
Wm. A. Hughes, Mitchell Vincent, W. S. Cooper, M. H. Pope,
Geo. Leavenworth, A. G. White, Peter Ward, H. S. Halligan,
James Davis, Frank H. Beecher, J. E. Buckley, F. A. Rugg.

HUMPHREY LODGE, No. 26, K. OF P.

INSTITUTED FEB. 8TH, 1871.

CHARTER MEMBERS.

S. H. Canfield, C. W. James, F. H. Beecher,
W. G. Mitchell, W. N. Storrs, V. H. McEwen,
George Rogers, S. C. Tucker, George Smith,
F. M. Lum, Charles French, D. C. Castle,
M. R. Castle.

WORTHY CHANCELLORS.

1871, First term, Samuel P. Davis, Second term, George A. Rogers,
1872, " " W. G. Mitchell, " " William S. Cooper,
1873, " " William N. Storrs, " " William H. Williams,
1874, " " William H. Williams, " " Charles Short,
1875, " " William H. Williams, " " Virgil H. McEwen,
1876, " " Frank H. Beecher, " " Frank H. Beecher,
1877, " " William H. Williams, " " William H. Williams,
1878, " " William H. Williams, " " Joseph H. Smith.

UPSON POST, No. 40, G. A. R.

ORGANIZED IN 1873.

Wm. S. Cooper, post commander; Joseph Ineson, adj.

RE-ORGANIZED FEB. 16TH, 1876.

1876, Horatio S. Chamberlain, post commander; Wooster B. McEwen, adjutant.

1877, James E. Buckley, post commander; Edward S. Downs, adjutant.

1878, Henry R. Chamberlain, post commander; James E. Buckley, adjutant.

FRIENDLY SONS OF ST. PATRICK.

This society is composed of members of Irish birth and their descendants, without reference or regard to religion or politics.

The society was organized at Strapp's Hall, Nov. 2nd, 1872, by the following-named persons: William Hayes, Dennis O'Callaghan, Matthias Bunyan, Francis McMorrow, Charles McCarthy, Michael Regan, Patrick Mahoney, Daniel Mahoney, William Mahoney, Jeremiah Driscol, John Coleman, John Bradley, Timothy O'Brien, Peter Sullivan, Edward Strapp, William Colbert.

At the first meeting the following officers were elected: President, William Hayes; vice-president, Peter Sullivan; secretary, Matthias Bunyan; treasurer, Dennis O'Callaghan; marshal, Francis McMorrow; standing committee, Edward Strapp, William Colbert, William Mahoney, Charles McCarthy.

At the last last annual meeting held May 4th, 1878, the following officers were elected: President, Patrick Sheehan; vice-president, Jeremiah Driscoll; treasurer, Dennis O'Callaghan; secretary, William O'Donnell; marshal, Patrick Mahoney; standing committee, Daniel McCarthy, Charles McCarthy Patrick Mahoney, Patrick Crowley.

SEYMOUR BIBLE SOCIETY.

Joshua Kendall, president; Rev. S. C. Leonard and Rev. J. Vinton, vice-presidents; T. B. Minor, secretary; H. A. Radford, treasurer; L. A. Camp, depository.

ELECTORS OF SEYMOUR, Nov. 5th, 1878.

Emery E. Adams,
James K. Adams,
Daniel Agnew,
Rufus Alcott,
Jeremiah Andrews,
Denizen D. Andrews,
Richard Aspden,
Morris Atwood,
Heman R. Atwater,
Frank P. Aylesworth,
Gustave A. Becker,
Alonzo Baldwin,
Edwin Baldwin,
Edward M. Baldwin,
William J. Barr,
George H. Bartlett,
Charles H. Bassett,
Edward F. Bassett,
Elliot R. Bassett,
Frank G. Bassett,
Isaac Bassett,
John W. Bassett,
Noyes E. Bassett,
Samuel Bassett,
Wilbur Bassett,
William R. Bates,
Charles Bay,
Samuel A. Beach,
Sharon D. Beach,
Sharon Y. Beach,
Burr P. Beecher,
Frank H. Beecher,
Frederick Beecher,
Henry B. Beecher,
Philo Beecher,
Virgil M. Beecher,
Abel J. Beers,
Charles M. Beers,
Herschel G. Beers,
William Bell,
David Betts,
William Blake,
Winfield Blake,
George Blakesley,
Frederick Boeker,
Albert Booth,
John Bowen,
Lyman Botsford,
Lucius Botsford,
Smith Botsford,
Harvey L. Botsford,
Edwin Botsford,
Charles S. Botsford,
Henry Botsford,
Charles Bradley,
Edward B. Bradley,
Henry Bradley,
John H. Bradley,
Leonard Bradley,
Abraham H. Bristol,
Nicholas Brockway,
Nicholas Brockway, Jr.,
Edward C. Brown,
Valentin Buchele,
Edwin Buckingham,
Henry Buckingham,
Isaac Buckingham,
Virgil Buckingham,
Willis Buckingham,
James E. Buckley,
Matthias Bunyan,
George W. Burroughs,
Nathan A. Brushell,
Samuel Butler,
Dennis Cahill,
Dennis Callahan,
Lewis A. Camp,
Samuel P. Camp,
DeForest Canfield,
Frank E. Canfield,
Samuel Canfield,
Samuel H. Canfield,
Carl Carlson,
Harvey Carpenter,
Heber P. Carpenter,
Jay Carpenter,
Smith T. Carpenter,
Nicholas Cass,
DeWitt C. Castle,
John H. Castle,
Martin R. Castle,
Thomas W. Chadwick,
Henry R. Chamberlain,
Horatio S. Chamberlain,
Hiram Chatfield,
Howard Chatfield,
Joel Chatfield,
Joel R. Chatfield,
Heman Childs,
Charles Church,
Noyes Church,
John Clancy,
Albert E. Clark,
Daniel W. Clark,
Andrew J. Clearwater,
William H. Cleary,
Frederick M. Clemons,
Lyman A. Clinton,
Thomas P. Cochran,
John A. Cochran,
William Colbert,
James Condon,
James Condon, 2nd,
Patrick Condon,
William Coney,
Michael Conroy,
Owen Conroy,
David R. Cook,
Timothy Cooper,
William S. Cooper,
Frank Couverette,
Arvin N. Crittenden,
Daniel Crowley,
Florence Crowley,
Patrick Crowley,
Timothy Crowley,
William A. Crowther,
Dennis Crummy,
Stephen H. Culver,
S. Hart Culver,
Michael Cunningham,
Owen Cunningham,
John T. Curry,
John Daily,
John Davenport,
Burr S. Davis,
George S. Davis,
Henry P. Davis,
Isaac H. Davis,
John Davis,
John Davis, 2nd,

SEYMOUR AND VICINITY. 137

Leonard A. Davis,
Lewellyn Davis,
Marcus Davis,
Samuel P. Davis,
Zerah B. Davis,
Edmund Day,
Henry P. Day,
Austin G. Day,
Theodore L. Decker,
John W. DeForest,
Samuel R. Dean,
Alva G. DeWolf,
William W. Dibble,
George A. Divine,
George W. Divine,
George P. Doolittle,
Oliver Doolittle,
James Donahue,
Walter W. Dorman,
Henry Downs,
Isaac Downs,
William A. Downs,
Jeremiah Driscol,
Albert B. Dunham,
Henry A. Dunham,
Daniel T. Dunham,
Joseph E. Dupee,
Jeremiah Durand,
Charles Edwards,
George S. Edwards,
Horatio N. Eggleston,
Adolph F. Eibel,
Frederick Emery,
Richard J. W. Emery,
David Evans, Jr.,
Jacob Faber,
Ebenezer Fairchild,
Ira G. Farrell,
Patrick Fitzgibbons,
Michael Fogarty,
Frank J. Ford,
John B. Ford,
Lyman H. Ford,
Philo James Ford,
Samuel C. Ford,
John T. Forsey,
George Fowler,
Thaddeus Fowler,
Raymond French,
Carlos French,
Adonijah French,
Charles H. French,
Hiram French,
John W. French,
Warren French,
Dwight Garrett,
George B. Garrett,
Lewis Garrett,
Frank C. Gerard,
David Geary,
Eli Gillett,
Lucius Gillett,
Thomas F. Gilyard,
William F. Gilyard,
Stephen B. Gregory,
Charles H. Guild,
Joseph Hagan,
Albion A. Hall,
William P. Hall,
Harvey S. Halligan,
William Halligan,
Alfred E. Hanchett,
Charles Hanchett,
Charles F. Hard,
Cornelius Hard,
Frederick Harris,
Charles Hawkins,
Joseph Hawkins,
Samuel Hawkins,
William Hayes,
Robert Healey,
Wilson E. Hendryx,
Samuel Hickox,
David R. Hill,
George H. Hill,
Charles N. Hinman,
Joseph Hitchcock,
Edward L. Hoadley,
Andrew Holbrook,
Charles F. Holbrook,
Horace Holbrook,
Nathan Holbrook,
Philo Holbrook,
Thomas C. Holbrook,
William Holbrook,
Willis R. Holbrook,
John Holloway,
William K. Holmes,
George H. Homan,
George W. Homan,
Charles D. Houghtaling,
Wm. N. Houghtaling,
Burton C. Hotchkiss,
Harvey Hotchkiss,
Burr A. Howard,
James Howard,
Sidney A. Hubbell,
William Howes,
DeWitt C. Hull,
John C. Hull,
Charles R. Hurlburt,
Thomas E. Hurlburt,
Charles L. Hyde,
Henry J. Iles,
Jerred Iles,
Joseph Ineson,
Cornelius W. James,
Thomas L. James,
George A. James,
David Johns,
Thomas Johns,
David Johnson,
John R. Johnson,
Sheldon C. Johnson,
Thomas James,
William B. Johnson,
William C. Johnson,
John Kelleher,
Charles D. Kelsey,
F. Xavier Kempf,
Joshua Kendall,
Roswell N. Kinney,
Walter S. Kenney,
Henry Kershaw,
John King,
Frederick Kokenwrath,
Theodore S. Ladd,
Martin Laughlin,
George Leavenworth,
Geo. B. Leavenworth,
William Leahy,
George E. Lester,
Stephen C. Leonard,
Evans Llewellyn,
Evans A. Llewellyn,
Edmond Libby,
Washington I. Lines,
Albert A. Lockwood,
Charles H. Lockwood,
Henry B. Lockwood,
Isaac Losee,
Isaac Losee, Jr.,
William Losee,
Frederick G. Losee,
Albert W. Lounsbury,
John Lounsbury,
Ernest Luedus,
James Lyon,
John Lyon,

Patrick Mahoney,
Eli Mallory,
Charles Manweiller,
Henry Manweiller,
John R. Matthews,
Robert A. Matthews,
Robert McKay,
George C. Munger,
John McLane,
Charles McCarty,
Daniel McCarty,
John McCarty,
Hugh McCormick,
Virgil H. McEwen,
Michael McNurney,
John T. Miles,
Sheldon Miles,
John H. Miller,
Thomas B. Minor,
Howard F. Moshier,
William Molan,
James Morris,
John E. Morris,
William Morris,
Harris B. Munson,
Harris B. Munson, Jr.
Dennis H. Munson,
Michael Nagle,
Julius H. Newton,
Michael Ney,
William B. Nichols,
Henry D. Northrop,
John O'Brien,
William O'Donnel,
Frederick O'Meara,
Josiah A. O'Meara,
Charles J. Osborn,
Noah A. Osborn,
John Owens,
John F. Parker,
Briggs M. Parmelee,
Ira A. Parmelee,
Ira B. Parmelee,
Wallace A. Parmelee,
John J. Peck,
Frederick C. Peck,
Edward G. Peck,
Jesse D. Perkins,
Henry Perthes,
Charles H. Pickett,
Christian Pickhart,
Richard Pierson,
Matthew H. Pope,

Frederick Popp,
Jabez E. Pritchard,
Frederick W. Pulford,
Horace A. Radford,
Edward H. Randall,
Hiram W. Randall,
Samuel H. Rankin,
Joseph Reigel,
Charles E. Reynolds,
William B. Reynolds,
Henry A. Rider,
Harpin Riggs,
John H. Riggs,
William J. Roberts,
George F. Robinson,
Harvey N. Rogers,
Isaac Rogers,
John W. Rogers,
Isaac Rood,
Henry Rose,
Samuel Roselle,
Frederick A. Rugg,
Harvey Rugg,
Frank H. Russell,
Stephen D. Russell.
Patrick Ryan,
Thomas Ryan,
Thomas Ryan, 2nd,
William Ryan,
James Samuels,
Sheldon Sanford,
Henry C. Schneider,
John Schofield,
David Scranton,
Thomas Sharpe,
William C. Sharpe,
John Shay,
Michael Shay,
Patrick Sheehan,
Terrence Sheridan,
William B. Sherman,
Charles J. Short,
George A. Simpson,
Burton W. Smith,
Charles Smith,
Edwin Smith,
George Smith,
George A. Smith,
George H. Smith,
George W. Smith,
James M. Smith,
John W. Smith,
Joseph H. Smith,

Matthew Smith,
Robert N. Smith,
Samuel R. Smith,
Theodore L. Smith,
Traver Smith,
Wilbur W. Smith,
William Smith,
William C. Smith,
Abel V. Somers,
Charles Spencer,
Charles E. Spencer,
James S. Spencer,
Willard James Spencer,
George C. Sperry,
Marcus Sperry,
Norman Sperry,
John Spiers,
Henry Spoonheimer,
Henry J. Spoonheimer,
John Spoonheimer,
Timothy Squires,
Frank E. Steele,
Jeremiah Stever,
Thomas Stoddard,
Arthur L. Storrs,
Ashbel Storrs,
Charles W. Storrs,
William N. Storrs,
Henry W. Stratton,
Ira A. Stuart,
Levi B. Stuart,
John Sullivan,
Peter Sullivan,
James Swan,
William B. Swan,
Daniel S. Swan,
Smith Terrell,
Theodore S. Terrell,
Benjamin B. Thayer,
Gotlib Theurer,
Daniel B. Tolles,
Edwin Tomlinson,
James W. Tomlinson,
William R. Tomlinson,
William E. Treat,
Charles C. Trumpbour,
David Tucker,
Medad K. Tucker,
Sheldon C. Tucker,
Cornelius Turk,
Thomas Urel,
James H. Van Buren,
Joseph Vinton,

SEYMOUR AND VICINITY.

Peter Ward,
Egbert R. Warner,
Charles F. Warren,
Wilford I. Warren,
George H. Washband,
Charles H. Weaver,
Lazarus G. Weaver,
Charles Weidlich,
William J. Welch,
Charles S. Weller,
Andrew W. Weston,
Frederick Weston,
Wilson Weston,
Henry Wheeler,
Charles P. White,
George B. White,
Nathan F. White,
Joseph Whitely,
Joseph J. Wilcoxson,
Frank G. Williams,
Leroy Williamson,
Bennett Wooster,
Charles A. Wooster,
Nathan R. Wooster,
Eugene A. Wyant,
Frank H. Wyant,
Henry L. Wyant,
Leonard Wyant,
Wilson Wyant,
Samuel L. Bassett.

Total, 489.

BUSINESS DIRECTORY.
MERCHANTS.

ATWOOD & BETTS, dealers in Clothing, Books and Stationery, No. 3 Davis' Block.

E. F. BASSETT, dealer in Furniture and House Furnishing Goods, and General Furnishing Undertaker, Maple street, near First.

S. Y. BEACH, dealer in Coal and Lumber, corner of Main and Maple streets.

BURR P. BEECHER, dealer in Groceries and Provisions, Main street.

HENRY BRADLEY, dealer in Millinery and Fancy Goods, Hull's Building.

S. W. BUCKINGHAM, dealer in Beef, Pork, Poultry, &c., No. 4 Davis' Block.

JOHN A. COCHRAN, Agt., dealer in Groceries and Provisions, corner of Hill and Pearl streets.

HENRY A. DUNHAM, dealer in Groceries and Provisions, Main street, near depot.

GEO. S. EDWARDS, dealer in Stoves, Tinware, Crockery, Hardware, Cutlery, &c., corner of Maple and Second streets.

JAMES HOWARD, dealer in Meat, &c., Main street, below Hill street.

MCEWEN & CAMP, dealers in Dry Goods, Groceries, School Books, &c., Maple street, near First.

J. N. POPP, Merchant Tailor, Third street.

M. M. RANDALL, dealer in Dry Goods and Groceries, corner of Main and Broad streets.

JAS. L. SPENCER, dealer in Beef, Pork, Lard, &c., Main st., south of depot.

C. W. STORRS, dealer in Dry Goods, Hardware, Newspapers, Magazines, &c., James' Building, next door to post-office.

DAVID TUCKER, dealer in Flour, Grain, Feed and Fertilizers, corner of Main and Broad streets.

WOOSTER, DEAN & BUCKINGHAM, dealers in Dry Goods, Hardware, Lumber, Coal, etc., Brick Store, opposite the depot.

PHYSICIANS.
*MEMBERS OF THE CONNECTICUT MEDICAL SOCIETY.

S. C. JOHNSON,* house corner of Church and West streets.

JOSHUA KENDALL,* house corner of Church and West streets.

F. W. PULFORD, Homeopathic, house on Pearl street.

THOMAS STODDARD,* house corner of Main and Pearl streets.

EGBERT R. WARNER, house corner of Maple and Second streets.

DRUGGISTS AND APOTHECARIES.

S. H. CANFIELD, James' Building, Main street.

GEORGE SMITH, No. 1 Davis Block.

SEYMOUR AND VICINITY.

HOTELS.

WOOSTER HOUSE, A. B. Dunham, Proprietor, corner of Second and Raymond streets.
SEYMOUR HOUSE, Peck & Riggs, Proprietors, Broad street.
HUMPHREY HOUSE, J. W. Meredith, Proprietor, First street.

LIVERY AND FEED STABLES.

A. B. DUNHAM, corner of Second and Raymond streets.
JOHN HOLLOWAY, Broad street, east of Congregational church.
H. A. RIDER, Main street, near foot of Hill street.
JOHN SPIERS, Derby Avenue, south of Congregational church.

MISCELLANEOUS.

F. P. AYLESWORTH, Plain and Ornamental Hair-work, Church street.
WILBUR BASSETT, Painter, Hill street, south of Pearl street.
MRS. WILBUR BASSETT, Dressmaker, Hill street, south of Pearl street.
N. A. BRUSHELL, Barber and Hair-dresser, Main street, near post-office.
SMITH T. CARPENTER, General Carting, Pearl street.
MRS. G. W. DIVINE, Dressmaker, house Maple street.
E. FAIRCHILD, Carriage Making and Repairing, Maple street.
MRS. GEORGE FOWLER, Dressmaker, residence on First avenue.
PHILIP HEILMAN, Boot and Shoemaker, No. 2 Davis' Block, room 4.
W. I. LINES, Painter, Chestnut street.
ISAAC LOSEE, Boot and Shoemaker, No. 1 French's Building.
MICHAEL MCNURNEY, Blacksmithing and Repairing, Maple street, near covered bridge.
SHELDON MILES, manufacturer of Clock Cord, Banding, Fish Lines, &c.
JOHN H. MILLER, Shoemaker and dealer in Confectionery, Broad street.
WILLIAM MORRIS, Harnessmaker, corner of Maple and First streets.
H. B. MUNSON, Attorney at Law, office James' Building.
HENRY SCHNEIDER, Barber and Hair-dresser, No. 5 Davis' Block.
A. H. SCRANTON, Newsdealer, No. 3 French's Building.
THOMAS SHARPE, Carpenter and Builder, corner of Hill street and Washington Avenue.
W. C. SHARPE, Printer and Publisher, No. 2 Davis' Block, second floor.
B. W. SMITH, Insurance Agent and Notary Public, corner of Derby Avenue and Grove streets.
JAMES SMITH, Machinery and Repairing, Factory street, foot of Raymond st. General Blacksmithing in shop attached to Machine Works.
G. C. SPERRY, Painter, house Mill street.
ASHBEL STORRS, Carpenter and Builder, house North street.
L. B. STUART, Jeweler, No. 3 French's Building.
B. B. THAYER, Truckman, residence Derby avenue.
W. H. WILLIAMS, Attorney at Law, office James' Building.

JAMES SWAN'S CHISEL WORKS.
MILL STREET, SEYMOUR.

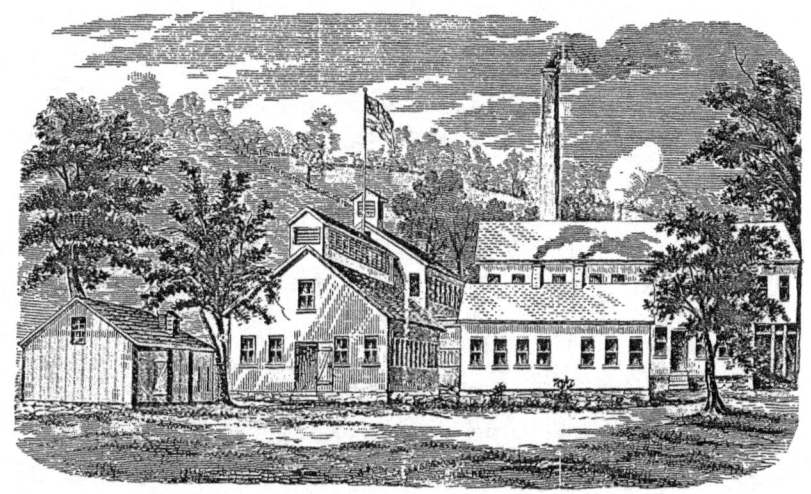

WORKS OF
JAMES SWAN,
SUCCESSOR TO
THE DOUGLASS MANUFACTURING COMPANY,
(ESTABLISHED IN 1856),
MANUFACTURER OF
AUGERS, AUGER BITS, GIMLETS, HOLLOW AUGERS, EXPANDING BITS, PATENT AUGER HANDLES, BORING MACHINES, CHISELS, GOUGES, DRAWING KNIVES, SCREW-DRIVERS, REAMERS, ETC.

H. B. BEECHER,
SUCCESSOR TO FRENCH, SWIFT & CO.,
(ESTABLISHED IN 1847),
MANUFACTURER OF
AUGERS, AUGER BITS, HOLLOW AUGERS, &c.

HUMPHREYSVILLE MANUFACTURING CO.
MANUFACTURERS OF
AUGERS, AUGER BITS, &c.

GEORGE H. ROBINSON,   NORMAN SPERRY,
DAVID R. COOK,   MARCUS SPERRY.

THE NEW HAVEN COPPER COMPANY.

THOMAS JAMES, President.
FRANKLIN FARRELL, Secretary and Treasurer.
Directors: Thomas James, Franklin Farrell, E. C. Lewis, Thomas L. James and Alton Farrell.

THE FOWLER NAIL COMPANY,

CARLOS FRENCH, President.   LEWIS H. BRISTOL, Secretary.

MANUFACTURERS OF

VULCAN HORSE-SHOE NAILS.

UNITED STATES PIN COMPANY.

HENRY L. HOTCHKISS, President.   LEWIS H. BRISTOL, Secretary.
CARLOS FRENCH, Treasurer.

H. P. & E. DAY,

MANUFACTURERS OF

RUBBER PEN-HOLDERS, PROPELLING PENCILS, SURGICAL APPLIANCES, &c.

S. Y. BEACH,

MANUFACTURER OF

PRINTING AND COLORED PAPERS.

CARLOS FRENCH,

MANUFACTURER OF

CAR SPRINGS.

W. W. SMITH,

MANUFACTURER OF

MANILLA PAPER.

RAYMOND FRENCH,

MANUFACTURER OF

PLAIN AND STEEL PLATED OX SHOES.

AUSTIN G. DAY,
MANUFACTURER OF
SUBMARINE TELEGRAPH CABLE.

GARRET & BEACH,
MANUFACTURES OF
GERMAN GIMLET BITS, CAST STEEL REAMERS AND SCREW DRIVER BITS.

Lewis L. Garrett.   Samuel A. Beach.

THE SEYMOUR RECORD,
Published every Thursday morning at
THE SEYMOUR PRINTING OFFICE,

No. 2 Davis' Block.   W. C. Sharpe, Editor and Publisher.

INCIDENTS OF THE REVOLUTION.

WHEN the war of the Revolution broke out, the Churchmen of Waterbury, of Connecticut, of New England were seen ranged upon the side of the parent country, and against the rebel colonists. They were royalists, or tories. They had reasons satisfactory to themselves for their opinions and conduct. They wished the success of the British government because on that success depended their hopes of worldly distinction and religious privilege. On that they supposed that they must rely for the permanent ascendancy of the Episcopal Church in America—its doctrines, its faith, and its worship. To England they were bound by the strongest ties. From that country their parish clergymen had from the first received a great part of their support. They owed it a debt of gratitude, which if they could not repay, they were unwilling to forget. They had always been the weaker party, had been ridiculed in their weakness, and sometimes voted out of their just rights. Their feelings had not been conciliated, and they had come to hate the whigs heartily. They now hoped that their wrongs would be redressed. The Episcopal clergy of Connecticut and of New England took the lead in opposition to the war. They kept up a correspondence with the Society [for Propagating the Gospel] at home, of which they were beneficiaries, in which they expressed their views freely of the merits of the controversy, and gave information of the state of the country. The loyalty of their own church was a subject for frequent comment and congratulation. Dr. Richard Mansfield, of Derby, wrote in December, 1775, that he had preached and taught quiet subjection to the king and parent state, and that he was well assured that the clergy in general of the colony of Connecticut had done the same. Of the one hundred and thirty families under his charge, one hundred and ten, he continued, are firm and steadfast friends to government, and detest and abhor the present unnatural rebellion, and all those measures which led to it. Further on, he remarked " that the worthy Mr. Scovill [of Waterbury], and the venerable Mr. Beach [of Newtown] have had still better success, scarcely a single person being found of their congregations but what hath persevered steadfastly in his duty and loyalty."—[History of Waterbury.

Among those who sympathized with and gave aid to the British forces were Henry Wooster, who lived about a mile below the Falls, a brother of John and Thomas Wooster who lived in what is now Oxford, and David Wooster, Jun., who lived in Gunntown, in what is now Naugatuck, near his father, David Wooster, Sen. Upon the bluff east of the Naugatuck, and about a quarter of a mile below the Falls, stood, in 1780, a tavern kept by Turel Whittemore—in fact it is still standing in the house now occupied by Martin Castle, having been raised a story and enlarged. One Saturday evening in March, 1780, there were gathered in the little barroom, Henry Wooster, Jun., his cousin David Wooster, Jun., from Gunntown; Samuel Doolittle, living not far distant but within the limits of New Haven, and others of the neighborhood. Alexander Graham, having a commission from the British General Howe, made his appearance and sought to raise a party among the tories present, for an expedition to Bethany to rob the house of Capt. Ebenezer Dayton, previously a merchant of Brookhaven, L. I., who had brought his family and goods from Long Island for safety. With him had come other patriots and left their valuables in the house taken by him, so that the tory conspirators expected to secure valuable booty by despoiling this refuge of the whigs during the absence of its defenders. A party was formed, consisting of Alexander Graham, David Wooster, Henry Wooster, Jun., Samuel Doolittle, and three others. The next Tuesday evening they proceeded to Dayton's house in Bethany, he being in Boston. About midnight they burst into the house, seized and bound Mrs. Dayton, ransacked the house, and carried off about £450 in gold and silver, and other valuables, after destroying much property which they could not carry away. Hastening towards Naugatuck, they met a young man named Chauncey Judd, and, lest he should expose them, they compelled him to go with them. The robbers hid several days in the house of David Wooster, Sen., Gunntown. From there they went to the house of John Wooster, known as "Capt. John," who kept a tavern in the southern part of Oxford. The house stood just back of where the house of David C. Riggs now stands, and was pulled down but a few years since. This Capt. Wooster was a great hunter, and had inclosed several hundred acres on the hills in the rear of his house, as a deer park, and the place is still known as "The Park." After being warmed and fed, they went to a barn a little ways south of the house belonging to Daniel Wooster, where they remained during the night and the next day, and after several narrow escapes, made their way to Derby, and, taking a boat, rowed down the river, closely pursued by horsemen on the shore. They arrived at the mouth of the river but just ahead of their pursuers, and escaped across the sound to Brookhaven. A pursuing party crossed the sound at night and captured the robbers, except one who escaped through a window into the woods. Chauncey Judd was released and the stolen goods retaken. Graham was found to be a deserter from the continental army, with a British commission in his pocket, and was sent to Morristown, tried by court martial, condemned and executed. The others were put on trial in the Superior Court at New Haven, with David Wooster, Sen., Noah Candee, Daniel Johnson, William Seeley, Francis

Noble, and Lemuel Wooding, Whittemore's barkeeper. Two of the accused, Scott and Cady, were allowed to turn state's evidence. All the others were found guilty. David Wooster, Henry Wooster, Jun., and Samuel Doolittle were each sentenced to a fine of £50, and imprisonment for four years in the Newgate state prison. Noah Candee and David Wooster, Sen., were fined each £500 and imprisoned nine months in Hartford jail. Daniel Johnson was fined £250 and imprisoned nine months. Francis Noble was fined £50 and imprisoned one year. William Seeley was fined £25 and imprisoned nine months. Lemuel Wooding was fined £25 and imprisoned six months. In addition, Capt. Dayton recovered heavy damages in civil suits against the different parties, amounting to several thousand pounds. Mr. Judd also recovered £800 from the robbers and their accessories, for damages to his son. This summary punishment was as discouraging to the tories of the vicinity as it was encouraging to the struggling patriots.

NAMES OF SOLDIERS IN ADDITION TO PREVIOUS LISTS.

WAR OF THE REVOLUTION.

DR. JESSE BALDWIN, surgeon.
ABRAM BASSETT, son of Abraham Bassett.
JOSEPH SANFORD.

WAR OF 1812.

DAVID SANFORD, son of Capt. Raymond Sanford.
CAPT. ENOS LUM, son of William Lum, of Great Hill.

WAR OF THE REBELLION.

CHARLES D. HOUGHTALLING, enlisted from Greenfield, Mass., first in receiving ship Ohio, and transferred to gunboat Azalea, as landsman. Discharged at navy yard, Philadelphia.

THEODORE S. LADD, Company H, 15th Connecticut Volunteers. Mustered in from Naugatuck, July 25th, 1862. Discharged on account of disability, August 10, 1863, at Hampton, Va. Re-enlisted September 3, 1867, and served until the close of the war.

JULIUS H. NEWTON, Company H, 20th Connecticut Volunteers. Mustered in from Bethany, August 15, 1862. Mustered out June 13, 1865, at Washington, D. C.

CHARLES H. PICKETT, Company H, 15th Connecticut Volunteers. Mustered in from Naugatuck, August 5th, 1862. Mustered out June 27th, 1865, at Newburn, N. C.

CARL CARLSON, Company A, 3rd Vermont Volunteers, enrolled August 23rd, 1864. Discharged July 11th, 1865, at Hall's Hill, Va.

NOTES FROM THE SCHOOL RECORDS.

GREAT HILL DISTRICT, No. 1.

THE following particulars are from a book in the possession of Mr. Samuel P. Davis of Great Hill, consisting of the records of the 8th District of the town of Derby, afterward the first district of the town of Seymour, from 1766 to 1810.

June 26, 1767, Henry Tomlinson elected district committee, Samuel Basit, collector.

Dec. 8, 1769, at house of H. Tomlinson, B. Tomlinson, moderator. Voted to hire a Master for the winter and that what overplus there might be should be used to pay a Mistress in the summer.

From the record of the meeting held Dec. 12, 1770, at the school-house, at 5 P. M., it appears that it was not the custom to hire the teacher for the winter until December. The meetings were usually held in the afternoon.

Jan. 13, Jonathan Miles, moderator. A motion was made to divide the school. The meeting adjourned to the first Monday in March, at 4 P. M., at which adjourned meeting an adjournment was again made to March 23rd, when it was voted "that those persons that send their children to Henry Wooster's school shall have their proportion of the school money according to their list."

At the meeting held Nov. 2, 1772, Benjamin Tomlinson, moderator, no action is recorded, except to instruct the committee to hire a teacher for the winter, at his discretion.

The next meeting recorded was held Dec. ye 14th, 1774. Micah Pool was chosen "one of the committee," and Samuel Russell, clerk.

It was voted that warnings of the next meeting be posted at the houses of Joseph Canfield, George Beard and Capt. John Lum, six days before the meeting.

Nov. 13, 1775, B. Tomlinson, moderator; Christopher Smith was chosen one of the committee.

Probably owing to the troublous times at the beginning of the Revolution, no meeting seems to have been held in 1776, but Nov. 27, 1777, B. Tomlinson was again moderator. An adjournment was taken from the schoolhouse to the house of George Bard, Dec. 11, but no business transactions recorded.

Sept. 2, 1778, voted to hire a schoolmaster three months, "and pay the master pr. the poll of the scholer after the publick money is gone."

June 12, 1780, Micah Pool, moderator; adjourned to June 19th, and voted to hire a mistress at six shillings pr. [torn off—probably *week*] "and to pay schoolmistress pr. the pool of the schollers."

Oct. 10, 1780, at the house of James Manvil; Mica Pool, moderator; Henry Tomlinson appointed collector.

Feb. 15, 1781, Joseph Tomlinson, moderator; voted to hire a master until April 1, and pay by "poll of the scholars." Daniel Tomlinson voted clerk.

Nov. 14, 1781, Philo Holbrook voted clerk. The next record is Nov. 23, 1784, when peace again prevailed, and the school, which very likely had been suspended by the necessities of the war for independence, was again awarded the attention it deserved, by those lovers of home, church, school, and free government. The meeting was held at the house of Geo. Bard; Zachariah Fairchild, moderator. It was "voted to build a schoolhouse on the highway near Mr. John Hawley's." Building committee, Ebenezer Lues, Webb Tomlinson, —— Hawkins, Jonathan Lum, Jr., and ——Pool. "Voted Mr. George Bard, Mr. Jonathan Lum, Jr., Mr. Rusil Tomlinson, Committe."

Nov. 28, 1785, Webb Tomlinson, moderator; voted a rate of six pence on the pound be collected on the list of 1784 to finish the schoolhouse, John Hawley, collector. Voted that the warnings for meetings be put up at the schoolhouse and Geo. Bard's shop. Voted Sam'l Russel be one of the committee in place of Jonathan Lum, Jr.

March 20, 1786, at the house of John Hawley; Henry Tomlinson, moderator; John Hawley voted "committyman in room of Joseph Hawkins, also Russell Tomlinson, Sam'l Russell and James Manville, Committee."

Nov. 22, 1787, Josiah Nettleton, moderator.

Dec. 26, 1788, Christopher Smith, moderator, rate laid of 3d. on the £, list of 1788, Webb Tomlinson, collector. Samuel Russell, Russell Tomlinson and James Manville, committee.

"OCTOBER THE 25, A. D., 1790.

"At a lawful meeting lawfully warned and attended, voted Mr. Samuel Russel moderator. 2nd voted Mr. Henry Tomlinson a school Committee in the room of Mr. Samuel Russel. 3d voted Mr. Abel Holbrook clerk for this eighth School district, it fourthly voted that the committee should hire a school master for this school according to their discretion for the ensuing year and pay the Master by the pool of the scholar."

Mar. 21, 1794, voted Nathaniel Holbrook, Russel Tomlinson and Jonathan Lum, committee.

Nov. 9, 1795, voted Enos G. Nettleton, clerk; R. Tomlinson, J. Lum, Jr., and James Bassett, committtee.

Nov. 6, 1796, J. Lum, Nathan Mansfield and N. Holbrook, committee; Enos G. Nettleton, clerk.

HISTORY OF SEYMOUR. 151

Nov. 27, 1797, voted E. G. Nettleton, J. Lum and N. Holbrook, committee; voted to hire a master four months " by the poll of the scholar."

Nov. 6, 1798, Amos Bassett, moderator; Abram English, clerk; voted that the eighth district be divided into two districts.

Oct. 11, 1799, J. Lum, moderator; Abram English clerk; J. Lum, N. Holbrook and Ephraim Wooster, committee; voted to hire a master five months.

Dec. 3, 1800, Eleazer Lewis moderator; David Tomlinson clerk; A. English, Moses Fenton, and Richard Holbrook, committee; Nathaniel Holbrook, collector.

Dec. 23, 1800, voted Reuben Lum and Wilson Hurd committee in addition to above; and to hire another master and to " divide the money according to the poll of the scholars belonging to the *first* district."

March 14, 1801, voted to hire a teacher twelve months, the school to be kept in the meetinghouse as long as the weather will permit, then to be continued in the school-house.

Nov. 5, 1801, voted John Lum, Jr., Moses Fenton and Isaac Bassett, committee; David Tomlinson, clerk.

From the record of the meeting held Nov. 12, 1802, it was voted that " the public money of the Great Hill School Society shall be applied to such schools as the committee think proper," and a provision was made that those who were unable to pay the schooling of their children should not be assessed therefor, thereby manifesting their belief that it was for the public good that the free education of the children of the poor should be provided for.

April 25, 1803, voted that a rate of six mills on the dollar be laid to repair the school-house.

Oct. 18, 1803, David Tomlinson, collector; J. Lum, Richard Holbrook and James Bassett, Committee. Voted to hire a teacher for five months.

" At a legal meeting of the First School District in Great Hill School Society, holden at the school-house in said District, Monday, the 18th of March, 1805. First, voted Mr. Abner Tibbils, moderator; 2nd, voted David Tomlinson, clerk; 3rd, voted Mr. Johnathan Lum, Benjamin English and Wilson Hurd a school committee for the first district; 4th, voted Mr. Benjamin English a collector of Miss Rebecca French's bill; 5th, voted Ephraim Wooster collector for the year ensuing."

Nov. 4th, 1805, J. Lum, moderator; David Tomlinson, clerk; J. Lum, A. English and Wilson Hurd, committee. Doct. Lum to see to the schoolhouse.

Nov. 19th, 1806, same clerk and moderator elected; Richard Holbrook and Abm. English committee.

Nov. 30th, 1810, John Smith, moderator; D. Tomlinson, clerk; adj. to W. A. Gillett's; Jared Mansfield and John Smith, committee; Capt. J. Nettleton, collector. " Voted that wood pr. load should be 84 cts. and boarding teacher 7 cts. per meal or 87½c. per week.

HISTORY OF SEYMOUR.

SHRUB OAK SCHOOL.

	Committee,	Teachers, Summer.	Teachers, Winter.
1847–9,	Lyman Botsford,		Frederick Durand.
1850,	Warren French,	Frances Wooster.	
1851,	Hiram Upson,		
1852–3,	Charles Swift,		
	January 4th, 1852, voted to unite with other districts in forming a Union School.		
1854,	Warren French,		
1855,	David Lounsbury,	Augusta Sanford,	Leverett Mallory.
1856,	" "	Leverett Mallory.	
1857,	Chas. R. Hurlburt,		
1858,	James E. Fisher,		
1859,	Charles Daniels,		
1860–4,	Stephen R. Rider,		
1865,	Amos G. White,	1866,	B. W. Smith,
1867,	Joseph J. Wilcoxon,	1868,	Charles W. Storrs,

BELL SCHOOL, No. 5.

	Teachers, Summer,	Teachers, Winter.
1832,	Mrs. Travis,	Isaac Sperry.
1833,	Miss Platt,	Ann Benham.
1834,	Miss Williams,	John Northrop.
	Miss Williams kept a select school, 1835-7.	
1835,	James Green,	John Lindley.
1836,	Miss Huntington,	John Northrop.
1837,	Miss Williams,	John Lindley.
1838,	Miss Benham,	Wales Buckingham.
1839,	Miss White,	Mrs. Wheeler.

CENTER DISTRICT, No. 6.

	Committee.	Teachers, Summer.	Teachers, Winter.
1846,	John Bodge.		P. B. Buckingham.
1847,	Ransom Tomlinson,	P. B. Buckingham.	P. B. Buckingham.
1848,	Crownage Lounsbury.		P. B. Buckingham.
1849,	Frederick Lord,	Jane M. Wooster.	
1850,	Elijah Losee,	Charles W. Sharpe.	
1851,	Nathan Tomlinson,		Stephen S. Mallet.
	School Building moved north of the house of S. Y. Beach.		
1852,	Albert Allen.		
1854,	S. Y. Beach,	Laura A. Sperry,	E. M. Bradley.
1855,	Thomas James,	E. M. Bradley.	
1856,	" "	School-house moved to its present location.	
1857,	Peter Worth,		Betsey Leek.
1858,	" "		
1859,	" "	M. A. Wilcox,	E. L. Tuttle.
1860,	Evan Llewellyn,	Cornelia E. Sherwood,	Cornelia E. Sherwood.
1861,	Philo B. Buckingham,	" "	Rhoda Kendall.
1862,	David Betts, Jr.,	Rhoda Kendall,	" "
1863,	Ira E. Parmelee,	" "	" "
1864,	Henry Kershaw,	" "	
1865,	Mark Lounsbury,	" "	
1866,	" "		
1867,	Christian Quering,	Miss Coltingham.	

GENEALOGIES.

"THE sacred tie of family, which reaching backward and forward, binds the generations of men together, and draws out the plaintive music of our being from the solemn alternation of cradle and grave—the black and white keys of life's harpsichord; the magical power of language, which puts spirit in communion with spirit in distant periods and climes; the great sympathies of country, which lead the Greek of the present day to talk of 'the victories *we* gained over the barbarians at Marathon'; the mystic tissue of race, woven far back in the dark chambers of the past, and which after the vicissitudes and migrations of centuries, wraps up great nations in its broad mantle; those significant expressions which carry volumes of meaning in a word—Forefather, Parent, Child, Posterity, Native Land: these all teach us, not blindly to worship, but duly to honor the past, to study the lessons of experience, to scan the high counsels of man in his great associations, as those counsels have been developed in constitutions, in laws, in maxims, in traditions, in great, undoubted principles of right and wrong, which have been sanctioned by the general consent of those who have gone before us; thus tracing in human institutions some faint reflection of that divine wisdom which fashioned the leaf, that unfolded itself six weeks ago in the forest, on the pattern of the leaf which was bathed in the dews of Paradise in the morning of creation."—HON. EDWARD EVERETT.

GENEALOGICAL research is becoming more frequent and the data are more highly valued with the lapse of years. The following collection is made up from town records, family records, old manuscripts, colonial and town histories, and the recollection of our older citizens. Where descendants of the old settlers have interested themselves to furnish additional particulars, or where the records have been more full, the genealogies are more complete. The following abbreviations are used; b. for born; m. for married; d. for died. D. R.—Derby Records; ^{bmd}—volume of births, marriages and deaths. The figures preceding names indicate the individuals descended from the same ancestor, and are for convenience of reference. The figures on the right indicate the generation, thus—John^4 indicates the fourth generation from the first of the name given.

FRENCH.

FRANCIS,[1] one of the first settlers of Derby, (see p. 41,) m. Lydia ———. Children: [3]Lydia, b. Aug. 21, 1662, d. Sept. 7, 1664; [4]Elizabeth, b. June 20, 1664; [5]Anna, b. Aug. 10, 1666; [6]Mary, b. Sept. 4, 1668, d. Oct. 26, 1677; [7]Dorah, b. Sept. 20, 1670; [8]Samuel, b. Jan. 6, 1672; [9]Susannah, b. June 6, 1675; [10]Francis, b. Feb. 11, 1677; [11](Name torn off the record), Nov. 1, 1679. Frances[1] died Feb. 14, 1699.

[10]FRANCIS,[2] m. Anna Bowers, Sept. 2, 1703. Children: [13]Nathaniel, d. Nov. 13, 1770, aged 64; [14]Samuel, d. Feb. 2, 1783, aged 78; [15]Charles, town clerk of Derby thirty-four years, d. Nov. 9, 1783, aged 79; [16]Israel.

[16]ISRAEL[3] was one of the first settlers of the north part of Derby, now Seymour, Sarah Loveland, Sept. 11, 1739. Children: [17]David, b. 1741, d. Aug. 4, 1821; [18]Israel; [19]Enoch, the miller; [20]Bowers; [21]Charles, b. Dec. 19, 1765.

[17]DAVID,[4] the oldest son of [16]Israel, married Lois Lines of Bethany. He first lived on Nyumphs Hill, but after a while built in Bethany, then the north part of Woodbridge, at the place now occupied by Justus Peck. His children were: [22]David, [23]Adonijah, [24]Luther (of Beacon Hill), [25]Asaph, [26]Harry, [27]Sarah, [28]Hannah, [29]Dorcas, [30]Hepzibah, [31]Lydia, [32]Lois.

[22]DAVID[5]. Children: [35]Stiles (of New Haven); [36]Charles; [37]Hannah, m. Sheldon Clark; [38]Emma, m. Joel White of Oxford; [39]Eliza, m. John Sanford, d. 1877; [40]Hannah, m. ——— Doolittle, lived in Hamden.

[23]ADONIJAH[5] was a justice of the peace and several times one of the representatives of Woodbridge. Children: [42]Adonijah, [43]Miles, [44]Lois; [45]Harriett, m. Jared K. Ford.

[21]CHARLES,[4] b. in town of Derby, Dec. 19, 1765; Anna Woodcock, b. in Milford, Aug. 20, 1763, m. Feb. 23, 1784; Charles,[4] d. April 14, 1814; Anna, d. Dec. 24, 1859. Children:

[50]Sally, b. Nov. 14, 1784, m. Erastus Sperry, Dec. 20, 1803.

[51]Polly, b. Oct. 26, 1786, d. Nov. 11, 1794.

[52]Wales, b. Oct. 12, 1788, m. Betsey Hitchcock, April, 1810, died in N.Y. March 5, 1814. His widow died in New Milford in 1820.

[53]Grant, b. Oct. 13, 1790, d, Sept. 29, 1794.

[54]Raymond, b. July 29, 1792, d. Sept. 27, 1794.

[55]Alfred, b. Aug. 22, 1794, m. Lydia Hotchkiss, d. June 23, 1859.

[56]Grant, b. July 28, 1796.

[57]Polly, b. Aug. 28, 1798, m. Joseph Russell, Dec. 23, 1817, d. May 27, 1865.

[58]Susan b. July 28, 1800.

[59]Harriett, b. March 20, 1803, d. May 5, 1804.

[60]Raymond, b. Jan. 7, 1805, m. Olive Curtiss, Dec, 11, 1833.

[61]Charles, b. Oct. 1, 1807, m. Julia Sperry, Aug. 20. 1831.

HISTORY OF SEYMOUR. 155

[70]NATHAN, m. Lucy Johnson, Sept, 2, 1773. Children : [71]Eunice, b. May 8, 1775 ; [72]Asa, b. March 26, 1777.

[54]RAYMOND, son of Charles and Anna French, m. Olive Curtiss, Dec. 11, 1833. Children :—
Carlos, m. Julia H. Thompson of New Milford.
Ann, m. Cornelius W. James of Seymour.
Sarah, m. Judge W. B. Stoddard of New Haven.
Harriett, m. Samuel H. Canfield of Seymour.

[19]ENOCH[4] m. Comfort ——, died Sept. 27, 1852. Children : [73]William, b. Sept. 29, 1783, d. Oct. 16, 1823 ; [74]Nancy, b. Dec. 22, 1785, m. William Bassett, Jan. 29, 1811 ; [75]Bird, of Salisbury, b. Oct. 1, 1797, m. Eliza Tharp, Aug. 2, 1822 ; [76]Pamelia, b. Sept. 16, 1799, m. Isaac Bassett, Sept. 8, 1822 ; [77]Enoch, b. Jan. 8, 1803, d. May 12, 1824 ; [78]Israel, b. Jan. 29, 1805, m. Caroline Tolls, Feb. 8, 1829.

[80]WALTER FRENCH married Laura Storrs, and came to Humphreysville from Mansfield. He first introduced the manufacture of augers in what is now Seymour. The first were made in the old shop corner of Hill and Pearl streets, Mr. F. being associated with Col. Ira Smith. Soon after, Mr. F. built the house on West street formerly occupied by John Washburn, and built a shop a little east of the house now occupied by Warren French. He afterward superintended the works of Gen. Clark Wooster, whose shop stood on the river bank opposite where the works of James Swan now stands. His shop was closed in 1844, and Walter French returned to Westville, to commence the manufacture of augers there. Wales French bought the shop by the saw-mill, and, with his brother Warren, carried on the business about two years, when Wales sold out and removed to Westville. The children of Walter French were : [82]William, [83]Warren, [84]Watson, [85]Wesley, [86]Wales, [87]Washington ; [88]Eliza, m. Levi Gilbert of New Haven ; [89]Emily, m. Henry McCoy of Branford ; [90]Emmeline, m. Lemuel Bliss of Humphreysville.

[82]WILLIAM, m. Milenna Martin. Children : [91]Isabel, m. S. C. Ford ; [92]Samuel.

[83]WARREN, b. Nov. 10, 1804, m. Lucinda Riggs, Nov. 21, 1823. Children : [93]Harpen R., [94]Herman B., [95]Laura M., [96]Walter J.

[85]WESLEY, m. 1st, Harriet, daughter of Rev. Samuel Hickox, 2d, Mary Boughton.

BOOTH.

1, RICHARD BOOTH,[1] was born in England in 1607, came to Stratford, Conn, in 1640, m. Elizabeth Hawley. Children: 3, Elizabeth, b. Sept. 12, 1641, m. John Minor; 4, Anna, b. Feb. 14, 1643; 5, Ephraim, b. Aug. 1, 1648; 6, Ebenezer, b. Nov. 19, 1651; 7, John, b. Nov. 5, 1653; 8, Joseph, b. March 8, 1656; 9, Bethia, b. Aug. 18, 1658; 10, Johannah, b. March 21, 1651.—[Stratford Records, vol. 1, p. 24.

6, EBENEZER,[2] m. Sarah Fairchild. Children: 12, Ebenezer, b. 1681, d. 1729; 13, Benjamin; 14, Edward; 15, Deborah; 16, Elizabeth; 17, Abigail. Ebenezer[2] was made a freeman in Hartford court, May 13, 1765, from Stratford.

12, EBENEZER,[3] m. Maria Clark, Sept. 8, 1709, settled in Newtown, d. in 1729. Children: 18, Ebenezer, b. 1710; 19, Deborah; 20, Ann; 21, Mary; 22, Eunice; 23, Abia; 24, Abner.

18, EBENEZER.[4] Children: 25, Ann, b. Dec. 4, 1740, d. 1741; 26, Ebenezer, b. Aug. 27, 1743; 27, Elijah, b. Oct. 30, 1745; 28, Ashbel, b. Oct. 19, 1747; 29, David, b. Oct. 4, 1749, d. 1753; 30, Nathan, b. July 19, 1751; 31, Amos, b. Aug. 17, 1752; 32, David, b. Oct. 8, 1754; 33, Amos, b. Dec. 18, 1758; 34, Amy, b. March 8, 1760; 35, Mary, b. March 17, 1762.

26, EBENEZER,[5] m. Olive Sanford, Nov. 20, 1766, lived in Newtown, and was by trade a cabinet maker, d. June 4, 1740. Olive, b. March 27, 1744, d. June 16, 1805. Children: 37, Amy, b. Wednesday, Aug. 12, 1767, m. —— Sherman, d. April 29, 1798; 38, Joel b. Saturday, June 17, 1769, d. Oct. 4, 1794; 39, Olive, b. Thursday, Nov. 7, 1771, m.[40] —— Glover, d. June 17, 1794; 41, Rachel, b. Sunday, Oct. 16, 1774, d. Jan. 31, 1777; 42, Rachel, b. Oct. 6, 1777, m. —— Glover, d. Feb. 23, 1801; 43, Ebenezer, b. Sunday, Dec. 24, 1780, d. Oct. 17, 1836.

43, EBENEZER,[6] m. Anna Han, Jan. 11, 1802.

Anna Han was the daughter of Michael Han, who emigrated from Germany in 1752. He worked for Capt. Johnson of "Poverty" district, Newtown, several years, then removed to South Britain, and tended mill. He married Ruth Squire, sister of Solomon Squire, about 1760. He was one of the first members of the South Britain Presbyterian church, having been one of the petitioners to the General Assembly for the division of the Southbury church. (Hist. Woodbury, p. 232) He was early among the defenders of his adopted country, having been at the battle of Crown Point. N. Y., May 10, 1775, under the command of Col. Seth Warren. He died June 19, 1816, and was buried in the graveyard in Pierce Hollow, about a mile north of South Britain. His children were Mary, Benedict, Michael, Rosanna, Ruth, Olive, Jacob, James, and Anna who was born Sept. 12, 1779, and died Nov. 18, 1867.

Children of Ebenezer[6] and Anna Booth:

44, Charles, b. October 21, 1802, m. Maria Booth, daughter of H. Treat Booth of Woodbridge, who was the son of Dr. Peter Booth of Milford. Charles died in Seymour, Dec. 12, 1848. Children: 45, Henry Treat, b. May 12, 1820, d. in Washington, D. C., Jan. 4, 1863; 46, George, 47, Louisa.
48, Olive Maria, b. July 31, 1804, m. Lugrand Sharpe, d. March, 8, 1864.
49, Rosette, b. July 3, 1807, m. Wilson E. Hendryx, m. Oct. 14, 1830. Children: [50]Harry E., [51]Andrew B., [52]James W., [53]Wilbur A.
54, Mary Ann, b. Nov. 23, 1815, m. David Sackett.
55, Harry, b. Oct. 2, 1813, d. Oct. 2, 1825.

HISTORY OF SEYMOUR. 157
BALDWIN.

[1]HENRY[1], and his wife Alice, of Dundridge, England, in his will dated 1599, mentions his sons [2]Richard, [3]Sylvester, [4]John and [5]Robert.

[3]SYLVESTER[2] m. Jane Willis in 1590, d. in 1638. Children: [6]John, [7]Henry, [8]Richard, [9]William, [10]Sylvester.

[10]SYLVESTER[3] m. Sarah Bryan. He sailed for America on ship Martin, and died on the passage in June, 1638. Children: [11]Sarah, baptised April 22, 1621; [12]Richard, baptised in England, Aug. 25, 1622, d. in Milford, July 23, 1665; [13]Mary, Feb. 19, 1625; [14]Martha, baptised April 20, 1628; [15]Samuel, Jan. 1, 1632, buried June 4, 1632; [16]Elizabeth, baptised Jan. 25, 1633; buried Jan. 31, 1633; [17]John, [18]Ruth.

[12]RICHARD[4] was a leading man in Milford and one of the purchasers of Paugassett from the Indians. (See page 42.)

[19]BARNABAS[5], youngest son of [12]Richard, was born in 1665, d. 1741. Children: [20]Timothy; [21]Theophilus, b. 1699; [22]Sylvanus, b. 1706, m. Mary, daughter of Francis French[2].

[20]TIMOTHY[6], son of Barnabas, b. 1695, d. 1766.

[23]CAPT. TIMOTHY[7], son of [20]Timothy[6], b. Dec. 15, 1722, m. Sarah Beecher, Jan. 15, 174⅘, who died in 1794, in her 74th year. Children: [24]Sarah, b. April 11, 1746, m. Simeon Wheeler of Derby, Oct. 10, 1764; [25]Timothy, b. 1749, m. 1st, Sarah, daughter of Murray Lester of Poughkeepsie, 2d, Charity Somers, and left no children; [26]Thaddeus, b. June 22, 1751; [27]Anne, b. Feb. 24, 1757, m. Edmund Clark of Derby.

[28]ISAAC[7], the miller, son of [15]Theophilus[6], b. April 18, 1740, m. Philene Pardee of Derby, Dec. 24, 1766, lived in Woodbridge, Bethlehem and Derby, d. Jan. 4, 1799. Philene d. July 1826. Children: [29]Rachel, b. Sept. 30, 1767, d. 1786; [30]Rachel, b. Sept. 30, 1769; [31]Isaac, b. Nov. 24, 1780, m. Louina Rowe, removed to Litchfield; [32]Elias, b. Jan. 16, 1773; [33]Elizer; [34]Eunice; [35]Louis, b. Nov. 17, 1780; [36]Eliphalet, b. 1785; [37]Lyman, Aug. 1, 1786.

[38]CHARLES[7], son [22]Sylvanus[6], b. 1751.

[39]SEYMOUR[8], son of Charles, b. 1807, m. Mary Candee of Oxford.

[40]CHARLES C.[9], son of [39]Seymour[8], b. 1834, residence Cleveland, Ohio, attorney at law, secretary of the Western Reserve and Northern Ohio Historical Society, and author of the Genealogy of the Baldwin Family.

[37]LYMAN[8], m. Nancy Candee, daughter of Moses Candee of Oxford. Children: [41]Dr. Edwin C., of Baltimore; [42]Julius, of Beach Pond, Pa.; [43]Alvin, [44]Amanda, m. —— Cushman; [45]Mary, m. —— Huntington; [46]Emily M., m. —— Olmstead, of Youngsville, Sullivan Co., Ohio.

[35]LOUIS, m. 1st, Maria Somers. Ch.: [47]Aleta, b. 1808, m. Smith Clark; m. 2nd, Lorinda, daughter of Jesse Baldwin. Ch.: [49]Albert L., m. Delia Youngs; [50]George W., [51]Ann Maria, m. Edwin Hyde of New Haven; [52]Mary, m. Thomas Cypher of New York; [53]Editha, m. —— Allen, of New Haven; [55]Charles.

BEACH.

¹Samuel Beach, who came to New Haven from England, married first, Miss Sanford, second, Miss Potter.

²Benjamin, only son of Samuel, m. Miss Blackley and had three sons, of whom Benjamin, 2d, the first settled preacher in what is now Seymour, was one.

³Benjamin. Children: ⁴Giles, died in North Haven at the age of 82; ⁵Lydia; ⁶Titus, who built the first mill where Sharon Y. Beach's papermill now stands, d. in Clymer, Chatauque Co., N. Y.; ⁷Mercy; ⁸Joel; ⁹David, d. in Oxford; ¹⁰Simeon; Benjamin, 2d, died in Cornwall at the age of 79 years.

⁴Giles, m. Mary Dayton. Children: ¹¹Bedy, b. April 1, 1790, m. Samuel Hemingway of Montowese; ¹²Joseph B., m. Julia Curtiss; ¹³Benjamin H.; Abram, m. Rhoda Dorothy, lived in Fair Haven; ¹⁴Ancy, b. June 1, 1805, m. George Minor of Montowese; ¹⁵Sharon Y. Beach, b. May 21, 1809.

¹⁵Sharon Y. Beach⁵, has been engaged in the manufacture of paper in this place for nearly forty years, (see page 120,) and has been a zealous advocate of the temperance reform. During the existence of the Baptist church of Seymour, he was one of its most efficient supporters. He was one of the first in Seymour to move in calling public meetings in aid and support of the government at the breaking out of the rebellion, contributing liberally of his time and means, and when Company H. of the 20th C. V. was being organized he offered an additional bounty of $10 for each man who should enlist in the quota of Seymour, and when the company was completed he went to the camp and gave the sum promised to each man from Seymour, to the amount of $270. He was one of the selectmen of the town in 1852 and 1870, justice of the peace a number of years, one of the school visitors of Seymour five years, and a member of the Board of Education most of the time since the consolidation of the districts in 1868. He married Adaline Sperry, Oct. 4, 1832. Children:

¹⁶George W. Beach, born in 1833. In 1850 he entered service of the Naugatuck Railroad Company as clerk at Seymour, and also filling any place upon the road as called upon. This position he filled with success, familiarizing himself with the details of the business and the methods of railroad work. In 1851 he was placed in the office at Waterbury as second clerk, but was frequently sent to various stations on the road, thus becoming acquainted all along the line. In 1855 he was appointed agent at Naugatuck, and in 1857 he was called upon to act as conductor of a passenger train, taking charge of the general ticket agency. In 1861 he became agent at Waterbury, and in 1868 succeeded Charles Waterbury as superintendent of the road, which office he has since held, and in which he has become generally and favorably known throughout the Naugatuck valley. He is a deacon of the First

HISTORY OF SEYMOUR. 159

Congregational church in Waterbury, superintendent of its Sunday school, and was one of the delegates to the convention in New York which organized the Christian Commission for the relief of soldiers during the War of the Rebellion. He represented Waterbury in the legislature in 1870 and 1871.

[17] ANDREW Y. BEACH, for some years general ticket agent of the Naugatuck Railroad, and now general freight agent of the Consolidated Railroad at Springfield, Mass.; m. Mary Woodford.

[18] EMELINE E.

[19] SHARON D. BEACH, paper manufacturer, Seymour, m. Elizabeth, daughter of Stephen R. Rider.

[20] Theodore B. Beach, ticket agent of the Naugatuck Railroad at Waterbury.

RICHARD BEACH[1] was one of the early settlers of New Haven, and marthe widow of Andrew Hull about 1640. Children: Mary, b. June, 1642; Benjamin, b. Oct. 1644; Azariah, b. July, 1646; Mercy, 1648.

AZARIAH,[2] settled in Killingworth. Children: Richard, b. Oct. 19, 1677; Thomas, b. Oct. 5, 1679; Benjamin, b. Jan. 14, 1682.

BENJAMIN,[3] m. Dinah Birdsey of Stratford. Children: Joseph, b. Oct. 24, 1710; Abel, b. Feb. 9, 1712.

JOSEPH,[4] m. Experience ———, lived in Durham and Torrington. Children: Miriam. b. Dec. 5, 1734; Hannah, b. May 17, 1736; Phebe, b. April 4, 1738; Benjamin, b. March 25, 1740; Experience, b. Sept. 10, 1744; Dinah, b. Nov. 2, 1751; Joseph, b. July 26, 1753.

JESSE BEACH, Esq., of Derby, m. Sally Wheeler, July 30, 1792. Children; Lucy Mariah, b. Feb. 23, 1794; Sally Keziah, b. Sept. 9, 1796. (D. R.bmd, p. 210.) Jesse Beach was chosen moderator of the town meeting, Dec. 11, 1809.

DURAND.

Three Huguenot brothers came over from France and settled—one in Milford, one in Derby, and one in Oxford.

2, JOSEPH,[2] of Derby, d. Aug. 6, 1792, aged 81. Anna, wife of Joseph, d. Feb. 14, 1788, aged 64.

4, NEHEMIAH,[2] son of John, of Oxford, b. Dec. 8, 1753, d. Aug. 10, 1824; m. Ruth Jones, b. Dec. 9, 1758, d. May 25, 1816. Children:

    6, Hannah, b. May 12, 1789, d. Nov. 18, 1818.

    7, Polly, b. 1791, m. Isaac Kinney, d. Sept. 23, 1827.

    8, John, b. 1796, d. Oct. 3, 1819.

    10, Jeremiah, b. March 22, 1800.

10, JEREMIAH,[3] m. Betsey Maria Kenney, Dec. 25, 1827. Children:

    11, Mary Elizabeth, b. Nov. 2, 1828, m. Edwin A. Lum, of Waterbury.

    12, Maria A., b. Feb. 22, 1831, d. Aug. 29, 1848.

    13, Charles William, b. Oct 2, 1834, m. Maria Hill of Oberlin, Ohio.

Mercy, daughter of Noah and Damaris Durand, d. May 8, 1748.—D. R., vol. 6, p. 2.

HOLBROOK.

JOHN,[1] m. Abigail.

JOHN.[2] m. —— Nichols, daughter of Rev. Mr. Nichols of Newtown. Children : [5]Philo, [6]Abel, [7]Richard, [8]Nathaniel, [9]Austin. They were all in the Revolutionary war. Philo was at Danbury when General Wooster was killed. Nathaniel served through the whole of the war, and was present at the surrender of General Burgoyne. He brought home a musket, through the breech of which a ball from a " King's arm " passed at Saratoga, as he raised it to his shoulder to take aim. He had sons named [10]Daniel[4], [11]Cyrus[4].

John[2] had a negro slave named Titus, who wished to go and fight for the independence of the colonies, but as the sons were all gone, John told him that if he would stay and help him till the war was over he would then give him his freedom and a tract of land. He did so, and the road which passed the land which was given to him is still known as Titus' lane.

[5]PHILO[3] m. Eleanor Wooster, daughter of Squire John Wooster. Children : [14]Abijah, [15]Sarah, [16]Eunice, [17]Sabra, m. 1st, Ebenezer Riggs, 2d, Curtiss Lindley.

[14]ABIJAH,[4] m. Sarah Webster. Children : [18]Thomas W. and [19]Sarah.

[7]RICHARD,[3] m. 1st, Mrs. Sarah Lum, Sept. 13, 1797, d. Nov. 21, 1798, 2d, Gracey Hawkins, Oct. 6, 1799. Children : [25]Daniel Lum, b. Nov. 21, 1798; [26]Sarah, b. July 31, 1800; [27]Philo, b. March 12, 1802; [28]Austin, Jan. 21, 1804 ; [29]Richard, Nov. 19, 1805. D. R.bmd p. 230.

[34]CAPT. JOHN HOLBROOK died Jan. 28, 1801, aged 74. Esther, his wife, died Feb. 5, 1795, aged 63.

[35]JOHN HOLBROOK, JR., m. Huldah Fox, July 7, 1774. Huldah died April 1, 1796. Children : [36]Hannah, b. Jan. 6, 1775 ; [37]John, b. April 29, 1777 ; [38]Benjamin, b. Oct. 26, 1780 ; [39]David, Dec. 27, 1782 ; [40]Nabby, b. Jan. 24, 1785 ; [41]Sally, b. June 9, 1787, d. May 27, 1788. D. R.bmd p. 230.

[6]CAPT ABEL,[3] m. Hannah Clark, of Oxford. Children : [42]Thomas C. ; [43]Patty, m. Joseph Platt of Southbury ; [44]Sir William, [45]Hannah, [46]Abel, [47]Esther.

[46]ABEL[4] m. Olive Pierce of Southbury. Children : [48]Nathan, m. Ellen, daughter of William R. Tomlinson ; [49]Esther, m. Lawrence Mitchell of Newtown.

[27]CAPT. PHILO HOLBROOK[4], who died Nov. 17, 1878, was for some years in command of a vessel sailing between New Haven and the West Indies. He became a member of Morning Star Lodge, F. and A. M., Oct. 10, 1826, was one of the original stockholders of the Seymour Savings Bank in 1852, justice of the peace from 1852 to 1858, one of the selectmen of the town of Seymour in 1855 and in 1865, and represented the town in the legislature in 1869. He was held in high respect by his fellow townsmen, who had so often called upon him to fill offices of trust and honor.

[42]THOMAS C.[4], m. Maria Benham. Children : [50]William E., [51]Charles F., [52]Noyes B.

HISTORY OF SEYMOUR.   161

⁶¹COL. DANIEL HOLBROOK², son of ⁶⁰Daniel¹, m. —— Hitchcock, built place now occupied by Joel Chatfield for his oldest son. Children: ⁶²Daniel, ⁶³David, ⁶⁴Josiah, ⁶⁵Abel.

⁶²CAPT. DANIEL³, m. Elizabeth M. Riggs. Children: ⁶⁶Daniel, ⁶⁷Harry, ⁶⁸Samuel.

⁶⁶DANIEL⁴, m. Harriett, (b. 1798), daughter of Moses Riggs. Served in the company of Capt. Abraham Hubbard, Conn. Militia, in the war of 1812. Children:

⁶⁹Willis, b. Aug. 19, 1818, m. M. Maria Smith.
⁷⁰Horace, b. Jan. 18, 1821, m. Mary A., daughter of Styles Tucker.
⁷¹David, b. June 24, 1826, m. Cynthia Smith.
⁷²Eliza, b. May 16, 1829, m. Clement A. Sargent.

⁶⁷HARRY, son of Capt. Daniel³, m. Nancy Davis. Children: ⁷³Nancy M., ⁷⁴Mary.

WHEELER.

¹JAMES WHEELER, m. Sarah Johnson, May 19th, 1736. Children:— ²Sarah, b. Dec. 27, 1737, d. March 31, 1764; ³Samuel, b. Sept. 24, 1739; ⁴Simeon, b. Apr. 15, 1741; ⁵Ruth, May 20, 1743, d. Sept. 1, 1764; ⁶James, b. Apr. 6, 1745; ⁷a daughter b. March 1, 1747, d. in infancy; ⁸Joseph, b. May 14, 1748; ⁹Moses, b. July 28, 1750; ¹⁰Anna, b. Aug. 10, 1752; ¹¹David, b. May 14, 1754; ¹²John, b. June 2, 1756; ¹³Elijah, b. Dec. 22, 1758; ¹⁴Hannah, b. May 25, 1761; ¹⁵Sarah, b. Apr. 15, 1764. ¹James, Sen., d. in May, 1768, aged 52 years. Sarah, his wife, d. in Sept., 1812, aged 92 years. Mrs. Lois Wheeler, the mother of James Wheeler, died Sept. 11, 1767, aged 87 years.

¹²JOHN WHEELER, m. Sybil Todd. Child:—¹⁶John Todd, b. in 1777.

¹⁶JOHN TODD WHEELER, m. Sally Clark, who died in 1824, leaving an only child, ¹⁷John Clark Wheeler.

¹⁷JOHN C. WHEELER, m. Charlotte Chatfield, who died in 1831. Children: ¹⁸Henry, ¹⁹Frances, ²⁰John, ²¹Sarah.

Children of ¹⁷John C. and Charlotte Wheeler.

¹⁸HENRY, m. Nancy Hotchkiss. Children:—²²Charlotte, ²³Frances, ²⁴Mary, ²⁵Henry, ²⁶Elizabeth, d. aged two and a half years; ²⁷John, d. aged eight years.

¹⁹FRANCES, m. O. C. Putnam. Children: ²⁸Flora, ²⁹Linda, ³⁰Frank.

162   HISTORY OF SEYMOUR.

²⁰JOHN, m. Alice Stanbury of N. Y. Children :—³¹Josephine, ³²Alice, ³³Elizabeth, ³⁴Marie.

²¹SARAH, m. Charles E. Converse. Children :—³⁵Charles, ³⁶Almira, ³⁷Alfred.

Children of ¹⁸Henry and Nancy Wheeler.

²²CHARLOTTE, m. Charles L. Lockwood. Children :—³⁸Fanny, ³⁹Louise, ⁴⁰Bessie, ⁴¹Mamie, ⁴²Flora.

²³FRANCES, m. George W. Ely. Children :—⁴³Henry, ⁴⁴Leonard, ⁴⁵Agnes.

²⁴MARY, m. William E. Lowe. Children :—⁴⁶Gerald, ⁴⁷Henry, ⁴⁸Charlotte.

²⁵HENRY, unmarried.

Children of ¹⁹Frances and O. C. Putnam.

²⁸FLORA, m. V. S. Woodruff. Child :—⁴⁹Frances.

²⁹LINDA, m. V. S. Woodruff.

³⁰FRANK, died aged nine years.

Children of ²⁰John and Alice Wheeler.

³¹JOSEPHINE, d. in 1853, aged 2 years and 3 months.

³²ALICE, m. O. M. Bogart, Jr. Child :—⁵⁰Alice.

³³ELIZABETH, unmarried.

³⁴MARIE, d. in 1876, aged 12 years.

Children of ²¹Sarah and Charles E. Converse.

³⁵CHARLES, m. Addie Shultz. Child :—⁵¹Sally.

³⁶ALMIRA, m. George Claflin. Child :—⁵²John.

³⁷ALFRED, unmarried.

JOHN TODD WHEELER, who died in 1868, aged 91, was an old resident of the town of Seymour, and was born in the northern part of the old town of Derby, then called Nyumphs, now Beacon Falls. His father, John Wheeler, removing to the then great west, left him then a babe with his grand-parents Todd, who lived at Derby Landing, who brought him up until their death, which left him to be hired out until he was of age. At twenty he purchased his time and married Sally Clark of Woodbridge and settled in Humphreysville, now the town of Seymour, following the vocation of a merchant until within a few years of his death, being one of the town's most energetic and best citizens. His only child, a son, JOHN C. WHEELER, at an early age entered into business with him, was a merchant and manufacturer of augers and paper for many years, until he removed to the city of New York, where he now lives, aged 82. He had six children by Charlotte Chatfield, his wife, four of whom are still living; the eldest, Henry, now a resident of Seymour, and John, Francis and Sarah all living in the city of New York.

JOHN WHEELER, youngest son of John Todd Wheeler, born in Humphreysville in 1823, removed to New York in 1843, early in life took much interest in public affairs as a democrat, in 1852, at the age of 27, was elected to

HON. JOHN WHEELER.

Congress from New York City, and took an active part in the exciting times upon the question of the Repeal of the "Missouri Compromise," otherwise called the "Kansas and Nebraska bill," in the 33d Congress. Upon its being made a party question, admitting slavery north of Missouri, he, with a few other democrats, took bold and open ground against it, and was the only member from the city of New York (of six democrats) who voted against the bill. He was re-elected to the 34th Congress—was renominated by the democracy in 1856 for the 35th Congress, but declined; was a war democrat when it required nerve so to be, was a strong opponent of the Tweed Ring, going out of Tammany Hall and joining with the honest portion of the democracy and other citizens for their overthrow. He was one of the most active of the famous Committee of Seventy which overthrew that infamous ring, was one of the leaders in the movement which elected William H. Havemeyer mayor, and one of the men who obtained from the Legislature at Albany the Charter of 1873. On the passage of that Charter, Mayor Havemeyer appointed him President of the Department of Taxes and Assessments, one of the Board of Estimate and Apportionment, and a Commissioner of Accounts, which positions he has held from May, 1873, for over six years, doing his utmost for a reduction of the expenses and taxes of the city. He was prominently named among the candidates by the regular democracy and independent citizens in 1878, for Mayor, but declined to enter the contest.

The following extract from the *N. Y. Tribune* of May 19th, 1879, will show the estimation in which Mr. W. is held in New York. Referring to his appointment by the General Assembly of the State of New York as a member of the Commission to Revise the Tax Laws, the *Tribune* said:—
"Mr. Wheeler is well and most favorably known for his administration of the Tax Office, and it is to him that the people of this city will chiefly look perhaps for such a reasonable and prudent re-adjustment of the tax system as will divide the burden fairly among all classes of property."

Mr. Wheeler is a modest, unassuming man, an Episcopalian, having been Vestryman and Senior Warden of the Anthon Memorial Church for many years, and Superintendent of the Sunday School of said church for twelve years.

⁴SIMEON WHEELER, m. Sarah, daughter of Capt. Timothy Baldwin. Children:—⁵³Ruth, b. Sept. 17, 1765, m. Dea. Bradford Steele, d. Feb. 20, 1856; ⁵⁴Nathan, m. Experience Washburn; ⁵⁵Timothy, ⁵⁶Sarah, m. Eli Sanford, d. May 23, 1820, aged 80; ⁵⁷David, d. Dec. 21, 1829, aged 53, unmarried.

⁸JOSEPH WHEELER, m. Lucy ———. Children:—⁵⁸Sally, b. Oct. 2, 1774, m. Jesse Beach July 30, 1792; ⁵⁹William, b. Apr. 3, 1779; ⁶⁰Nancy, b. Mar. 1, 1782; ⁶¹Whittelsey, b. Sept. 19, 1784; ⁶²Joseph, b. Aug. 11, 1787; ⁶³Polly, b. May 19, 1791.—(D. R.,ᵇᵐᵈ p. 212.

UPSON.

¹THOMAS UPSON was a resident of Hartford in 1638, and afterward an original settler and proprietor of Farmington. He married Elizabeth Fuller in 1646 and died July 20, 1655. Children:—²Thomas, ³Stephen, ⁴Mary, ⁵Hannah, ⁶Elizabeth.

³STEPHEN,² of Waterbury, m. Mary Lee, Dec. 29, 1682, and died in 1735, aged 85. Children:—⁷Mary, ⁸Stephen, ⁹Elizabeth, ¹⁰Thomas, b. Mar. 1, 169$\frac{2}{3}$, ¹¹Hannah, ¹²Tabitha, ¹³John, ¹⁴Thankful.

¹⁰THOMAS,³ of Wolcott, m. Rachel Judd, May 28, 1749. Children:— ¹⁵Thomas, ¹⁶Mary, ¹⁷John, ¹⁸Josiah, ¹⁹Asa, ²⁰Timothy, ²¹Amos, ²²Samuel, b. Mar. 8, 1737, ²³Freeman.

CAPT. ²²SAMUEL,⁴ of Wolcott, m. Ruth Cowles, Apr. 5, 1759, d. Feb. 25, 1816, aged 79. Children:—²⁴Mary, ²⁵Archibald, ²⁶Isaac, ²⁷Obed, b. Jan. 2, 1767; ²⁸Harvey, ²⁹Samuel, ³⁰Ruth, ³¹Jerusha, ³²Manly, ³³Betsey.

²⁷OBED,⁵ b. in Wolcott, m. Sybil Howe and lived in Waterbury. Children:—³⁴Laura, ³⁵Hiram, ³⁶Maria, ³⁷Lena, ³⁸Garry, ³⁹Luther, ⁴⁰Isabel, ⁴¹Eunice, ⁴²Caroline, ⁴³Charlotte.

³⁵HIRAM⁶, m. Sarah Harrison. Children:

⁴⁴Harriett, m. Harpin Riggs of Seymour.
⁴⁵Charles N., of Waterbury, m. Juliette Warner.
⁴⁶William A., lives in Kensington, m. Sarah Terrill.
⁴⁷Martha Maria, m. James Smith of Derby.
⁴⁸Hiram, Jr., killed in the war of the rebellion.
⁴⁹George F., lives in Springfield.
⁵⁰Edwin Leroy, d. aged 2½ years.
⁵¹Sarah, m. George W. Beach of Waterbury.
⁵²Henry H., d. aged 17 years.
⁵³Esther P., m. Leroy Upson.

ELLIS.

REV. THOMAS ELLIS was born in Martyn, Flintshire, North Wales, Jan. 1, 1800. He emigrated to America Apr. 1, 1824, settled in Humphreysville and married Charlotte Clinton, Apr. 19, 1829. He joined the M. E. church in 1829 and in 1833 received a license as local preacher. He joined the New York conference in 1839 and became an efficient minister of the gospel. His children were—Mary J., m. William S. Eno of Pine Plains, N. Y.; Adam C. and Matthew H., lawyers of New York, all born in Humphreysville. Rev. Mr. Ellis died at Pine Plains, N. Y., May 31, 1873. His wife died at Hyde Park, N. Y., June 8, 1860, aged 51 years.

ABIRAM STODDARD, M. D.

The Coat of Armes of the Antient Family of Stoddard, of London.

Sa. 3, Estoiles and a bordure gu, Crest out a ducal coronet a demihorse salient, erm.

MOTTO :—*Festina Lente.* Be in haste, but not in a hurry.

The name Stoddard is derived from the office of Standard-Bearer, and was anciently written De-La-Standard.

In the office of Heraldry, England, the following origin of the Stoddard Family is found :

WILLIAM STODDARD, a knight, came from Normandy to England, A. D., 1066, with William the Conqueror, who was his cousin. Of his descendants, we find record of RUKARD STODDARD, of Mottingham, Kent, near Eltham, about seven miles from London Bridge, where was located the family estate of about four hundred acres, which was in possession of the family in 1490, how much before is not known, and continued till the death of NICHOLAS STODDARD, a bachelor, in 1765.

THOMAS STODDARD, of Royston.
JOHN STODDARD, of Grindon.
WILLIAM STODDARD, of Royston.
JOHN STODDARD, of Royston.
ANTHONY STODDARD, of London.
GIDEON STODDARD, of London.
ANTHONY STODDARD, of London.
WILLIAM STODDARD, of London.
ANTHONY STODDARD, of London.

166 HISTORY OF SEYMOUR.

[1]ANTHONY STODDARD came from England to Boston about 1639. He was admitted Freeman in 1640, was a representative in 1650, 1659, 1660, and during twenty successive years from 1665 to 1684. He married first, Mary, daughter of Hon. Emanuel Downing of Salem, who, with Lucy his wife, was admitted to the church in Salem Nov. 4th, 1638, and sister of Sir George, afterward Lord George Downing, by whom he had three sons:

[2]Solomon, b. Oct. 4, 1643, d. Feb. 11, 1729.

[3]Samson, b. Dec. 3, 1645, d. Nov. 4, 1698.

[4]Simeon, b. 1650, d. Oct. 15, 1730. Simeon was member of an artillery company in 1675. He had three sons: Anthony, b. Sept. 24, 1678, d. Mar. 11, 1748; David, b. Dec. 5, 1685; Jonathan, b. Feb. 5, 1688.

He married second, Barbara, widow of Capt. Joseph Weld of Roxbury, who died April 15, 1654, by whom he had two children:

[5]Sarah, b. Oct. 21, 1652.

[6]Stephen, b. Jan. 6, 1654.

He married third, Christian (about 1655), whose family name is unknown, by whom he had ten children, as follows:

[7]Anthony, b. June 16, 1656.

[8]Christian, b. Mar. 22, 1657, m. Nathaniel Peirse.

[9]Lydia, b. May 27, 1660, m. Capt. Samuel Turell.

[10]Joseph, b. Dec. 1, 1661.

[11]John, b. April 22, 1663.

[12]Ebenezer, b. July 1, 1664.

[13]Dorothy, b. Nov. 24, 1665.

[14]Mary, b. Mar. 25, 1668.

[15]Jane, and Grace, b. July 29, 1669.

Anthony Stoddard, Sr., d. Mar. 16, 168$\frac{6}{7}$.

[2]SOLOMON, graduated at Harvard in 1662 and was librarian of the college from 1667 to 1670, preached two years in Barbadoes to the dissenters, and in 1672 became the settled minister of Northampton, Mass. He married Mrs. Esther Mather, Mar. 8, 1680. Children:

[16]Mary, b. Jan. 9, 1761, m. Rev. Stephen Mix, who graduated at Harvard in 1690.

[17]Esther, b. June 2, 1672, m. Nov. 6, 1694, Rev. Timothy Edwards, who graduated at Harvard in 1691. Their fifth child, Johnathan, b. Oct. 5, 1703, graduated at Yale in 1720, elected president of Nassau Hall College in 1757, and became president of Princeton College in Jan., 1758, in which position he continued until his death.

[18]Samuel, b. Feb. 5, 1674, d. Mar. 22, 1674.

[19]Anthony, b. June 6, 1675, d. June 7, 1675.

[20]Aaron, b. Aug. 23, 1676, d. Aug. 23, 1676.

[21]Christain, b. Aug. 23, 1676, m. Rev. William Williams, who graduated at Harvard in 1683, and was settled as minister in Hatfield 66 years.

JOSEPH NETTLETON STODDARD.

HISTORY OF SEYMOUR. 167

²²Anthony, b. Aug. 9, 1698, d. Sept. 6, 1760.
²³Sarah, b. Apr. 1, 1680, m. Rev. Samuel Whitman, who graduated at Harvard in 1696 and settled as minister in Farmington.
²⁴John, b. Feb. 17, 1682, graduated at Harvard in 1701, for many years one of the Governor's council, also Chief-Justice of the Court of Common Pleas, Judge of Probate, &c.
²⁵Israel, b. Apr. 10, 1684, d. a prisoner in France.
²⁶Rebecca, b. 1686, m. Joseph Hawley, d. January, 1766.
²⁷Hannah, b. Apr. 21, 1688, m. Rev. William Williams, who graduated at Harvard in 1705 and settled as minister in Weston, Mass.

²²ANTHONY³, graduated at Harvard in 1697 and settled as minister in Woodbury, where he continued sixty years, m. first, Oct. 20, 1700, Prudence Wells, who died in May, 1714; second, Jan. 31, 1715, Mary Sherman, who died Jan. 12, 1720. Children:
²⁸Mary, b. June 19, 1702.
²⁹Solomon, b. Oct. 12, 1703, d. May 13, 1727.
³⁰Eliakim, b. Apr. 3, 1705, m. Joanna Curtiss, d. in 1750.
³¹Elisha, b. Nov. 24, 1706, m. Rebekah Sherman, resided in Woodbury, d. in 1766.
³²Israel, b. Aug. 7, 1708, d. May 30, 1727.
³³John, b. Mar. 2, 1710.
³⁴Prudence, b. Oct. 12, 1711, m. Joseph Curtiss.
³⁵Gideon, b. May 27, 1714, m. Olive Curtiss.
³⁶Esther, b. Oct. 11, 1716, m. Preserved Strong.
³⁷Abijah, b. Feb. 28, 1718, m. Eunice Curtiss.
³⁸Elizabeth, b. Nov. 15, 1719, m. Daniel Munn.

³⁰ELIAKIM⁴, m. Joanna Curtiss in 1729, resided in Woodbury. Children:
³⁹John, b. Jan. 26, 1730, d. Jan. 22, 1795.
⁴⁰Israel, b. Jan. 28, 1732, m. Elizabeth Reade, d. Aug. 8, 1794.
⁴¹Anthony, b. Oct. 21, 1734, m. Phebe Reade, d. in 1785.
⁴²Joanna, b. July 16, 1738, m. Reuben Squares.
⁴³Prudence, b. Sept. 24, 1740, m. John Marchant.
⁴⁴Eliakim, b. July 25, 1742, d. in childhood.
⁴⁵Seth, b. Dec. 2, 1744, m. Hannah Noyes.
⁴⁶Abigail, b. Aug. 2, 1747, m. Israel Woodward, d. Dec. 18, 1703.
⁴⁷Eliakim, b. Dec. 11, 1749, d. in Canada.

³⁹JOHN⁵, m. Mary Atwood, resided in Watertown. Children:
⁴⁸Samson, b. Oct. 25, 1752, d. Nov. 11, 1809.
⁴⁹Abiram, b. Oct. 25, 1756, d. Oct. 25, 1776, in the revolutionary army.
⁵⁰Wells, b. July 1, 1759, m. Sarah Hickox, d. in 1840.
⁵¹Phebe, b. Feb. 19, 1760, m. Josiah Hickox, d. Sept. 25, 1827.
⁵²John, b. July 1, 1763, m. Sarah Woodward, d. Feb. 24, 1821.
⁵³Submit, b. Mar. 17, 1766, d. Sept. 7, 1775.

HISTORY OF SEYMOUR.

[54]Joanna, b. Feb. 19, 1767, m. Eri Parker, d. June 5, 1847.

[55]Mary, b. June 11, 1771, m. Randall Judd of Woodbury, d. in 1845.

[56]Sarah, b. May 13, 1773, m. James Williams, d. Dec. 20, 1809.

[57]Israel, b. Feb. 15, 1776, m. Polly Wilson, lived in Camden, N. Y., was Supervisor nineteen years, Justice of the Peace twelve years, member of Assembly four years, and County Judge eight years, d. Apr. 4, 1859.

[58]Eliakim, b. Aug. 10, 1779, m. Lois Matthews, d. Feb. 28, 1860, was a Methodist minister.

[48]SAMSON[6], m. first, Susannah Nettleton, who died Apr. 24, 1779; second, Amy Goodwin, who died Sept. 16, 1827, whose ancestors came in the Mayflower. He resided at Watertown, Ct. Children:

[59]Prudence, b. Aug. 11, 1775, m. James Atwood of Woodbury, d. Feb. 19, 1833.

[60]Abiram, b. Jan. 27, 1777, d. Nov. 26, 1855.

[61]Susannah, b. Mar. 26, 1779, m. Wheler Atwood of Woodbury, d. June 15, 1833.

[62]William, b. Sept. 29, 1781, graduated at Yale in 1804, m. a Miss Stone, was a physician, died in Mobile, Ala., in 1817.

[63]Goodwin, b. May 8, 1783, m. Ann Warner, was a Methodist preacher and Presiding Elder in Oneida Conference.

[64]Harvey, b. Apr. 14, 1785, m. Selima Martin, residence, Waverly, Ill.

[65]Anna, b. Aug. 17, 1788, m. William Tolls, d. Sept. 24, 1846.

[66]Samuel, b. Aug. 6, 1791, m. Phebe Minor, d. Aug. 4, 1828.

[68]ABIRAM[7], graduated at Yale in 1800, m. Eunice Clark and settled in Humphreysville as physician. He was representative from Oxford in the General Assembly in 1814 and held offices of public trust in Derby for many years. He was a man of large intelligence and great energy and endurance. Children:

[69]Theresa, b. Jan. 26, 1806, d. in 1814.

[70]Jonathan, b. Oct. 9, 1807, graduated at Yale College in 1831, was a lawyer, and successfully followed his profession for many years in New Haven, Conn., was appointed U. S. District Attorney for the District of Connecticut by President Polk in the year 1845, which office he held four years; was appointed District Attorney for the county of New Haven, 1853, and continued in said office till July 20, 1854; d. April 28, 1855.

[71]Susan H., b. Aug. 3, 1809, m. Sheldon C. Johnson, M. D., of Seymour.

[72]Thomas, b. Mar. 11, 1813, m. Esther Ann Gilbert.

[73]Joseph Nettleton, b. Nov. 12, 1815, d. Nov. 28, 1859.

[74]William, b. Jan. 6, 1818, studied law in New Haven, where he continued to reside till the time of his death, gained many friends by his genial and social manners, and earned the reputation of a thorough scholar and an able advocate, d. in New Haven, Ct., Mar. 16, 1858.

MARIA THERESA STODDARD.

GENEALOGY.

[75]Maria Theresa, youngest daughter of Abiram and Eunice Stoddard, b. June 2, 1825, went to Maryland during the War of the Rebellion, to aid in caring for the sick and wounded soldiers, contributing liberally of her ample means for their comfort and for the alleviation of their sufferings.

---

[72]THOMAS, son of Abiram and Eunice Stoddard, graduated at Yale Medical School in 1836, m. Apr. 19, 1839, Esther Ann Gilbert, b. July 31, 1819. Children:

    [76]Francis Eunice, born Jan. 13, 1840, married Nov. 30, 1861, Samuel L. Bronson, born Jan. 12, 1834, graduated at Yale, 1855; at the Law School, 1857; was Judge of the New Haven City Court and afterward Judge of the Court of Common Pleas for several years; now practicing law at New Haven.
    Children: (77) Thomas Stoddard, (78) Josiah Harmar, (79) Mary Esther, (80) Sarah Frances, (81) Ezekiel Stoddard.
    [82]Sarah G., b. Apr. 6, 1842.
    [83]Ezekiel, b. Nov. 14, 1844, wholesale merchant in New Haven and a director of New Haven County National Bank; m. Mary De Forest Burlock.
    Children: (84) Thomas Burlock, (85) Esther Ann, (86) Mary, (87) Louis Ezekiel.

---

[73]JOSEPH NETTLETON, son of Abiram and Eunice Stoddard, m. Dec. 10, 1838, Sophia Buddington, b. June 2, 1818, resides in Westville. Children:
    [88]William B., b. Sept. 27, 1839. Resides in Westville.
    [89]Henry, b. Mar. 22, 1843. Studied law in Albany Law School.
    [90]Sophia Theresa, b. Mar. 9, 1845.
    [91]Goodwin, b. Apr. 2, 1847.
    [92]Robert J., b. Aug. 2, 1855.
    [93]Joseph E., b. Feb. 13, 1859.

SAMUEL HICKOX.

SAMUEL HICKOX, of Waterbury, appears to have previously resided at Farmington, died in 1693. Children, with ages in 1694:
    Samuel[26], Hannah[24], William[22], Thomas[20], Joseph[17], m. Ruth Fairchild Nov. 3, 1697, and settled in Woodbury; Mary[14], Elizabeth[12], Stephen[11], Benjamin[9], m. Hannah Skeel and settled in Woodbury; Ebenezer[2]. The sons spelled the name Hickcock.

170   HISTORY OF SEYMOUR.

REYNOLDS HICKOX of Torrington, m. Oct. 8, 1770; d. Sept. 13, 1828. His wife d. Sept. 18, 1832. Children :
Randall, b. Oct. 15, 1786; d. May 8, 1836.
Olive, b. Mar. 10, 1782; m. Sheldon Morris of Middlebury; d. in May, 1845·
Samuel R., b. in Torrington, Jan. 12, 1790; d. Mar. 14, 1861.

REV. SAMUEL R., a local preacher, son of Reynolds Hickox, removed from Torrington to Waterbury, then to Southbury, and in 1828 to Seymour. He married Sarah Osborn, who was born Mar. 28, 1789, and died Jan. 26, 1868. Children :
Harriett, b. Sept. 19, 1810, m. John Wesley French, d. Oct. 16, 1837.
Samuel, b. Feb. 20, 1814; m. 1st, Elizabeth Spencer Jan. 6, 1839; who d. Dec. 9, 1841, aged 26, leaving one child, Harriett E.; m. 2nd, Eliza M. White, Nov. 9, 1854.

DAVIS.

COL. JOHN DAVIS, son of Joseph and Mary Davis of Oxford, b. Feb. 2, 174$\frac{8}{9}$, m. Apr. 10, 1782, Mehitable, daughter of Reuben Thomas of New Haven. Children :
Sarah, b. Mar. 31, 1783, d. Dec. 6, 1808.
Anson, b. Sept, 5, 1785, m. Sally Prudden of Milford.
Truman, b. Mar. 13, 1787, m. Mary Allen of Woodbridge.
John, b. Sept. 8, 1788, m. Laura Riggs, Oct. 16, 1813, d. Aug. 8, 1848.
Lucretia, b. Sept. 22, 1790, m. Samuel Mallory and went west.
Mary, b. May 28, 1792, m. Abijah Hyde of Oxford.
Chary, b. Feb. 8, 1794, m. Peter Prudden of Milford.
Nabby, b. Dec. 21, 1795, m. Harvey Osborne of Oxford.
Nancy, b. Dec. 21, 1795, m. Cyrus Humphrey of Oxford, d. Aug. 25, 1826.
Children :—Bernard, m. Sarah, dau. of Denzel Hitchcock, d. in January, 1854.
Nancy, m. G. Burton Robinson, d. in February, 1854.
Joseph Wheeler, b. Aug. 13, 1798, m. Henrietta Newton of Woodbridge.
Children :—Jonah N., m. —— Bassett, moved west.
Dewitt, a lawyer, residence Milwaukee, Wis.
Joseph Burritt, d. Nov. 4, 1854.
Sheldon, b. Sept. 3, 1800, d. May 30, 1813.
Lewis, b. Jan. 26, 1803, m. Lucinda Perkins of Oxford. Children :
Dr. Henry, of Wallingford, m. —— Beecher of Bethlehem.
Mary, m. Charles W. Storrs of Seymour.
Frank, m. —— Lane of Oxford,
Burritt, b. July 12, 1806, m. Sarah Electa, dau. of Hiram Osborn of Oxford. Children :
Jay, m. Anna Fairchild; Sarah, m. Frederic Cable; and Bernard, all living in Owego, N.Y.
Julia Maria, b. July 4, 1810, m. Ebenezer Riggs of Oxford, d. Aug. 9, 1844.
Col. John Davis was born Sept. 27, 1755, d. Nov. 27, 1848, aged 93 years. His wife was born Apr. 12, 1764; d. Dec. 27, 1852, aged 88 years.

GENEALOGY.

ANSON DAVIS, son of Col. John Davis of Oxford, m. Sept. 5, 1811, Sally, daughter of Samuel Prudden of Milford. Children:

Sheldon, b. Jan. 1, 1813, m. Marietta, dau. of Abel Church.
Sarah Ann, b. Mar. 10, 1815, m. Luman Chapman.
Anson Riley, b. Mar. 30, 1818, m. Mary Newton Alling.
Marcus, b. Oct. 9, 1820, m. Sarah M. Greene.
Delia Maria, b. Oct. 25, 1822, m. John F. Coxhead of Poughkeepsie, d. in April, 1878.
Harpin, b. Feb. 24, 1825, m. Mary Chatfield of Chestnut Tree Hill.
Homer, b. Oct. 15, 1827, living in Nevada.
Samuel Prudden, b. Sept. 1, 1831.
Martha Ellen, b. July 11, 1834, principal of St. Catharine's Hall, Augusta, Me.
Victoria Sophia, b. Sept. 21, 1837, m. John F. Coxhead.

JOHN DAVIS, JR., son of Col. John Davis, m. Laura, daughter of John Riggs; d. Aug. 8, 1844. Mrs. Laura Davis d. Feb. 20, 1855. Children:

John, m. Jennette, dau. of Lyman Wheeler, d. in 1872. Lived in Oxford.
Isaac B., m. Ann, daughter of Sheldon Tucker. Lives in Hartford.
Otis, d. in 1842.
Wm. Hart, m. Frances Mallett.

CAPT. TRUMAN DAVIS, son of Col. John Davis, m. 1st, Dec. 6, 1808, Mary, dau. of Roger Allen of Woodbridge, who died Feb. 13, 1832; 2nd, Mar. 18, 1832, Statira Ball of Bethany, who died Apr. 24, 1854; 3rd, Oct. 24, 1854, Sophia Mallory of Milford. He died May 19, 1868, aged 81 years. Children:

Emily, b. Aug. 19, 1810, m. Aug. 5, 1830, C. Lockwood Adams, d. Feb. 2, 1854. C. L. Adams d. May 25, 1841.
David Allen, b. July 29, 1812, d. Mar. 20, 1847.
Clark, b. Mar. 31, 1815, m. Jan. 23, 1842, Mary A. Toffey of N. Y.
Marietta, b. Aug. 22, 1817, m. May 6, 1838, Nathan W. Morgan of Pa., d. July 24, 1855.
An infant, b. Sept. 25, 1819, d. Dec. 20, 1819.
Emerette, b. Jan. 24, 1821, m. Jan. 10, 1841, Harrison Tomlinson, who died Nov. 25, 1855.
John, b. Oct. 7, 1823, m. Oct. 13, 1847, Jennette G. Allen.
Lydia Perkins, b. Feb. 15, 1826, m. Jan. 1, 1845, John R. Tomlinson, d. Nov. 2, 1852.
Burr, b. Jan. 7, 1828, m. Mar. 31, 1850, Mary J. Mallett.
Lucy, b. Feb. 19, 1830, m. Nov. 22, 1848, Hart C. Hubbell.

Benjamin, son of Nathan and Eunice Davis, b. Mar. 20, 1746.

HULL.

ALFRED HULL, a descendant of Joseph Hull, 3rd, the father of Gen. William Hull and grandfather of Commodore Isaac Hull, was born Oct. 25, 1785, m. Oct. 21, 1806, Sally, daughter of Jonathan Lum. Children:
John Clark, b. Jan. 25, 1808, m. July 25, 1830, Sarah Tomlinson.
Eliza, b. Feb. 27, 1814, m. Amos Glover Bassett.
<small>Frances, m. Judge James G. Haswell of Hardinsburgh, Ky.; Anna.</small>
Sarah, b. Oct. 21, 1820, m. Sept. 12, 1841, John J. Rider, d. Aug. 21, 1864. Children:
<small>Harriett Elizabeth, b. Aug. 12, 1842.
John Alfred, b. Apr. 12, 1844.
Mary Bennett, b. Jan. 7, 1846.
Ellen Frances, b. Mar. 17, 1847.
Charles Augustus and Eliza.   John J. Rider was born Jan. 20, 1820, died Jan. 7, 1871.</small>
William, b. July 7, 1825, m. Eliza, dau. of Amos Smith of Woodbridge. Residence, New Haven.

JOHN CLARK HULL, son of Alfred and Sally Hull, m. July 25, 1830, Sarah, dau. of David and Sarah Tomlinson, b. Dec. 5, 1814. Children:
Mary, m. Egbert Coggswell of New Preston.
Charles, m. 1st, Isora Taylor of Oregon, d. Jan. 27, 1868; 2nd, Lilly, dau. of Marcus Davis of Great Hill. Residence, Ansonia.
De Witt, m. Juliette Brown of Harwinton. Residence, Seymour.

BROADWELL.

LEWIS BROADWELL, a soldier of the War of 1812, m. Betsey, only daughter of Abiel and Mary Canfield, and made scythes with Ira Smith in a shop on the bank of Little river, opposite where the auger works of James Swan now stand, using the first triphammer ever set up in the place. He died Sept. 6, 1844, aged 53 years. Betsey d. March 10, 1821. Children:
Luther, born in 1811, m. ——— Twitchel of Oxford. Residence, Ohio.
David B., b. in 1813, m. Catharine Schermerhorn, d. June 19, 1879.
James, b. 1815, m. Margaret Skiene, removed to Ohio.
Lewis, b. in 1817, m. Mary A. Lyon.
Sarah, b. in 1819, d. in 1837, aged 18 years.
Jacob, b. in 1821, m. Susan Henry, removed to Ohio, d. in 1871.

LEWIS[2], son of Lewis and Betsey Broadwell, m. Mary A. Lyon. Children:
Homer, m. Ellen Clark of North Haven. Child:
<small>Alice May, born in 1867, died in 1868.</small>
Mary A. Residence, Fair Haven.

THE METHODIST EPISCOPAL CHURCH.

In 1791, Rev. Jesse Lee, the pioneer of Methodism in New England, came to Derby, and—hiring a bellman to ring the people out—he preached to them in the shade of some trees in what is now known as Derby Uptown, on the east side of the Naugatuck, then deeper than now, and navigable to that place. The seed then sown by the wayside has brought forth an hundred fold. Among the hearers were John Coe and Ruth, his wife, who invited him to preach in their house on his next visit. This invitation he accepted a few weeks later, and extended his work to Chusetown, by which name the settlement at the Falls of the Naugatuck was then known. From that time Derby was included in the circuit, which embraced nearly all of what now constitutes the New Haven an Bridgeport districts.

In 1792, Middletown was made the head of the circuit, which embraced a large part of Middlesex and New Haven counties. This section was no exception to the general persecution of the new denomination, and from pulpit and fireside warnings were given against the innovators, but Lee and his co-laborers, like brave men of God as they were, continued to sow broadcast the seeds of truth. John and Ruth Coe, and Mr. and Mrs. Hinman, were the first fruits of their labors here, and soon brought their infant sons for baptism at the hands of Rev. Jesse Lee. Mr. Coe's son was baptised John Allyn, and Mr. Hinman's son Jesse Lee. John A. Coe grew to manhood as an earnest, efficient Christian, and settled in what is now Beacon Falls, where one of his grandsons still resides, and is one of the most honored residents of that place, having been repeatedly elected to the legislature and various offices of trust in the town.

The first society in Derby was formed in 1793, with John Coe as leader, and was visited by the venerable Bishop Asbury. Those of the members who lived in Chusetown were first organized as a separate society in 1797. The members were Jesse Johnson, Isaac Baldwin, Esther Baldwin, Sarah Baldwin and Eunice Baldwin. Daniel Rowe of Derby was the leader. The following names were soon added: George Clark, Lucy Hitchcock, Silas Johnson

174   HISTORY OF SEYMOUR.

and Olive Johnson. The ministers preached where they found open doors, once or more in Mrs. Dayton's tavern, the house now owned by William Hull, at the corner of Main and Pearl streets, also in the house of Mr. Stiles, now the residence of Dr. Stoddard. Some years later they preached in the ballroom of the Moulthroup tavern on the northeast of Hill and Pearl streets. The preachers upon the circuit from 1791 to 1800 were,—

1792, Rev. Richard Swain and Rev. Aaron Hunt.
1793, Rev. Joshua Taylor and Rev. Benjamin Fisler.
1794, Rev. Menzies Raynor and Rev. Daniel Ostrander.
1795, Rev. Evan Rogers and Rev. Joel Ketchum.
1796, Rev. Joshua Taylor and Rev. Lawrence McCombs.
1797, Rev. Michael Coate and Rev. Peter Jayne.
1798, Rev. Augustus Jocelyn.
1799, Rev. Ebenezer Stevens.
1800, Rev. James Coleman Rev. Roger Searle.

Rev. Jacob Brush, Rev. George Roberts, Rev. Jesse Lee, Rev. Freeborn Garrettson and Rev. Sylvester Hutchinson served as elders.

These itinerants were generally stalwart men, strengthened by daily horseback rides and hardened by exposure to all extremes of the weather. Most of them were men of fair culture, of great mental strength, of ready wit and glowing oratory, of fervid piety, and of marked success as evangelists. Many of them attained a good old age, and the churches which they organized have grown into large and powerful congregations.

For a long time the society continued small, and encountered much prejudice and some persecution. At one time while a meeting was being held in the house of Isaac Baldwin, which stood on the flat east of H. B. Beecher's augur factory, the persecutors went up on a ladder and stopped the top of the chimney in time of preaching, so that the smoke drove the people out of the house. Squibs of powder were often thrown into the fire in time of worship, to the great annoyance of the people. One who was acquainted with the subquent life of many of these disturbers of worship, relates that a curse seemed to follow them, and that most of them died in the prime of life. The preachers on the circuit from 1801 to 1810 were,—

1801, Rev. Abijah Bachelor and Rev. Luman Andrus.
1802, Rev. Abner Wood and Rev. James Annis.
1803, Rev. Abner Wood and Rev. Nathan Emory.
1804, Rev. Ebenezer Washburn and Nathan Emory.
1805, Rev. Ebenezer Wasburn and Rev. Luman Andrus.
1806, Rev. Luman Andrus and Rev. Zalmon Lyon.
1807, Rev. Wm. Thatcher, Rev. R. Harris and Rev. O. Sykes.
1808, Rev. James M. Smith and Rev. Phineas Rice.
1809, Rev. Noble W. Thomas and Rev. Coles Carpenter.
1810, Rev. Oliver Sykes and Rev. Jonathan Lyon.

HISTORY OF SEYMOUR. 175

The elders of the district were, Rev. F. Garrettson in 1801-2; D. Ostrander in 1803-5; William Thatcher in 1806; and Joseph Crawford from 1807 to 1810.

Among the early Methodists living on Great Hill were Anson Gillette and wife, with five sons and two daughters: Mrs. David Tomlinson, with one son and three daughters; Capt. Isaac Bassett and wife, with one son and six daughters; and James Tomlinson and wife.

Freeborn Garrettson held the first quarterly meeting in this place in the old Congregational meeting-house in 1803. Moses Osborn, a zealous local preacher residing in Southbury, by his faithful labors in Derby and vicinity during four or five years, prepared the way for a great revival in 1809, when seventy persons were converted in the Neck school-house. Most of these joined the Congregational church, but several families joined the M. E. church, and added to its influence in the town. For several years the work went on; now in Stratford, then at Humphreysville, and then at Nyumphs, and in other places. In 1811 the preachers were Rev. Zalmon Lyon and Rev. Jesse Hunt; in 1812, Rev. Aaron Hunt and Rev. Arnold Scholefield. In 1813 Middletown circuit was divided, and Stratford was made the head of the new circuit, and Rev. Ebenezer Washburn and Rev. James Coleman were the preachers. Stratford, Milford, Derby, Humphreysville, Nyumphs, Great Hill, Quaker's Farms, George's Hill, Bridgewater, Brookfield, Newtown, East Village, Stepney and Trumbull, were included in the circuit.

In 1814, Rev. Nathan Bangs was presiding elder of the New Haven District, and Rev. Elijah Woolsey and Rev. Henry Ames were the preachers on this circuit. This year, preaching was divided—half a day at Humphreysville, half a day at Nyumphs, and once a fortnight at Derby Neck. It was a revival year at the Neck and on Great Hill. The two brothers, Samuel and David Durand, and their wives, were added to the little church in the little red school-house which stood a lttle north of where the Great Hill church now stands. Samuel was a good singer. In 1815, Rev. Elijah Hebard and Rev. Benoni English were the preachers on this circuit—but Mr. English soon located at Humphreysville and went into business. This year Walter French, a resident of Humphreysville, received license to exhort, and afterwards a license to preach, and was very useful here and in other parts of the circuit. He had a good memory, a ready utterance, and often spoke with great power and success. He died in 1865, aged over eighty years.

When Rev. Nathan Bangs was presiding elder, in 1816, he came and preached in the Bell school-house, and made his home with Stiles Johnson, on the Skokorat road, opposite Thomas Gilyard's place. After some cautions from careful brother Johnson against doctrinal preaching, the elder went down in the evening and preached a free salvation to a crowded house, giving Calvinism its portion in due season, as was the custom, and such was the power of his words on the congregation, that when the preacher, in closing, inquired

"Who will have this salvation? Let those who will seek it arise," the whole congregation stood up with one accord and a revival ensued. In 1817 the society numbered fifty-six members.

The legislature of the state authorized the division of the shares of its surplus war tax of 1812 among the religious denominations of the state; but the Methodists refused their portion of the money. At a quarterly conference held at East Village, January 9, 1818, Rev. O. Sykes was appointed to communicate with the trustees of the state on the subject, but no person had been authorized to receive rejected funds. The afflicted brother returned, still burdened with unwelcome charity. At the quarterly conference of August in the same year, held at Humphreysville, Rev. Aaron Pierce and two others were appointed a committee to write to the treasurer of the state, and if he could not receive the Methodist portion of the money, to draw up a petition in behalf of this circuit, to the General Assembly, for liberty to return their proportion of said money. Liberty was granted and the funds returned to the state. The rising church, though struggling with crushing difficulties, would not sacrifice her honest independence of the state. The fathers were fully committed to the voluntary principle for the support of the Gospel.

An extensive revival commenced at a watch meeting in the old meeting-house, on New Year's eve of 1818. In this year the Congregational Society conveyed the "meeting-house" to the Methodist Society. (See page 66.) Jesse and Stiles Johnson, sons of Isaac Johnson, who died in 1813, with their wives and many of their relations had joined the Methodist society. Jesse Johnson was afterwards a local preacher, and a close student of the Bible, but became insane, and after a long confinement died in 1829. The two brothers were buried in the cemetery in the rear of the church. Stiles, who died Oct. 4, 1818, by his will gave the land on which the church stands to the Methodist society, and also $334 in money. (See page 68.) The old meeting-house was soon after made a two-story building, but no paint was used inside or outside. In 1819 the members of the church constituted three classes. The leaders were Robert Lee, Timothy Hitchcock and Orrin Peck, the latter class being in Woodbridge. The members of the class of Timothy Hitchcock were, Cynthia Johnson, widow of Stiles Johnson, Thomas and Lois Gilyard, Jared and Sally B. Bassett, (daughter of Stiles Johnson,) Timothy and Urania Hitchcock, Anna Davis, widow of Reuben Davis, Bezaleel and Martha Peck, Alva Davis, and his wife Polly, daughter of Capt. Daniel Holbrook, Hepzibah Johnson, daughter of Jesse Johnson, and Sheldon Hitchcock, son of Timothy Hitchcock. The circuit preachers from 1816 to 1820 were Rev. Nathan Emory, Rev. Arnold Scholefield, Rev. Reuben Harris, Rev. Ezekiel Canfield, Rev. Samuel Bushnell, Rev. Aaron Pierce, Rev. Beardsley Northrop, Rev. David Miller and Rev. Bela Smith. The circuits were large, and two preachers were usually appointed to each circuit each year, to alternate at the different stations.

HISTORY OF SEYMOUR. 177

The quarterly meetings of those times were largely attended and exceedingly interesting, the people going from all parts of the circuit on Saturday, and putting up with the people in the vicinity of the place where the meetings were to be held, so as to be ready for the services of the Sabbath. In the afternoon they heard a sermon, after which came the quarterly conference, composed of all the stewards, class leaders, exhorters and preachers on the circuit. The presiding elders were present on such occasions and drew large congregations, the people usually expecting to hear strong doctrinal sermons, which were usually very effective. At one of these meetings on Great Hill, in 1820, Rev. E. Washburn, presiding elder, fifteen persons were converted in one afternoon.

From 1821 to 1830, the membership on the circuit was much increased as the fruit of revival in different places. The preachers were Rev. James Colman, Rev. Laban Clark, Rev. E. Barnett, Rev. John Nixon, Rev. Eli Denniston, Rev. William F. Pease, Rev. Julius Field, Rev. Samuel D. Ferguson, Rev. Valentine Buck, Rev. John Luckey, Rev. Nathaniel Kellogg, Rev. Reuben Harris, Rev. John Lovejoy and Rev. Laban C. Cheney. The presiding elders were Rev. Samuel Merwin, Rev. Samuel Luckey, Rev. D. Ostrander and Rev. Laban Clark.

In 1828 this part of the circuit was separated and called Humphreysville and Hamden. Samuel R. Hickox, a local preacher from Southbury, moved into Humphreysville in 1828, and had charge of a grist mill on the falls, keeping boarders from the cotton mill. He was a good preacher and was a great help to the church in this place. In 1829 Thomas Ellis, a Welshman and a spinner in the cotton mill, was converted and joined the church here, of which his wife was already a member. He had been a wild young man and a great singer. It was said that he could sing all night without repeating a song. But in two years after his conversion he had forgotten them all. He was an important addition to the church on account of his musical ability.

In 1831 Daniel Smith was appointed to the circuit, and was assisted by William Bates, a local preacher residing in Humphreysville. In that year a camp meeting was held in a woods west of where the Catholic church of Birmingham now stands, and continued eight days. On the Sabbath ten thousand people were supposed to be present, and the fruit of the meeting was about one hundred converts. Rev. Sylvester Smith, afterwards long identified with the interests of the church, was present during the whole of that remarkable meeting. In this year the churches in South Britain and Middlebury were built, and the foundation of one at Waterbury laid, and the building of a parsonage in Humphreysville commenced. Three hundred dollars worth of books were sold on the circuit; a large amount of missionary money raised, and the preachers' salaries paid in full. In April, 1832, Sylvester Smith, a local preacher from Hotchkisstown, now Westville, where he was first licensed in March, 1830, moved into this village. Rev. Daniel Smith was continued on the circuit, and Rev. Robert Travis was preacher in charge. The parsonage was not quite ready for Mr. T., but in a few days after his arrival in town he moved into it. It was built by the two brothers Lane, from Monroe. After this time the church was an ecclesiastical society under the statute and known as the Methodist society of Humphreysville.

In 1833, Rev. Thomas Bainbridge and Rev. Chester W. Turner were the preachers on the circuit—Mr. B. occupying the parsonage. Turner was a single man, who afterwards married the sister of Rev. J. D. Smith, of the Episcopal church. Mr. B. was a good preacher and a sweet singer. The next year Rev. Humphrey Humphries and Rev. John Crawford were the preachers, Mr. H. moving into the parsonage. Rev. Josiah Bowen had charge of the circuit in 1834-5. In the middle of 1836 he moved out of the parsonage into a house at Derby Neck, where he remained until he died not long since. On the first of October, 1836, Rev. Sylvester Smith moved into the parsonage and occupied it four years at an annual rent of fifty dollars. Rev. David Miller was preacher in charge two years, residing at Great Hill, and closing his term of service in May, 1839. Rev. Owen Sykes had been an assistant preacher for several years. Thomas Ellis received license to preach in 1833, and did good service on the circuit until 1838, when he joined the conference and became a successful itinerant. He died in triumph, in May, 1873, aged sixty-eight.

Since 1839 Birmingham was a station separate from us, so it was with Waterbury. Middlebury and South Britain sustained a pastor ; so that only Humphreysville, Great Hill, Pleasant Vale and Pinesbridge remained in the Derby circuit.

In 1840 and 1841 Rev. Thomas Sparks was the preacher in charge, residing at South Britain, and Rev. Ezra Jagger in 1842 and 1843, residing at Great Hill and assisted in his second year by Rev. M. Blydenburgh. L. Atwater, a student at Yale, was also a very effective assistant.

On Saturday, March 19, 1842, a quarterly meeting commenced at Southford. Presiding Elder Carpenter being absent, Sylvester Smith preached. Sunday morning was very pleasant, and after love feast, it was found impossible for more than half the people to get into the chapel. Sparks occupied the pulpit, and Smith went below and took his stand in the school-room and preached with half his congregation outdoors. It was a memorable time. These were prosperous years for the church at Humphreysville, after a period of depression. Rev. Moses Blydenburgh was pastor in charge in 1844, and lived on Great Hill. Mr. B. died in 1848, aged 31 years, leaving a wife, and one son, now a lawyer in New Haven. The next two years Rev. George L. Fuller had charge of the circuit, residing on Great Hill. Three of his children were buried there. In the fall of 1846 a subscription was opened for a new church edifice, and Sylvester Smith led with the sum of six hundred dollars. The burning of the paper mill of which he was half owner, involving a heavy loss, did not abate his zeal; for, during the year he increased his subscription to eight hundred dollars. One brother who did not at first set down his name, gave one hundred dollars; another man changed from twenty to one hundred dollars, and a good woman changed her subscription from ten to eighty dollars.

Rev. Charles Stearns moved into the parsonage in May, 1847, and remained two years in charge of this circuit. He found the society commencing the new church. The old meeting-house was sold for one hundred dollars, and torn down, and the new one built in the same place. Jared Bassett, assisted by Isaac Bassett, built the stone work, and all labored to the extent of their ability, giving what they could in money and then turning out and laboring with a zeal and ardor worthy of the cause. The corner stone was laid on Saturday, June 19, 1847. Rev. E. W. Smith, of Birmingham, was the speaker. Sylvester Smith deposited the case under the stone after announcing its contents. Rev. Charles Stearns, pastor, conducted the services, and was assisted by Rev. Wm. B. Curtiss, of the Congregational church. Amos Hine, of Woodbridge, was the contractor for the building, except the stonework. (See p. 74.) The bell, from Meneely's foundry in Troy, was raised to its place in November. Its weight was eleven hundred and fifty pounds. In this year a board of trustees was first appointed by the pastor in charge, and vacancies were afterwards filled by the official board.

The church was dedicated on Tuesday, January 18, 1848, by Bishop Janes, who preached from Ezra vi, 16. In the evening he preached again. The collections amounted to $292.83. The whole cost of the house, bell, and furniture, was $5,800, and of this the society owed $800. On the day of dedication, the slips rented for $580, and the average amount of annual rents in the first ten years was about $550.

All the elm trees near the church were obtained and set within a year after the dedication, under the direction of Rev. Sylvester Smith, by his son William E. Smith, who was killed in the war, Sept. 1, 1864. The first two in front nearest the house of Mr. Tucker, were set on the day of the presidential election in 1848.

In May, 1849, Rev. Seneca Howland was in charge of what in the next year was set off from Derby as the town of Seymour. He remained two years, and some additions were made to the church. Twenty-three came forword as seekers at his first watch meeting. Rev. David Osborn was pastor of Seymour and Ansonia one year, from April 1851 to April 1852, and it was a prosperous year in both places; over one hundred conversions reported. The second year the Great Hill church was in a separate charge. His successor for two years was Rufus K. Reynolds, an energetic and useful man.

Rev. William T. Hill was the pastor in 1855-6 for the two churches—Seymour and Great Hill. In his first year, (this being his first appointment,) there were sixty-seven conversions and fifty additions to the church.

Fifteen adults were baptized at one time. Twenty-four of the converts were from the Sunday school.

Rev. Thomas Stevenson was pastor in 1857-8. He was a good and successful preacher. Rev. L. P. Perry was the pastor in 1859-60, confining his labors to this village, and was a faithful and useful minister. Albert Booth was the pastor in the conference year commencing in April, 1861.

At the Conference of 1862 George Lansing Taylor was appointed to Seymour, this being his first itinerant work. In his first year the missionary collection was increased from $28 to over $100. In his second year the Society raised $1,200 dollars towards paying off the church debt, and there were a number of conversions. He was an earnest and fearless defender of the "stars and stripes," and in those troublous days spoke boldly for "the Union, one and inseparable."

In the summer of 1864, in the pastorate of Rev. A. B. Pulling, a festival was held in a car shop on the flat, and later in the season, another in the Messrs. Day's new brick factory above the paper mill. The net proceeds of the two were $800, and the church was out of debt. Mr. P. remained until the spring of 1866, when Sylvester Smith was appointed to the charge for one year, and the church edifice was painted outside. It being the centennial year of American Methodism, Mr. Smith preached eight sermons on the subject. Nineteen persons who had on the previous year joined on probation were received into full membership. Rev. Joseph Pullman was pastor in 1867-8, and was eminently successful, receiving sixty-five probationers at one time near the close of the first year. Rev. Bennett T. Abbott was pastor in 1869-70.

Rev. Joseph Smith was pastor the next three years, 1871-3, and proved himself an able minister of the New Testament. Previous to 1864 two years was the limit of the pastoral term in the M. E. Church. In 1864 the General Conference extended the limit to three years. Rev. Joseph Smith was the first pastor who preached in the Seymour M. E. Church three consecutive years, and when his time expired by limitation, he was generally beloved and esteemed by the members of the society for which he had labored faithfully, earnestly and impartially. In former years Mr. Smith, as a local preacher, residing in Waterbury, had done much good service here in connection with our pastors. E. H. Frisbie and James Wiswel, local preachers in New Haven, also rendered much good service. Sylvester Smith, during his forty years residence here was a most active laborer and liberal giver in the church.

Rev. William R. Webster officiated as pastor of the church from April, 1874, to April, 1875, laboring with much zeal wherever there seemed to be a prospect of doing good. The lot east of the church was purchased of Edwin Smith for $500 in 1870, with the intention of building a parsonage thereon as soon as should seem practicable. Mrs. M. A. Sackett canvassed the society for funds to pay for it, and by her zealous perseverance succeeded in collecting the larger portion of the amount. The balance was paid subsequently from funds received from the legacy of Mrs. Kirtland. In the spring of 1875 the subject of building a parsonage adjoining the church was agitated and finally at an official meeting, consisting of the stewards, class-leaders, trustees and superintendent, held at the parsonage, April 26th, 1875, the pastor presiding, it was voted to offer the "Kirtland Place" and the old parsonage for sale, preparatory to building a new parsonage. An offer being received the board of trustees met and appointed Warren French an agent to sell the old parsonage for $2,000, and Lugrand Sharpe, Warren French and W. C. Sharpe were appointed a building committee. Plans and estimates were obtained and the contract was awarded to Thomas Sharpe for $2,300. A large and commodious parsonage was erected, the total cost for the building, fence, well, &c., being $2,630, of which $2,000 was met by the sale of the old parsonage. The parsonage, with the handsome shade trees around it, is said to be the pleasantest in the Naugatuck valley.

In April, 1875, Rev. E. H. Dutcher was sent by the conference for the ensuing year. The dissensions which seemed at the time of his coming to be ended, rapidly revived during his pastorate, and had a disastrous effect upon the interests of the society. Under his influence the annual meetings of the society, which had for so many years been held under the sanction of the laws of the commonwealth, were discontinued, and a ruling was made by him and sustained by the presiding elder that there was under the law of the church no such thing as a Methodist society, and that the separate organizations could only be known as Methodist churches. During his pastorate the amount contributed by the membership for the missionary cause dwindled to $13, including $3 interest on the Gilyard legacy. During the eight years previous, when Lugrand Sharpe was collector, the amounts contributed were —year commencing in April of 1867, $65.75; 1868, $107.33; 1869, $91.95; 1870, $158.73; 1871, $64.50; 1872, $68.22; 1873, $67.00; 1874, $61.00; as shown by the published minutes of the New York East Conference.

In April, 1876, the conference appointed Rev. Charles A. Tibbals, for the ensuing conference year. In December he very abruptly resigned to join the Protestant Episcopal communion. Rev. A. B. Pulling, who was pastor of the society in 1864-5, was appointed by the presiding elder to fill the vacancy until the next session of the conference, and—notwithstanding his failing health—labored earnestly and efficiently for the good of the society.

The old pulpit was removed in the spring of 1876 at the request of Mr. Tibbals, and in February, 1877, an elegant black walnut pulpit was presented to the society by H. B. Beecher, Esq. It was first occupied Feb, 4th by Rev. Aaron Pierce of East Village, who was the pastor of the church in 1848, and his aged form and hoary locks, white with the frosts of eighty-nine winters, as he preached from 2 Tim., 4-7, constituted an occasion long to be remembered.

In the spring of 1877 Rev. J. Vinton became pastor of the church. In the following fall, in connection with an effort to advance the temperance cause, a revival commenced. Arthur J. Smith, the first convert, son of Rev. Joseph Smith, had long been a leader among the young people, and was then instrumental in leading many of his old associates to the cross. Feeling called to the ministry he left the RECORD office, where he had been employed, to attend the Collegiate Institute at Hackettstown, N. J., preparatory to entering college. This revival resulted in the conversion of about thirty persons. During the following winter there were several conversions at Great Hill, under the labors of Rev. J. Vinton.

The year 1868 was a notable one in the history of the church. It was decided to renovate the church, and on Sunday morning, June 27th, an appeal was made for funds for the work, and $225 was quickly pledged. The work was soon commenced and in all about $900 was raised and laid out in frescoing the audience room, repairing and refurnishing the lecture and class rooms, repainting the whole interior, putting on a new roof, &c. At a festival held adjoining the church July 4th $103 was raised, and $283 was subscribed at the re-opening Aug. 11th, and the whole expense of the improvements was soon paid. There were several conversions during the year. In the two years—April, 1867, to April, 1869, about fifty united with the church on probation, of whom nearly forty have been received into full membership.

The finances of the church, under the efficient direction of the pastor, have been well kept up and notwithstanding the extensive outlay there has been no increase of debt. The contributions of the church for regular expenses, repairs, &c., from April, 1878, to April, 1879, were over $2,000, with a total membership at the close of the year of one hundred and sixty.

The whole church property, at Seymour and Great Hill, is estimated at $13,000, with a debt of only $662, on the parsonage.

TRUSTEES.

Oct. 31, 1818, Stiles Johnson, Bezaleel Peck, Robert Lees, Thomas Gilyard and Timothy Hitchcock.

Wales French was elected a trustee April 2nd, 1840.

Sylvester Smith was elected April 10th, 1843.

Jan. 26th, 1846, Rev. George L. Fuller appointed trustees as follows:— Thomas Gilyard, Jared Bassett, Merritt Osborn, Samuel R. Hickox, Sylvester Smith, Warren French, Burritt Hitchcock, William B. Watson and Wilson Wyant. Apr. 3, 1846, Lyman Hartson vice Thomas Gilyard, resigned. Sheldon Miles vice Wilson Wyant, resigned.

1861, Jared Bassett, Sylvester Smith, Warren French, Sheldon Miles, Henry W. Benedict, Smith Botsford and William N. Storrs.

Sept., 1866, elected for one year, Albert W. Lounsbury, Sheldon Miles and Willis Umberfield. For two years, Jared Bassett, Smith Botsford and

HISTORY OF SEYMOUR. 183

Wilson E. Hendryx. For three years, Sylvester Smith, William N. Storrs and Warren French.

Since 1866 three trustees have been elected by ballot annually in September, by the adult male members of the church.

1867, Sheldon Miles, Willis Umberfield, W. W. Dibble.
1868, Smith Botsford, A. W. Lounsbury, C. C. Nugent.
1869, Sylvester Smith, Warren French, W. N. Storrs.
1870, Sheldon Miles, S. H. Rankin, W. W. Dibble.
1871, W. C. Sharpe, Lyman Botsford, T. S. Ladd.
1872, H. B. Beecher, Warren French, W. N. Storrs.
1873, Lugrand Sharpe, A. W. Lounsbury, William Gilyard.
  Edwin Smith, elected to fill vacancy vice Lyman Botsford, resigned.
1874, W. C. Sharpe, William B. Johnson, James K. Adams.
  T. S. Ladd, elected to fill vacancy vice William Gilyard, resigned.
1875, H. B. Beecher, W. N. Storrs, Sheldon Miles.
1876, W. W. Dibble, H. C. Rogers, D. H. Munson.
1877, W. C. Sharpe, James K. Adams, Joseph Hitchcock.
1878, H. B. Beecher, W. N. Storrs, Sheldon Miles.
  Warren French, elected to fill vacancy vice H. C. Rogers, removed.

THE SUNDAY SCHOOL.

George Kirtland came to Seymour in 1825, and in 1826 or 1827 he started a Sunday school with five children of his own, the number increasing the first year to 27. He tried to establish a library for the Sunday school, both himself and a Mr. Fisher contributing books and money. He kept up the school six or seven years, when it was discontinued for a time.

The Superintendents since the re-organization of the school, so far as I have been able to learn, are:

1841-2, Samuel R. Hickox.
1843-8, Lugrand Sharp.
1852, John Adams.
1853, Frederick Durand.
1854, William A. Hughes.
1855, William Mallory.
1856-7, Albert W. Lounsbury.
1858, William Mallory.
1859, Warren French.
1860-1, William N. Storrs.
1862-5, Henry W. Benedict.
  In 1862 there were 777 volumes in the library. In 1865, 851 volumes.

1866-7, William N. Storrs.
1868, Sheldon Miles.
1869, William C. Sharpe.
1870-1, William N. Storrs.
1872, William W. Dibble.
1873, Samuel Butler.
1874, Charles N. Blanchard.
1875, Samuel Butler.
1876, Edward N. Botsford.
1877, Henry C. Rogers.
1878, Samuel Butler.
1879, George E. Stockwell.

REV. JOHN BOWER,

FIRST MINISTER AT DERBY.

The first clergyman of Derby was Rev. John Bower, who was settled there in 1672 and died in 1688. He was a graduate of Harvard College, class of 1649. He was a son of George Bower, or Bowers, found in Scituate, Mass. in 1637, in Plymouth in 1639, and who removed to Cambridge. George lived in Cambridge on the east side of North Avenue, not far from the railroad bridge. There his wife Barbara died, 25th March, 1644. He m. 2nd Elizabeth Worthington, and had Jerathmeel, b. 1650. George Bowers had some trouble with his son Benamuel, for in May, 1652, he was complained of for rending a deed with several articles between them. Yet in 1656 he conveyed twenty acres in Charleston next Cambridge line to Benamuel. He voted several years but at the same court in 1652 was fined for it, not being a sworn freeman. Both offences were complained of by Thomas Danforth, who apparently made it warm for him. He died late in 1656, his will of 8th Nov. being proved 30th Dec. of that year, and his widow married 25th June, 1657, Henry Boutell or Boutwell. He had two daughters—Patience, m. Humphrey Bradstreet, and Silence; and by his first wife two sons, undoubtedly born in England. Benamuel of Cambridge, who suffered imprisonment, whipping and fines as a quaker, and Rev. John, graduated at Harvard College in 1649. John was a school master in Plymouth, perhaps (says Savage) the earliest in the business.

New Haven was early ambitious to have a classical school, which however was maintained with difficulty, so few wished to study "Latten."

"8th Nov., 1652, the Governor informed the Court that the cause of calling this meeting was about a school master to let them know what he hath done in it; he hath written a letter to one Mr. Bower, who is school master at Plymouth and desireth to come into these parts to live."

Dec. 20th, 1652, the Governor had received a letter from Mr. Bower, who was willing to come but could not until spring because he was engaged in Plymouth until April and he wished to know what the town expected. The town declared he might "for the worke and the paye" have the terms Mr. Hanford had. The terms with Hanford in 1651 were, he was "to have "£29 a yeare and the towne to pay for his chamber and dyet, (which they "have agreed with Mr. Atwater for, for 5s per week.) That his paye bee "goods and some of it such as wherewith he may buy bookes and defraye "charges in his travel. That he have libertie once a yeare to goe see his "friends which was propounded to be in harvest time. That if he be called "away (not to the same worke) but some other employment which may be "for the honor of Christ he may have libertie, and for this he will teach the "children of this towne, (having the benefit of strangers to himself) after "they are entered and can reade in ye Testament to perfect them in English "and teache them their latin tongue as they are capable and to wright."

The arrival of Mr. Bower is noticed 21st June, 1653, and he boarded with Thomas Kimberly. His predecessor had trouble with scholars not far enough advanced for his school, and May 1st, 1654, a complaint was made that Mr. Bower was so employed in teaching children their letters that the "Lattin" suffered, so two townsmen were deputed to send such children home. 3rd April, 1660, Mr. Bower informed the town that there were in this high school, only eighteen scholars, and sometimes but six or eight present, and he wanted to know "whether they would have a schoole or no schoole." This year closed his seven years service. We hear of him next in Guilford, where in 1660, says Smith, he purchased an estate and supplied the pulpit for three or four years until Mr. Joseph Elliot was settled, which was in 1664. In another place Mr. Smith says John Cotton and Mr. Bower jointly supplied the pulpit. He was not as popular as Mr. Elliot after him.

In 1666 on the removal of a part of the planters of Branford to New Jersey, with their pastor, Mr. Pierson, he engaged Mr. Bower to preach in his place, and himself paid him to the end of that year. The people gave a formal call to him Jan. 6th, 1667, to become their pastor, voting to allow him for the next year forty pounds and a days work from every planter. They renewed it year by year adding to the salary.

In May, 1671, he was invited to settle there and accepted Dec. 3rd of that year but left in 1672. He had previously meditated removing to Derby, as 18th April, 1671, Derby granted him twelve acres for a home. 18th Nov., 1673, the planters there voted to build him a house, and it is recorded next that the first year Mr. Bower is willing to take what the inhabitants would voluntarily give, as they are at great expense in building.

In 1681 and again in 1682 they voted him fifty pounds for a years salary. Mr. Bower's will is recorded in Derby records as well as at New Haven. It is dated Jan. 8th, 1684, (1685).* It is very short, speaking of him as being

---

*A copy of Mr. Bower's will—from the Town Records of Derby—no date to the record.

The last will and testament of Mr. John Bower of Derby, being very weak of body but of perfect understanding and memory, do leave these lines as my last will and testament.

Impri. My will is yt after my decease, my dearly beloved wife, Bridget Bower, shall have ye disposal of my whole estate, to dispose of it amongst our children, as she shall see cause, he desiaring yt ye birthright may be remembered if he cary it well to his honored mother, as witness my hand, this eight day of jenuary, one thousand, six hundred eighty four,

ABELL GUN.
JOE FRISBIE.
John Bower.

The will no doubt was written by another, while Mr. Bower was sick, and signed by him, and the bad spelling may be due to the scribe or recorder.

HISTORY OF SEYMOUR. 187

very weak in body and giving his wife Bridget the full disposal of his estate, care of the children, &c., desiring y^t ye birthright, (ie. double portion) may be remembered if he carry it well to his honored mother." He died 14th June, 1687. His widow continued to reside in Derby, where she died 19th May, 1720. Her house is mentioned in 1701, the pound being "as you go to Mrs. Bower's, her house."

In 1676 he joined with the Rev. Zachariah Walker of Woodbury in a letter urging defence of Woodbury and Derby "as would be the first attacked."

He married at New Haven, Bridget Thompson, daughter of Anthony Thompson of New Haven. Mr. and Mrs. Bower's had at least the following children, perhaps more.

Ruth, bapt. 20th Dec., 1657, m. 2nd Dec., 1674, John Frisbie of Branford, and had children—John, 23rd May, 1676; Edward, 24th Jan., 1678; Rebecca, 14th Nov., 1679; Hannah, 18th Jan., 1681; Samuel, 10th Feb., 1683; Ruth, 6th Dec., 1685, d. 26th May, 1688; Joseph, 15th Aug., 1688. As widow and administratrix of her husband, she deeds 20th Jan., 1700, to her son Samuel, with assent of her son John. Mr. Savage says she m. 2nd, William Hoadly.

Mary, m. 1682, Samuel Nichols.

Samuel, 5th Nov., 1665.

John, born at Guilford, 3rd Dec., 1667.

Ann, m. 2nd Sept., 1703, Francis French of Derby.

Nathaniel. The latter does not appear in Savage's Dictionary, but 29th Dec., 1707, Mrs. Bridget Bower deeds to "my beloved son Nathaniel Bower of Greenwitch, in the county of Fairfield." He removed to East New Jersey and in the grant for Derby appear the minor heirs of Nathaniel Bower in East New Jersey, deceased. He was Rev. Nathaniel, minister of the first church in Greenwich in 1700. He succeeded Mr. Wakeman at Newark, New Jersey, and was succeeded shortly after Aug., 1716, by Mr. Whittlesey in Newark. He is beyond all question the Rev. Mr. Bower of Rye—in 1696, and remaining there until 1700, when he was "settled" at Greenwich. The period of his stay at Rye was while the people of Rye "revolted" from New York to Connecticut, which revolt apparently arose in considerable degree at least, from religious feeling. In 1700 the town ordered his salary to be paid "in specie as followeth, wheat at five shillings per bushel, and all other provisions pay equivalent." His salary was fifty pounds.

SAMUEL, born in 1665, m. 1st, in 1687, Ruth Wooster of Derby, daughter of Edward Wooster from Milford. He m. 2nd, 4th Nov., 1691, Lydia French, daughter of Francis and sister of the husband of Ann Bower. She was born 28th Sept., 1670. He was several times constable, (then an office of high honor), and was alive as late as 1708. He had children at least

Lydia, born Aug. 2nd, 1692.

Rebeckah, born March 9th, 1694, died Dec. 7th, 1712.

Kezziah, born March 2nd, 169⅜.
Miriam, born April 5th, 1703, m. Oct. 7th, 1724, Ephraim Washbon.
Samuel, born Dec. 2nd, 17—(torn off) who m. a wife Sarah, and had a daughter born in Derby, Jan. 8th, 1729.

JOHN, born in 1667, appears in Derby in 1693, and continued there, holding various places of trust. He was surveyor in 1705, collector in 1706, deputy to the legislature in May, 1708, dying in September of the same year and styled Mr. He is identified beyond question by a deed from his mother in 1707. It is generally said that he was minister for a while in Rye. This is a mistake, originating with Mather in his Magnalia, who put at Rye in 1696, Mr. Bower, H. C. (Harvard College). This was John the first, but out of date. Trumbull in his history of Conn. says *John* Bower removed from Derby and settled at Rye about 1688. Mr. Savage makes it the Sen. John—but it appears plainly in Mr. Baird's History of Rye, p. 281, that the only Bower of Rye was Nathaniel. Mr. Baird adds he knows nothing of Nathaniel's antecedents which we here set forth.

To help the confusion that has existed as to the Johns—there was in Greenwich a John Bower, neither of these as in Vol. IV of Fairfield Probate Records is his will 1693, who gives to his daughter-in-law Judah Renolds and sister Hester Bukley ? John of Greenwich was 43 years old in 1681. There was also in 1672 a Mr. John of Oxford, Mass., who had a son in South Middletown, Conn. I do not know what children this second John of Derby had, but a third Mr. John m. Nov. 22nd, 1732, Sarah Riggs, died 26th Jan., 173⅞, and April 18th, 1739 his widow married Rev. Mr. Daniel Humphreys. They had at least a daughter, Sarah, born Aug. 18th, 1736.

Rev. Daniel Humphreys and his wife Sarah above named were parents of General David Humphreys, born 1752 or 1753—from whom Seymour was first named Humphreysville.

Anthony Thompson of New Haven, (the father of Bridget, wife of John Bower), with his wife, two children and brothers John and William embarked at London in 1637, on board the Hector with Gov. Eaton, Rev. Mr. Davenport and others of the New Haven colony, arriving at Boston June 26th, 1637. They were among the first settlers at New Haven, where he signed the compact, June 4th, 1639.

Anthony died March 23rd, 1647, making a nuncupative will in the presence of Rev. Davenport and Robert Newman, which was proved May 27th, 1650. He left fifteen pounds to Bridget, (daughter of his first wife), to be paid her at the age of eighteen years, provided she disposed of herself in marriage with the consent and approbation of her mother and the elders of the church then being. As she married a clergyman and the classical school teacher of New Haven, it is to be hoped the widow and elders were not averse to the match.

Anthony had children, John and Anthony, when he came. Bridget was born here. He married 2nd, Catherine, and had two daughters by her;

Hannah, who married a Staunton; and Lydia, who married Isaac Crittenden; and one son, Ebenezer, 15th Oct., 1648, who was born some months after the will and probably posthumous.

He remembered the daughters and the widow while she was his widow. She forfeited her share by marrying Nicholas Camp in 1652, but she was still loved by her step children, for Anthony gave his property to his brother John, sister Bridget, his three half sisters, children of "Goodwife Camp," and his "mother-in-law," ie. step-mother.

William, the brother of the first Anthony, died 24th April, 1683, leaving neither wife or children. He gave property to his nephews and neices, calling them cousins, and among them his "beloved cousin Bridget Bower."

The Thompsons might be presumptively from the neighborhood of many of the New Haven emigrants, to-wit: Kent, London and Hertfordshire, but Bridget's brother Ebenezer died in Guilford in 1676 and is called a Scotchman. Possibly the Thompsons had moved from Scotland to London. Anthony evidently was respected in New Haven, for it appears by the Colonial Records that he was very often chosen by the court as a committee man or an arbitrator in case of doubt or trouble.

In March, 1643, he was with several others at training fined "6d for foole (foul) guns." There were fined in all, thirty-eight men, so we judge the service was not much better than Falstaff's motley company. In 1647 it was charged that "the last night he watched he fell asleep." The only effect seems to have been that Richard Osborne who made the charge, was made to " pay 40s. fine to the town for his slanderous reproach layed on the watchmasters, which he was not able to make out or prove." Osborne had also to acknowledge his "sinne" in general court. In 1648, Anthony Thompson having deceased, another was chosen in his place as " collector for the colledge corne."

His nuncupative will, made May 27, 1650, was not allowed as a legal will, but it was ordered that the wife should administer upon the estate "according to the particulars in this writing contained," which would seem about as well as if it was a legal will. This left out poor Ebenezer as though he had no business to be born after his father died. Barnabas Baldwin, b. September, 1665, son of Richard, the "moderator," of Derby, who died intestate in July of the same year, was similarly punished.

PETITION FOR A CHURCH AT DERBY.

For the following petition to the general court at Hartford we are indebted to Hon. Charles J. Hoadley of Hartford. It is written and signed by Mr. Bower.

To the Hon^{r}able Gen^{ll} Court at Hartford we humbly crave leave to pr sent as followeth :

We may truly say as sometimes said good Nehemiah in somew^t a like case, that G^d hath put into o^r hearts & y^t for some space of time and desirous we are all now & y^t as one man to build the L^d o^r G^d an house & to end^{or} the enjoy^{mt} of a cch state according to ye order of the Gospell amongst o^{r}selves in this place where divine providence hath cast us, wch if the L^d shall grant unto us, we shall say wth the psalmist y^t our lives are fallen in pleasant places & y^t we have a goodly heritage, especially if y^t ye name of o^r little citty, (if it shall co'e to y^t) may be Jehovah Sham'ah the L^d is there.

The causes moving hereunto are

1 Gods com'and 1. Hagg 8. Go build the house wch relates to Christ's visible cch so termed : 1 Tim : 3, 15 : The house of G^d wch is ye cch of ye living God.

2 Christ's com'and : 6 Math : 33 : first seek the kingdo'e of G^d wch relates to a church State : the vissible cch of Christ on earth being ye kingdo'e of he a' or of G^d on earth 25 Math ; 1.

3 The great cont^{mt} G^d takes to breathe in ye counsi' of saints in a ch state & y^t above all other societies 87 ps 2 : 132 ps 13 so on : That is my rest etc.

4 The promise of G^{ds} presence w^{ch} & blessing upo' his cch : 20 Exo^d 24 : 87 ps 5. 6.

5 The practise of true beleving ones in primitive times to embody yms in a cch state though but few : of wch ye N. T. gives abundant proof

6 We desire to be under a cch watch, wch of all watches is the most strict 12 Heb 15. Looking diligently.

These & such like consideratio's have put us upo' our forementioned desires & in order to the further prosecution of ye same, we did in the 1st place make our addresses unto the throne of grace for guidance & to seek of G^d a right way for us and our little ones After this we sent unto the churches of Christ next adjacent & we have (as will appear by y^r letters) their consent and advice to up and bee doing in wch respect we may set up o^r Ebenezer & say hitherto ye L^d hath helped & set before us an open door And hereby we are the more embolned according to o^r boundin duty humbly to entreat (Hon^{rs} fathers of the Com'onwealth & nourishers of Gods Israel) that you wil please to cast a favorable aspect upo' these o^r desires & y^t o^r looking w^{t}ever of obliguity or human frailty yor honors may have espyed or may now in these, wch might justly impedim^t, and give us leave to build an house for o^r God and with y^{or} leave under God by his assistance we will say : as 15 Exod 2 he is o^r God and we will prepare hi' an habitatio' our fathers God & we will exalt hi'.

Hon^{ro} fathers, if G^d shall so dispose of yor hearts as to abbet, encourage, assist, protect us in this matt^r we wil yet againe set up o^r Ebenezer & say behold he hath set before us an open door & no man can shutt it. If it shall be object^d, we are poor : A. G^{ds} ordinances will enrich us, 6 Math : 33 : 3. Pro. 9, 10 but if you are few & small : we would answer in the Lords own words 4 Zach : 10, who hath dispised the day of small things. We read y^t instruments have been too maney, never too few for G^d to work by : & therefore through G^d we shall do valliantly.

Y^{or} hon^{rs} humble supplicants & faithful servants in the name of the rest of o^r brethe' & neighbo^{rs}

Derby: the 6th of May, 1678.

John Bower.

JOHN HULLS,
JOSEPH HAWKINS.

NOTE.—In the original m and other letters are frequently omitted and the omission is indicated by a wave line over the preceding letter. No such type being available, the omissions have here been indicated by apostrophes.

TROUBLE WITH INDIANS.

In the first volume of Cothren's History of Woodbury is an interesting letter from Rev. Mr. Walker of Woodbury, and Rev. Mr. Bower of Derby, relating to the removal of inhabitants from their places on account of the Indians and securing of these two plantations. The original is on file in Hartford in the handwriting of Mr. Walker and signed by both:

"To ye Honoured Gen^r Court convened at Hartford Octob^r 12th 1676 we whose names are hereunto subscribed do humbly propose as followeth :

That whereas ye providence of God hath so ordered that by means of late troubles brought upon ye country we the inhabitants of Woodbury and Derby have been necessitated to remove from o^r dwellings And a more favorable aspect of Providence at ye present inviting us to a return & ye necessity of many of o^r families in part inforcing it yet forasmuch as we cannot be assured but ye like danger may again arise we make bold before such o^r return to request this honoured Court to resolve us in one important inquiry viz in case the war wth ye indians should be again renewed what we may expect & trust to from ye authority of this Colony in order to o^r protection & safety ? We humbly request that o^r inquiry may neither be judged offensive nor concluded irrational till ye following grounds of it be considered :

1 First we cannot be insensible of o^r former experience viz : that in a time when danger threatened ye loudest & o^r two plantations afores^d were probably in greatest hazzard we were not only without any other help but o^r own for ye guarding of o^r ould place but o^r own also wch were indeed too few were taken from us time after time being pressed from ye sea-side towns when occasionally they came thither about necessary business whereby we had more proportionally to o^r members from o^r two plantations imployed in ye publick service then (we suppose) any other town of ye Colony ; And as by ye means we were forced to a removall so y^r in we had not the least benefit of any guard for ye safety of o^r persons or goods.

2 Neither can we be insensible how unable many persons will bee after a second remove to those plantations without ruine to ye families to return again to these older plantations ; partly by means of ye chargeableness of such removes & partly by means of what disapointments we have already met with.

3 Thirdly we desire ye mutuall obligation betwixt rulers & subjects may be considered viz: y^t as ye latter owe subjection respecting both ye persons & estates; so ye former are obliged to protect both according to ye best ability providing that they may lead a quiet & peceable life.

4 Let it be considered; that though formerly the country had cause enough because sin enough to beget an expectation of affliction yet y^r was little or no expectation y^t it should arise from such means before it did begin; the experience y^r fore of so unexpected an affliction affords (notwithstanding a present seeming cessation) ye more cause to expect ye like again sooner or later especially so little of refformation any where appearing: If therefore new-begun & remote plantations may not in such hazzards have any promise of just protection ye non-encouragin^t of such (as will endanger their desertion) so it will discourage any other persons from erecting any other for ye inlargement of ye Colony & whether y^t will not be much to ye disadvantage of ye Colony we leave upon inquiry.

5 The secureing of those two plantations of Woodberry & Darby will according to second causes be one of ye most considerable securities in a time of such dangers unto ye two western counties viz, of New Haven & Fairfield for it can hardly be expected y^t any strength of indians will adventure to set upon any lower plantation till they have attempted ours above & if they fail they will be ye more shy of pounding themselves by coming lower.

6 Though we cannot affirm yet we are not without some reason to suspect (& y^t fore only propound it as a conditionall argument) that ye charges expended in other colonies for garrisoning some of their out towns & fetching offe ye persons & goods of some others will come upon account in ye publick charges of ye war to be proportionably borne by ye three Colonies which if it be this Colony will not be so much ye shorter in ye bill of expenses because they have not done ye like & vertually fined to ye other Colonies because they had not as extensive & generall a care of y^r out plantations y^t were most exposed to danger as other Colonies had of theirs.

We humbly request yor consideration of ye premises & y^t yor worships will so far regard o^r infant plantations as to afford us some intimation of yor pleasure concerning this o^r inquiry.

Yours in all due observance

John Bower. in ye behalfe of Derby.

ZECHARIAH WALKER in ye behalfe of Woodberry.

CANFIELD.

THOMAS CAMPFIELD was in Milford as early as 1646, and in 1668 his name appears as proprietor of the home lot No. 55 in the original town plot. In 1669 he was recorded a freeman, and May 13, 1669, he was confirmed "Serjeant of the Train Band" of Milford. He was admitted into the church at Milford in 1657. In 1686 he was taxed on £154. His will is dated Feb. 23, 1687. In his inventory, dated Aug. 22, 1689, (£482,1s.,2d.,) are mentioned his three married daughters, Sarah, Phebe and Elizabeth, his daughter Abigail, and three unmarried daughters, and his two sons as executors. He married Phebe ———. Children: ²Thomas, b. Oct. 14, 1654; d. in 1712; ³Mary, b. Jan. 1, 165$\frac{6}{7}$; ⁴Elizabeth, b. Feb. 14, 16$\frac{59}{60}$; ⁵Hannah, b. Nov. 20, 1667; ⁶Mehitabel, b. July 2, 1671; ⁷Jeremiah, ⁸Abigail; ⁹Sarah, m. Josiah Platt, Dec. 2, 1669; and ¹⁰Phebe.

---

²THOMAS, Jr., son of Thomas and Phebe, (spelled his name Camfield), had children: ¹¹Rebecca, b. Jan. 23, 1682; ¹²Thomas; ¹³Israel, b. May 24, 1684; ¹⁴Abiel. Milford Records of Apr. 30, 1712, speak of land deeded by Israel and Abiel, sons of Thomas Camfield, late deceased, to Thomas, their older brother.

---

¹⁴ABIEL³, son of Thomas, (name spelled Canfield,) removed to Derby and m. Ruth Washborn Sept. 12, 1717. The name occasionally appears upon record as Abiram. Children:

¹⁵Joseph, b. Oct. 1, 1719, m. Sarah Stilson Sept. 3, 1746, d. July 14, 1784.
¹⁶John, b. Mar. 31, 1721.
¹⁷Abiel, b. May 30, 1723, d. Mar. 13, 1741.
¹⁸William, b. Oct. 29, 1725; m. Hannah Lumm, d. Sept. 30, 1761.
¹⁹Samuel, b. Dec. 26, 1727, m. Mary Bassett Apr. 3, 1754.
²⁰Josiah, b. Dec. 22, 1729, d. Jan. 1, 1737.
²¹David, b. Feb. 5, 1734, d. Nov. 23, 1741.
²²Dr. Josiah, b. Dec. 31, 1739, m. 1st, Jan., 1, 1767, Anne Nichols, who died Oct. 20, 1768; 2nd, Feb. 28, 1769, Mrs. Naomi Davis; child, ²³Abigail, b. Sept. 9, 1770.

194   HISTORY OF SEYMOUR.

Abiel[3] gave to his son Joseph a house and land on Bungay as appears by the deed which reads as follows:

Received to Record December 2d, 1754, and Recorded in page 295 of Derby 6 Book, by me.
CHARLES FRENCH, Clerk.

TO ALL PEOPLE TO WHOM THESE PRESENTS SHALL COME GREETINGS

Know ye that I Abial Canfield of ye Town of Derby in ye County of New Haven in his Majesties Collony of Connecticut in New-England Do for ye Parential love good will and affections that I have and do bear to wards my Son Joseph Canfield of s^d Derby with other good Causes and considerations me hereunto moveing: Do by these presents Give: Grant. Bargain, Alien: make Over convey and Confirm unto to him ye s^d Joseph Canfield and to his heirs and assigs for ever one certain percell of Land Scituate within ye Town Ship of Derby above s^d. Lying and being within that tract of Land called Camps Mortgage: Containing by Estimation Thirty Acres be it more or less Bounded East and Westerly on High ways: Northerly or ye Land of m^r John Brinsmaid Southerly on ye Land of Sar^{nt} Jonah Smith together with one Dwelling H^{o}use and orchards thereon Standing: Withall ye previlidges and Appurtenances there unto belonging to Have And to Hold all ye above Granted and Bargained premises withall ye privilidges and Appurtenanc^{es} thereof unto him ye s^d Joseph Canfield and to his heirs and assigns for Ever: to his and their own proper use & benifit as a good Indefeasiable Estate in Fee Simple: Without any manner of trouble or Molestation Given by me ye s^d Abial Canfield or any other person or persons in Name or Steed In confirmation of ye premises I ye s^d Abiall Canfield have hereunto Set my hand and Seal this twenty fourth Day of June in ye Twenty first year of ye Reign of our soverign Lord George ye Second of Great Brittian King &c A,: D. 1747.

ABIEL CANFIELD

Signed Sealed and Delivered) EBENEZER KEENEY
In presence of   ) ABIGAIL RIGGS juner

Derby in ye County of New Haven on ye Day and Date above written then and there Mr Abill Canfield personly appeared and Acknoledged ye Above written Instrument with ye signing and Sealing ye Same to be his own free act and Deed before me   SAM^{ll} RIGGS Justice of Peace

Abiel[3] died in 1772 and his will was proved at New Haven in June of that year, John Canfield, executor. In it he mentions his grandson Samuel, son of Dr. Samuel of Derby, deceased, also his grandson Abel, son of William. Ruth d. Sept. 24, 1784, aged 87 years.

---

[15]JOSEPH[4], oldest son of Abiel and Ruth, m. Sept. 3, 1746, Sarah, daughter of Moses Stilson, b. Apr. 23, 1726, d. Jan. 25, 1793. Children:

[24]Ruth, b. Feb. 7, 1748, d. Oct. 31, 1749.
[25]Ruth, b. Feb. 20, 1750.
[26]Anne, b. Oct. 17, 1751.
[27]Abiel, b. Apr. 6, 1753, m. Mary Barlow, d. Dec. 6, 1812.
[28]Sarah, b. Mar. 19, 1755.
[29]Charity, b. Feb. 1, 1758, d. Feb. 2, 1758.
[30]Abraham, b. June 20, 1759, m. Oct. 6, 1784, Mabel, dau. of Isaac and Lois Johnson, b. Nov. 27, 1766, and had children;
31, Ethelinda, b. Feb. 12, 1786, (32) Urania, b. Mar. 6, 1788.
[33]Daniel, b. Mar. 21, 1761, m. Anna Hurd, d. Dec. 25, 1818.

GENEALOGY. 195

[27]ABIEL[5], oldest son of Joseph and Sarah Canfield, m. Mary Barlow of Stratford Dec. 23, 1779. See page 126. Children:

[34]Abiel, m. Eunice, daughter of Capt. Bradford Steele, removed to Ohio.
[35]Samuel, b. 1797, m. Mary Allen, d. Apr. 17, 1879.
[36]Clark, [37]Lewis.
[38]Betsey, m. Lewis Broadwell, d. in 1821.
[39]Lockwood, b. 1782, d. Feb. 18, 1803.

Abiel Canfield made many purchases of land on the west side of the Naugatuck and south of Little river, among which were the following, which may help to give an idea of the "ancient landmarks":

May 10, 1784, from Theophilus Miles, a piece of land "lying at a place called Camp's mortgage, containing twenty rods of land, begining at the northeast corner of said peace of land, neare to a well in the highway, and then runing northwesterly by the highway ten rods to a heap of stones, and then runing southerly three rods to a heap of stones, and then runing easterly ten rods to a heap of stones, and then runing northerly one rod to the first mentioned corner; bounded north on high way, west and south and east on my own land." Witnessed by James Riggs and Thomas Clark, Justice of the Peace.

Dec. 6, 1790, from James Pritchard of Bethlehem, Litchfield co., for the consideration of £20, "one certaine peace or parcel of land situate in the Township of Derby, containing three acres, be it more or less, lying in Camp's Mortgage on the Little River Road, said peace of land being part of the land owned by Nathaniel Wooster, Decst.—bounded East on highway, north on Susannah Cornishes land, west on Johnathan Miles' land, south on Daniel Wooster land." Witnessed by John Davis and Thomas Clark, Justice of the Peace.

Aug. 22, 1791, from Samuel Sanford, for £17, one piece lying southward of John Cornishes house, the other west of sd. Cornishes house, commencing at corner of John Rowe's land, running westward 44 rods on highway, southward 35 rods on Johnathan Miles' land, thence eastward 21 rods on Abiel Canfield's land and northward 9 rods on John Rowe's land; witnessed by Simeon Curtiss and Thomas Clark, Justice of the Peace.

July 2, 1796, from Jesse Smith, nine rods of land between lands of said Canfield and Smith, witnessed by Jesse Baldwin and Levi Tomlinson, Justice of the peace.

Feb. 9, 1805, from George Steele, for $500, a piece of land bounded northerly and westerly by highway, easterly on land of the heirs of Isaac Baldwin, 1¼ acres with house and barn; and two acres bounded southerly by highway and northerly and easterly on Johnathan Miles' land. Witnesses, Philo and Levi Tomlinson.

The same date, from George Steele, Wm. and Milo Keney, for $650, one piece bounded westerly on highway, southerly on land of Abijah Hull, easterly on Naugatuck river, northerly on land of heirs of Isaac Baldwin and said Steele, 5¼ acres; and 14 acres bounded southerly on highway and land of Leverett Pritchard, westerly on land of sd. Pritchard and Josiah Washborn, northerly on land of Philo Holbrook, and easterly on land of Johnathan Miles.

---

[35]SAMUEL[6], son of Abiel and Mary Canfield, m. Mary Allen, who died Oct. 5; 1841, aged 38 years. Children:

[40]Ann, d. Jan. 16, 1858, aged 30 years.
[41]John M., d. Apr. 14, 1858, aged 29 years.
[42]Elsie, d. Sept. 10, 1848, aged 18 years.
[43]George, d. May 25, 1853, aged 18 years.
[44]Harriett, m. Henry T. Booth. Children:
   45, Alida; (46) Hattie, m. Frank A. Cotter of Ansonia; (47) Lottie E. and (48) Mary.
[49]Samuel H., m. Harriett, daughter of Raymond French, Esq.
[50]Edwin U.

At the time of the second war with Great Britain, Samuel Canfield was an apprentice learning the trade of machinist with Elias Gilbert. He was drafted, and Mr. Gilbert hired a substitute rather than lose his assistance. Years after, in company with Hiram Upson, he carried on the manufacture of augers in what are now James Swan's chisel works, and afterwards worked for Dwight and French and the Humpreysville Manufacturing Company about twenty years. For the twenty years preceding his death he lived in retirement at his residence near Trinity church. He died April 17, 1879, aged 82 years.

---

[33]DANIEL,[5] third son of Joseph and Sarah Canfield, m. Feb. 11, 1789, Anna, d. of Zedock Hurd of Woodbury, b. Aug. 13, 1765. Lived on Bungay, south of the schoolhouse. Children:

[52]Esther, b. Mar. 5, 1790, m. Sheldon Kinney.
[53]Charity, b. Oct. 24, 1792, d. Oct. 1, 1793.
[54]William, b. Sept. 18, 1792.
[55]Joseph, b. Sept. 29, 1796, m. Frances Eason.
[56]Julia Ann, b. Apr. 10, 1799.
[57]Almira, b. Dec. 5, 1801, m. Charles Bradley.
[58]Sarah, b. Jan. 5, 1804.
[59]Caroline, b. Sept. 26, 1806, m. Treat Botsford.
[60]Judson, b. April 8, 1806, m. Sarah Miles.

---

[16]JOHN[4], son of Abiel and Ruth Canfield, m. 1st in March, 1751, Elizabeth Johnson, who died Sept. 8, 1751; 2nd, Mrs. Martha Judd, Nov. 20, 1753. Children: David, b. Nov. 6, 1754; Bette, b. Mar. 26, 1756; Molle, b. June 1, 1758; Eunice, b. Nov. 17, 1760. *Derby Records.*

---

[18]WILLIAM[4], m. Hannah Lumm Mar. 6, 1774. Children, Abel, b. May 29, 1755; Hannah, b. May 30, 1756.

---

[19]DR. SAMUEL[4], son of Abiel and Ruth Canfield, m. Apr. 3, 1754, Mary Bassett, and d. in 1766. Children: Samuel, b. July 13, 1756; Sabra, b. Feb. 15, 1758; Suze, b. Nov. 6, 1759; Seba, b. Jan. 2, 1762; Salle and Silva. *Derby Records.*

GENEALOGY.

RIGGS.

•EDWARD RIGGS settled in Milford in 1640, and was afterwards one of the first settlers of Derby. Savage says Samuel Riggs of Milford m. in 1667 a daughter of Richard Baldwin and removed to Derby.

EDWARD RIGGS of Derby, probably a descendant of Edward of Milford, and Lois Osborn of Waterbury were married by Rev. Mr. Mansfield May 19, 1759. Children:
    Moses, b. Apr. 10, 1760, m. Susannah Tucker.
    Edward, b. Jan. 24, 1762.
    David, Thomas and Isaac.

MOSES RIGGS, son of Edward and Lois, a soldier of the Revolution, m. Susanna, daughter of Samuel Tucker. Children:
    Sheldon, m. Rebecca Lingham.
    Leman, m. Patty Clark.
    Moses, m. Gracie Holbrook.
    Simon,
    Thomas, m. Watie G. Smith.
    Clara, m. 1st, David Johnson; 2nd, John Nichols.
    Susan, m. Ezra Bassett.
    Harriett, m. Daniel Holbrook.
    Eliza, m. Levi Johnson.
    Garry, m. Sally Clark.

EBENEZER RIGGS, m. Rachel Peck of Waterbury July 5, 1733. Children:
    Rachel, b. May 31, 1734, d. May 25, 1740.
    Esther, b. July 24, 1736.
    Ebenezer, b. Nov. 17, 1738, d. May 29, 1740.
    Rachel, b. Jan. 23, 1741.
    Louis, b. July 25, 1743, d. Aug. —, 1751.
    Eunice, b. Oct. 14, 1745.
    Ebenezer, b. Jan. 22, 1748.
    Jeremiah, b. July 1, 1750.
    Joseph, b. Aug. 17, 1753.

EBENEZER RIGGS of Oxford m. Julia M., dau. of Col. John Davis. Children:
    Lucinda, m. Henry, son of Sheldon Church of Seymour.
    Dewitt, unmarried.

Homer, m. Mary E. Davis of New Rochelle, N. Y., daughter of Capt. Clark Davis, and granddaughter of Capt. Truman Davis. Resides at Washington, D. C.
Bernice, m. Charles Meiggs of Oxford.
N. Clark.

JOSEPH RIGGS, m. Mabel Johnson Feb. 20, 1739. Children:
Hannah, b. Dec. 21, 1740.
John, b. Apr. 10, 1742.
Joseph, b. July 21, 1746.
Samuel, b. Nov. 21, 1750, d. Sept. 21, 1766.
Mabel, b. May 5, 1759.

JOHN RIGGS, Esq., son of Joseph and Mabel, m. Elizabeth Hawkins. He died June 18, 1814, and his wife died Oct. 3, 1815. Children:
John, b. Dec. 22, 1771, m. Jan. 1, 1793, Mary Beecher.

JOHN RIGGS, son of John and Elizabeth, m. Jan. 1, 1793, Mary, dau. of Isaac and Hannah Beecher. Children:
Maria, b. May 7, 1793, d. June 4, 1813.
Laura, b. May 7, 1795, m. John Davis Oct. 16, 1813, d. in 1854.
Mary, b. Mar. 13, 1798, m. John S. Moshier, Oct. 27, 1816, d. Feb. 9, 1877.
John H., b. Jan. 6, 1801, d. Oct. 10, 1805.
Lucinda, b. May 20, 1804, m. Warren French, Nov. 21, 1823; d. $\frac{3}{4}$ 20, '76.
Thirza, b. Oct. 26, 1807, m. 1st, John Humphrey, 2nd, Joshua Kendall.
John, b. Oct. 25, 1811, d. Nov. 14, 1855.
Harpin, b. Dec. 9, 1813, m. Harriett Upson May 17, 1840.
Henry, b. Jan. 15, 1816, m. Mary Ann Bradley, d. in 1864.
John m. 2nd, Mar. 6, 1829, Betsey Hawkins, b. Apr. 26, 1786, d. July 18, 1849.

HARPIN RIGGS, son of John and Elizabeth, m. Harriett, dau. of Hiram and Sarah Upson May 17, 1840. Children:
John H., b. Apr. 5, 1841, m. Adella Kennedy May 17, 1866. Children:
Alice Louisa, Lizzie Atwood, John Harpin.
Royal B., b. Oct. 6, 1844, m. Mary Dunn.
Hiram U., b. Dec. 20, 1846, d. July 4, 1852.
Louiza B., b. Sept. 4, 1849, m. Norman Sperry Nov. 24, 1869.
Sarah M., b. June 5, 1852, m. Geo. A. James May 26, 1875. Child:
Florence H.
Harriett, b. Apr. 2, 1856, m. Joseph G. Redshaw of Ansonia Sept. 18, '78.
Mary B., b. Feb. 4, 1859, m. Gilbert E. Osborne of New Haven, Nov. 7, '78.

GENEALOGY.

GILLETTE.

CAPT. GILLETTE was taken by the British at the time of the Revolution as he was returning with a valuable cargo after an absence of four or five years. His vessel and cargo were held by the enemy, but he was after a time released.

ANSON, son of Capt. Gillette, b. Feb. 3, 1773, m. 1st, Oct. 11, 1795, Sarah Hull, b. Jan., 1769, d. Aug. 28, 1800; 2nd, Mar. 10, 1801, Betsey Mansfield, b. Nov. 30, 1777. Children:
    David, b. Dec. 16, 1796, d. in Golconda, Ill., in 1822.
    William, b. Aug. 16, 1798, d. Sept. 11, 1803.
    Sally, b. Dec. 23, 1801, m. Judson English, Mar. 23, 1828.
    William, b. July 31, 1804, m. Amaritta Johnson.
    Isaac, b. Dec. 7, 1805, m. Harriett Hurd, d. May 22, 1833.
    Eli, b. June 1, 1810, m. Eliza Bassett.
    Lucius, b. June 11, 1812, d. Nov. —, 1878.
    Philo, b. Sept. 30, 1814, m. Mary Bassett.
    Mary, b. Dec. 23, 1816, d. May 26, 1817.
    Charles, b. May 15, 1818, d. Mar. 13, 1819.
    Mary, b. Sept. 8, 1820, m. Albert J. Downs of Squantuck.
    Betsey, b. Apr. 8, 1823, m. Abner White, moved to Bradford co., Pa., d. Mar. 8, 1848.

ELI GILLETTE, son of Anson and Sarah, m. Eliza, dau. of Ezra L. Bassett of Oxford. Children:
    Emily, m. F. M. Clemons. Children:
        Bertha, m. Apr. 20, 1879, Walter W. Radcliffe of Oxford; Arthur F. and Walter.
    Wilbur F., m. Amelia Rice. Residence, New Haven.
    Sarah A., m. Edwin W. Clark of Derby.
    Lillie M.,
    Augusta, d.

EPHRAIM GILLETTE, m. Pervis ———. Children:
    Freelove, b. Aug. 10, 1729.
    Mary, b. Mar. 10, 1726-7.
    Joseph and } b. Aug. 7, 1744.
    Benjamin,

PHILO GILLETTE of Rocker's Hill, m. Mary, dau. of Ezra Bassett. Children:
    Martha, m. David Hawley of Oxford. Child, Clifford.
    Dexter, m. Emaretta Sperry. Child, Walter.

JOHNSON.

PETER JOHNSON[1] of Fairfield, had three sons.
Moses, with his wife Mary, removed to Woodbury, and died Oct. 30, 1713, aged 62.
Ebenezer m. Elizabeth Wooster and removed to Derby.
John, d. in 1659.

COL. EBENEZER JOHNSON[2] m. Nov. 23, 1671, Elizabeth, dau. of Edwin Wooster; removed to Derby in 1676. Children:
Elizabeth, b. in 1672.
Eunice, b. Aug. 22, 1678.
Hannah, b. Dec. 6, 1680.
Peter, b. Oct. 9, 1684.
Ebenezer, b. Feb. 22, 1686.
Israel, b. Apr. 13, 1689.

Ebenezer, Sr., was a freeman in 1678, long one of the chief men of Derby, and its representative to the General Assembly in 1685. His name is recorded in the list of the proprietors of Derby in 1717. Among the many purchases from the Indians made by him was one April 15, 1700, recorded in D. R., Book 1, p. 52, from Cockupatain and Ahuntaway, of "a certain quantity of land at Rimmon, bounded southward with ye little River, Eastward & northward with David Wooster his land & ye afors^d Captaine & Ensigne their land, Naucatug River Westward, & Northward with Tobie ye Indian's purchase."

On the 18th of April, 1704, he purchased from James Howd "a certain parcell of upland lying & being easterly of Road that goeth to Woodbury against ye land called Quakers Farme, bounded Northerly with a splitt Rocke & stones in ye cleft thereoff, easterly with a white oake tree, westerly with a chestnut tree, southerly with a chestnut tree, eighty rods long on each side, 62 rods wide att each end, containing 31 acres more or lesse." D. R., Book 1, p. 80.

In D. R., Vol. 3, p. 43, is a record of a sale to Ebenezer Johnson in 1709, on account of a squaw, of land extending from the Naugatuck river east to Milford bounds, and from Beacon Hill Brook to Lebanon Brook.

LIEUT. EBENEZER JOHNSON[3], son of Ebenezer and Elizabeth, m. Hannah ———, d. in 1751. Children:
Benajah, b. in 1704; d. Apr. 13, 1763.
Timothy, m. Abigail Brewster, Feb. 21, 1725. They had but one son,
    [12]Alexander, b. in 1730, d. in Sept., 1817.
.... m. John Riggs.
Ann m. Samuel Hitchcock.
Sarah m. James Wheeler, May 19, 1736.

GENEALOGY.

BENAJAH JOHNSON[4], son of Ebenezer and Elizabeth, m. Oct. 10, 1728, Mrs. Sara (Brewster) Hawkins, who died May 7, 1763, aged 72 years. Children:
  Isaac, b. in 1735, m. Lois Hopkins, d. Apr. 10, 1813.
  Zeviah, b. in 1739, m. Abiel Fairchild, d. May 29, 1816.

Benajah Johnson bought of Johnathan Lum for £200 a tract of land " lying in the North purchase near Bladens Brook, so called, containing ninety-six acres, be it more or be it less, bounded northward on the land of Sam^n Tomlinson, eastwardly on common land, southwardly on land of Daniel Wooster, late of Derby, deceast, westerly on highway." Dated "ye seventeenth day of December, in the ninth year of the Reign of our Sovereign Lord, George ye Second of Great Britain, King, & A. D. 1735." D. R., Vol. 4, p. 157.

ISAAC JOHNSON, son of Benajah, m. Lois Hopkins, who was born in 1738, and died Oct. 16, 1814, aged 76 years. Isaac d. Apr. 10, 1813, aged 78 years. Children:
  Susannah, b. Nov. 24, 1763.
  Ruth, b. Mar. 31, 1765.
  Mabel, b. Nov. 27, 1766.
  Jesse, b. in 1773, d. Oct. 21, 1829.
  Stiles, b. in 1782, d. Oct. 4, 1818.

ALEXANDER JOHNSON[5], son of Timothy and Abigail, m. Hannah .... He lived at Pinesbridge, in the house still standing a little north of the house of William Gillette, and gave the land for the Pinesbridge cemetery. Children:
  Timothy, b. Jan. 21, 1766, d. Jan. 21, 1836.
  David, Elijah, Nathaniel, Charles.
  Abigail Brewster m. Moses Clark of Nyumphs.
  Ruth, b. in 1693, m. Thomas Leavenworth.

ASAHEL JOHNSON m. Lois .... Children:
  Lois, b. Mar. 11, 1766.
  Elisha, b. Oct. 27, 1767.

GIDEON JOHNSON, son of Jeremiah, m. Lydia Beecher of New Haven, Mar. 24, 1749.
A sister of Gideon m. Thaddeus Baldwin of Woodbridge.

EBENEZER BEECHER JOHNSON, b. Nov. 24, 1763, m. May 25, 1785, Hannah P. Clark, b. Aug. 13, 1766. Children:
  Garry, b. Nov. 5, 1792, m. Harriett Hotchkiss.
  Chary, b. Jan. 27, 1795, m. James Downs of Monroe, Oct. 14, 1815.
    Children, Clark B., b. Oct. 3, 1816; Chary Ann, b. June 16, 1818; James B., b. Feb. 21, 1822.

Hannah Betsey, b. Mar. 23, 1802, m. June 15, 1820, David Beach, d. Oct. 9, 1822. Child, Hannah B.
Ebenezer B. Johnson d. Sept. 17, 1846. His wife Hannah d. July 24, 1847.

GARRY, son of Ebenezer B. and Hannah P. Johnson, m. May 1, 1817, Harriett Hotchkiss, b. Mar. 29, 1798. Children:
Garry B., b. Apr. 9, 1817, m. Huldah Dolittle. Residence, Bethany.
David, b. Mar. 11, 1819, m. Ruth Ann Scott. Residence, Seymour.
Mary Ann, b. Nov. 7, 1821, m. Robert Hodge.
Andrew, b. Oct. 5, 1823, m. Elizabeth Davis.
Betsey, b. Oct. 21, 1825, m. John Scott.
Harvey, b. Dec. 17, 1827.
Clark, b. May 4, 1830, m. Mrs. Eliza Snell.
Albert, b. Oct. 17, 1833, m. Eliza J. Tuttle, residence Ansonia.
Noyes, b. in 1836, m. Julia ....
Harriett E., b. Oct. 1839, m. Geo. G. Lewis. Residence, Shelton
Martha A., m. Fred Neuschler. Residence. Ansonia.

ISRAEL JOHNSON, m. Elizabeth Wakling May 28, 1740. Children:
Charles, d. Oct. 28, 1763, aged 22 years.
Elijah, d. Nov. 11, 1763, aged 18 years.
Elizabeth, d. Nov. 15, 1763, aged 2 years.

REV. JESSE JOHNSON, son of Isaac and Lois, m. Hepzebath ...., d. Oct. 21, 1829. Hepzebath d. Apr. 13, 1824. Children:
Sally B., b. Sept. 6, 1797, m. Jared Bassett.
Isaac, b. Apr. 2, 1799.
Jesse, Jr., b. Mar. 28, 1801.
Hepzibah, b. Jan. 28, 1803.
Harry, b. Mar. 30, 1805.
Sally, b. July 12, 1807.
Lois Emily, b. Feb. 24, 1810.
Stiles, b. May 14, 1813. D. R.^{bmd}, p. 433.

HEZEKIAH JOHNSON m. Rebecca Johnson Dec. 12, 1784. Children:
Elizabeth, b. Nov. 26, 1786.
Newel, b. May 22, 1789, d. in Westville June 11, 1879.

EBENEZER JOHNSON, b. in 1761, d. Sept. 25, 1792. Buried in the Cemetery adjoining the M. E. Church.

GENEALOGY.

GIDEON JOHNSON, son of Ebenezer, m. Sarah, dau. of Dr. Crittenden of New Haven, m. in 1835, aged 86 years. His house stood in the angle of the road where Day and Pearl streets meet. Died in 1835, aged 36. Children: Sheldon Crittenden, m. Susan H. Stoddard.
Hopie, m. Henry L. Noble, d. in Cleveland, O., in 1869.

SHELDON C. JOHNSON, son of Gideon, m. May 19, 1828, Susan H., dau. of Abiram and Eunice Stoddard. Residence, Seymour, Ct. Children:
Charles Napoleon, born March 4, 1829. Graduated in Yale College, 1857. Studied law in Tolland with Judge Waldo, and engaged in practice in New Haven in 1857, died Nov. 12, 1867.
Henry, born Nov. 10, 1830, married Oct. 10, 1853, Ellen E. Botsford, who died July 21, 1861. He resided in Seymour, Conn., till 1861, when he removed to New Haven. Is a merchant. He represented the town of Seymour in the Legislature in 1857, was one of the committee to locate the new county jail at New Haven, and was appointed on other important trusts while a member of the Assembly.
Oscar, born Jan. 10, 1833, died Oct. 17, 1833.
Oscar F., born March 13, 1834, died Nov. 29, 1836.
Oscar Eugene, born Nov. 28, 1836. Removed to San Francisco in 1862.
Josephine W., born Oct. 10, 1838, married April 9, 1863, Gustavus R. Elliot, Esq., a lawyer in New Haven.
Harold St. Clair, born Jan. 29, 1841.
Louis Le Grand, born Feb. 18, 1843, died May 14, 1843.
Susan Stoddard Clark, born Sept. 15, 1844.
Sarah Crittenden, born Sept. 20, 1851, m. John T. Forsey.

STEELE.

JOHN STEELE[1], b. in Essex co., Eng., appears first on the records at Dorchester in 1631, only ten years after the arrival of the Mayflower. He was one of the proprietors of Cambridge in 1632, as were also George and Henry Steele. In 1635 he led a band of emigrants through the then pathless wilderness to the bank of the Connecticut river, where they laid the foundation of the city of Hartford. For twenty-three years he represented the new settlement in the Colony Court and for twenty years he was the recorder of the town of Hartford. His last years were spent in Farmington, where he died Nov. 25, 1665. He m. 1st, Rachel, who died in 1653; 2nd, Mercy Seamer, who died in 1665. He had eight children, among whom was

HISTORY OF SEYMOUR.

JOHN STEELE[2], m. Mercy Warner in 1645, and d. in 165¾. They had six children, among whom was

SAMUEL STEELE[3], b. Mar. 16, 1652, lived in Hartford, m. Sept., 1680, Mercy, dau. of Major Wm. Bradford. She died in 1720. He died in 1710, had five sons and two daughters, among them Thomas and Lieut. John.

THOMAS STEELE[4], son of Samuel and Mercy, b. Sept. 9, 1681, m. May 10, 1709, Susannah Webster, who d. Nov. 27, 1757. He lived in West Hartford, had eight children, died in 1757.

CAPT. BRADFORD STEELE, b. in 1735, m. 1st, Mary ...., d. Oct. 16, 1788, aged 56 years; 2nd, Sarah Wheeler. Capt. Bradford d. Apr. 18, 1804, aged 69 years. Sarah died May 13, 1826, aged 80 years.

DEA. BRADFORD STEELE, son of Capt. Bradford, m. Mar. 9, 1785, Ruth, dau. of Simeon Wheeler. Children:

Edmund, b. Apr. 4, 1788, m. Anna Tucker, d. Apr. 8, 1840.

Sally, b. May 7, 1791, m. Chester Jones Nov. 20, 1808. Children:
Susan Minerva, b. in Aug. 1809, m. William Brewster of Erie, Pa.
Sarah Maria, d. Nov. 18, 1877.
Mary Ann, b. in August, 1811, m. Clark McSparren of Erie, Pa.
Julia Malinda.
Ruth Emmeline, m. W. C. Curry of Erie, Pa.
Chester Bradford, m. Caroline Smith, lives in East Saginaw.
Louisa, m. Dr. Wm. Magill of Erie, Pa.

Ashbel, b. Aug. 8, 1793, d. Sept. 23, 1794.

William, b. Feb. 14, 1798, m. Betsey Northrop Nov. 1, 1819; d. Nov. 24, 1874. Children:
John, Truman, Walter (living in Ansonia), George, Mary.

Burr, b. June 7, 1800, m. Betsey Mallett Nov. 7, 1822, d. Aug. 11, 1823.
Child, Burr S, b. Mar. 19, 1824, d. Sept. 4, 1844. Betsey d. Apr. 7, 1824.

Susan, b. Dec. 17, 1802, d. Oct. 11, 1804.

Almyra, b. Feb. 22, 1810, m. 1st John W. Holcomb Nov. 23, 1832; 2nd, Henry P. Davis Sept. 2, 1849.

Mrs. Ruth Steele was born Sept. 17, 1765, and died Feb. 20, 1856, aged 90 years and 5 months.

EDMUND STEELE, son of Dea. Bradford and Ruth, m. Nov. 24, 1809, Anna, dau. of Zephaniah Tucker, b. Nov. 27, 1783. Children:

Albert J., b. Feb. 22, 1812, d. Jan. 6, 1878.

John Burton, b. June 10, 1814, d. Aug. 22, 1854.

ALBERT J. STEELE, son of Edmund and Anna, m. Feb. 11, 1835, Julia, dau. of Chester and Sally Jones, who died July 29, 1863. Children:

Sarah Ann, b. Oct. 17, 1836.

Susan Maria, b. Mar. 28, 1840.

Julia Frances, b. May 2, 1843, d. Feb. 29, 1844.

HISTORY OF SEYMOUR.   205 b

HENRY P. DAVIS, born May 16th, 1818, in Smithtown, Montgomery Co., N. Y., and Catharine Crandall, born Dec. 16th, 1816, were married in Cohoes, N. Y., April 16th, 1840, by Rev. Mr. Westcott. Children:
   [1] Amanda M. Davis, born in Trenton, N. J., Aug. 14, 1841; died Feb. 20, 1851.
   [2] Sarah J. Davis, born in Trenton, May 8th, 1843.
   [3] Anna C. Davis, born in Trenton, Sept. 15, 1845.
   [4] Charles H. Davis, born in Humphreysville, Ct., Jan. 7th, 1848.
Mrs. Catharine C. Davis died Feb. 27. 1849.

Henry P. Davis married, second, Mrs. Almira Holcomb, Sept. 2, 1849. Residence, Seymour, Conn. Children:
   [5] George Smith Davis, born May 24, 1850.
   [6] Burr Steele Davis, born Dec. 22, 1851.
   [7] Alice Almira Davis, born Feb. 2, 1854.

SARAH JANE DAVIS, daughter of Henry P. and Catharine C. Davis, and Henry Carrington of Woodbridge, were married Jan. 9th, 1862, by Rev. Mr. Booth. Children:
   Fannie Carrington, died Mar. 27, 1870, aged 7 years and 4 months.
   Silas Carrington.
   Royal Carrington, b. Mar. 25, 1871.

Mrs. Sarah Jane Carrington married, second, Andrew Wheeler of Orange, July 8th, 1880.

ANNA C. DAVIS, daughter of Henry P. and Catharine C. Davis, and Wm. Webster Cowell of Woodbridge, were married May 21, 1874, by Rev. Mr. Martin. Children:
   Henry David Cowell, born Mar. 2, 1875; died Mar. 7, 1875.
   Burton Webster Cowell, born Nov. 18, 1876.
   Henry Archie Cowell, born July 2, 1879.
   Leon Daniel Cowell, born July 25th, 1881; died Oct. 6, 1882.

CHARLES HENRY DAVIS, son of Henry P. and Catharine C. Davis, enlisted in Co. C., 1st Conn. Heavy Artillery, Dec. 4, 1863; served till the close of the war, and was honorably discharged Sept. 25, 1865. He married Mrs. Mary Jane Finch, Mar. 21, 1868; lived in Oshkosh, Wis., until 1883, moved to Wittemburg, Wis. Children:
   Zella May Davis, born Feb. 20. 1869.
   Nellie Davis.

GEORGE SMITH DAVIS, son of Henry P. and Almira Davis, married Martha M. Cushen of Ansonia, Oct. 2, 1872. Children:
   Charles Henry Davis, born Aug. 10, 1873.
   George W. Davis, born Jan. 8, 1876.
   Willie Cushen Davis, born Mar. 3, 1879; died April 26, 1879.

BURR STEELE DAVIS, son of Henry P. and Almira Davis, m. Frances E. Waterman of Orange, Nov. 17, 1880 Children:
   Florence Orie Davis, born Oct. 1, 1882.

ALICE ALMIRA DAVIS, daughter of Henry P. and Almira Davis, married Joseph T. Beard of Milford, Mar. 27, 1872. Children:
   Nellie S. Beard, born Mar. 21, 1873.
   Ernest Treat Beard, born Nov. 24, 1874.
   Alice May Beard, born Feb. 19, 1877.
   Warren W. Beard, born June 9, 1880.

GENEALOGY. 205

Albert Edmund, b. Oct. 29, 1845, d. Oct. 19, 1858.
Oriana Louisa, b. July 2, 1852.

JOHN BURTON STEELE, son of Edmund and Anna, m. May 11, 1845, Emmeline A. Stuart of Bridgewater, b. July 13, 1819. Children:
Celestia, b. Sept. 29, 1846, m. Edward B. Bradley Nov. 29, 1866.
Frank E., b. Aug. 20, 1848.

ALMIRA STEELE, daughter of Dea. Bradford and Ruth, m. 1st, Nov. 23, 1832, John W. Holcomb, b. Jan. 16, 1812. Children:
George S., b. Dec. 23, 1835, d. Oct. 17, 1842.
John W., b. Nov. 2, 1843, m. Rhoda L. Langdon, Sept. 24, 1867.
Mary B., b. Apr. 1, 1838, m. Samuel Howd, July 4, 1871.
Married 2nd, Sept. 2, 1849, Henry P. Davis, b. May 16, 1818. Children:
George Smith, b. May 24, 1850, m. Martha M. Cushen Oct. 2, 1872.
Burr Steele, b. Dec. 22, 1851.
Alice Almira, b. Feb. 2, 1854, m. Joseph T. Beard Mar. 27, 1872.

JOHN W. HOLCOMB, son of John W. and Almira Holcomb, served four years in Co. E. 5th C. V.; m. Rhoda Langdon, b, in Burlington, Iowa, Feb. 25, 1844. Residence in 1883, Cincinnati, Ohio. Children:
1. Emma Almira, b. in Newport, Ky., July 14, 1869.
2. Blanche Irene, b. in Cincinnati, Ohio, Aug. 20, 1870; d. Aug. 3, 1871.
3. Alice May, b. in Cincinnati, Mar. 12, 1872; d. Nov. 29. 1875.
4. Frank Wilbur, b. in Columbia. Ohio, Oct. 20. 1880.

BASSETT.

SAMUEL BASSETT m. Sarah ———. Children:
John, b. Nov. 14, 1751.
Abraham, b. Mar. 21, 1753, d. Nov. 17, 1833.
Eunice, b. Jan. 9, 1759.
Sarah, b. Feb. 14, 1761.

ABRAHAM BASSETT, son of Samuel and Sarah, m. Mary ———. Lived on Bungay in house now occupied by Robert Healey. Mary Bassett died Dec. 25, 1849, aged 90 years. Children:
Abram, d. Nov. 17, 1853.
Samuel, m. 1st, Mary Lyman; 2nd, Laura Phanton.
Abel, m. Martha Peck, d. Mar. 23, 1863, aged 78.
Jared m. Sally, d. of Jesse Johnson.
Marcus, m. Mary Ann Rogers.
Glover, m. 1st, Elizabeth Baldwin; 2nd, Nancy Gilyard.
Grace m. Bronson Wheeler of Southbury.
Lucinda, d. Oct. 8, 1878, aged 90 years.
Harvey,
Abijah, m. Polly Durand.

GLOVER BASSETT, son of Abraham and Mary, b. Oct. 19, 1793, m. 1st Oct. 5, 1820, Elizabeth Baldwin, b. Oct. 17, 1793, d. Oct. 1, 1838; 2nd, Oct. 21, 1839, Nancy Gilyard. Children :
Amos, b. Oct. 5, 1820, m. Keziah H. Rowe Sept. 11, 1845, d. Aug. 31, 1862.
Jane, b. Oct. 23, 1822, m. Willis Baldwin and d. Sept. 8, 1849.
Louisa, b. July 6, 1825, d. Feb. 10, 1826.
Elizabeth A., b. Apr. 4, 1829, d. May 17, 1853.
James Harvey, b. Oct. 25, 1835, d. Nov. 22, 1872.
William G., b. May 8, 1844, d. Dec. 2, 1862.

AMOS BASSETT, son of Glover and Elizabeth, m. Sept. 10, 1845, Keziah H. Rowe, who died Oct. 26, 1873. Children :
Frank G., b. Sept. 28, 1847, m. Hattie L. Storrs Jan. 9, 1878.
Isaac H., b. Apr. 30, 1849, m. Sarah Sanford July 31, 1869.
Alice J., b. Apr. 30, 1851, m. Robert Healy Sept. 13, 1866.
Mary E., b. Apr. 14, 1854, d. Sept. 2, 1874.
George A., b. Dec. 30, 1857, d. Sept. 15, 1858.
Hattie K., b. Oct. 10, 1860.

JARED BASSETT, son of Abraham and Mary, m. Sally, daughter of Rev. Jesse Johnson. Children :
Julius, m. 1st Augusta Ann Lake; 2nd, Sarah Lum. Children :
Frederick B., Heber L., Sarah E., Augusta A., Flora.
George, m. Laura Tomlinson. Children:
Minerva M., Elizabeth E.
Sheldon, m. Elizabeth Sperry, lives in Woodbridge. Children :
Ida A., Hattie.
Sarah, m. Sylvester P. Smith of Birmingham. Children:
Elizabeth, Joseph H.
Thomas G., m. Catharine A. Lake. Child :
Nellie C.

JOSEPH BASSETT, m. Sarah Hawkins Nov. 16, 1748. Children: Samuel, b. June 25, 1751; Tafeene, b. Jan. 12, 1762; Sarah, b. Feb. 12, 1764; Rhode, b. Feb. 12, 1769.

JOHN BASSETT, m. Naomi Wooster Oct. 6, 1743.
SAMUEL BASSETT, m. Sarah Bochford Oct. 26, 1748.

JOSEPH BASSETT and Molly Henman were married March 18, 1779. Children :
Sheldon, b. Feb. 14, 1780.
Nancy, b. Mar. 22, 1782. D. R., bmd, 156.
Laurey, b. Mar. 13, 1784.

SHARPE.

THOMAS SHARPE, born in England about 1580, was appointed assistant to Endicott, the new Governor of Massachusetts, in 1629. He sailed from London on the Arabella in the fleet with Winship, and was present at the court held on the Arabella March 23rd, 1629. He was the sixth member of the Boston Church.

He filled his office of Assistant to the Governor, as it was then termed, and member of the Council of Massachusetts Colony without interruption until 1631, when he embarked at Salem with Sir Richard Saltonstall and family on board the Lions Whelp, April 1st, and arrived in London April 30th.

Winthrop's New England, Young's Chronicles of Massachusetts, etc.

THOMAS SHARPE came from England in 1700, settled in Stratford, m. Lydia, daughter of Wm. Dickinson, and granddaughter of Rev. Frederick Dickinson, in 1701, and in 1708 was one of the thirty-six men to whom the General Assembly granted the township of Newtown. He sold the lands he had purchased in Stratford and removed to Newtown. Among the transfers made by him at this time was one of land in Stratford to Samuel Hawley of Derby in exchange for said Hawley's right in the town of Derby, Jan. 23, 170$\frac{5}{6}$, recorded in Derby Records, book 2, p. 101, land records. At a town meeting (in Newtown) held Sept. 4, 1711, Thomas Sharpe was appointed surveyor of highway, an office which was then no sinecure, as the town records of the highways laid out through the lands until then almost untrod by the feet of white men will attest. By the several divisions among the proprietors of various tracts of land as fast as surveyed during two or three years following, he and his heirs acquired several hundred acres of land, the larger part of the township being still unsurveyed and undivided. He died in 1712, leaving five children. His wife Lydia survived him about forty years. A protest made by her Dec. 15, 1751, still appears on the Newtown records, relative to lands of which she was unjustly deprived.

Thomas, b. Mar. 18, 1702, died April 17, 1765, aged 63 years.
Mary, b. Oct. 10, 1703.
William, b. Aug. 19, 1705.
John, b. Feb. 1, 1708.
Elizabeth, b. Apr. 18, 1712.

THOMAS SHARP, son of Thomas and Lydia, m. Feb. 17, 1745, Sarah, dau. of Richard Crozier and granddaughter of William Crozier, lived in Newtown. Children:

Thomas, b. May 28, 1746, m. Mary Treadwell, d. Mar. 14, 1805.
Lydia, b. Dec. 16, 1748.

208   HISTORY OF SEYMOUR.

John, b. Nov. 12, 1750, m. Phedina Lake Nov. 23, 1772, d. at Harlem in 1777. Children:
Lucy, born Oct. 11, 1773; Rena, born Aug. 4, 1776.
Eliakim, b. Dec. 5, 1752, m. Hester Wetmore Nov. 25, 1773.
Jesse, b. Jan. 30, 1755.
Sarah, b. Mar. 25, 1760, m. John Blake Vose. Children:
John, Abby (m. ——— Smith of Stratford), Lucy, Lydia, Ruth.

THOMAS SHARP, son of Thomas and Sarah, m. Mary Treadwell, removed to Ridgefield and afterward to Oxford, near Zoar Bridge, where he died Mar. 14, 1805. Children :

Polly, b. June 30, 1771, m. Frederick Galpin of Woodbury, d. Oct. 30, 1851.
Children : Stephen, Curtiss, Polly, Maria and Leman.
Lydia, b. Apr. 18, 1774, d. Jan. 28, 1778.
Floranna, b. Feb. 20, 1778, m. Corydon Kelsie of Vermont, d. in 1841.
Mary Ann, b. July 11, 1781, m. Joseph Thompson of West Haven, d. Mar. 23, 1765. Children:
Fanny, Cynthia, (m. Sherwood E., Stratton), Louisa, Jeduthun, Charles, George, Lucinda, Joseph and Jane.
Amy, b. July 11, 1783, m. Seth Sherwood Stratton, d. Aug. 6, 1843.
Daniel, b. Apr. 22, 1785, m. Polly Bennett, d. Mar. 28, 1870, æ 84y, 11m.
Children: Sherman Judson, m. Aphia E. Wheeler; and Legrand, father of Samuel and Jane (m. Ira Beardsley of Monroe).
Philander, b. Mar. 24, 1787, m. Sarah Davis, d. Apr. 30, 1859, aged 72.
Children : Eugene, George, Alfred, Eliza, m. ——— McEwen.
Henry, b. Oct. 7, 1789, m. Polly Sherman, d. Oct. 27, 1823, aged 33.
Children: Urzelia, m. Rev. Thomas Clinghan ; Henrietta, m. William Wakeman of New Haven ; Walker.
Hannah, b. Dec. 7, 1791, d. May 20, 1820, aged 28.
Abia, b. Dec. 7, 1791, d. June 28, 1817, aged 25.
Lugrand, b. in Ridgefield June 1, 1797, d. May 1, 1876, aged 78 y. 11 m.

LUGRAND SHARP, son of Thomas and Mary, m. Sept. 28, 1823, Olive M. Booth, daughter of Ebenezer and Anna Booth of Southford, who d. Mar. 8, 1864. He purchased a homestead in Southford, where he lived until Apr. 1843, when he removed to Seymour. Children:

Mary A., m. John James of Ansonia.
Olive Maria, m. Albert W. Lounsbury of Seymour.
Elizabeth, m. Rev. Walter Chamberlin of the Newark Conference.
Henry, d. in Southford, Apr. 10, 1832, in his second year.
John Wesley, d. in Seymour, Jan. 29, 1849, aged 16.
Thomas, m. Lottie McLain ; residence, Seymour.
Daniel Smith, d. in Seymour, Aug. 27, 1849, in his 13th year.
William Carvosso, m. Vinie A. Lewis of Monroe, residence, Seymour.
Andrew Benedict, d. in Southford, Nov. 27, 1842, in his 2nd year.
David Watson, m. Emily Lewis of Monroe, residence, New Haven.

W. C. SHARPE.

GENEALOGY. 209

ELIAKIM SHARP of Monroe, son of Thomas and Mary, m. Nov. 25, 1773, Hester Wetmore, b. Sept. 16, 1756, d. in Mar. 1839. Children:
Andrew, b. Aug. 17, 1775, d. Nov. 26, 1790.
Betsey, b. Nov. 5, 1776, m. Burr Tomlinson.
Mabel, b. Oct. 11, 1779.
Ruth Ann, b. June 10, 1784.
Lydia Ann, b. Mar. 22, 1788, d. Feb. 7, 1817, buried in Huntington.
Mary, b. Oct. 18, 1789.
John W., b. Aug. 10, 1791, d. Nov. 7, 1815, in Liverpool, Eng., where he had gone in a vain endeavor to recover the family estate.
Annice, b. Aug. 10, 1791, m. John W. Robert and removed to Ohio.

JESSE SHARP had children:
Sally, m. .... Yale.
John, b. 1690, m. Kate Dawson, d. Oct. 27, 1825.
William, m. the daughter of Moses Beardsley.
Lydia, m. William Dart.
Nancy, m. .... Dart, brother to William.
Hepsey, m. Israel Calkins.
David, went to sea while young and never returned.

In Vol. 11, p. 126 of Derby Records, Jesse Sharp is named as one of the original proprietors of the "Quaker Farms Purchase," and a tract of land was set off to him "at a place called Good Hill Rocks, on the easterly side of the highway adjoining the Great River, beginning at Joseph Wooster's northwest corner at sd. river, bearing northerly ninety-two rods to a heap of stones on a rock, thence eighty-two rods easterly to Joseph Twitchell and Joseph Wooster's corner, thence to the bounds begun at one hundred and thirty-two rods, * * * a middle bound at the end, of sixty rods upon the highway on the River, * * * likewise another piece of land lying westerly on highway next to the River for the purpose of a fishing place, forty-four rods long, bounded at the north end at a little brook at butnut tree, with a bowing line to a middle bounds at Wickup tree, thence southerly to a great rock with stones on it."
ZACHARIAH HAWKINS, }
JOHN TOMLINSON, } Com't.
JOHN HOLBROOK. }

John Sharp sold land Nov. 4, 1807, to William Sharp as follows: "lying in said Derby at the lower end of Paul's Plain so-called, bounded westerly on Ousatonick River, southerly on a small brook, easterly on the Ousatonick Turnpike road & Northerly part on Philo Bassett's land & part on Russel Tomlinson's land." A subsequent transfer of this land is witnessd by David Sharp and Philo Bassett. Aug. 16, 1811, John Sharp bought of David Judson "a certain piece of land lying in Derby at a place called Falls Plain Rocks and is bounded West on highway, south on lands formerly belonging to Russell Tomlinson."

AMY SHARP, dau. of Thomas and Mary, m. Seth Sherwood Stratton of Bridgeport. Children:
Seth Legrand, m. Nancy Stetson of Boston. Children:
Joan, Nancy and Jane died young.
Augusta, m. ——— Marks of Stratford.
Adaline, m. Maria Hinman.
Legrand, m. ——— Hubbell.
George, was in the army; John.
Sherwood Edward, m. Cynthia, daughter of Joseph and Mary Ann (Sharp) Thompson of West Haven. Children:
Jane, Elizabeth, Charles S., (Tom Thumb), and William.
Laurena, m. Shelton B. Stratton. Children:
Charles T.; Shelton B.; and Francis, m. Daniel Bostwick.

210 HISTORY OF SEYMOUR.

Lossena, m. Elijah Peet. Children:
    Laura Ann, m. ...... Beach; Harriet Lossena, m. Lemuel Sherman; Jane Eliza, m. Elihu Taylor of Easton.

Daniel, m. Susan Curtiss of Stratford. Children:
    Elizabeth m. Frank Booth of Stratford, and has three children, Freddie, Susan, Flora. Edward Curtis.

Henry T., m. Caroline Mills of Westport, d. Nov. 29, 1874. Children:
    Antoinette Amelia, m. Benjamin Anson Fields; Frederick Thomas, Emma Caroline, Alice Louisa, Frank Sherwood.

SHERMAN SHARP, son of Daniel and Polly, m. Aphia Emmeline Wheeler, d. in Seymour in Dec., 1866. Children:
    Minot, m. Jane Hawkins of Quaker Farms. Children:
        Frank Newton and Carrie Estella.
    Rev. Charles W., graduated at Yale, in 1861, m. Helen Bradford of Binghampton, N. Y.; now principal of Boydton Institute, Boydton, Va.

TOMLINSON.

JONAS TOMLINSON[1], emigrant, settled on Great Hill about 1680. He had two sons, Jonas[2] and Agur[2].

HENRY TOMLINSON[3], son of Jonas[2], m. Sybil[3], dau. of Agur[2]. Children:
    Elizabeth, m. ...... Thorpe.
    Annie, m. ...... Nathan Mansfield.
    ...... m. ...... Givens.
    ...... m. ...... Waters. whose dau. m. Dea. Nehemiah Botsford.
    Patience, m. Yelverton Perry.
    Henry, Jr., m. Sally, dau. of Benjamin Davis.

HENRY TOMLINSON[4], son of Henry and Sybil, m. Sally, dau. of Benjamin Davis. Children:
    William, m. Amy Curtiss. Children:
        Harry and Russell of Bridgeport.
    Sheldon.
    Marcus, m. Polly Driver. Children:
        Sheldon, m. Rhoda Farrington of Boston, lived in Charleston, Mass. Nathan, Jennette and Rhoda.
    Russell, b. Dec. 23, 1754, d. June 22, 1809.
    Charles.
    Henry.
    Permelia, m. Joseph Vicker.

GENEALOGY. 211

RUSSELL TOMLINSON[5], Esq., of Great Hill, son of Henry and Sally, m. Apr. 26, 1779, Agnes Cortelyou of New Utrecht, L. I., b. Mar. 10, 1764. Lived for a time where Samuel P. Davis now lives. Children:
Sarah, b. Mar. 14, 1780.
Isaac, b. May 26, 1782.
Peter, b. Nov. 18, 1784, m. Esther Holbrook, d. Dec. 17, 1823.
Simon, b. May 22, 1787, m. Charity Hurd, d. Aug. 25, 1818.
James, b. Aug. 18, 1789, drowned in the Housatonic Apr. 22, 1804.
Betsey, b. Apr. 29, 1792, m. Charles Bacon.
Russell, b. Mar. 27, 1801, m. Sarah Burwell of Brookfield.
They had one daughter, Mary.
James C., b. Mar. 4, 1806, m. Laura Tomlinson.

DAVID TOMLINSON, b. Feb. 5, 1778, m. Sept. 26, 1779, Sarah[6], dau. of Russell Tomlinson, b. Mar. 14, 1780. David Tomlinson died Aug. 3, 1862, aged 84 years and 6 months. His wife Sarah died April 16, 1867, aged 87 years and 1 month. Children:
Eliza, b. May 4, 1801, m. Elijah Baldwin Jan. 6, 1820, d. June 4, 1822.
Mary, b. Mar. 5, 1803, d. Oct. 4, 1803.
David, b. Sept. 1, 1804, m. Nancy Hayes Sept. 24, 1825.
Augustus, b. Nov. 12, 1806, m. Dorcas English Apr. 17, 1830.
Jane, b. Nov. 7, 1808, m. 1st, John Lane Nov. 24, 1831; 2nd, Roger Newton Whittelsey Aug. 19, 1838; 3rd, Samuel Camp May 15, 1843.
Charles, b. Nov. 6, 1810, m. Jane, dau. of Sheldon Canfield, Nov. 10, 1831, d. July 18, 1839.
Betsey, b. Sept. 21, 1812, m. 1st, Samuel Russell Apr. 21, 1833; 2nd, Edward Russell Dec. 17, 1849.
Had one dau., Mary E., m. Benjamin Bristol Nov. 7, 1878.
Sarah, b. Dec. 5, 1814, m. John C. Hull July 25, 1830.
Isaac, b. May 24, 1817, m. Eliza Baytis Oct. 15, 1839, d. Oct. 31, 1853.
Simon, b. Apr. 11, 1820, m. Maria Lewis Apr. 23, 1843.

PETER TOMLINSON[6], son of Russell and Agnes, m. Esther Holbrook, b. Sept. 7, 1783, d. Feb. 10, 1854. Children:
Williard, b. Aug. 22, 1820, d. Dec. 7, 1832.
Peter and Edwin, b. Dec. 17, 1823.

SIMON TOMLINSON[6], son of Russell and Agnes, m. Aug. 28, 1806, Charity Hurd, b. July 3, 1780, d. in April, 1842. Children:
Agnes, b. Jan. 22, 1808, m. George Wagner of Southbury.
William R., b. Sept. 15, 1809, m. 1st, Phebe, 2nd, Hannah, daughters of Edwin Bassett.
Catharine A., b. Oct. 5, 1811, m. Wm. Shelton of Ohio.

212   HISTORY OF SEYMOUR.

Charles H., b. May 11, 1813, m. Esther, dau. of Wm. Smith, removed to Indiana.
George, b. Sept. 29, 1814, m. Delia, dau. of Arad Skeels of Birmingham.
Mariette, b. Feb. 2, 1816, m. 1st, Harry Johnson, 2nd, Legrand Bennett.
Sarah, b. Sept. 22, 1818, m. Charles Benton of Sharon.

ISAAC TOMLINSON[6], son of Russell and Agnes, m. Grace, dau. of Reuben Lum. Children:
Jennette, m. Sherman Prescott of New Haven.
James, m. Milly Miles of Derby.
Mary, m. Anson F. Colt of New Haven.
Peter, m. .... Canfield of Derby.
Betsey, m. .... Canfield of New Haven.
Isaac, died in childhood.

JAMES C. TOMLINSON[6], son of Russell and Agnes, married Laura Tomlinson. Children:
Agnes, Elizabeth, \/ Mary A., Williard, Edward, Isaac, Laura.
John R., m. Lydia, dau. of Capt. Truman Davis of Naugatuck.

ANNIE TOMLINSON[4], dau. of Henry[3] and Sybil, m. Nathan Mansfield. Children:
Betsy, b. Nov. 30, 1777, m. Anson Gillette.
Sally, m. Cyrus Holbrook.
  Had one son, and one daughter who married Benjamin Chatfield. Both died young.
Annie m. Wm. Dyer of Berlin, Ct. Had three sons.
Jared m. Eunice Jennings. Children:
  Stephen, Nathan and Eliza Ann, who m. Abram Fowler.

ISAAC TOMLINSON, m. ...... Hawkins. Children:
Isaac, m. Lucretia Webster of Oxford.
Grace, m. Samuel Lake. Children:
  Jennette, d. unmarried; George, lives in New Haven.
Ammon, m. Hannah ......
Silas, m. Polly Hawkins.
Truman, b. July 7, 1780, m. Nancy Perry, d. Dec. 25, 1846.
Laura, m. David Beecher.

TRUMAN TOMLINSON, son of Isaac, m. Nancy, dau. of Yelverton Perry and Patience Tomlinson of Oxford. Mrs. Nancy, d. Nov. 8, 1841. Children:
  Born in Castleton, Vt.
Ransom, b. Apr. 29, 1808, m. Nancy Bates of Oxford, d. in July, 1872.
  Children: Martha, m. William Riggs, living in Orange.

GENEALOGY.

Nancy, m. —— Wolfe, living in Hoboken, N. J.
Perry, m. Emma ——, living in Portland, Oregon.

Mary, b. Jan. 16, 1810, m. Joel R. Chatfield. Children:
  John, m. Anna Leigh.
  Edwin, m. Kate Tomlinson.
  Hiram.
  Ransom, m. Sarah, dau. of William Gilyard.
  Mary.
  Charlotte, m. Jerred Kimberly.
  Hattie.
  Joel, m. —— Keast.

Emily, b. Jan. 24, 1812, m. Capt. Philo Holbrook, d. in Nov. 1859.
  Children: Frederick, m. Dotha Kimberly.
  Andrew.
  Royal.
  Julia, m. Howard F. Moshier.
  Philo, Jr., living in Oregon.
  Daniel.
  Nebraska.
  Hermon.

Harrison, b. Apr. 25, 1814, m. Jan. 14, 1841, Emerett, dau. of Capt. Truman Davis of Naugatuck, d. Nov. 25, 1855. Children:
  Mary, Emma S., Hattie, m. Horace D. Chatfield of Birmingham; Clara and Henry Harrison, died in infancy.

Laura, b. Aug. 4, 1816, m. George Bassett of Seymour, d. in Meriden Mar. 25, 1855.
  Born in Monckton, Vermont.

Minerva, b. Dec. 7, 1818, m. Benjamin Nichols of Oxford. Children:
  Nancy M., m. George A., Tomlinson of Ansonia.
  Arthur, died in infancy.
  John, unmarried.
  Born in Oxford, Ct.

John Givens, b. Mar. 23, 1821, resides in Portland, Oregon.

One Jonas Tomlinson d. Oct. 2, 1796. One Agur had a negro slave Feb. 7, 1791. D. R.^{bmd} 139.

LEVI TOMLINSON, Esq., m. Amelia ...... Children:
Urania, d. Oct. 1, 1794, aged 1 year and 11 months.
Amelia, d. Sept. 29, 1794, aged 16 years.
Levi, d. Sept. 23, 1794, aged 9 years.
Phebe, May 11, 1794, aged 3 years and 10 months.

PERRY.

ARTHUR PERRY[1] came to Stratford about 1675 and married Anna, only daughter of Joshua Judson, about 1676. He had thirteen children, viz.:
  William, b. in June, 1677.
  Anna, b. in Jan., 1679.

Samuel, b. in Feb., 1681, m. Elizabeth ———
Sarah, b. in Jan., 1682.
Elizabeth, b. in Sept., 1684.
Yelverton, b. in Aug., 1686.
Seth, b. in Jan., 1688.
Ruth, b. in May, 1690.
Daniel, b. in Apr., 1692.
Joshua, b. in Dec., 1694, d. at Ripton in 1688.
Caleb, b. in Aug., 1696.
Deborah, b. in Mar., 1698.
Josiah, b. in Aug., 1699.

It is thought that the Arthur above mentioned was a son of Arthur Perry of Boston, 1638 to 1652, born too near his father's death to be mentioned in his will.

———

SAMUEL PERRY[2], son of Arthur, born in Stratford, m. Elizabeth ——— had a son Abner[3], who had a son Caleb[4], the father of Yelverton Perry[5], m. 1st, ——— Hawley of Huntington, by whom he had one daughter, Sally, who married Silas Hawkins of Oxford; 2nd, Patience, dau. of Henry and Sybil Tomlinson of Derby, by whom he had four sons and three daughters, John[6], Frederic[6], Hermon[6], Azariah Hawley[6], Laura[6] and Nancy[6], b. Oct. 1, 1783, d. Nov. 8, 1841.

———

JOHN PERRY[6], b. in Oxford, Oct. 19, 1767, married Anna Beardsley, who died Nov. 26, 1836. He died March 13, 1852. Children:

Charles[7], b. Apr. 24, 1796, in Oxford, d. in fall of 1861. Married Mary Ann Paine. Children:
Frederick, Charles, Harriet, Adam Clark. All dead but youngest.

Philo[7], b. Feb. 11, 1798, drowned June 12, 1800.

John[7], b. Nov. 12, 1801, d. July 15, 1839, leaving one child,
Charles, b. Sept. 20, 1835, d. Sept. 12, 1842.

Nancy[7], b. Sept. 3, 1803, m. Cornelius Pugsley of Stamford, Dutchess co., N. Y., Sept. 14, 1831. Children:
Henry, Cornelia, Van Allen, Jacob, Charles.

———

FREDERICK PERRY[6], of Southbury, m. Mary Strong. Children:

Andrew, resides at Southbury, unmarried.

Betsy, m. ——— Smith, then Osborne. Left no children. Died in Southbury in 1874.

Charles, m. Maria Curtiss of Southbury.
Had one son, Hermon, who married Josephine Mitchell of South Britain.

Sophia, m. ——— Raymond.
Dau. Mary, m. ——— Stone of Southbury.

GENEALOGY. 215

HERMON PERRY[6], of Baltimore, Md., m. Susannah Henry. Children:
  Hermon, died unmarried.
  William, died unmarried.
  Albert, m. —— Lake.
  Susannah, m. Geo. W. Waters.

LAURA PERRY[6], m. David Smith of Kent, Ct., removed to Dutchess co., N. Y., and died there.

AZARIAH HAWLEY PERRY[6], born in Oxford Sept. 21, 1780, m. Mar. 6, 1809, Polly Leavenworth, b. Aug. 27, 1789, in Huntington. He died Nov. 21, 1826. She died May 31, 1871. Had one child, Jane[7], b. in Huntington, Mar. 11, 1811, m. David Shelton of Huntington May 4, 1830. David Shelton died June 2, 1872. They had one daughter, Mary Jane[8], born Feb. 8, 1833, who married Edwin Wooster of Birmingham May 23, 1860; died June 4, 1864. Edwin Wooster was drowned in the Housatonic river near Birmingham, Apr. 20, 1876.

NANCY PERRY[6], m. Truman Tomlinson. See Tomlinson Genealogy.

KINNEY.

EBENEZER KINNEY, b. in 1718, m. Betty Davis Dec. 7, 1738. He died Jan. 10, 1795. She died in Nov., 1784. Children:
  Lucy, b. Dec. 3, 1739, d. Nov. 27, 1861.
  Comfort, b. Oct. 11, 1741, d. May 2, 1771.
  Eunice, b. Aug. 31, 1743.
  Betty, b. Sept. 20, 1745.
  Sarah, b. Oct. 3, 1748.
  Ebenezer, b. Oct. 27, 1750, d. in May, 1777.
  Abigail, b. Feb. 11, 1753, d. Oct. 4, 1769.
  Ethel, b. Mar. 17, 1755, d. in Oct., 1838, aged 82 years.
  William, b. July 16, 1757, d. Jan. 7, 1845, aged 87.
  Medad, b. May 31, 1759, d. in May, 1794, aged 35 years.
  Lucy, b. Sept. 20, 1761.   D. R.[bmd] p. 7.

WILLIAM KINNEY, son of Ebenezer, m. Millie Steele, b. Dec. 15, 1760, d. Mar. 9, 1827. Children:
  Ebenezer, b. Nov. 28, 1779, m. Betsey Buckingham, d. Apr. 2, 1851. She d. Dec. 29, 1846.

HISTORY OF SEYMOUR.

Sheldon, b. Oct. 12, 1781, m. Esther, dau. of Daniel Canfield, d. June 13, 1873, aged 91 y. and 8 m. She was b. Mar. 6, 1790, d. May 30, 1852.

William, b. Aug. 20, 1783, m. Anna Smith, d. June 25, 1856. She died Sept. 28, 1867, aged 76 years.

Betsey, b. Sept. 10, 1785, m. Anson Chatfield, d. June 28, 1863.
Children: Divine, Marietta, Susan.

Sally, b. Nov. 10, 1787, m. Sheldon Nichols, d. Oct. 25, 1863. Children:
Sheldon, William, Lucena.

Isaac, b. Feb. 13, 1790, d. Aug. 18, 1875.

Lucinda. b. Oct. 2, 1792, m. Capt. William Lum, d. Aug. 9, 1825.

Medad, b. Dec. 18, 1794, m. Rebecca White, d. Feb. 6, 1830. She died May 2, 1826, aged 32. Children:
Roswell, Mary, Polly, Ann, John.

EBENEZER KINNEY, son of William, m. Betsey Buckingham, b. Apr. 19, 1783. Children:
Betsey M., b. Jan. 29, 1804, m. Jeremiah Durand.
William, b. Sept. 27, 1806, d. Jan. 1, 1847.
George, b. Nov. 2, 1816, d. Oct. 16, 1847.
Lester B., b. Feb. 4, 1819.

WILLIAM KINNEY, son of William, m. Anna Smith. Lived in the house on Hill st., now occupied by John Kelleher. Children:
Mary Jane, m. James Johnson of Bridgeport.
Sarah Grace, m. Isaac White, lived in Derby.
Miranda, m. Clark Lum of New Haven.
Esther Ann, m. Medad K. Tucker.

DEA. ISAAC KINNEY, son of William and Mille, m. 1st, Polly Durand, b. July 3, 1796, d. Sept. 23, 1827; 2nd, Dec. 16, 1828, Anna Church, b. Sept. 20, 1803, d. Jan. 24, 1868. Children:
Isaac Heber, b. Mar. 7, 1830, d. Feb. 13, 1851.
Charles D., b. Mar. 27, 1832, living in New Haven.
Frederick C., b. Nov. 28, 1836, died July 30, 1854.

CHARLES D. KINNEY, son of Isaac and Anna, m. 1st, Jan. 25, 1857, Martha J. Wilder, b. Dec. 3, 1835, d. Oct. 23, 1871; 2nd, July 16, 1874, Ella A. Burwell. Children:
Frederick N., b. Feb. 2, 1860.
Charles H., b. Feb. 17, 1866.

GENEALOGY.

LOUNSBURY.

JOSIAH LOUNSBURY came from Rye, Westchester co., N. Y., to New Haven, m. Ruth Lines May 7, 1724, removed to Bethany, lived nearly opposite where Wm. Lounsbury now lives. Children:

   Timothy², m. Hannah Smith and lived to be 86 years of age. Children:
      ——, a boy, died young.
      Timothy.
      Eri,
      Lucy, m. James Hotchkiss, moved to Homer, N. Y.
      Eunice, m. Truman Prince, had but one child, Castle, died young.
   Stephen², m. —— Sperry. Children:
      Elias, m. 1st, Appalina Judd, 2nd, Mary Perkins.
      Hezekiah, father of Mrs. Thomas Cochran.
      Peany and Irena.
   John², b. Jan. 18, $172\frac{4}{5}$, m. Ruth Perkins Apr. 4. 1751. Children:
      Jairus, b. Jan. 14, 1752.
      Benjamin, b. Apr. 11, 1753.
      Richard, b. Aug. 20, 1754.
      Ethal, went west.
      Ethan, d. a bachelor.
   Mary², b. Feb. 12, $172\frac{7}{8}$.
   Josiah², b. Aug. 5, 1729. Children:
      Linus, m. Prudence Scott. Children:
         Josiah, father of Ransom, Calvin, Obadiah, Ancel.
      Amelia, m. Daniel Davis.
      Esther, m. Edmund Mallory of Hull's Hill.
      Patty, m. Titus Smith.
   Samuel², was a soldier of the Revolution, died in Farmington over 80 years of age.
   Ruth²., m. —— Tolles.

TIMOTHY LOUNSBURY³, son of Timothy² and Hannah, m. Hannah French. Timothy lived to be nearly 86 years of age, his wife nearly 70. Children:
   Dorcas⁴, m. Jabez Wilcox.
   Timothy, m. Mary Ann Clark.
   Lewis, m. Charity, dau. of Amos Clark of Nyumphs.
   Daniel, m. Sarah, dau. of David Wooding of Bethany.
   Jesse, m. Bede, dau. of Jesse Bradley of Bethany.
   Hannah, m. Herschel Sanford of Prospect.
   Smith, m. Jennette Tomlinson.
   Allen, m. Maria, dau. of Elam Cook of Cheshire.
   Eunice, m. 1st, Vincent Brown, 2nd, McDonald Fisher.
   Mary, m. Burritt Hitchcock, son of Timothy.
   Dr. John of Oxford, m. Mary, dau. of Wm. Church. Children:
      Emma, Tully.
   George, m. —— Austin of Prospect.

HISTORY OF SEYMOUR.

Eri, m. Sally Carrington. Children:
Polly, Sarah, Rebecca, Abraham, Lucy, Isaac, Lucretia, Harriet, William, Harlo.

The preceding portion of the Lounsbury genealogy was furnished by Dr. John Lounsbury of Oxford.

JAIRUS LOUNSBURY was said by his sons to have come from Vermont to New Haven and settled near where the jail now stands. He married Amelia Chapman who died at the age of 83 years. He was in the Revolutionary service, and died aged 96. Children:

Collins[4], b. July 19, 1783, m. and lived in Vermont, d. aged 80.
Clarissa, b. Feb. 11, 1791, m. John Gamsby. Children:
Albert, John Henderson, Alfred, Edwin, Sarah, Lucius.
Betsey, b. Oct. 11, 1794, m. Harvey Finch. Child:
Crownage.
Victory, b. Sept. 8, 1795, m. Loraine Baldwin.
Sally, b. Apr. 13, 1800, m. Russell Moulton. Children:
Ann Julia, m. Elijah Losee of Norwich.
Amanda, m. Capt. Alden Powers. Children:
Frank, Sarah, Luthera, Benjamin.
Benjamin, shot in San Francisco, Cal.
Mary.
Crownage, b. May 20, 1803, m. Samantha Hotchkiss, d. Feb. 28, 1879, aged 76 years. She died Feb. 28, 1877. Children:
William H., m. Julia Ann Ladue of Mattawan. Child, Jennie.
Mark, m. Ann Webster of Thompsonville. Children: Annette Eliza, Etta Maria, Norman Webster.
Sarah, m. Chauncey Hooker, near Holyoke, Mass.
David, b. Aug. 15, 1805, m. Jane Patchen died in New Haven April 1, 1877, aged 72 years. Children:
Lewis, Martha, Eliza, Mary, Maria.

Probably Jairus was the son of John, (2), of Bethany and went from there to Vermont, where he married Miss Chapman, whose father was killed by the Indians when she was an infant.

VICTORY LOUNSBURY, son of Jairus and Amelia, m. Loraine, dau. of James and Sarah Baldwin, who d. Nov. 25, 1868, aged 73 y. and 8 m. Children:
Fanny, b. Feb. 2, 1817, m. Byron Tucker. Child:
Lillie, m. Oscar L. Woodruff; child, Bernice.
George W., b. Aug. 27, 1819.
John, b. Sept. 8, 1821, m. Lucinda Summers. Child:
Gertrude, m. Matthias Smith; child, Maud Lizette.
Charles W., b. Jan. 23, 1824, d. Oct. 13, 1826.
Albert W., b. Jan. 6, 1826, m. Olive Maria Sharpe.
Henry W , b. June 29, 1829, m. Dec. 20, 1850, Mary A., dau. of Benjamin and Harriett Bradley of New Haven, d. Aug. 14, 1862. Children:
Charles, living in New Haven, Mich.
Harriet Jane, m. July 22, 1874, David Evans, Jr.
Children: David Otis and Benjamin Bradley.
Edward Benjamin.
Jane, b. Nov. 6, 1832, m. Lucius Canfield of New Haven, Mich.
Children: Alanson, Horatio, Oscar.

GENEALOGY. 219

Mary, b. Feb. 8, 1834, m. David W. Riggs of Pinesbridge. Children:
  Francis, m. Harris Osborne.
  Fred O., m. Sarah Isbell, who d. in Apr., 1879.
  Elmer, Edward, Dudley.
Sarah, b. Dec. 12, 1836, m. John H. Miller, d. May 2, 1867. Children:
  George B., d. Aug. 2, 1867, aged 3 years; Eda.
Charles, b. Sept. 4, 1838, d. Sept. 15, 1850.
Ellen, b. Sept. 14, 1843, m. Frank Couvrette, d. Apr. 12, 1878, aged 34 years. Children:
  Arthur B., Alice B., d. in July, 1873, aged 11 months.

ELIAS LOUNSBURY[3], son of Stephen[2], m. 1st, Appolina Judd. Child: Elias, father of Elizur of Westville.
Married, 2nd, Mary Perkins. Children:
Major, Newel, Marlin, Belus, Ursula.

TUCKER.

DANIEL TUCKER came from Long Island, m. Elizabeth ———. Children:
  Capt. Ruben, b. Mar. 1, 1744/5.
  Gideon, b. Apr. 17, 1746.
  Joseph, b. July 1, 1748.
  Zephaniah, b. in 1759.

ZEPHANIAH TUCKER, blacksmith, lived uptown, Derby, d. Sept. 18, 1848, aged 89 years. Children:
  Sheldon, b. Mar. 6, 1786, d. Jan. 5, 1843.
  Anna, b. Nov. 27, 1783, m. Edmund Steele.
  Betsey, m. Rev. Nathaniel G. Huntington.

SHELDON TUCKER, m. Nancy Kinney, b. Nov. 23, 1793, d. Sept. 19, 1831. Children:
  Medad K., b. Jan. 28, 1815.
  Mariah A., b. Sept. 23, 1819, m. Isaac B. Davis.
  Sheldon, b. Mar. 6, 1824, d. Aug. 18, 1825.

MEDAD K. TUCKER, son of Sheldon, m. Esther A. Kinney. Has one son, Sheldon, m. Mary E., dau. of Henry B. Beecher.

HITCHCOCK.

EBENEZER HITCHCOCK[1] of New Haven, m. Rebecca Thomas, Mar. 23, 1747. Their son, Timothy[2] was born Nov. 8, 1748.

TIMOTHY HITCHCOCK[2] of Bethany, son of Ebenezer and Rebecca, m. Abigail ———, who d. aged 99 years and 7 months. He d. Aug. 5, 1820, aged 72. Children:
    Timothy.
    Denzil H., b. Dec. 7, 1786, d. Jan. 24, 1850, aged 63.
    Clark, m. Abigail Perkins, removed to Baltimore.
    Abigail, d. in 1873, unmarried.
    Anna, m. Dilavan Wooster of Watertown.
    Elizabeth, m. Darius Driver of Bethany.
    Thyra, m. Arlon Hine, removed to Cleveland, Ohio.
    Lydia, m. Samuel Driver of Bethany.

The following inscription from a Bible shows the excellent character of the writer:

"This Bible is the Gift of Timothy and Abigail Hitchcock to their son Denzil Hitchcock, who was born Dec. 7th, A. D., 1786, in the Parish of Bethany, town of Woodbridge, county of New Haven and State of Connecticut.

"My son, I beseech you not to let this Book lie by you neglected; read it with care and attention; meditate on the truths and doctrines it contains with delight; and endeavor to govern your life and conversation agreeable thereto.

"That God may grant you Grace to avoid sin; Patience under trials; quiet resignation to Providence; A Prosperous life; and a happy Eternity, is the earnest Prayer of your Affectionate Father, Timothy Hitchcock."

DENZIL HITCHCOCK[3], son of Timothy[1], m. Betsey, dau. of Elias Carrington of Milford. Children:
    Henry Nelson, d. Mar. 25, 1825, aged 2½ years.
    Henrietta.
    Sarah C., m. 1st, Oct. 24, 1847, Bernard Humphreys, who d. Jan. 9, 1854; 2nd, George B. Robinson Dec. 4, 1854.

Bernard Humphreys bought out Albert Steele's cabinet business and at one time was engaged in papermaking in company with Andrew De Forest.

TIMOTHY HITCHCOCK[3], b. in August, 1781, m. 1st, Rayner Twitchell; 2nd, Mrs. Amanda Bassett; d. in New Haven Dec. 5, 1878, aged 97 y. and 4 m. Children:
    Sheldon, m. ——— dau. of Capt. Auger of New Haven, d. in New Haven in Aug., 1877.
    Burritt, m Mary, dau. of Dr. Timothy Lounsbury, of Bethany. Residence, New Haven.
    Sarah, m. Clark Webster of Oxford.
    Lucinda, m. Joel Chatfield. Children:
        Clark and Lucinda.

Jonathan Hitchcock m. Abigail Beecher Jan. 21, 1747.
Samuel Hitchcock m. Ann Johnson Jan. 20, 174$\frac{7}{8}$. Child:
    Samuel, b. June 8, 1750.   D. R., Vol. 6, p. 2.

GENEALOGY.

BEECHER.

A Mr. Beecher, with his wife and son, from county Kent, England, is said to have embarked in the first ship which brought emigrants to New Haven. (The first settlers came overland from Massachusetts.) He died before the vessel sailed. His wife was persuaded by the other emigrants to continue with the company, with her son Isaac, from whom all the New Haven families of the name are said to have descended, and from whence the name has spread throughout the country, numbering among the direct descendants the Rev. Henry Ward Beecher of Brooklyn. For her services as physician and midwife, the first Mrs. Beecher had a portion of land voted to her by the town of New Haven, which remained in the family until quite recently. On a part of it the City Hospital now stands.

JOHN BEECHER, lived in New Haven. Children:
John, b. Aug. 9, 1671.   Jemima, b. Feb. 11, 1681.
Mary, b. Feb. 23, 1672.   Joseph, b. Feb. 13, 1683.
Johanna, b. July 21, 1677. Ebenezer, b. Apr. 12, 1686.

JOSEPH BEECHER, son of John, lived in New Haven. Children:
Allis, b. Jan. 28, 1695.   Hezekiah, b. June 14, 1703.
Joseph, b. Nov. 22, 1698.   Nathaniel. b. Mar. 7, 1706.
Lydia, b. Feb. 15, 1700.   Eliphalet, b. May 31, 1711.

JOSEPH BEECHER, 2nd, m. Sarah Ford May 15, 1729, lived in New Haven. Children:
Joseph, b. Feb. 14, 1731/2, m. Esther Potter Feb. 28, 1754.
Moses, b. Feb. 2, 1733/3.
Timothy, b. Feb. 8, 1734/5.
Abel, b. Nov. 17, 1737.
Titus, b. July 5, 1740.
Amos, b. June 10, 1743.

New Haven Records, Vol. 1.

ISAAC BEECHER of Derby, m. Hannah Ball, d. in Sept., 1789. Child:
Mary, b. July 3, 1775, m. John Riggs Jan. 1, 1793, d. Dec. 16, 1827.

EZRA BEECHER of West Haven m. Mary Trowbridge, who died in Southbury aged 92 years. His son, Nathaniel, m. Dinah Smith of West Haven and lived in Southbury.

LEWIS BEECHER, son of Nathaniel and Dinah, m. Martha Peck. Children:
Louis L., m. Polly Fairchild, lived in New Haven.
Sarah M., m. ——— Bartholomew, lived in New Haven.
Henry B., auger manufacturer of Seymour.
Eliza A., m. Major Russell Norton of New Haven.
Mary J., m. George Fowler of New Haven. Child:
    Frederick, m. Mary Root.

HENRY B. BEECHER, son of Lewis and Martha, m. 1st, Betsey A. White; 2nd, Mary Fairchild. Children:
    Ann, m. William W. Joy of Ansonia. Children:
        Frederick and Willie.
    Frank H., m. Nellie A. Thompson.
    Mary E., m. Sheldon Tucker of Seymour.

STEELE.

ADDITIONAL.

WALTER W. STEELE of Ansonia, son of William Steele, b. Jan. 28, 1824. m. Mary E. Carter of Wolcott, Sept. 23, 1850. He died Sept. 20, 1874. Children:
    Arthur Willis, b. Mar. 18, 1852, d. Aug. 24, 1852.
    Mary Frances, b. Apr. 5, 1855.
    Truman Bradford, b. Aug. 21, 1858.

JOHNSON.

ADDITIONAL.

HEZEKIAH JOHNSON m. Dec. 12, 1784, Rebecca Tuttle, dau. of Abraham and Elizabeth Tuttle, b. Feb. 14, 1756, d. May 1, 1830. Hezekiah, b. Nov. 6, 1749, d. Nov. 15, 1826.

NEWEL JOHNSON, son of Hezekiah and Rebecca, b. May 22, 1788, d. June 11, 1879; m. 1st, Oct. 21, 1809, Betsey, dau. of Benjamin and Martha Molthrop, who d. Feb. 7, 1810; 2nd, Sept. 2, 1810, Esther Carrington, dau. of Elias and Content Carrington of Milford, who d. Mar. 9, 1866. He removed from Humphreysville to Westville in 1833. Children:
    Sheldon N., b. May 5, 1811, d. Jan. 27, 1853.
    Betsey Julia, b. May 1, 1813, d. July 6, 1872.
    Richard Miles, b. Nov. 8, 1814, d. Jan. 26, 1874.
    Esther Ann, b. Apr. 7, 1817.
    Almira Minerva, b. Jan. 6, 1821.
    Eliza Augusta, b. Sept. 10, 1836.

WOOSTER.

SAMUEL WOOSTER, m. Mary ———. Children :
  Nathaniel, b. Nov. 25, 1761, d. Nov. 24, 1855.
  Milton, m. ——— Welton.
  Dilavan, m. Anna, dau. of Timothy Hitchcock.
  Josiah, m. Elizabeth Terrill.
  Philo, m. Sarah, dau. of Philo Hawkins.

NATHANIEL WOOSTER of Quaker Farms, son of Samuel and Mary, m. Feb. 5, 1788, Charity ———, b. July 26, 1767. Children :
  Mamie, b. Sept. 23, 1788.
  Grace, b. Jan. 9, 1791, m. John Smith.
  Anna Maria, b. Nov. 13, 1793; d. Oct. 29, 1794.
  Bennett, b. Oct. 13, 1795; m. Sarah, dau. of Truman Bassett. Child:
    Charles B., m. Mary A. Booth. Residence, New Haven.
  Clarissa Maria, b. Mar. 4, 1796, m. Lewis Buckingham of Oxford. Children:
    Mark, living in Ansonia.
    Martha, m. Styles French of New Haven.
    Henrietta, went west.
    Henry.
    Joel, killed in the war of the rebellion.
  Nathan R., b. Nov. 18, 1810, m. Antoinette, dau. of Truman Bassett.
  Mark, b. Jan. 26, 1815, d. July 2, 1839.

GRACE WOOSTER, dau. of Nathaniel and Charity, m. John Smith of Quaker Farms. Children:
  Edwin, m. Betsey A., dau. of Harvey Johnson of Ansonia. Residence, Seymour. Child:
    Frances, m. Robert N. Smith.
  Lucy, died young.
  Mary, m. Joel Wheeler of Oxford.
  Laura.
  Bennett, died young.
  George, m. ———, dau. of Luther Moulthrop. Residence, Ansonia.

BALDWIN.
ADDITIONAL.

JAMES BALDWIN m. Sarah Perkins. Children :
  Elias.
  Anson.
  Stephen, m. Betsey Hubbell.
  Loraine, m. Victory Lounsbury.
  Jesse, m. Jane, dau. of Capt. Isaac Botsford. Child: Jabez.
  Charlotte.

STEPHEN BALDWIN, son of James and Sarah, m. Betsey Hubbell. Children
George R., m. Emily Grace Sperry of Oxford.
Eliza Ann, m. 1st, Lewis Williams of Naugatuck; 2nd, Jabez Pritchard.
Lucy Jane, m. Hobart Churchill of Waterbury.
Sarah Maria, m. Robert Twitchell of Naugatuck.
Frederick L., m. Addie Way, lives in Oxford.

MOULTHROP.

MATHEW MOULTHROP, m. Jane ——— and removed from New Haven to Sterrey River in 1662. Children:
Mathew, Jr., m. Hannah Tompson.
Elizabeth, m. John Gregory in 1663.
Mary.

MATHEW MOULTHROP, 2nd, m. Hannah Tompson in 1662. Children:
Hannah, b. Apr. 20, 1665.
John, b. Feb. 5, 1667, m. Abigail Bradley.
Matthew, 3rd, b. July 18, 1670.
Lydia, b. Aug. 8, 1674.
Samuel, b. Apr. 13, 1679.
Keziah, b. Apr. 12, 1682.

JOHN MOULTHROP[3], m. Abigail Bradley June 29, 1692. Children:
Abigail, b. Aug. 12, 1693.
John[4], b. Mar. 17, 1696.
Mary, b. in 1698.
Sarah, b. in 1701, m. Adonijah Morris.
Dan[4], b. Dec. 1, 1703; m. 1st, Hannah Belcher, 2nd, Lydia How. Children:
Dan, Charles, lost at sea; Timothy; Hannah m. Israel Lindsley; Enos, Enoch; Sarah, m. Elisha Andreas; Eli, m. Mary Moulthrop; Lydia; Mabel.
Israel[4]. b. June 7, 1706.
Joseph and Timothy.

JOHN MOULTHROP[4], m. Sarah ———. Children:
John[5], Stephen, Mehitabel.
Sarah, m. 1st, Timothy Russell, 2nd, John Pardee.
Mary, m. John Dawson, Jr.
Abigail, m. Dan Goodsell.

GENEALOGY.

JOHN MOULTHROP[5], m. Abigail Holt. Children:
David[6], m. Hepsibah Hotchkiss. Child: David[7].
John.
Reuben, m Hannah Street Nov. 18, 1792. Children:
Daniel Bowen, Maria, Clarissa, Daniel, Delia, Sydney, Reuben.

ENOCH MOULTHROP[5], son of Dan[4], m. Mary Hotchkiss. Children:
Dan, Lydia, Mary, Betsey, Silas, Timothy.

ISRAEL MOULTHROP[4], m. Lydia Page. Children:
Samuel, m. Sarah Dennison.
Jacob, died in the French war.
Timothy; Lydia, m. John Fuller in 1766.
Loris, m. Charles Page in 1765.

SAMUEL MOULTHROP, m. Sarah Dennison. Children:
Josiah, b. May 30, 1754, m. Mrs. Lydia Smith July 4, 1792. Children:
Desire, b. Apr. 16, 1793; Jared, b. Mar. 9, 1795; Samuel R., b. May 5, 1797.
Desire, b. Nov. 16, 1756, m. Moses Tompson in 1775.
Jared, b. Jan. 20, 1759.
Jacob, b. Aug. 29, 1762, m. 1st, Abigail Pardee; 2nd, Elizabeth Goodrich. Children:
Abigail, Betsey, Eunice, Leonard, Bela, Sarah, Damaris.
Sarah, b. Aug. 13, 1764.
Mercy, b. Sept. 9, 1767.
Lydia, b. Aug. 7, 1769.
Samuel, b. Sept. 1, 1773.
James, b. Oct. 14, 1776.
Israel, b. in Sept., 1779.

JOSEPH MOULTHROP, m. Mary Wheden. Children: Elihu, Jude; Adonijah, lost in French war; Hannah, Rhoda, Mary, Lucretia, Abigail.

JOSEPH MOULTHOP, m. Lucretia Bradley in 1766. Children: Abijah, Joseph, Jared, Rhoda, Irene, Chauncey.

ELIHU MOULTHROP, m. Mary ———. Children: Jared, Polly, Adonijah, Elihu; Esther and Matthew, 3rd, who m. Mary ———. Children:
Jane, b. Dec. 13, 1694, m. Thomas Hodge; Matthew, b. in Sept., 1696; Joseph, b. in Oct., 1698; Mary, b. June 1, 1701, m. Gideon Potter; Martha, b. Feb. 18, 1703; Mathew, b. Feb. 1, 1705; Benjamin, b. Mar. 2, 1707; Asher, b. Jan. 28, 1710; Dorothy, b. Dec. 1, 1712, m. Isaac Granniss.

MATHEW MOULTHROP, 4th, m. Sarah Granniss. Children: Thankful, b. in Nov., 1728; Joseph, b. in Dec., 1730; Sarah, b. in Jan., 1732; Mabel, b. Sept. 6, 1735; Mathew, b. Nov. 9, 1743; 2nd wife, Hannah Way, had David, b. March 23, 1748. David, m. Rachel Swayne. Children: John, Martin, Major, Polly, Swayne.

BENJAMIN MOULTHROP, son of Elihu, had Benjamin July 20, 1735, Elizabeth, Mary, Benjamin.

BENJAMIN MOULTHROP, JR., m. Thankful Granniss in July, 1761. Children:
Benjamin.
Seba, b. Nov. 23, 1770, d. July 8, 1831, aged 60.
Mary and Elizabeth.

SEBA MOULTHROP, son of Benjamin and Thankful, m. Catharine Fowler, b. Aug. 16, 1780, d. May 22, 1859. He built the hotel, or tavern, as it was then called, corner of Hill and Pearl streets, in 1812, and kept it about twenty years, when he died. Children:
William Fowler, b. Aug. 3, 1798, m. Eunice Bassett Sept. 2, 1821, d. in April, 1864.
Luther, b. Nov. 17, 1800, d. in 1866, m. Jennet Candee Dec. 19, 1830.
Huldah, b. Jan. 26, 1803 m. Jan. 19, 1852.
Mary, b. June 28, 1806, m. Amos Wheeler Apr. 24, 1825.
Clark, b. Dec. 6, 1812.
Betsey, b. Sept. 8, 1820, d. Aug. 5, 1847.
Grannis, b. Nov. 17, 1822.

HULDAH MOULTHROP m. Isaac Rowe Apr. 4, 1824. Isaac Rowe, Sr., and his twin brother Fred, born Aug. 16, 1799, came from Brattleboro, Vt., with Gen. Humphrey in 1811. Isaac was born Aug. 16, 1799; drowned in Lake St. Clair, Mich., Dec. 15, 1830. Children:
Huldah Keziah, b. Feb. 17, 1825, d. Oct. 26, 1873.
Isaac Thomas, b. Sept. 22, 1828; m. Sarah A. McGraw in Seymour Mar. 16, 1851.
Catharine, b. Jan. 4, 1831; m. George S. Wyant Dec. 24, 1850. Children:
Frank H., Eugene A., m. Mary Hard; Helen I., d. Apr. 17, 1859; Nettie E., George E.

SHELDON CLARK, ESQ.

Condensed from a sketch by Prof. Silliman kindly loaned for the purpose by the Secretary of Yale College.

A little beyond our northern boundary, in Chestnut-tree Hill, is a tract of land owned by Yale College, given by one who is well worthy of a sketch in these pages. Sheldon Clark, a brother of Mrs. Abiram Stoddard of Seymour, was born in Oxford Jan. 31, 1785, and died April 10, 1840, aged 55 years. His father died when he was very young and he was adopted by his grandfather, Thomas Clark, Esq., with whom he remained until the death of this venerable ancestor at the age of 82, April 5, 1811. The grandson wished to obtain a liberal education, but his grandfather disapproved of such a course as a waste of time and money, and he had no extraordinary opportunities for education except about a year at South Farms, in Litchfield, in 1805 and 1806. But his active mind prompted him to diligently read such books as he could obtain and thus cultivated habits of intellectual exercise and independence of character. The death of his grandfather left him free to pursue such a course as his own judgment dictated, and he applied for advice to Prof. Silliman of Yale College and passed the autumn and winter of 1811–12 in a course of study in connection with the recitations and discussions of President Dwight. Among his numerous manuscripts is one dated January, 1812, giving an account of a dream or vision of the general judgement. The language is elevated and beautiful and the imagery splendid and sublime. It is remarkable for deep seriousness and reverence for the heavenly world. Ten years later he called on Prof. Silliman and stated that the twenty thousand dollars left him by his grandfather he had by industry and economy increased to twenty-five thousand, that he had no family, and might never have one, and that he was disposed to appropriate at least a part of his estate to the encouragement of learning. He therefore deposited $5,000, to be placed at compound interest until it should amount to a sufficient sum for the establishment of the Clark professorship. In 1824 he gave $1,000 for the purpose of establishing a scholarship. This new instance of liberality excited additional interest in the hardworking Oxford farmer, whose example had now placed him at the head of the benefactors of this ancient literary institution. In 1829 he presented to the College an excellent telescope, with a focal length of ten feet and an aperture of five inches, made to his order, and costing over $1,000. He was elected to the legislature from Oxford in 1825 and for several succeeding years. His sentiments and mode of thought may perhaps best be expressed in his own words, as in the following extract from a letter written by him in reply to acknowledgments of one of his bequests:

"OXFORD, Nov. 29th, 1832.

"RESPECTED FRIENDS—Man is a child of circumstances. While some are born to ease and plenty, seldom meet with disappointments, are surrounded by benevolent friends, always ready to assist, to comfort, and to afford them the most ample means of enjoying the highest degree of mental culture; others are born to poverty and servitude, unassisted, even by their nearest relatives, and denied the privilege of obtaining a good common school education, and are often dispirited by disappointments.

"It was my destiny to belong to the latter class. Early in life I had a tender father, who was in possession of a large amount of property. He intended, and often promised, that I should have a liberal education—but, alas, before I was old enough to prepare to enter College, he died, and the *estate proved to be insolvent.*

"Thus all my fond hopes of having a liberal education were frustrated, and I was left fatherless and penniless in a hard, unfeeling, selfish world, to provide, by my own industry, to satisfy those positive wants congenial to poor human nature. It fell to my lot to live, till I was of age, with my grandfather, a hard working, parsimonious farmer, but I was allowed the privilege of reading occasionally, on Sundays, stormy days, and in the long nights of winter. From these opportunities of reading, I was soon convinced that the power, the honor, and glory of nations, consisted in, and depended upon, their great men. What has Greece, or Rome, or any nation of antiquity transmitted to posterity, worthy of esteem and admiration, but the achievements of their heroes, and the productions of their artists, poets, and philosophers? And what else can we transmit to succeeding ages, to distinguish us from the unlettered savages that roamed at large in the uncultivated wilds of America when discovered by our fathers? Full of this idea, and animated with an ardent desire to promote the honor and happiness of my own native country, I felt determined to do all I could to patronize and encourage literature and science, to provide the means of affording our literary and scientific genius a finished education.

"Oft when toiling with ceaseless assiduity to accomplish that object, I have been pointed at, by my fellow-citizens, with the finger of scorn, and taunted by the tongue of ridicule. But for all this I felt a reward in the anticipation of promoting the honor, and glory, and happiness of my beloved country. I never dreamed of personally receiving the grateful acknowledgments of one of the most respectable collegiate classes in the world. This I assure you, my dear friends, is a full, a rich compensation for all the labor, the hardships and privations I have suffered."

From his will, made in 1823, the following is taken:

"Knowing the uncertainty of life—thinking that we must always be prepared to die—feeling that it is our duty to do all the good in our power, and believing that part of my property will do more good if given to encourage literature than it would to descend according to law, I, Sheldon Clark, of Oxford, am voluntarily and of my own accord, disposed to make the following will:

"I wish to be buried in a decent manner, and to have decent grave-stones at the discretion of my executors. It is my will, that my just debts and my funeral expenses be paid out of my movable estate. I give and bequeath to the Corporation of Yale College in New Haven, all my homestead farm where I now live, with its buildings and appurtenances—also, all the land that was given to me by my grandfather, Thomas Clark, Esq., on the east side* of the road that runs north and south of Mr. Samuel Tucker, with its buildings and appurtenances—also, all my land that lies north of the road that runs by where George Drake now lives—also, my meadow that lies a few rods west of Rimmon school-house, and also, all my Red Oak farm, &c.

"Funds being so liable to be lost by bad security, it is my will, that the lands I have given to said Corporation shall never be sold, but that they shall be let or rented, in such way and manner, as the President and Fellows of said Yale College, and their successors, forever, shall judge to be for the best interest of said institution. It is my will, that the annual income of said lands shall be annually appropriated for the advancement of literature in said Yale College, in such a manner, as its President and Fellows, and their successors forever, shall deem the best and most beneficial for said institution; but no part of said donation or income shall ever be appropriated to erect or repair buildings.

"I also give and bequeath to the Corporation of Yale College in New Haven, all the money I shall have on hand and all the notes I shall have due me at the time of my decease, (except three hundred and thirty-four dollars for Chesnut-tree hill school district,) to be appropriated for the benefit of said Yale College, as its President and Fellows, and their successors forever, shall think shall be for its best good, and the most conducive to its prosperity and honor."

---

*The house and homestead farm were on the west side of the road.

He then gives in form, and with certain conditions, the above named sum to the Chestnut-tree hill school district. He gives also to his three sisters a valuable farm, which fell to him from his and their brother, besides other lands acquired after his will was made; also, all his personal estate not otherwise disposed of; and on his death bed he expressed a wish, that the sisters should receive each one thousand dollars.

He named Abel Wheeler, Esq., of Oxford, and Benjamin Silliman of New Haven, his executors, but Judge Wheeler did not survive him. He died April 11, 1840, from injuries received by a fall from a scaffolding in his barn. Under his extreme sufferings not a word escaped him as to his future prospects: he remarked only, that he had endeavored to do all the good in his power, and as these pages show, his efforts were not in vain.

A large concourse of friends and neighbors and people of the vicinage, with several of the officers of the college and the clergy attended him to his last home. A long retinue of rural vehicles wound slowly down the high hills and along the deep valleys to a secluded burying ground, which he had been instrumental in arranging, on a quiet and beautiful plain, shaded by pines and watered by the murmuring current of a branch of the Housatonic. A neat marble slab records his name as "a distinguished benefactor of Yale College." Such indeed he was. His benefactions to the institution, including the funded interest that had accumulated to the time of his death, amounted to full thirty thousand dollars—three times as much as any other individual had ever given.

This object was not accomplished without a long course of stern self-denial—with great industry and severe economy. Mr. Clark expended very little on his own personal accommodation. The plain farmer's house remained as his grandfather left it, without decoration and almost without repair; the furniture was of the humblest kind, but a warm welcome was given to his friends and to strangers, with ample provision not only of the produce of a farmer's cultivation and care, but occasionally, with a free hospitality in rarer things.

His policy was, to augment as far and as fast as possible, his productive capital; he attempted no improvements in his agriculture; he hardly preserved fences and buildings *in statu quo;* little return of manure was made to his hard worked soils, and even his wood and timber, were, to a certain extent, sold for money and cleared away for market, by other hands. He kept his money always at work—loaned all the cash he did not need, (and his personal wants were few)—required his interest and payments at the day—but was exactly just in his dealings—prompt to give his advice when desired, and kind in his treatment of all. His hoarding was not for himself; wife and children he had none, and he laid by his thousands—the results not of traffic or speculation, but of laborious thrifty industry—to furnish the means of a superior education to the children of others, and to generations yet unborn.

SEYMOUR AT THE CENTENNIAL.

NAMES OF VISITORS.

James K. Adams,
Morris Atwood,
Miss Flora Bassett,
Edward F. Bassett,
Samuel A. Beach,
Mrs. M. A. Beach,
Harry R. Beach,
C. E. Beach,
Sharon Y. Beach,
Mrs. S. Y. Beach,
Sharon D. Beach,
David Betts, Jr.,
Mrs. David Betts,
Lottie E. Booth,
Edward N. Botsford,
Edward B. Bradley,
Mrs. E. B. Bradley,
Edward C. Brown,
Lewis A. Camp,
Samuel H. Canfield,
DeWitt C. Castle,
John Castle,
Martin R. Castle,
Mrs. O. S. Chatfield,
Sheldon Church,
J. A. Clark,
F. M. Clemons,
Mrs. S. A. Cooke,
Burr S. Davis,
John Davis, 2d,
Mrs. Martha E. Davis,
Nettie E. Davis,
Samuel P. Davis,
Zerah B. Davis,
Austin G. Day,
Mrs. A. G. Day,
Edmund Day,
Mrs. Edmund Day,
Henry P. Day,
Theodore Decker,
A. G. DeWolfe,
H. H. DeWolfe,
Mary Dibble,
Sarah G. Dibble,
M. A. Doolittle,
Mary Doolittle,
Mrs. E. L. Doolittle,
Albert B. Dunham,
Daniel T. Dunham,
Geo. S. Edwards,
Mrs. Geo. S. Edwards,
Charles Edwards,
Horatio N. Eggleston,
Mrs. H. N. Eggleston,
Ada M. Eggleston,
Mrs. Josephine Elliott,
Mrs. S. E. Fairchild,
G. B. Flagg,
Hattie Ford,
Mrs. S. C. Ford,
Friend C. Ford,
Mrs. Friend C. Ford,
John T. Forsey,

HISTORY OF SEYMOUR. 231

Mrs. J. T. Forsey,
Lewis L. Garrett,
Dexter A. Gillette,
Harvey S. Halligan,
Frederick Hilton,
Andrew Holbrook,
Charles F. Holbrook,
Rilla Hurlburt,
Thomas E. Hurlburt,
Thomas James,
George A. James,
Lizzie E. James,
N. A. Johnson,
Mrs. S. C. Johnson,
Susie S. Johnson,
Marie Kissam,
Fannie Kissam,
Theodore S. Ladd,
George Leavenworth,
Libbie O. Lockwood,

Virgil H. McEwen,
Mrs. V. H. McEwen,
Bernard H. Merrick,
Frank K. Mitchell,
Sheldon Miles,
Mrs. Sheldon Miles,
W. C. Noyes,
Mrs. Noyes,
Josephine L. Northrop,
Christian Pickardt,
Horace A. Radford,
Mrs. C. C. Radford,
S. H. Rankin,
Martha E. Reynolds,
Minnie E. Reynolds,
Sarah L. Reynolds,
William B. Reynolds,
George A. Rider,
William C. Sharpe,
Burton W. Smith,

James Smith,
Mrs. Sara Smith,
William Smith,
John Spiers,
H. V. Swift,
James Swan,
Wm. B. Swan,
Rev. Chas. A. Tibbals,
Emma Tomlinson,
Lloyd L. Weaver,
Mrs. Lloyd L. Weaver,
Lazarus G. Weaver,
Charles H. Weaver,
Henry Wheeler,
Mrs. Henry Wheeler,
Nellie White,
Charles H. Williams,
Eugene A. Wyant.

GREAT HILL ECCLESIASTICAL SOCIETY.

At a General Assembly of the Governor and Company of the Colony of Connecticut, holden at New Haven on the second Thursday of October, A. D., 1775.

Upon the memorial of Timothy Russell and others, inhabitants of Derby, living within the limits of the first Ecclesiastical Society, and in the limits of Oxford, showing that their situation is such that they cannot conveniently attend public worship in said societies, especially in the winter season, praying that they may be exempted from Ministerial Taxes to each of their respective societies for four months in each year, and that they may be empowered to tax themselves for the support of the gospel among themselves for said term as per mem[1] on file.

Resolved by this Assembly, That the memorialists and all such persons living in the following limits, (viz.) beginning at the Five Mile Brook, where the County Road that leads to Woodbury crosses said brook, and then down said brook to the Great River, from thence down said river to a small brook that falls into said river in Amos Bassett's farm, and from thence to the mouth of Haseky Meadow brook, where the same empties into the Naugatuck river, including the dwelling houses of Amos Bassett and Benjamin Bassett, and from thence up said Naugatuck river to the bridge by the falls, and from thence up the road to the corner of Daniel Wooster's meadow by the Little river, and from thence to the dwelling house of Abner Johnson (excluding said house), and from thence to the first mentioned station; be, and are hereby empowered to tax themselves for the support of public worship among themselves for the term of four months months in each year, and they are hereby exempted from paying any ministerial taxes, during said term towards the support of the gospel in each of the other societies; this act to continue during the pleasure of this assembly, provided and on condition they uphold, support and carry on public worship among themselves as proposed.

A true copy of Record. Examined by   GEORGE WYLLYS, Secret.

At a General Assembly of the Governor and Company of the State of Connecticut, holden at Hartford on the second Thursday of May, 1779.

Upon the memorial of John Holbrook and others, inhabitants of the southwesterly part of the township of Derby, praying this assembly to grant and enact that that part of the town of Derby laying within the following bounds, (viz.) beginning at the southerly corner of Benjamin Bassett's land by the Great river running thence a straight line to the mouth of Haseky Meadow's brook where it empties into the Naugatuck river, thence up said river to the New Great bridge, thence running northwesterly as the county road runs, to the easterly corner of Daniel Wooster's meadow, thence running to Abner Johnson's dwelling house, leaving the same on the north side of said line, from thence to the five-mile brook, where it crosses Woodbury road leading to Derby, thence down said brook to the Great river, and from thence down said river to the first mentioned boundary, be constituted and made an Ecclesiastical Society by the name of the Great Hill Society, with all the privileges, immunities and advantages that other Ecclesiastical Societies by law have and enjoy.

Resolved by the Assembly, That all the inhabitants dwelling in that part of the township of Derby, laying within the above described lines and boundaries be, and the same are hereby constituted and made an Ecclesiastical Society by the name of the Great Hill Society, with all the priviledges, immunities and advantages that all other Ecclesiastical Societies by law have and enjoy.

A true copy of Record. Examined by   GEORGE WYLLYS, Secret.

INDEX.

The lists of names on pages 136 to 139 and 230-1, being arranged alphabetically, are not indexed.

Abbott, C. F., 112, 117.
  Rev. B. T., 180.
  Robert J., 73, 79.
Acly, Rev. Charles G., 28.
Adams, James K., 99, 134, 183.
  C. Lockwood, 171.
  John, 76, 78, 183.
Adamson, Rev. Mr., 15.
Adye, John, 21.
Allen, Albert, 152.
  Ephraim, 106, 157.
  Jennette G., 171.
  John, 110.
  Mary, 170, 171, 195.
  Roger, 171.
Alling, Gideon, 52.
  Ichabod E., 92.
  Mary Newton, 171.
American Car Co., 86.
Ames, Rev. Henry, 175.
Amity, 53.
Anderson, Ahira, 56.
Annis, Rev. James, 174.
Andreas, Elisha, 224.
Andress, Samuel, 52.
Andrus, Rev. Luman, 174.
Armstrong, J., 117.
Atwater, L., 178.
  Mr., 185.
  S. A., 118.
Atwood, Henry C., 132, 133.
  James, 168.
  Lucy A., 111.
  Mary, 167.
  Wheler, 168.
Atwood & Betts, 139.
Auger, Capt., 220.
Austin, Miss, 217.
Aylesworth, F. P., 99, 140.

Bachelor, Rev. Elijah, 174.
Bacon, Charles, 211.
Bainbridge, Rev. Thomas, 178.
Baird, Mr., 188.
Baker, Capt. James, 90, 102.
Ball, ———, 51.
  Hannah, 221.
  Statira, 171.
BALDWIN FAMILY, 157, 223.
  Anson, 63.
  Barnabas, 42.
  E. C., Rev., 14.
  Edward N., 183.
  Edward, 93.
  Elias, 56, 68.
  Elijah, 211.
  Elizabeth, 205, 206.
  Esther, 57, 173.
  Eunice, 57, 173.
  Isaac, 21, 54, 56, 57, 173, 174, 195.
  James, Sergt. 51, 218.
  Jesse, 51, 56, 63, 157.
  Jesse, Dr., 147.
  John, 92.
  Loraine, 218.

Baldwin, Lorinda, 157.
  Nathan, 40.
  Philena, 68.
  Reuben, 45.
  Richard, 42, 197.
  Sarah, 57, 163, 173, 218.
  Silas, 45, 56, 113, 114.
  Stephen, 108, 109.
  Thaddeus, 46, 48, 201.
  Timothy, 16.
  Timothy, Capt., 21, 46, 163.
  Willis, 206.
Bangs, Heman, Rev., 119.
  Nathan, Rev., 175.
Bank of North America, 85.
Baptist Church, 82, 89.
Barlow, Mary, 126, 194, 195.
Barnett, Rev. E., 177.
Barnes, Abraham, 52.
  Minot, 132.
Bartholomew, Mr., 222.
Bartis, Mary, 113.
Bartist, Samuel, 56.
Bartlett, George H., 99.
  Henry W., 112, 182, 183.
Barr, Mrs. E. C., 15.
  William J., 15.
  Andrew, 16.
Bassett & Smith, 73.
BASSETT FAMILY, 205.
  Abel, 63.
  Abram, 51, 128, 147.
  Abraham, 45, 46, 147.
  Amanda, Mrs., 220.
  Amos, 151, 221.
  Amos G., 172.
  Andrew, 87.
  Benjamin, 48, 231.
  Capt. Elliott, 89, 119.
  Capt. Isaac, 119, 175.
  Edward, 52.
  Edward F., 74, 85, 102, 104, 139.
  Edwin, 211.
  Eliza, 199.
  Elliott R., 90, 101, 102, 103, 108, 119.
  Eunice, 226.
  Ezra, 197, 199.
  George, 111, 213.
  Hannah, 211.
  Hattie, 110.
  Isaac, 151, 155, 179.
  James, 150, 151.
  Jared, 75, 112, 176, 179, 182, 202.
  John, Lieut., 48.
  John W., 89, 103, 104, 108, 116, 117.
  Josiah, 108, 109.
  Julius, 76, 78, 92, 112, 134.
  Lorenzo M., 92, 112.
  Martin B., 80.
  Mary, 193, 196, 199.
  Minerva, 111.
  Noyes E., 93.
  Phebe, 211.

Bassett, Philo, 209.
  Rosetta, 110, 111.
  Samuel, 9, 40, 42, 63, 71, 72, 85, 87, 121, 128, 149.
  Sally B., 176.
  Sheldon, 92.
  Truman, 223.
  Wilbur, 140, Mrs., 140.
  William, 63, 155.
Bates, Ella A., 216.
  Nancy, 212.
  William, 70, 120, 121, 177.
Baytis, Eliza, 211.
BEACH FAMILY, 158.
  Andrew Y., 19, 108.
  Benjamin, Rev., 10, 11, 17, 113.
  Betsey, 128.
  David, 56, 84, 89, 114, 115, 117, 202.
  Emma E., 16.
  George W., 164.
  Jesse, 163.
  Lucy M., Mrs., 29.
  Samuel A., 92, 103, 104, 108, 124.
  Sharon Y., 10, 19, 72, 81, 82, 84, 87, 89, 102, 105, 107, 108, 116, 117, 120, 139, 152.
  Simeon, 113.
Beach's Paper Mill, 81, 120.
Beacon Falls, 37, 39.
Beacon Hill, 6.
Beard, George, 48, 149, 150.
  Joseph T., 205.
  William, 56.
Beardsley, Anna, 214.
  Ira, 208.
  Moses, 209.
Becker, Gustave, 105.
Beebe, Joel, 10.
  Martin, 25.
  Sheldon, 132. Mrs. 128.
BEECHER FAMILY, 221.
  Abraham, 45, 46.
  Abigail, 220.
  Burr P., 139.
  Edgar, 99.
  Frank H., 134.
  Hannah, 198.
  Henry B., 74, 103, 105, 137, 141, 174, 181, 183, 219.
  Henry Ward, Rev., 221.
  Isaac, 46, 48, 198.
  Lydia, 201.
  Mary, 198.
  Philo, 82.
  Sarah, 42, 157.
Beement, Jonathan, 114.
Beers, A. J., 134.
  Henry B., 92.
Bell, Catharine, 15.
  Rev. Robert C., 15, 19, 20.
  William 15,
Bellamy, Rev. Mr., 19.
Benedict, George A., ———.
  Henry W., 183.

HISTORY OF SEYMOUR.

Benham, Ann, 152.
Bennett, 92.
  Charles, Mrs., 128.
  Maria, 160.
  Marietta, 111.
  Mrs. Charles, 128.
  Sarah, 109.
Benton, Charles, 212.
Bennett, Legrand, 212.
  Polly, 208.
Bethany, 6, 41, 70.
Bethany Church, 127.
Betts, David Jr., 80, 101, 104, 105, 152.
  William F., 102, 104.
Bidwell, James H., 77.
Bigelow, Lottie E., 118.
Birdseye, Ephraim, 116.
Birdsey, Dinah, 159.
Birmingham, 38.
Bissell, W. D., 134.
Black, Nathaniel, 52
Blackley, Miss, 158.
Blackman, Alfred, 84
  Ethel, 132.
  John E., 89.
  Lucius, 79.
Blacksmith Shop, 58.
Bladen's Brook, 6, 115, 116.
Blake, Isaac, 116.
  Rubin, 56.
  William, 99.
Blakeslee, David, 52.
Bliss, Howard, 92.
  Lemuel, 74, 155.
  Mrs. 70.
  Mrs. Charles, 15.
  Mrs. Emeline, 14.
Blueville, 72, 73.
Blydenburgh, Rev. Moses, 32, 33, 34, 72, 178.
Board of Education, 107.
Bochford, Sarah, 206.
Bodge, George E., 92.
  John, 121, 152.
Boeker, Mrs. F., 15.
  Rev. Edward, 25.
  Rev. Solomon, 26.
Bogart, O. M. Jr., 162.
Boudinot, Mr., 123.
BOOTH FAMILY, 156.
  Albert, 180.
  Anna, 208.
  Andres, 90.
  Ebenezer, 127, 208.
  Frank, 210.
  H. Treat, 93, 134, 156, 195.
  Huldah, 129.
  Lottie E., 110, 117.
  Maria, 156.
  Mary A., 223.
  Olive M., 208.
  Peter, Dr., 156.
Booty, Edward, 132.
Bostick, Isaac, 113.
Bostwick, Daniel, 209.
  Israel, 25.
Botsford, Charles S., 136.
  Cyrus, 119.
  Ellen E., 203.
  Grace E., 13.
  Harvey L., 93.
  Isaac, Capt., 223.
  John, 45, 47.
  Lyman, 152, 186.
  Nehemiah, 16, 19.
  Nehemiah, Dea, 210.
  Smith, 89, 90, 104, 111, 112, 121, 122, 182, 183.
  Treat, 196.
Bounties to Soldiers, 90, 91.
Boutwell, Henry, 185.
  Patience, 185.

Boutwell, Silence, 185.
Bowen, Merwin, 110.
  Rev. Josiah, 178.
BOWER FAMILY, 185.
  Anna, 154.
  John, Rev., 185, 192.
Bowman, James, 63.
Bradford, Helen, 210.
  Mercy, 204.
  William, Major, 204.
Bradley, Charles, 16, 196.
  Abigail, 224.
  Bede, 217.
  Benjamin, 218.
  Dorcas, 128.
  Edward B., 205
  Elephas, 113.
  Enos, 43.
  Harriett, 218.
  E. M., 152.
  H. & M., 71.
  Henry I., 93.
  Henry, 71, 84, 89, 90, 101, 102, 103, 105, 134, 139.
  Jesse, 217.
  John H., 99, 135.
  Leonard, 139.
  Lucretia, 225.
  Mary, 110.
  Mary Ann, 198.
  Merritt, 71, 133.
  Miss, 111.
Bradlew, Rev. Charles W., 27.
Bradstreet, Humphrey, 185.
Brassill, Matthew, 98.
Bray, Rev. John E., 12, 13, 19.
  William H., 93.
Brewster, Abigail, 39, 200.
  Nathaniel, 37.
  William, 204.
Bridges, 182.
Bristol, Aaron, 43.
  Benjamin, 211.
  Corp., 52.
  William, 110.
BROADWELL FAMILY, 172
  Betsey, 129.
  Lewis, 63, 129.
Bronson, Henry, 87.
  Miles, 109.
  Rev. David, 44.
  Rodney O., 93
  Royal L., 93.
  Samuel L., 89, 104, 169.
  William, 131.
Brown, Charles, 93.
  E. C., 134.
  Juliette, 172.
  Vincent, 217.
Brush, Rev. Jacob, 174.
Brushell, Nathan A., 140
Bryan, Sarah, 157.
Buck, Rev. Valentine, 177.
Buckingham, Betsey, 215, 216
  Edwin, 105.
  Ebenezer, Lieut., 45.
  Lewis, 223.
  Philo B., Col., 19, 84, 85, 87, 88, 89, 93, 107, 133, 152.
  Samuel, Sen., 6.
  Samuel W., 139.
  Wales, 152.
Buckley, Jas. E., 93, 105, 134, 135.
  Owen, 93.
Buddington, Sophia, 169.
Buffum, William, 73, 78, 79.
Bukley, Hester, 188.
Bunce, Lewis, 77, 79, 123.
Bungay, 47.
  George W., 77.
Bunyan, Matthias, 102, 105, 135
Burgoyne, Gen., 160.
Burlock, Thomas, 79.

Burlock, Mary DeForest, 169.
Burton, Henry, 109.
Burr, Thaddeus, 57.
Burritt & Lewis, 71.
Burroughs, George W., 99.
Burritt, William, 70.
Burwell, Catharine C., 15, 110.
  Ruth, 47.
  Sarah, 211.
Bushnell, Rey, Samuel, 176.
Business Directory, 139.
Butler, Ezra, 51.
  Samuel, 105, 134, 183.
Buxton, Henry, 132.

Cable, Frederic, 170.
  Roswell, 132.
Cadwell, Perry, 76.
Cady, ——, 147.
Caffrin, John Church, 56.
Calkins, Israel, 209.
Camp's Mortgage, 43.
Camp Lewis A., 104, 105, 135.
  N, D., Hon., 101.
  Samuel, 211.
Candee, Arthur L., 117.
  Benjamin, 131.
  Caleb, 56.
  Corp, 52.
  Daniel, 131.
  David, 128, 132.
  E. C., 131.
  Geo. B., 93.
  Gid. H., 110.
  Isaiah, 132.
  Jennette, 226.
  Judson, 110.
  Levi, 131, 132, 133.
  Lewis B., 87.
  Mary, 157.
  Moses, 131, 157.
  Nancy, 157.
  Noah, 146, 147.
CANFIELD FAMILY, 193.
  Abiel, 126, 172.
  Betsey, 172.
  Daniel, 216.
  Esther, 14, 216.
  Ezekiel, Rev., 176.
  Hannah, Mrs., 14.
  Joseph, 45, 149.
  Josiah, Dr., 42.
  Lucius, 218.
  Mary, 172.
  Reuben, 52.
  Roswell C., 15.
  Samuel, 64.
  Samuel H. 103,104,108,134,139
  Sheldon, 132, 211.
  ——, 212.
Capital Punishment, 125.
Carlson, Carl, 147.
Carpenter, Coles, Rev., 174.
  Henry, 56.
  Pearl, 80.
  Smith, 140.
Carrington, Albert,
  Betsey, 220.
  Content, 222.
  Elias, 220, 222.
  Esther, 222.
  Sally, 218.
Carroll, Wm., 93.
  Presiding Elder, 178.
Carter, Jacob, 78.
  Mary E., 222.
Cartright, Jonathan, 52.
Case, Annie, 129.
Cass, Nicholas, 93.
Castle, D. C., 134.
  Martin, 146, 134.
  S. J., Mrs., 15.
Cemeteries, Union, 71,

HISTORY OF SEYMOUR. 235

Cemetery, Pinesbridge, 38, 39.
Rimmon, 38, 39, 128.
Centennial Ex., Vis. to, 230.
Chadwick, Thomas, 93.
Chais, Isaac, 113.
Chamberlin, Betsey, 110.
  C., Rev., 15.
  E. B., Rev., 14.
  Henry R., 99, 135.
  Horatio S., 99, 105, 135.
  Walter, Rev., 208.
Change of Name, 84.
Chapman, Amelia, 218.
  Luman, 171.
Charter of the Town, 80.
Chatfield, Anson, 216.
  Benjamin, 212.
  Caleb, 52.
  Charlotte, 161, 162.
  Daniel, 45.
  Horace D., 213.
  Joel 1st, 25, 113, 129, 161, 220.
  Joel R., 103, 111, 112, 213.
  John, 90, 101, 102, 107.
  John R., 108.
  Leman, 81, 82, 83, 84, 104, 132.
  L. Cornelia, 112, 117.
  Maria, 110.
  Mary, 111, 112, 171.
  Miss, 117.
  Oliver, 52.
  Ruth, 129.
Cheney, Rev. Laban C., 177.
Chestnut-tree Hill, 7.
Chipman, Joseph, 84, 117, 133.
Church, Abel, 20, 25, 56, 171.
  Anna, 130, 216.
  Henry, 197.
  John, 46.
  Laura, 129.
  Marietta, 171.
  Mary, 217.
  Sheldon, 28, 72, 84, 89, 90, 105, 129, 197.
  William, 25, 56, 73, 217.
Churchill, Dr., 15.
  Hobart, 224.
  John, 56.
  Timothy, 56.
Chuse, 17, 36, 40, 41, 59.
Chusetown, 40, 57, 59, 17.
Chusetown District, 112, 115.
Claflin, George, 162.
Clark, Allan, Rev., 15, 102.
  Amos, 56, 217.
  Chauncey, 52.
  David B., 73, 117.
  David M., 132, 133.
  Edmund, 157.
  Edwin W., 199.
  Ellen, 172.
  Ellen M., 110, 117.
  Elias, 56.
  Eliza, 111.
  Eunice, 168.
  George, 52, 57, 173.
  George, Ensign, 6.
  Hannah, 160.
  Hezekiah, 39.
  Hezekiah, Jun., 56.
  John, 86.
  Joseph, 132.
  Laban, Rev., 177.
  Levy, 56.
  Maria, 156.
  Martin, 52.
  Mary Ann, 217.
  Moses, 21, 39, 201.
  Oliver, 113.
  Patty, 197.
  P. E., Mrs., 111.
  Rufus, 56.
  Russell, 115.

Clark, Sally, 161, 162, 197.
  Sheldon, 39, 227.
  Smith, 117, 132, 157.
  Susanna, 128.
  Thomas, Sen., 6. 40.
  Thomas, Esq., 45, 46, 56, 195, 228.
  Thomas, Capt., 45, 46, 52.
  Thomas, Lieut., 128.
  Timothy, 217.
  Walter B., 116, 117.
  William, 129.
  William A., 86.
  William, Capt., 45.
Clement, Eli, 94.
Clemons, Frederick M., 99, 105, 108, 199.
Clinghan, Rev. Thomas, 208.
Clinton, Charlotte, 164.
Coate, Rev. Michael, 57, 174.
Cochran, Thomas, 81, 82, 105, 116, 217.
  John, A., 89, 139.
Coe, John, 21, 45, 46, 173.
  Ruth, 173,
  John Allyn, 173.
Coggswell, Egbert, 172.
  Jeremiah, 71.
Coleman, Rev. James, 174,175,177
  John, 135.
Collin, Rev. H, P., 15.
Collins, Mrs. Sarah, 13.
  Amos, 52.
  Abraham, 94.
Colbert, William, 135.
Colt, Anson F., 212.
Cornish, Susannah, 195.
  John, 195.
Cotter Frank, A., 195.
Cortelyou, Agnes, 211.
Condon, Richard, 94.
Conference Room, 116.
Congdon, Jairus, 52.
Congregational Church, 9.
Connecticut Cents, 24.
Couvrette, Frank, 219.
Converse, Charles E., 162.
Conway, Richard, 94.
Cooper, Wm. S., 99, 105, 133-4-5.
Cook, Elam, 217.
Cornwall, William, 83, 87.
  Eli, S., 82, 85.
Cotton Factory, 78.
Cotton, John, 186.
Coltingham, Miss, 117, 152.
Cowles, Ruth, 164.
Cowel, Lydia, 113.
Cox, Reuben, 94.
Coxhead, John F., 171.
Crafts, Dr. Edward, 55, 57.
Crawford, Benjamin, 112.
  John, Rev., 113, 178.
  Joseph, 175.
Creelman, Eliza M., 16.
Cridenton, Worrin, 56.
Crittenden, Sarah, 203.
  Dr., 203.
Crosby, Seth, 132.
Cross, Frederick, 94.
Crowley, Patrick, 135.
Crozier, Richard, 207.
  William, 207.
  Sarah, 207.
Culver, Miles, 16, 19, 71, 84, 88, 106, 129.
  Laura, Mrs., 14.
  Stephen H., 103, 105, 112, 117.
Crummy, Dennis, 94.
Currency in 1695, 8.
Curry, W. C., 204.
Curtiss, Amy, 210.
  Eunice, 167.
  Joanna, 167.

Curtiss, John, 35.
  Joseph, 167.
  Julia, 158.
  Maria, 214.
  Olive, 154, 167.
  Simeon, 195.
  Simon, 109.
  Susan, 210.
  William B., Rev., 13, 19, 76, 78, 79, 179.
  William E., 94.
Cushen, Martha M., 205.
Cushman, Mr., 157.
Cutts, Rev. Wm., 127.
Cypher, Thomas, 157.
Dachester, George, 52.
Daggett, Judge David, 127.
Danforth, Thomas, 185.
Daniels, John L., 74, 76, 132.
  Charles, 152.
Dart, William, 209.
Daughters of Temperance, 78.
Davenport, Rev. Mr., 188.
DAVIS FAMILY, 170.
  Alva, 77, 176.
  Anna, 176.
  Anson, 106, 108.
  Benjamin, 25. 47, 57, 210.
  Betty, 215.
  Charles H., 94.
  Clark, Capt., 198.
  Daniel, 25, 47. 217.
  Elizabeth, 202.
  Ella, 117.
  Emerett, 213.
  Harpin, 134.
  Henry, 102, 104, 107, 108.
  Henry P., 105,117,134,204,205
  Henry W., 94, 103.
  Isaac B., 75, 82, 84, 105, 219.
  James, 79.
  John, 1st, 45, 46, 90.
  John, 2nd, 198.
  John, 3rd, 101, 105, 117, 134.
  John, Col., 170.
  Joseph, 46, 195, 198.
  L., 110.
  Lilly, 172.
  Lydia, 212.
  Marcus, 109, 137, 172.
  Martha E., 110.
  Mary E., 198.
  Miss, 110.
  Mrs. Henry P., 13.
  Mrs. Naomi, 193.
  Nancy, 161.
  Nathan, 131.
  Polly, 176.
  Reuben, 113, 176.
  Sally, 210.
  Samuel P., 102, 103, 105, 107, 108, 133, 149, 211.
  Sarah, 208.
  Sheldon, 56.
  Sophia, 110.
  Truman, Capt., 198, 212, 213.
  Virginia, 110.
  Zerah B., 94.
Dawson, John, Jr., 224.
  Kate, 209.
Day, Anstin G., 123, 143.
  Edmund, 104, 107, 108.
  H. P. & E., 123, 142, 180.
  Henry P., 104.
  Zelotes, 86.
Dayton, Capt. Ebenezer, 50,129. 146, 147.
  Mrs. 146, 174.
  Phebe, 113, 129.
  Mary, 158.
Deal, Charles, 113.
Deery, Mary R., 118.
DeForest & Hodge, 73, 122.

DeForest, Andrew, W., 16, 71, 77, 220.
David, 45, 46.
George F., 19, 83-4-5-6-7, 116.
George W., 116.
H. A., 20.
John H., 68, 69, 115,129, 132.
William, 85.
Derby Journal, 73.
Deremore, Joseph, 52.
Denney, Mrs. Harriett E., 14
Dennison, Sarah, 225.
Denniston, Rev. Eli, 177.
Devil's Jump, 6.
William, 79, 82.
DeWolfe, Alva G., 131.
Huldah, 15.
Mrs. Lucy, 15.
Dibblé, Capt. Amadeus. 63, 112, 113, 129.
Mary, 129.
Raymond, 129.
William W., 112, 134, 183
Dickerman, Capt. Isaac, 43, 44.
Dickinson, Rev. Frederick, 207.
Lydia, 207.
Dike, Veren, 131.
Divine, G. W., 73-4,101-2-3-5,133
Mrs. G. W., 140.
Dolittle, Huldah, 202.
Jane, 111.
Samuel, 146, 147.
Domingo, Chas., 94.
Donahue, Patrick, 94.
Dorman, Amos, 113.
Walter W., 16.
Dorothy, Rhoda, 158.
Douglass, Chas., 87.
Downing, Mary, 166.
Hon. Emanuel, 166.
Sir George, 166.
Downs, Albert J., 199.
Edward S., 135.
Emma J., 117.
James, 201.
Jarvis, 113.
Downs & Sanford, 79.
Drake, George, 220.
Driscol, Jeremiah. 135.
Driver, Darius, 220.
James, 71.
Polly, 210.
Samuel, 220.
Dunham, Albert B., 104, 140.
Henry A., 139.
Dunn, Mary, 198.
DURAND FAMILY, 159.
Anna, 129.
Charles, 14, 33, 87.
David, 175.
Ebenezer, 52.
Elizabeth, 110.
Frederick, 101, 107, 110, 111, 117, 118, 152, 183, 183.
Isaac, 52.
Jeremiah, 32, 69, 116, 216.
Joseph, 129.
Mrs. B. M., 13.
Polly, 205, 216.
Samuel, 52, 129, 175.
Dutcher, Rev. E. H., 181.
Dutton, Thomas A., 132.
Dwight, Pres. of Yale, 12,60,125.
John W., 72, 79, 83, 86, 87.
Timothy,72, 83,85, 86,87, 120.
Dwight & French, 78, 80,79, 196.
Dyer, William, 212.

Eagle Manufacturing Co , 85
Eason, Frances, 196.
Eastman, Vespatian, 52.
Eaton, Gov., 188.
Edwards, Charles, 131, 134.

Edwards, George S., 139.
Pierpont, 127,
Timothy, Rev., 166.
Ells, Samuel, 6.
Eggleston, Horatio N., 104.
Electors of Seymour, 135.
Elliot, Gustavus R., 203.
Joseph, 186.
ELLIS FAMILY, 164.
Thomas, 115, 177, 178.
William H., 86.
Ely, George W., 162.
Emancipation, 48.
Emory, Rev. Nathan, 174, 176.
English, Abel, 108, 109.
Abraham, 26.
Abram, 151.
Benjamin, 108, 109, 159.
Benoni, Rev., 175.
Dorcas, 211.
Judson, 69, 119, 199.
Eno, William S., 164.
Episcopal Church, 18, 25.
Evans, David Jr., 218.
Richard, 15.

Fairchild, Abiel, 38, 42.
Anna, 170.
Ebenezer, 89, 105, 137, 140.
Julia A., 110.
Miss, 111.
Nathan B., 132.
Ruth, 169.
Nathaniel, 40.
Sarah, 156.
William A., 102, 105
Zachariah, 45, 150.
Fairfield, 37.
Falls of the Naugatuck, 5, 40, 41
Farrell, Frank, 87.
Loren, 94.
Farrington, Rhoda, 210
Fengot Coal Co., 102.
Fenn, Benjamin, 6.
Fenton, Moses, 151.
Ferguson, Rev. Samuel D., 177.
Field, Julius, Rev., 177, 183.
Fields, Benjamin Anson, 210.
Fife, Mrs. William T., 15.
Finch, Joel. 129.
Harvey, 218.
Fisher,Ebenezer, 114-15, 120, 132.
James E., 89, 152.
Fisler, Rev. Benjamin, 174.
Fitch, Rev. J. W., 15.
Fitzpatrick, Hugh, 94.
Five Mile Brook, 7.
Foot, Corporal, 52.
Foote, Elihu D., 153.
Hattie M., 15.
Ford, Clark, 73, 100.
Jared K., 154.
Lyman H., 137.
Samuel C., 155.
Sarah, 221.
Forque, Frances, 21.
Forsey, John T., 203.
Foster, T., 121.
Four Mile Brook, 7.
Fowler, Abram, 212.
C. A., 110.
Catharine, 226.
De Grasse, 94.
George, 222.
George, Mrs., 14, 15.
Jane, 109.
John, Capt., 43.
Luther, 109.
Fox, Amos, 52.
Huldah, 160.
Freeman, Richard, 113.
Freemasonry, 131.
Freemen in 1708, 7.

FRENCH FAMILY, 154.
Asa, 56.
Adonijah, 101, 102, 105.
Alfred, 133.
Carlos, 65,89,102, 104,108, 139
Charles, 25, 40, 41, 42, 45, 94, 113, 134, 198.
David, 41.
David, Esq., 127, 129.
Enoch, 56, 113, 129.
Francis, 41, 157, 187.
Hannah, 217, 129.
Harpin R., 94.
Harriet, 195.
Herman, B., 94.
Hobart, 95.
Israel, 25, 41, 101, 102, 103, 105, 112, 113, 127, 133.
John W., 95, 170.
Laura, 111.
Lydia, 187.
Mary, 157.
Nancy, 129.
Nathaniel, 45, 129.
Noah, 45.
Raymond, 2, 10, 17, 42, 69, 70, 71, 72, 79, 83, 85, 86, 87, 102, 121, 195.
Raymond, Mrs., 15.
Rebecca, 151.
Samuel, 35, 45, 129.
Wales, 71, 182.
Walter, 50. 175.
Warren, 74, 152, 181-2-3, 198.
William, 129.
French & Dwight, 78.
French, R. & Co., 73.
French, Swift & Co., 74, 79, 83.
Freshets, 70, 71, 74, 81, 83, 84, 89, 101, 102.
Friendly Sons of St. Patrick, 135
Frisbie, Job., 186, 187.
E. H., 180.
Fuller, Elizabeth, 164.
George L., Rev., 119,178, 182
John, 225.

Gainsby, E., 78.
Galpin, Frederick, 208.
Garrettson, Rev. Freeborn, 174-5
Gay, Prof., 83, 118.
Gaylord, Ranson, 74.
William, 87.
Geissler, Robert H., 95.
Gerard, Frank C., 100, 105.
Gerling, Wm., 129, 132, 133.
Gilbert, Elias, 64, 113, 114, 196.
Esther Ann, 168, 169.
Ezekiel, 69, 71, 73, 129.
Isaac J., 116.
Levi, 155.
Sarah E., 110.
Gilbert, Beach & Co., 120.
Gilbert & Wooster, 70.
GILLETTE FAMILY, 199.
Anson, 119, 175.
Chas., 110.
Eli, 89, 103, 108, 137, 212.
Ephraim, 53.
Jeremiah, 25.
W. A., 151.
Wm., 201.
Gilyard, Anna, 129.
Lois, 176.
Nancy, 205, 206, 116, 120.
Sarah, 213.
Thomas, 62, 63, 115, 129, 175, 176, 182, 183.
William, 38, 41, 112, 213.
Givens, ——, 210.
Gleason, M. A., 111.
Glendining, Geo. B., 77, 78, 118, 132, 133.

HISTORY OF SEYMOUR. 237

Glendining, Nancy H., 77.
Glendining Academy, 77,78, 133.
Glover, ——, 156.
Goddard, William W., 87
Goodrich, Elizabeth, 225.
  Elizur, 63.
Goodsell, Dan, 224.
Gordin, William, 47.
Gorham, Joseph, 35.
Gough, John B., 77.
Graham, Alexander, 146.
  Andrew S., 108, 109.
  George R., 127.
Granby Copper, 23.
Grand List of Seymour,'69. 103.
Granniss, Isaac, 225
  Sarah, 226.
  Thankful, 226.
Gray, Rev. Mr., 15.
Great Hill Ecclesiastical Soc.,231
Great Hill M. E. Church, 119
Great Hill Road, 40.
Great Hill School, 19, 47, 108
Green, James. 152
  Sarah M., 171.
  Seth, 132.
Gregory, Hyatt, 95
  John, 224.
Grogan, Wm., 95.
Griffin, John, 25.
Grissell, Jeremiah, 56.
Griswold, Rev. Samuel. 26.
Gunn, Abel, 43, 186.
  Abigail, Mrs., 47.
  George, 132.
  Simon, 56.

Haines, Chauncey, 132.
Hall, Col. Benjamin, 43.
Halligan, Harvey, S., 134
  William, 100, 133.
Han, Michael, 156.
Hanford, Mr., 185.
Hanley, John, 95.
  Samuel, 40.
Hard, Charles, F., 15, 137.
  Cornelius, 137.
  Ellen, C., 16. 110.
  James, 7.
  Lydia, A., 16.
  Mary, 226.
Harden, Jonah, 56, 129.
Harding, James, 106.
Harger, Alfred, 132.
  Ebenezer, 7.
  Edward, 7.
  Henry, 110.
Harris, Mrs. A. A., 15.
  Reuben, Rev., 174.
Harrison, Rev. Mr., 14.
  Sarah, 164.
Hart, John M., 132, 133.
Hartshorn, Jesse, 63.
Hartson, John L., 82. 134.
  Lyman, 182.
Hassakee Meadow Brook,47,231. 232.
Haswell, James G., 172.
Hatch, Chauncy M., 63, 132. 133.
Hatte, Matilda, 129.
Havemeyer, William H., 163.
Hawes, David, 109.
Hawkins, Abraham, 45. 47
  Betsey, 198.
  Elizabeth, 198.
  Freegift, 45.
  Jane, 210.
  John, 38.
  Joseph, 38, 56, 150.
  Philo, 223.
  Polly, 212.
  Sara, Mrs., 201
  Sarah, 206.

Hawkins, Silas, 214.
  Truman, 108.
  Zachariah, 209.
  ——, 150.
Hawley, Benjamin. 25.
  David, 199.
  Elizabeth, 156.
  John, 150.
  Samuel, 40, 207.
  Samuel, Rev.,127.
  William, 95.
Hayden, Richard E., 95.
Hayes, Edward, 25.
  Eli, 77.
  Nancy, 211.
  William, 135.
Hayman, Mrs. Charlotte, 16.
Healey, Robert. 100, 134,205.206
Hebard, Rev. Elijah, 175.
Hedden, Thomas M., 132.
Heilman, Phillip, 140.
Hemingway, Samuel, 158.
Hendryx, James, W., 95.
  . W. E., 76,117,134,135.156,183
Hendryx & Peck, 103.
Henry, Susan, 172, 215.
Hermance, Miss, 101, 118
HICKOX FAMILY, 169
  Elizabeth, 129.
  Harriet, 155.
  Josiah, 167.
  Sarah, 167.
  Samuel R.,69,79,82,84,111-12.
    115-6, 127, 177, 182. 183.
High School, 77, 83, 101.
High School Association. 85
High School Room, 102.
Highways, 52, 60, 124
Hill, Maria, 159.
  Mary A., 16.
  William T., Rev , 179
Hill street, 87.
Hilton, John, 134.
Hine, Amos, 21, 75, 179
  Arlon, 220.
  Samuel B., 114
  Sylvester, 15.
  William, 56.
Hinman, Jesse L.. 173
  Maria, 209.
  Molly, 206.
  Philo, 21.
  Simeon, 109.
  William. 133.
HITCHCOCK FAMILY. 220.
  Betsey, 154.
  Burritt, 72, 77, 182, 217
  Daniel, 132.
  Denzel, 69, 82, 115, 170
  Gad, 132.
  John, 44.
  Jonathan, 45, 48.
  Joseph, 100, 183
  Lucy, 57, 173.
  Samuel, 200.
  Sheldon, 176.
  Timothy, 66, 129,176,182,223.
  Urania, 176.
Hoadley, Edward L., 90, 105.
  William, 187.
Hobart, Right Rev. John H., 26
Hodge, George L., 72. 82, 120.
  Mrs., 117.
  Robert, 202.
  Thomas, 225.
Hodge & Co., 72, 120.
Hog's Meadow Purchase, 53.
HOLBROOK FAMILY, 160.
  Abel, 82, 89,90,104-5,110,150.
  Cyrus, 212.
  Daniel, Capt., 47, 48, 52, 63,
    72, 129, 176.
  Daniel, Col., 161.

Holbrook, Daniel, Jr., 112, 113.
  Daniel L., 81, 82.
  Daniel, 4th,42, 45-6, 56, 82, 84.
  Daniel, 5th, 197.
  Esther, 211.
  Gracie, 197.
  John, 43, 219.
  John, Capt., 45, 46, 52, 160.
  Lois, 129.
  Louis, 10.
  Maria, Mrs., 13.
  Nathan, 101, 105, 108.
  Nathaniel, 25, 150, 151.
  Philo, 25, 85, 150.
  Philo, Capt., 46, 72, 82, 84,
    86, 102-3-4-5, 213.
  Richard, 151.
  Sarah, 71.
  Thomas W., 28, 160.
  William E., 111.
Holcomb, Annie, 111.
  John W., 95, 204, 205.
Holden, Mrs. Fidelia E., 13, 14.
Holeren, James, 95.
Holland, Charles B.. 95.
Holloway, John, 140.
Holmes, Samuel, 87.
  William K., 133.
Homan, George W., 95.
Hooker, Chauncey, 218.
Holt, Abigail, 225.
Hopkins, Dr. Samuel, 38.
  Lois, 201.
Hosmer, Stephen T., 131.
Hotchkiss, A. T., 110, 111.
  Charles T., 111.
  David, 116.
  Elias, 79.
  Harriet, 15, 201, 202.
  Harvey, 101, 105, 137.
  Hepsibah, 225.
  Levi, Lieut., 47.
  Lucy, 217.
  Lydia, 154.
  Mary, 225.
  Mary A., 117.
  Mr., 75.
  Nancy, 161.
  Reuben H., 87.
  Samantha, 218.
  Thomas, 21.
Houghtalling, Charles D., 147.
Housatonic Valley, 125.
Howard, James, 102, 108.
Howd, Edward, 45, 46, 63, 78.
  John, 40-1-2-5-6-8, 57-9.
  Samuel, 205.
Howe, Lydia, 224.
Sir William, 123.
Sybil, 164.
William, 123.
Howland, Andrew, Mrs., 159.
  Rev. Seneca, 179.
Hubbard, Abraham, Capt., 161.
  Calvin A., 95.
Hubbell, Harvey, 224.
  Hart C., 171.
  Lewis, 46.
  Phebe, A., 15.
  ——, 209.
Hughes, William A., 78,134, 183.
HULL FAMILY, 172.
  Abijah, 26, 46, 195.
  Alfred, 16, 19.
  Andrew, 159.
  Benjamin, 63.
  Isaac, 64.
  John Clark, 89, 211.
  Joseph, 35, 40, 41, 59.
  Juliette, Mrs. 15.
  Miss, 111.
  Samuel, 46, 56.
  Sarah, 199.

Hull, Wm. M., 14, 79, 86, 116, 174.
Hulse, Joseph, 52.
Humaston, Roswell, 82.
Humphrey & Wooster, 71, 79
Humphrey, proposed name, 84, 89
Humphrey Lodge, No. 26, K. of
  P., 134.
Humphreys, Aaron, Rev., 26.
  Bernard, 220.
  Cyrus, 133, 170.
  D., Rev., 17, 45, 48, 54, 188.
  David, Gen., 11, 17, 49, 59,
    64, 65, 113, 114, 120, 126,
    128, 129, 188.
  David, 2nd, 129
  David, 3rd, 129.
  David's, Gen., Flag, 65.
  Elijah, 69.
  George, 124
  John, 47, 52, 68, 69.
  John, Ensign, 46, 47
  John, Jr., Hon., 129, 114.
  John, Lieut., 52.
  William, 69, 115, 129.
Humphreysville, 60.
Humphreysville Academy, 77.
Humphreysville Copper Co., 79,
  83, 87.
Humphreysville Graveyard Association, 71.
Humphreysville Greys, 73,
Humphreysville High School
  Association, 85.
Humphreysville Library Co., 87.
Humphreysville Lyceum, 74.
Humphreysville Mfg. Co., 68, 70,
  85, 120.
Humphreysville & Salem Turnpike Co., 86.
Humphreysville Total Abstinence Society, 76.
Humphries, Rev. Humphrey, 178
Hunt, Rev. Jesse, 175.
  Aaron, Rev., 174, 175.
Huntington, Miss, 152.
  Nathaniel, Rev. G., 219.
Hurd, Anna, 194-5-6.
  Charity, 211.
  Harriett, 199.
  Henry G., 102, 105.
  James W., 132.
  Sarah, 129.
  Sheldon, 82, 121.
  Silas, 109.
  William, 131.
  Wilson, 25, 151.
  Zedock, 196.
Hurlburt, Charles R., 152.
  Mary A., 16.
  Orilla E., 14.
  Thomas, 95, 137.
Hutchinson, Rev. Sylvester, 174.
Hyatt, Daniel, 132.
Hyde, Abijah, 70, 77, 170.
  Charles L., 82.
  Edwin, 157.
  Marcus. 110.
  Mr., 77.
  Orson, 77.

Iles, Charles, 95.
Indians, 31 to 37.
Indian Lands, Sale of, 5, 6, 7, 63,
  40, 41, 42.
Indian Lands, Value of, 5.
Ineson, Joseph, 100, 135.
Isbell, Sarah, 219.

Jackson, Andrew, 95.
Jagger, Rev. Ezra, 178.
James, Cornelius W., 101-2-3-5-7,
  134.
  George A., 198.

James, John, 208.
  Thomas, 87, 89, 108, 152.
Janes, Bishop, 179.
Jardine, Mr., 27.
Jayne, Rev. Peter, 174.
Jennings, Eunice, 212.
Jewett, Rev. Stephen, 27, 69.
Jocelyn, Rev. Augustus, 174.
JOHNSON FAMILY, 200.
  Abner, 55, 231.
  Alexander, 25, 38, 39, 129.
  Amaritta, 199.
  Ann, 220.
  Asahel, 21, 45.
  Benajah, 37, 38, 41, 128, 129.
  Bertha E., 16.
  Capt., 156.
  Charles, 35.
  Chauncey, 56, 113, 129.
  Cynthia, 176.
  Daniel, 146, 147.
  David, 16, 45, 56, 74, 75, 112,
    128, 197.
  Ebenezer, 6, 36, 45, 48, 113, 200
  Ebenezer B., 21, 112.
  Ebenezer, Capt., 7.
  Ebenezer, Col., 8, 35, 129.
  Ebenezer, Maj., 7.
  Eleanor, 129.
  Elijah, 39, 56, 129.
  Elizabeth, 196.
  Gideon, 21, 41, 42, 45, 47.
  Hannah, 35, 39.
  Hannah P., 10.
  Harvey, 212, 223.
  Henry C., 84, 304.
  Henry S., 89, 104.
  Hepsibah, 129, 176.
  Hezekiah, 112, 113, 129.
  Hiram, 82.
  Isaac, 10, 51, 53, 113, 194.
  Jesse, Rev., 57, 113, 114, 121,
    173, 176, 129, 206.
  James D., 216.
  Jesse, Jr., 113, 130.
  Joseph, 25, 112, 113, 114, 130.
  Levi, 56, 197.
  Lois, 194, 129.
  Lucy, 155.
  Mabel, 194, 198.
  Nathaniel, Capt., 25, 26, 42,
    46, 48, 51.
  Newel, 69, 114, 115, 121, 132.
  Olive, 57, 174.
  Peter, 48.
  Phebe, 128.
  Philo, 45.
  Phineas, 51.
  Sally, 205, 206.
  Sarah, 38, 128, 129, 161.
  Sheldon C., 29, 79. 139, 168.
  Silas, 57, 173.
  Stiles, 68, 113, 114, 130, 175,
    182.
  Timothy, 25, 35, 37, 39, 56, 130
  William B., 95, 183.
  Zerviah, 130.
Jones, Anna, 204.
  Chester, 69, 70, 113, 114, 115,
    116, 132, 204.
  Ruth, 159.
  Sarah, 10, 204.
Jones & Keeney, 113.
Joy, Jesse, 132, 133.
  William W., 222.
Judd, Appalina, 217.
  Chauncey, 146.
  Ebenezer, 38.
  Lewis, 87, 102.
  Martha, Mrs., 196.
  Rachel, 164.
  Ralph, 95.
  Randall, 168.

Judson, Anna, 213.
  David, 209.
  Joshua, 213.
Justices of the Peace, 105.

Kalmia Mills, 103, 104.
Keast, Catharine, 213.
Kelleher, John, 216.
Kelley, John, 56.
  Martin, 89, 134.
Kellogg, Bela, Rev., 9, 12, 13, 19.
  Nathaniel, Rev., 177.
Kelsey, Charles D., 100.
  G. T., 100.
Kelsie, Corydon, 208.
  Dotha, 213.
Kendall, Joshua, 15, 16, 69, 74,
  76, 78, 89, 104, 107, 108,
  135, 102, 103, 139, 198.
  Rhoda, 152, 110.
Kennedy, Adella, 198.
Kershaw, Henry, 152.
Ketchum, Rev. Joel, 174.
Kilgore, Arthur, 118.
Killon, John, 110.
Kimberly, Jerred, 213.
  Liberty, 55.
  Thomas, 186.
KINNEY FAMILY, 215.
  Abraham, 130.
  Betsey Ann., 159.
  Ebenezer, 59, 40, 41, 47, 45, 194.
  Esther A., 219.
  Isaac, 27, 29, 69, 130, 116, 159
  Lydia, 57, 113.
  Medad, 21.
  Milo, 195.
  Nancy, 219.
  Roswell N., 13, 14, 105.
  Sheldon, 16, 19, 79, 82, 83, 86,
    87, 196.
  William, 16, 47, 68, 69, 130,
Kinneytown Dam, 72.
Kirtland, Elijah, 130.
  George, 35, 69, 70, 115, 183.
  Mrs., 181.
Knowles, Isaac, 43.

Ladd, Josie E., 110.
  Theodore S., 19, 105, 147, 183.
Ladue, Julia A., 218.
Lake, Augusta Ann, 206.
  Catharine A., 206.
  Miss, 215.
  Phedina, 208.
  Samuel, 212.
Lane, Brothers, 178.
  John, 211, 130.
Langdon, Rhoda L., 205.
Lathrop, Augusta, Mrs., 15.
  Simon, 96.
Leach, James, 51, 52, 113.
Leaming, J. Fisher, 68.
Leavenworth, Calvin, 64.
  George, 134.
  Isaac, 64.
  John, 35.
  Julia, 111.
  Mark, Rev., 38.
  Polly, 215.
  Thomas, 56, 201.
Lebanon Brook, 6.
Lee, Cyrus, 121.
  Jesse, Rev., 119, 173, 174.
  Mary, 164.
  Robert, 176, 182.
  William, 96.
Leek, Betsey, 152.
LeForge, Henry, 120, 132.
Leigh, Anna, 212.
  Lewis E., 96.
Leonard, Mrs. S. C., 16.
  Rev. S. C., 135.

HISTORY OF SEYMOUR.   239

Lessell, Rev. E. J. K., 96.
Lester, George E., 14, 19, 134.
 Murray, 157.
 Sarah, 157.
Lewis, Edward, 71.
 Eleazer, 45, 151.
 Emily J., 208.
 Geo. G., 202.
 Maria, 211.
 Vinie A., 208.
Lewis, E. & Co., 79.
Lindley, Curtis, 72.
Lindsley, Isaac, 82.
 Israel, 224.
 John, 71, 109, 110, 152.
 Miss, 117.
 Sabra, 88.
 Sarah, 110.
Lines, Calvin, 112.
 James, 52.
 Joseph, 21.
 Lois, 154.
 Sarah M., 16.
 Washington I., 140.
 Zebulon, 56.
Lingham, Rebecca,
Lissberger, Lazarus, 87.
Little River, 7.
Llewellyn, Evan, 70, 152.
Lockwood, Charles L., 162.
 Elizabeth O., 16, 112.
 Emma, 15.
 Henry B., 15.
 Mary, Mrs., 15.
Long Plain, 47.
Lopus, 39.
Lord, Frederick, 152.
Losee, Elijah, 152, 218.
 Isaac, 16, 64, 76, 115, 140
 William, Mrs., 14.
LOUNSBURY FAMILY, 217.
 Albert W., 96, 117, 182, 183, 208
 Crownage, 152.
 David, 152.
 Ethel, 56.
 Francis, 15.
 Henry W., 96.
 John L., 63.
 Levi, 16.
 Linus, 51.
 Mark, 152.
 Timothy, Dr., 220.
 Victory, 223.
Lovejoy, John, Rev., 177.
Loveland, Arnold, 131.
 Ashbel, 21, 45, 52.
 Joseph, 45.
 Sarah, 41, 154.
 Truman, 21, 51.
Lowe, William E., 162.
Lucket, David, 96.
Luckey, Rev. John., 177.
 Samuel, 177.
Ludlow, Roger, 37.
 Sarah, 38.
Lues, Ebenezer, 150.
Lum, Adam, 131.
 Bennett, 109.
 Clark, 110, 111, 216.
 Edwin A., 159.
 Eliza, 110.
 Enos, Capt., 147.
 Frank M., 134.
 Grace, 212.
 Hannah, 193, 196.
 John, Capt., 149.
 John, Jr., 150, 151.
 Joseph, Capt., 45.
 Jonathan, 7, 40, 150, 172, 201.
 Jonathan, Jr., 48.
 Mr., (teacher), 117.
 Philo, 109.
 Reuben, 25, 151, 212.

Lum, Sarah, 172, 206.
 Sarah, Mrs., 160.
 William, Capt., 216.
 William D., 109, 147.
Lyman, Annie E., 16.
 I. H., 86.
 Johnathan, Rev., 44, 52.
 Mary, 205.
Lynch, Rev. James, 84.
Lynde, Duane M., 96.
Lyon, Jonathan; 174.
 Mary L., 172.
 Zalmon, Rev., 174, 175.
Lyons, Charles B., 96.

Magill, Dr. William, 204.
Mahoney, Daniel, 135.
 Patrick, 135.
 William, 135.
Mallett, Betsey, 204.
 Frances, 171.
 Mary J., 171.
 Stephen S., 152.
Mallory, Edmund, 217.
 Leverett P., 117, 152.
 Nathan, 52.
 Samuel, 170.
 Sophia, 171.
 William, 117, 183.
Mansfield, Betsey, 199.
 Eliza, 110.
 Jared, 151.
 Nathan, 25, 45, 150, 210, 212.
 Rev. Mr., 197.
Manville, James, 25, 150.
Marchant, John, 167.
Marks, ——, 209.
Marshall, John F., 74.
Martin, Anna C., 114.
 Isaac N., 79.
 Jethro, 51.
 Milenna, 155.
 Mr., 75.
 Selima, 168.
Mather, Mrs. Esther, 166.
 John P. C., 81.
Matthews, Lois, 168.
 James R., 100.
Mauwehu, Eunice, 17, 36.
 Joseph, 17, 32, 33, 40, 51, 59.
 Richard, Dr., 25, 26, 44, 145.
McArthur, Albert, 96.
McCarthy, Charles, 135.
 Daniel, 135.
McCombs, Rev. Laurence, 174.
McCormick, 96.
McCoy, Henry, 155.
McEwen, David J., 132, 133, 208.
 Virgil H., 104, 106, 107, 108, 134
 Wooster B., 135.
 ——, 208.
McEwen & Camp, 139.
McGary, Henry A., 132.
McGraw, Sarah H., 226.
McKay, Kate, 111.
McLain, Lottie, 208.
McMorrow, Francis, 135.
McNurney, Michael, 140.
McSparren, Clark, 204.
Meacham, Mary F., 110.
Mechanics' Lodge, I.O.O.F., 134
Meigs, Charles, 198.
 Samuel, 80, 108, 132.
Merino Sheep, 59.
Merriam, Olive, 13.
Merrick, Capt., 121.
 George H., 82, 85, 87, 112.
 W. J., 134.
Merwin, Rev. Samuel, 9, 177.
 Lucy S., 118.
Meteorological Notes, 76.
Methodist Episcopal Church, 18, 37.

Methodist Episcopal Church,
 Bequest to, 68.
 Deeds to, 66, 75.
 Description of, 74.
 History of, 173-183.
 Maples by, 77.
Middlebury, 125.
Miles, Jonathan, 25, 42, 46, 47, 130, 149, 195.
 Milly, 212.
 Sheldon, 140, 182, 183.
 Theophilus, 25. 26,[41, 47, 51, 64, 130, 195.
Miller, David, Rev., 176, 178.
 John H., 140, 219.
Military Titles, 8.
Militia, 56.
 Officers of, 7.
Mills, Caroline, 210.
 Rev. J. L., 15.
Minor, George, 158.
 John, 156.
 Phebe, 168.
 Thomas B., 135.
Mitchell, Samuel W., 56.
 William G., 134.
Mix, Rev. Stephen, 166.
Morgan, Charles, 132.
 Nathan W., 171.
Morning Star Lodge, No. 47, F. & A. M., 131.
Morris, Adonijah, 224.
 Luzon D., 74, 84, 87, 104, 107.
 Martha, 118.
 Major, 52.
 Sarah, 196.
 Sheldon, 170.
 William, 100, 131, 132, 133.
Moshier, John S., 27, 64, 73, 97, 121, 132, 192.
 Howard F., 213.
MOULTHROP FAMILY, 224.
 Benjamin, 222.
 Lewis, 223.
 Seba, 56, 113, 114.
Moulton, Russell, 218.
Munn, Daniel, 167.
Munson, H. B., 79, 80, 81, 82, 83, 84, 90, 101, 102, 104, 105, 117, 133, 140.
 Byron W., 96.
 Charles, 131.
 Dennis H., 183.
 Marcus E., 96.
 Thomas, 111.
Murray, Abraham, 52.
Mygatt, Henry S., 86, 87.

Nathans, Isaac, 79.
Naugatuck Railroad, 73, 76, 78, 85.
Naukotunk, 17.
Nehawkumme, 42.
Nettleton, Enos G., 25, 150.
 Josiah, 26, 132, 150, 151.
 Susanna, 168.
Newel, Asahel, 52.
New Haven & Seymour Plank Road Co., 86.
Neuschler, Fred, 292.
Newheim, Adam, 102, 105.
Newman, Robert, 188.
Newton, Charles, 134.
 Fletcher, 52.
 Henrietta, 170.
 Julius H., 147.
Nicholas, Wm., 96.
Nichols, Abel, Rev., 27.
 Anne, 193.
 Benjamin, 213.
 John, 197.
 Rev. Mr., 160.
 Samuel, 187.
 Sheldon. 216.

Nichols, William B., 15.
Nixon, Rev. John, 177.
Noble, Francis, 147.
  Henry L., 203.
Northrop, Beardsley, Rev., 176.
  Betsey, 204.
  Ebenezer, 64, 301.
  H. D., Rev., 14.
  John, 152.
  Laura E., Mrs., 15.
  Mr., 115.
Norton, Lucy, 130.
  Major Russell, 222.
Noyes, Hannah, 167.
Nugent, C. C., 183.
Nyumphs, 39, 41.

Oatman, Chas., 111, 115.
O'Brien, George, 96.
  Timothy, 135.
O'Callaghan, Dennis, 135
Ockemunge, 42.
O'Claughessy, David, 96.
O'Donnell, William, 135.
Old Coins, 23, 24.
Old Field Brook, 109.
Olmstead, Mrs. C. J., 15.
  ——, 157.
O'Riley, Rt. Rev. Bernard, 84.
Ormsbee, Sarah L., 14.
Osborn, David, Rev., 179.
  Ebenezer, 56.
  Ensign, 52.
  Gilbert E., 198.
  Harry, 132, 218.
  Harvey, 170.
  Joseph, 43.
  Lois, 197.
  Mattie, 16.
  Merritt, 182.
  Moses, 175.
  Noah, 15.
  Sarah, 170.
  Sarah M., 110.
  Sarah S., 16.
  Thomas, 43.
Ostrander, Rev. Daniel, 174-5-7.
Oxford, 39, 88, 125.
  Incorporation of, 54, 55.
  Parish of, 43.
  St. Peter's, 44

Page, Charles, 224.
  Edmund, 57.
  Philo, 56.
Paine, Mary Ann, 214.
Papermaking in Seymour, 72, 120
Pardee, Abigail, 225.
  Austin R., 76.
  John, 224.
Park, 8, 47.
Parker, Eri, 168.
  Norman, 87.
  Salmon, 56.
Parmelee, Ira E., 152.
Patchen, Eleazer, 56, 113
  Jane, 70, 120.
Patcher, Jane, 218.
Patterson, Henry, 78.
Paugussett, 5, 6, 21, 43.
Pease, Rev. Wm. T., 177.
Peck, Bezaleel, 21, 54, 112, 113,
  Ebenezer, 113, 130. [176,182.
  Edward G., 138.
  Elbert A., 102.
  Justus, 154.
  Martha, 176, 205, 222.
  Naaman, 54.
  Nathan, Jr., 83.
  Noah, 52.
  Orrin, 176.
Peet, Elijah, 210.
Perkins, Abigail, 220.

Perkins, Jesse C., 117
  Lucinda, 170.
  Mary, 217, 219.
  Peter, 170.
  Ruben, 47.
  Ruth, 217.
  Sarah, 223.
Pero, 38.
PERRY FAMILY, 213.
  John, 56.
  Martin, 96.
  Nancy, 210.
  Rev. L. P., 180.
  Yelverton, 210, 212.
Pettingil, Rev. Amos, 13, 69.
Phanton, Laura, 205.
Phelps, Anson G., 72, 73, 85
  Charles B., 87.
  Edward D., 96, 134.
Pickett, John, 45.
  Rachel, 197.
Pickhardt, Carrie L., 16.
Pierce, Rev. Aaron, 176, 181.
Pierson, Aaron, 115.
  David, 46.
  Elizabeth C., 15.
  Lieut., 52.
  Nathan, Capt., 47.
  Rev. Mr., 186.
  Richard, 100.
Pinesbridge, 38, 39.
Pine Tree Shilling, 23.
Pitcher, Thomas, 56.
Pitt, John, 77, 130.
Plant, Ebenezer, 48.
Platt, Geo. B., 132.
  Josiah, 193.
  Miss, 152.
Poe, Edgar A., 127.
Poke By-law, 89.
Polly, Jarvis, 82.
Pool, Micah, 48, 149, 150.
Pope, M. H., 134.
Postmasters, 79.
Potter, Esther, 221.
  Gideon, 225.
  Miss, 158.
Pound By-law, 82.
Powers, Alden, 218.
Prescott, Sherman, 212
Priestly, John, 52.
Prince, Chas., 96.
  Truman, 217.
Prindle, Rev. Chauncey, 26, 44.
  John, 52.
Pritchard, Ennis, 47.
  Jabez E., 83, 84, 105, 224.
  Jabez, Lieut., 50, 52, 123, 138.
  James, Jr., 47, 195.
  Leverett, 21, 25, 56, 69, 76, 195.
  Olive, 160.
Prudden, Peter, 170.
  Sally, 170, 171.
  Samuel, 171.
Pugsley, Cornelius, 214.
Pulford, Frederick W., 139.
Pulling, Rev. A. B., 126, 180, 181.
Pullman, Rev. Joseph, 102, 180.
Purvis, Rev. John, 27.
Putnam, Daniel I., 76, 134.
  O. C., 161.

Quaker Farms, 40, 127.
Quaker Farms Purchase, 43.
Quick, Rev. A. J., 15.
Quiering, Freddie, 16.
  Christian, 152.

Radcliffe, Walter W., 199.
Radford, H. A., 74, 87, 105, 134, 135
Randall, Charles, 74.
  Hiram, 130.
  Hiram W., 69, 71, 84, 104.

Randall, M. M., 139.
Rankin, S. H., 183.
Ransom, Charles, 132, 133.
Raymond, ——, 214.
Raymond French & Co., 72.
Raynor, Rev. Menzies, 174.
Reade, Elizabeth, 167.
  Phebe, 167.
Redshaw, Joseph G., 198.
Regan, Michael, 135.
Representatives, list of, 105.
Revolution, Incidents of, 145.
Revolutionary period. 45-52.
  Soldiers, 38, 39, 49, 52, 147.
  Sufferings of, 123.
Reynolds, A. F., Prof., 118.
  Charles, J., 16.
  Ella F., Mrs., 15.
  John Y., 97.
  Judah, 188.
  Rufus K., 179.
  William B., 138.
Rheylee, Archer, 56.
Rice, Amelia, 199.
  George, 79. 85.
  Rev. Phinehas, 174.
Richardson, Mrs. James, 15.
Ricks, Mrs. Emmeline, 14.
Ricketts, Geo. R. A., 87.
Rider, Clara S., 110.
  Elizabeth, 159.
  Henry A., 69, 132, 133.
  John J., 78, 82, 86, 172.
  Mrs. H. A., 15.
  Stephen R., 101-2-5, 133, 152-8.
RIGGS FAMILY, 197.
  Abigail, 194.
  Anna, 128.
  Betsey, 130.
  David, 128.
  David C., 146.
  David W., 219.
  Ebenezer, 44, 46, 170.
  Ebenezer, Capt., 48.
  Elizabeth M., 161.
  Garey, 132, 133.
  Harpin, 28, 82-3-9, 103-4-7, 164
  Harriett, 110, 161.
  James, 195.
  John, 46, 58, 109, 121, 130, 171,
    200.
  John, Capt., 46, 47, 53, 56.
  John H., 97, 114, 138.
  Joseph, 53, 63, 128.
  Joseph, Capt., 55, 46.
  Joseph, Lieut., 52.
  Laura, 170, 171.
  Lowis, 47.
  Lucinda, 155.
  Lyman, 132.
  Mary, 130.
  Moses, 25, 58, 130, 161.
  Samuel, 53, 56, 114, 131, 132, 194
  Samuel, Ensign, 7.
  Sarah, 39, 110, 117, 188.
Riley, Horace, 77.
Rimmon Burying Ground, 39, 128
Rimmon Dam, 74, 78.
Rimmon District, 47.
Rimmon Hill, 39.
Rimmon Paper Co., 77, 123.
Rimmon Water Co., 102.
Roads Across Great Hill, 40.
Roads, Shrub Oak to Derby Narrows, 60.
Roads to Waterbury, 40.
Robbins, Nehemiah, 85.
Robert, John W., 209.
Roberts, Rev. George, 174.
  James, 89.
  Mrs. E. A., 15.
Rocker's Hill, 7, 40, 52.

HISTORY OF SEYMOUR. 241

Rock Rimmon, 39.
Rock Spring Division, 76, 78.
Rockwell, Jacob, 132.
Rogers, Ammi, Rev., 26.
   Evan, Rev., 174.
   Geo. A., 105, 134.
   H. C., 97, 183.
   John W., 105.
   Mary A., 205.
Roman Catholic Church, 18. 84.
Rood, Isaac, 138.
Root, Oliver, 52.
Rose, Henry, 97.
Roselle, Samuel, 72, 89. 105, 120.
Rowe, Daniel, 173.
   Isaac, 114, 226.
   John, 195.
   Keziah, 206.
Rubbermill Burned, 101.
Rugg, Fred A., 134.
   Harvey, 134.
Russell, Eliza, 109.
   Frank H., Mrs., 115.
   Henry, 74.
   Joseph, 46, 48, 154.
   Samuel, 45. 149, 150, 211.
   Stephen D., 28, 89, 90. 101, 102, 105, 133.
   Timothy, 224, 231.
Ryan, John, 97.
   Patrick, 97.
   William E., 97.

Sackett, David, 156.
   Mary A., 180.
Sage, Harlow P., 115.
Saltonstall, Sir Richard, 207.
Sanford, Augusta, 110, 152.
   A. H., Rev., 69.
   David, 70, 130, 132, 147.
   Eli, 163.
   Herschel, 217.
   Joseph, 52, 147.
   John, 56.
   Miss, 158.
   Moses, 56.
   Olive, 156.
   Raymond, Capt., 50, 147.
   Samuel, Dr.,25,54-5-7,130,195
   Sarah, 206.
   Sheldon C., 13.
   S. P., 39.
   Thomas, 86.
   Zadoc, 39.
Sargent, Clement A., 74, 161
Satterlee, Samuel K., 87.
Schermerhorn, Catharine, 172.
Schneider, Henry C., 140.
Scholefield, Rev. Arnold,175.176
Schools of Seymour, 106.
   Beacon Falls, 46.
   Bell, 112, 152.
   Bungay, 47, 110.
   Cedar Ridge, 111.
   Center, 107, 117, 152.
   Consolidation of, 103.
   First Intermediate, 117.
   Great Hill, 108, 150.
   High, 101, 108.
   Second Intermediate, 117.
   Shrub Oak, 47, 106, 110, 152.
   Squantuck District, 109.
School Societies, 106, 108.
School Visitors, 107, 118.
Scott, Henry, 109.
   Jesse, 131.
   John, 202, 204.
   Prudence, 217.
   Ruth Ann, 202.
   R. W., 134.
   ———, 147.
Scoville, Mr., 145.
Scranton, Amos H., 140.

Scranton. Monroe, 108.
Scucurra, 6.
Seabury, Rev. Geo., 29.
Seamer, Mercy, 203.
Searl, Rev. Roger, 174.
Seeley, William, 146, 147.
Segears, Edwin C., 15.
Selectmen of Seymour, 105.
Selleck, Joel F., 111.
Seymour, Mary, 63.
   Thomas H., 73.
Seymour and New Haven Plank Road Co., 86.
Seymour and Woodbury Plank Road Co., 87.
Seymour Bible Society, 135.
Seymour boundaries, change, 88.
Seymour in the Rebellion, 90.
Seymour Record, 143.
Seymour Savings Bank, 86.
Shannon, M. P., Mrs., 29.
   O. E., Rev.,28,29, 101,102.107
SHARPE FAMILY, 207.
   Charles W., Rev.,117,118,152
   David W., 97.
   Lugrand, 18, 117, 127, 156, 181, 183.
   Mary, 127.
   Olive Maria, 218.
   Thomas, of Boston, 207.
   Thomas, of Stratford, 207.
   Thomas, of Newtown, 127.
   Thomas, of Oxford, 208.
   Thomas, of Seymour, 140,181
   William C., 107, 108, 111. 139, 140, 181, 183.
Sheard, Charles, 16.
Shehan, Cornelius, 97.
Sheldon, Francis, 97.
Shelton, Ann Eliza, 110.
   Geo. P., 73, 74, 82, 84. 85, 86.
Shenson, John, 133.
Sherman, Charles, 15.
   C. S., Rev., 15.
   Lemuel, 210.
   Mary, 167.
   Polly, 208.
   Rebekah, 167.
   ———, 136.
Sherman & Beardsley, 79.
Sherwood, Cornelia E., 152.
Short, Sylvester, 97.
   Charles, 134.
Shubael, 38.
Shultz, Addie, 162.
Silliman, Benjamin, 229.
Simpson, Mrs. D., 16.
Skeals, Abial, 56.
Skeel, Hannah, 169.
Skeels, Jason, 130.
Skiene, Margaret, 172.
Skokorat, 6, 40, 41, 42.
Small Pox, 54, 57, 79.
Smith, Abner, Rev., 119.
   Abraham, 45.
   Albert E., 110.
   Almon, 115.
   Alonzo T., 78.
   Amos, 116, 172.
   Anna, 216.
   Anson, 97.
   Arthur J., 182.
   Bela, Rev., 176.
   Bevil P., 86.
   Burton W. 28-9,71-2-3-4-6-7-8-9 90, 101-2-4-5-7-9, 140, 152.
   Caroline, 204.
   Charlotte M., 111.
   Christopher, 108, 109,149,150
   Corporal, 52.
   Cynthia, 161.
   Daniel, 132.
   Daniel, Rev., 177.

Smith, David, 215.
   Dinah, 221.
   Edwin, 70, 89,105,180,183,223
   Elijah, 56.
   Eliza, 172.
   Emily, 110.
   Ephraim, 109.
   Ephraim G., Rev., 19.
   Esther, 212.
   E. W., Rev., 179.
   Frank A., 16.
   George, 134, 139, 223.
   George A., 97.
   Gibson, 113.
   Hannah, 217.
   Ira, Col., 10, 63, 113, 130, 155
   Ira, Rev., 19, 20, 68.
   Isaac, 45, 48.
   James, 140, 164.
   James M., Rev., 174.
   Jesse, 56, 69, 130, 195.
   John, 105, 110, 132, 151, 223.
   John D., Rev., 27, 178.
   John W., 103.
   Joseph H., 134.
   Joseph, Rev., 180, 182.
   Lydia, Mrs., 225.
   Lyman, 56, 70, 71, 114.
   Margaret, 16.
   Mary A., 109.
   Matilda, 110.
   Matthias, 218.
   M. Maria, Mrs., 161.
   Nathan, Major, 147.
   Samuel, Jr., 46, 113.
   Sarah, 130.
   Sylvester, Rev., 75, 77, 79, 82, 86-7, 102-3-4-7-9, 111, 112, 121,177-8-9, 180,182-3.
   Sylvester P., 206.
   Titus, 217.
   Watie G., 197.
   Wilbur W., Capt., 73, 97, 103, 108, 122.
   William, 52, 108, 212.
   William C., 82.
   William E., 179.
   Willis, 132.
   ———, 208, 214.
Smith & Bassett, 79, 121, 123.
Smith & Sanford, 114.
Smith's Papermill, 103, 121.
Soldiers of the Revolution, 38, 39, 49 to 52, 147.
   War of 1812, 63, 147.
   Mexican War, 73.
   War of the Rebellion,92, 147.
Somers, Elvira W., 110.
   Charity, 157.
Soule, Henchman S., 87.
South Britain, 125.
Southford, Union Church, 127.
Southbury, 125.
Sparks, Rev., Thomas, 178.
Spencer, Elizabeth, 170.
   James L., 15,16,74,76,130, 139
   Mary E., 16.
   John, 56.
   Rufus, 110.
Sperry, Adaline, 13, 158.
   Alexander, 52.
   Elizabeth, 206.
   Emmaretta, 110, 199.
   Emmeline, 13.
   Erastus, 19.
   Erazmass, 113.
   George C., 140.
   Grace, 224.
   Isaac J., 13, 114, 152.
   Jabin, 52.
   Job, 52.
   Joshua, 53.
   Jonathan, 52, 53.

242   HISTORY OF SEYMOUR.

Sperry, Julia, 154.
  Laura A., 152.
  Miss, 217.
  Norman, 102, 103,107,108,198
  Philo, 52, 53.
  Rufus, Mrs., 15
  Samuel, 53.
  Silas, 131.
  Shelton, David, 215
    William, 211.
Skeels, Arad, 212.
  Delia, 212.
Snell, Mrs. Eliza, 202.
Spiers, John, 140.
Squantuck, 7, 52.
Squantuck School, 109
Squares, Reuben, 167.
Squire, Ruth, 156.
  Solomon, 156.
Stanbury, Alice, 162.
Stanley, Celia A., 118.
Stearns, Rev. Chas., 79, 179
STEELE FAMILY, 203, 222.
  Albert J., 74, 75, 79, 117, 220.
  Ashbel, 47, 113.
  Deacon Bradford, 10, 16, 19,
    21, 39, 50, 58, 69, 113, 114,
    123, 126, 130, 163, 204
  Bradford, Lieut., 45, 52.
  Bradford, Capt., 21, 41, 45,
    46, 47, 50, 130, 195, 204
  Edmund, 114, 115, 219.
  Elisha, 21.
  Emmeline, Mrs., 14
  Eunice, 195.
  Frank E., 105.
  George, 56, 146.
  John B., 107, 117
  Mary, 130.
  Millie, 215.
  Norman, 130.
  Sarah, 10, 68.
  William W., 76.
Stetson, Nancy, 209.
Stevens, Ann S., Mrs., 62, 126-7.
  Edward, 127.
  James A., 76, 79, 134
  Rev. Ebenezer, 174
Stevenson, Rev. Thomas, 180
Stiles, Mr., 174.
  Nathan, 25, 113.
  Nathan Jr., 56.
  Phebe, 63.
Still, Jacob L., 97.
Stilson, Sarah, 193, 194
Stockwell, Geo. E., 183.
STODDARD FAMILY, 165.
  Abiram, Dr., 130, 203
  John, 82, 85, 130.
  Oliver, 112.
  Oliver H., 56, 132
  Eunice, 130, 203.
  Thomas, Dr., 17, 36, 79, 82,
    117, 139, 174
  Hannah, 113.
  Susan H., 203.
  William B., 101.
Stone, Leman, 57.
  Miss, 168.
  Noah, 132.
  Rollin S., Rev., 12, 13, 19
Stone Bridge, 46.
Storer, E. G., 133.
Storrs, Ashbel, 22, 87, 103, 112,
    122, 133, 140.
  Charles W., 73, 79, 103, 108,
    139, 152, 170.
  Hattie L., 206.
  John W., 74, 76, 77, 78, 79.
  John, 130, 132.
  Arthur L., 134.
  William N., 89, 105, 182, 183.
  Laura, 155.

Strapp, Edward, 135.
Stratford Bridge, 57.
Stratton, Seth Sherwood,208,209
  Shelton B., 209.
Streets, High, 82.
  Names of, 124.
  Humphrey, 72.
Strong, Josiah, 48, 56
  Leman, 56.
  Mary, 214.
  Preserved, 167.
Stuart, L. B., 140.
  Mr., (Teacher), 117.
Sullivan, Peter, 135.
Summers, Lucinda, 218
Sutton, Nancy, 110.
Swain, Rev. Richard, 174.
Swan, James, 15, 19, 104, 105,
    141, 155.
  Jessie, 16.
Swayne, Rachel, 226.
Swift, Charles W., 97.
  Charles, 74, 76, 152.
  Ephraim, Rev. G., 13, 19
  Hortie V., Mrs., 15
  John, 52, 60.
  Josiah, 26, 56, 113, 114.
  Mary A., 117.
  Sarah, 110, 111.
  Zephaniah, Rev., 10, 11, 12,
    13, 19.
Sykes, Rev. O., 71, 174, 176, 178.

Talmadge, James, 44.
Taylor, Elihu, 210.
  General, 77.
  Isora, 172.
  Rev. Geo. L., 180
  Rev. Joshua, 174.
Teacher's Institute, 101.
Teachers, names of, 109, 110,111,
    117, 118.
Temperature, Notes on, 84, 89.
Terrill, Elizabeth, 223
  Jane, 110, 111.
  Sarah, 164.
  Smith, 112.
  Solomon, 111.
Tharp, Eliza, 155.
Thatcher, Rev. William,174, 175
Thayer, Benjamin B., 100, 148.
  Mrs. B. B., 16.
  Reuben W., 97.
  William, 98.
The Fowler Nail Co., 122.
The New Haven Copper Co., 87,
    142.
Thomas, Francis N., 111
  George W., 131.
  Rev. Noble W., 174.
  Thadias, 56.
THOMPSON FAMILY, 188
  Anthony, 188.
  Bridgett, 187.
  Charles, Rev., 13, 19
  Cynthia, 209.
  Daniel, 114.
  Hannah, 224.
  Jabez, 48.
  James, Rev., 26.
  Joseph, 208, 209.
  Mary Ann, 209.
  Moses, 225.
Thomson, Rev. Wm. J., 16.
  Hezekiah, 113.
  Lois, 70, 120.
  Major Edgar, 45, 48.
  Mehitable, 170.
  Rebecca, 220.
  Reuben, 170.
Thorpe, ——, 210.
Tibbals, Rev. C. A., 181.
Tibbils, Abner, 151.

Tift, John, 43.
Titles, Civil and Military, 8.
Toby's Rock, 36, 39, 46.
Todd, Rev. Ambrose, 26.
  Sybil, 161.
Toffey, Mary A., 171.
Tolles, Miss, 217.
Tolls, Caroline, 155.
  William, 168.
TOMLINSON FAMILY, 210
  Agur, 45.
  Ammon, 109.
  Benjamin, 149.
  Betsey, 109.
  Burr, 209.
  Cyrus, 56.
  Daniel, 150.
  David, 47, 151, 172, 175, 211.
  David, Mrs., 175.
  Edwin, 105.
  Ellen, 160.
  Emma S., 110, 117.
  George A., 213.
  H. A., 110.
  Hannah, 7.
  Harrison, 73, 79, 83, 85, 86,
    116, 117, 171.
  Henry, 45, 150, 149, 214.
  James, 175.
  James C., 106.
  Jane, 109.
  Jennette, 217.
  John, 209.
  John R., 171.
  John, Capt., 45, 46, 47, 48.
  Joseph, 150.
  Kate, 213.
  Laura, 111, 206, 211, 212.
  Leroy, 112.
  Levi, 21, 25, 54, 113, 195.
  Mark, 130.
  Mary, 117.
  Nathan, 152.
  Noah, 46, 47, 48.
  Patience, 214.
  Phebe, 110.
  Philo, 195.
  Ransom, 73, 87, 98, 152.
  Rev. Nathaniel W., 9, 10.
  Russell, 25, 150, 209, 211.
  Samuel, 40, 201.
  Sarah, 172, 211.
  Sybil, 214.
  Truman, 215.
  Webb, 150.
  William, 7.
  William R., 52,56,105,109,160
Torrance, Thomas, 52, 53.
Touantic Brook, 47.
Towner, Joseph, 43.
Townhouse, 102.
Town Clerks, List of, 104.
Town Debt, 104.
Town Reports, 103.
Town Treasurers, List of, 104.
Tracey, Patrick, 89.
Training Day, 70.
Travis, Mrs., 152.
  Rev. Robert, 178.
Treadwell, Mary, 207, 208.
Treat, Robert, 6.
  David, 60.
Trinity Church, 25.
Trowbridge, Amasa, 122.
  Isaac, 43, 44.
  Mary, 221.
Truesdell, Lucius B., 98.
TUCKER FAMILY, 219.
  Ann, 111.
  Anna, 204.
  Byron, 98, 218.
  Daniel, Jr., 59, 60.
  David, 76, 89, 108, 134, 139.

HISTORY OF SEYMOUR.   243

Tucker, Frederick, 98.
  Maria M., 117.
  Mary, 161.
  Medad K., 75, 82, 117, 134, 179, 216.
  Reuben, Capt., 46, 60
  Samuel, 197, 228.
  Sheldon, 115, 130, 171.
  Sheldon C., 105, 134 219, 222.
  Styles, 161.
  Susannah, 197.
  William, 125.
  Zephaniah, 60, 130, 204.
Turkey Hill, 39.
Turner, Rev. Chester W., 178
Tuthill, William, 76, 82.
Tuttle, Abraham, 222.
  Benjamin, 56.
  E. L., 152.
  Eliza, 111, 115, 202.
  Lucius, 79, 82, 85.
  Rebecca, 222.
  Wallace M., 13, 14, 16, 19.
Tuttle & Bassett, 79
Twitchell, David, 47
  John, 43.
  Joseph, 209.
  Miss, 72.
  Rayner, 220.
  Robert, 224.

Umberfield, Catharine, 109.
  Willis, 182, 183.
Uminger, William, 98
Uncou, 37.
Union Bank, 26.
Union Mercantile Co., 86.
United States Pin Co., 142
UPSON FAMILY, 164.
  George, 134.
  Harriet, 198.
  Hiram, 79, 87, 98, 109, 112, 132, 152, 198.
  Leroy, 164.
  Miss, 111.
  Sarah, 198.
Upson Manufacturing Co, 87.
Upson Post, No. 40, G. A. R, 135

Value of Indian Lands, 5.
Vicker, Joseph, 210.
Village Directory in 1849, 79.
Vincent, Mitchell, 134.
Vinton, Rev. Joseph, 182, 135.
Vose, T. & Co., 126.
  Adam, 52, 53.
  John B., 210.

Wagner, George, 211.
Wainright, Rt. Rev. Bishop, 28
Wakelee, Lewis, 31.
Wakeley, Lilly, 109.
Wakeman, Mr., 187.
  William, 208.
Wakeman & Stoddard, 71
Waldo, Judge, 203.
Walker, Aaron, 98.
  Josephine A., 111, 112.
  Wm. L., Rev., 27, 77, 79.
  Zacharish, Rev., 187
Waln, Lewis, 68.
Ward, John, 115.
  Peter, 134.
  William, 53, 56.
  William S., 98.
  William H., 118.
Warner, Ann, 168.
  Ebenezer, 21, 47
  Egbert R., 139.
  Jacob, 56.
  Juliette, 164.
  Mercy, 204.
  William H., 118.

Warren, Henry, 111, 152.
  Col. Seth, 156.
  Wilford I., 16.
Washband, Bowers, 25.
  Eli, 52.
  John, 42.
  Josiah, 47.
Washbon, Ephraim, 188.
Washborn, Josiah, 95, 57.
Washburn, Bowers, 42, 52.
  Ebenezer, Rev., 174, 175, 177
  Ephraim, 44.
  Experience, 163.
  George, Mrs., 13.
  John, 155.
  Josiah, 56, 57
  Ruth, 193.
  Smith, 130.
Washington, Gen., 123.
Waters, George W., 215.
  ——, 210.
Waterbury, Charles, 158.
Watson, Wm. B., 78, 112, 182.
Wattles, Maria, 109.
Way, Ad ie, 224.
  Hannah, 226.
Weaver, Robert A., 16.
Webster, Aaron, 52.
  Ann, 218.
  Clark, 220
  Rev. Wm. R., 180.
  Sarah, 160.
  Susannah, 204.
  ——, 212.
Weed, John, Jonas, Joseph, 43.
Weld, Capt., Joseph, 166.
  Barbara, 166.
Wells, Prudence, 167
Welton, Miss, 223.
Wesquantuc, 52.
Weston, Wilson, 78, 139.
  Jube, 106.
Wetmore, Hester, 208, 209.
Wheden, Mary, 225.
WHEELER FAMILY, 161, 39
  Abel, 56, 131, 133, 229.
  Almira, 130.
  Amos, 226.
  Aphia E., 210.
  Bronson, 205.
  David, 52.
  Edwin, 76.
  Experience, 59.
  Henry, 25, 139.
  James, 200.
  Joel, 223.
  John C., 113, 114, 121, 162.
  John, Hon., 162.
  John T., 39, 113, 115, 130,162.
  Lyman, 171.
  Moses, 56.
  Mrs., 152.
  Nathan, 21, 59.
  Robert, 48.
  Ruth, 204.
  Samuel, Lieut., 46, 47.
  Sarah, 204.
  Sarah C., 130.
  Sally, 10, 159.
  Simeon, 204.
  Simon, 130, 157.
White, Abner, 199.
  Amos G., 134, 152.
  Augustus, 98.
  Calvin, Rev., 26.
  Charles P., 134.
  Daniel, 19,74,114,116,117,121.
  Daniel, Mrs., 12.
  Eliza M., 170.
  Isaac, 111,112,115,130,132,216
  James, 98.
  Joel, 19, 111.
  John, 25, 51, 113, 130.

White, Miss, 152.
  Nathan, 78.
  Rebecca, 216.
  W. W., 134.
Whiteley, Joseph, 139.
Whitfield, Rev. George, 19,127.
Whiting, Mr., 27.
Whitlock, Leman, 102.
Whitman, Rev. Samuel, 167.
Whitney, John, 15.
  Henry, 45.
  Ranford, 47.
Whittemore, Ebenezer Turel, 21, 45, 146, 147.
  David, 52.
  W. H., 134, 140.
Whittlesey, Roger Newton, 211.
Wilcox, Jabez, 217.
  M. A., 152.
  Miss, 117.
Wilcoxson, Nathan J., 132.
  Joseph J., 89, 90, 101, 102, 103, 105, 152.
Wild Animals, Bounty for killing, 7.
Wilder, Martha J., 216.
  Elizabeth, 202.
Wildman, Sidney R., 132.
Williams, David, 15.
  James, 168.
  Lewis, 114.
  Miss, 152.
  Rt. Rev. Bishop, 28.
  William, Rev., 166.
Willis, Jane, 157.
Wine, Samuel, 108, 128, 132, 133.
Winterbottom, John. 62, 126.
Winthrop, John, 37.
Wiswel, James, 180.
Wolfe, ——, 213.
Wood, Rev. Abner, 174.
  Samuel, 52.
Woodbridge, 6, 41, 63.
  Rev. Benjamin, 53.
Woodbury and Seymour Plank Road Co., 87.
Woodcock, Anna, 154.
Woodford, H. A., 117.
  Mary, 159.
Woodin, Hezekiah, 21, 47, 52.
  Thomas, 56.
Wooding, David, 217.
  Lemuel, 147.
Woodruff, John W., 134.
  Oscar L., 218.
  V. S., 162.
Woodward, Israel, 167.
  Sarah, 167.
Woolsey, Rev., Elijah, 119, 175.
WOOSTER FAMILY, 223.
  Abraham, 47.
  Bennett, 70, 75, 82, 104, 116.
  Charles A., 101, 102, 105.
  Charles B., 82,84,89,90,104,107
  Clark, Gen., 71, 74, 79, 85,90, 104, 128, 155.
  Daniel, 146, 195, 201, 231,232.
  David, 6, 146, 147, 200.
  David, Jun., 146, 147.
  Dilavan, 220.
  Edward, 187.
  Edwin, 200, 215.
  Eleanor, 160.
  Eleazer, 46.
  Elizabeth, 131, 200.
  Ephraim, 25, 151.
  Eunice, 131.
  Francis E., 110, 152.
  Grace, 130.
  Henry, 56,110,116,130,132,145
  Henry, Jun., 146, 147, 149.
  Jane M., 110, 152.
  John, 40, 41, 100, 131, 145,160.

244 HISTORY OF SEYMOUR.

Wooster, John, Capt., 48, 146.
   Joseph, 209.
   Juliette, 110.
   Leslie B., 98.
   Mary A., 111.
   Naomi, 206.
   Nathaniel, 195.
   Nathan R., 89,102,103,104,105
   Philo, 132.
   Ruth, 187.
   Samuel, 47.
   Silvester, 40.

Wooster, Simeon, 42.
   Thomas, 146.
   Timothy, 43.
   Walter, 47.
Wooster, Dean & Buckingham, 139.
Wooster Park, 8.
Worrull & Hudson, 120.
Worth, Mrs. Mary, 14.
   Peter, 103, 108, 152.
Worthington, Elizabeth, 185.
Wyant, Frank E., 16.

Wyant, George S., 98, 226.
   Leonard, 101, 102.
   Polly, 168.
   Wilson, 73, 76, 98, 105, 112, 182.
Wyllis, George, 232.

Yale, M. D., 74, 79, 209.
Yatman, James, 52.
Youngs, Delia, 157.

Zurcher, Carl, 103.

ERRATA AND ADDITIONS.

Page 41, fourth line from bottom of page, the term King was applied to David, *son* of Squire David.
Page 72, tenth line, *Randall* should be *Lindley*.
Page 90, eighth line, after "April 7th," insert "1862."
Page 108, under "Great Hill School," second line, for pages 19 and 20, and 149 to 151.
Page 134, add H. B. Beecher to list of charter members of Mechanics' Lodge, and Samuel P. Davis and and W. C. Sharpe to list of charter members of Humphrey Lodge.
Page 162, third line from bottom, for *John Todd Wheeler* read *John C. Wheeler*.

ILLUSTRATIONS.

VIEW OF THE FALLS AND VICINITY,	Frontispiece.
PINE TREE SHILLING,	PAGE 23
GRANBY COPPER,	23
CONNECTICUT CENT.,	24
GENERAL HUMPHREY,	49
HUMPHREYSVILLE IN 1815,	67
HUMPHREYSVILLE IN 1838,	70
LUGRAND SHARP,	127
JAMES SWAN'S MECHANICS' TOOL WORKS,	141
HON. JOHN WHEELER,	163
ABIRAM STODDARD, M. D.,	165
COAT OF ARMS OF THE STODDARD FAMILY,	165
JOSEPH NETTLETON STODDARD,	166
MARIA THERESA STODDARD,	168
SHELDON CLARK, ESQ.,	227
CENTENNIAL ART GALLERY,	230

www.ingramcontent.com/pod-product-compliance
Lightning Source LLC
Chambersburg PA
CBHW070336240426
43665CB00045B/2085